KEY TREATIES
for the
GREAT POWERS
1814-1914

Volume 2   1871-1914

KEY TREATIES
for the
GREAT POWERS
1814-1914

Volume 2   1871-1914

(pages 459-948, including Index to Volumes 1 and 2)

Selected and Edited by

MICHAEL HURST MA, FRSA, FR Hist S

Fellow in Modern History & Politics

St John's College, Oxford

DAVID & CHARLES : NEWTON ABBOT

ISBN 0 7153 5633 X

Set in Imprint & Times by C. E. Dawkins (Typesetters) Limited,
London SE1
and printed in Great Britain by
Redwood Press Limited, Trowbridge, Wiltshire
for David & Charles (Publishers) Limited
South Devon House Newton Abbot Devon

CONTENTS
VOLUME 2

[A full list of contents appears in volume 1]

93 DECLARATION OF LONDON

DECLARATION between Great Britain, Austria, France, Italy, North Germany, Russia, and Turkey, as to non-Alteration of Treaties without consent of Contracting Parties. London, 17th January, 1871.

THE Plenipotentiaries of North Germany, of Austria-Hungary, or Great Britain, of Italy, of Russia, and of Turkey, assembled to-day in Conference, recognize that it is an essential principle of the Law of Nations that no Power can liberate itself from the engagements of a Treaty, nor modify the stipulations thereof, unless with the consent of the Contracting Powers by means of an amicable arrangement.

In faith of which the said Plenipotentiaries have signed the present Protocol.

Done at London, 17th January, 1871.

BERNSTORFF.

APPONYI.

GRANVILLE.

CADORNA.

BRUNNOW.

MUSURUS.

13th March, 1871. BROGLIE.

94

CONVENTION OF ARMISTICE between France and the Germanic Confederation. Signed at Versailles, 28th January, 1871.

BETWEEN Count Bismarck, Chancellor of the Germanic Confederation, acting in the name of His Majesty the Emperor of Germany, King of Prussia, and M. Jules Favre, Minister for Foreign Affairs of the Government of National Defence, furnished with the necessary Powers, have decided upon the following Conventions:

TABLE.

1. Armistice to last to the 19th February. Armies to preserve their positions. Armistice to apply to Naval Forces. Captures made after conclusion of Armistice to be restored, as well as Prisoners. Military operations in Departments of the *Doubs, Jura*, and *Cote d' Or*, as well as the seige of *Belfort*, to continue until arrangements are made.

2. Armistice concluded to enable Government of National Defence to convoke an Assembly to decide on Peace or War. Assembly to meet at *Bordeaux*.

3. Fortresses round *Paris* to be occupied by *German* Troops.

4. *German* Army not to enter *Paris* during Armistice.

5. The enclosure shall be disarmed of its cannon, and the carriages sent into the Forts.

6. Armed Garrisons to be Prisoners of War, except 12,000 Men for internal Service in *Paris*. Arms to be delivered up. Soldiers to be interned and delivered up as Prisoners of War if Peace is not concluded. Officers to preserve their Arms.

7. National Guard, &c., charged with Maintenance of Order to preserve Order. Rifle Corps to be disbanded.

8. Facilities to *French* Commissioners for the revictualling of *Paris*.

9. Revictualling of *Paris* after delivery of Forts, &c.

10. Permits for leaving *Paris*.

11. City of *Paris* to pay War Contribution of 200,000,000 francs.

12. Public Securities not to be removed during Armistice.

13. Import of Arms, &c., into *Paris* during Armistice interdicted.

14. Exchange of Prisoners of War.

15. Postal Service for unsealed Letters.

ANNEX. *Demarcation of Armies before Paris. Surrender of Forts and delivery of Armament. 29th January, 1871.*

1. Lines of Demarcation before *Paris*.
2. Roads by which Persons may pass the Line of Demarcation.
3. Surrender of Forts and Redoubts.
4. Delivery of the Armament and Material.

Done at Versailles, 28th January, 1871.

    (L.S.) JULES FAVRE.   (L.S.) v. BISMARCK.

ANNEX.

(ARTS. I to IV. Matter of a minor importance.)

    Versailles, 29th January, 1871.

    (L.S.) JULES FAVRE.   (L.S.) v. BISMARCK.

[Conventions for fixing the line of Demarcation between the French and German Armies were signed on the 31st January and 5th February, 1871.]

95

ADDITIONAL CONVENTION between France and the Germanic Confederation for extending the Armistice to the Departments of the Doubs, the Jura, the Côte d'Or, and before the Fortress of Belfort. Signed at Versailles, 15th February, 1871.

Reference to Convention of 28th January, 1871.

THE Undersigned, furnished with Powers in virtue of which they concluded the Convention of 28th January, 1871; considering that by the said Convention it was reserved to a subsequent understanding to terminate the Military Operations in the Departments of the Doubs, Jura, Côte d'Or, and before Belfort, and to trace the Line of Demarcation between the German occupation and the positions of the French Army, commencing at Quarré-les-Tombes, in the Department of the Yonne, have concluded the following Additional Convention:

1. Surrender of Fortress of *Belfort* with War Material. Garrison to leave with Honours of War. Commanders of *Belfort* and of besieging Army to Settle Details.
2. *German* Prisoners in *Belfort* to be set at Liberty.

3.
&
4. } Line of Demarcation between the *French* and *German* Armies.

5. Departments of the *Jura*, *Doubs*, and *Cote d'Or* to be included in

Armistice Convention of 28th January, 1871.
Done at Versailles, 15th February, 1871.

> (L.S.)   JULES FAVRE.
> (L.S.)   v. BISMARCK.

Conventions for the suspension of Hostilities, and for the surrender of the Fortress of Belfort, were signed at Belfort on the 13th and 16th February, 1871.

96   PRELIMINARY PEACE OF VERSAILLES

PRELIMINARY TREATY OF PEACE between France and Germany. Signed at Versailles, 26th February, 1871. Ratifications exchanged at Versailles, 2nd March, 1871.

BETWEEN the Chancellor of the Germanic Empire, Count Otto de Bismarck-Schönhausen, furnished with Full Powers from His Majesty the Emperor of Germany, King of Prussia; the Minister of State and of Foreign Affairs of His Majesty the King of Bavaria, Count Otto de Bray-Steinburg; the Minister for Foreign Affairs of His Majesty the King of Wurtemberg, Baron Auguste de Wächter; the Minister of State, President of the Council of Ministers of His Royal Highness the Grand Duke of Baden, Monsieur Jules Jolly, representing the Germanic Empire, on the one part; and on the other part, the Chief of the Executive Power of the French Republic, Monsieur Thiers, and the Minister for Foreign Affairs, Monsieur Jules Favre, representing France; the Full Powers of the two Contracting Parties having been found in good and due form, the following has been agreed upon, to serve as a Preliminary Bases to the Definitive Peace to be concluded hereafter.

Renunciations by France in favour of Germany.
ART I. France renounces in favour of the German Empire all her Rights and Titles over the Territories situated on the East of the Frontier hereafter described.

Line of new Frontier between France and Germany.
The Line of Demarcation begins at the North-west Frontier of the Canton of Cattenom, towards the Grandy Duchy of Luxemburg, follows on the South the Western Frontiers of the Cantons of Cattenom and Thionville, passes by the Canton of Briey, along the Western Frontiers of the Communes of Montjois-la-Montagne and Roncourt,

as well as the Eastern Frontiers of the Communes of Marie-aux-Chenes, St. Ail, Habonville, reaches the Frontier of the Canton de Gooze, which it crosses along the Communal Frontiers of Vionville, Bouxières, and Onville, follows the South-west Frontier, south of the District of Metz, the Western Frontier of the District of Chateau-Salins, as far as the Commune of Pettoncourt, taking in the Western and Southern Frontiers thereof to follow the Crest of the Mountains between Seille and Moncel, as far as the Frontier of the District of Sarreburg, to the South of Garde. The demarcation afterwards coincides with the Frontier of that District as far as the Commune of Tanconville, reaching the Frontier to the North thereof, from thence it follows the Crest of the Mountains between the Sources of the White Sarre and Vezouze, as far as the Frontier of that Canton of Schirmeck, skirts the Western Frontier of that Canton, includes the Communes of Saales, Bourg-Bruche, Colroy-la-Roche, Plaine, Ranrupt, Saulxures, and St. Blaise-la-Roche of the Canton of Saales, and coincides with the Western Frontier of the Departments of the Lower Rhine and the Upper Rhine as far as the Cantons of Belfort, the Southern Frontier of which it leaves not far from Vourvenans, to cross the Canton of Delle at the Southern Limits of the Communes of Bourogne and Froide Fontaine, and to reach the Swiss Frontier skirting the Eastern Frontiers of the Communes of Jonchery and Delle.

International Boundary Commission to be appointed.

The German Empire shall possess these Territories in perpetuity in all Sovereignty and Property. An International Commission, composed of an equal number of Representatives of the two High Contracting Parties, shall be appointed immediately after the exchange of the Ratifications of the present Treaty, to trace on the spot the new Frontier, in conformity with the preceding stipulations.

Duties of Commissioners.

This Commission shall preside over the Division of the Lands and Funds, which have hitherto belonged to Districts or Communes divided by the new Frontiers; in case of disagreement in the tracing and the measures of execution, the Members of the Commission shall refer to their respective Governments.

Map of Frontier.

The Frontier, such as it has just been described, is marked in green on two identic copies of the Map of the Territory forming the Government of Alsace, published at Berlin in September, 1870, by the Geographical and Statistical Division of the Staff, and a copy of which shall be annexed to both copies of the present Treaty.

Alteration in Boundary Map. France to retain Town and Forts of Belfort.

Nevertheless, the alteration of the above tracing has been agreed to by the two Contracting Parties. In the former Department of the Moselle, the Villages of Marie-aux-Chênes near St. Privat-la-Montagne, and Vionville to the west of Rezonville, shall be ceded to Germany. In exchange thereof, France shall retain the Town and Fortifications of Belfort, with a Radius which shall be hereafter determined upon.

Indemnity to be paid by France.

ART II. France shall pay to His Majesty the Emperor of Germany the sum of 5,000,000,000 Francs (5 milliards).

Time of Payment of Indemnity.

The Payment of at least 1,000,000,000 (one milliard) Francs shall be effected within the year 1871, and the whole of the remainder of the Debt in the space of 3 years, dating from the Ratification of the present.

Evacuation of French Territory by German Troops.

ART. III. The Evacuation of the French Territory occupied by German Troops shall begin after the Ratification of the present Treaty by the National Assembly sitting at Bordeaux. Immediately after that Ratification, the German Troops shall quit the interior of Paris, as well as Forts on the Left Bank of the Seine, and within the shortest possible delay agreed upon between the military authorities of the two Countries, they shall entirely evacuate the Departments of Calvados, Orne, Sarthe, Eure et Loire, Loiret, Loire et Cher, Indre et Loire, Yonne, and also the Departments of the Seine Inférieure, Eure, Seine et Oise, Seine et Marne, Aube, and Côte d'Or, as far as the Left Bank of the Seine. The French Troops shall fall back at the same time behind the Loire, which they shall not be allowed to pass before the signature of the Definitive Treaty of Peace. The Garrison of Paris is excepted from this disposition, the number of which shall not exceed 40,000 men, and the Garrisons indispensably necessary for the safety of the strongholds.

Gradual Evacuation according to Payments made.

The Evacuation of the Departments between the Right Bank of the Seine and the Eastern Frontier by German Troops shall take place gradually after the Ratification of the Definitive Treaty of Peace and the payment of the first 500,000,000 (half milliard) of the contribution stipulated by Article II, beginning with the Departments nearest to Paris, and shall continue gradually, according to the proportion of the Payments made on account of the Contribution; after the first Payment of a 500,000,000 (half milliard) that Evacuation shall take place in the following Departments: Somme, Oise, and the parts of the Departments of the Seine Inférieure, Seine et Oise, Seine et Marne, situated on the Right Bank of the Seine, as well as the part of the Department of the Seine, and the Forts situated on the Right Bank.

Conditions for Payment of the last 3,000,000,000 (3 milliards) of Indemnity.

After the payment of 2,000,000,000 (two milliards), the German occupation shall only include the Departments of the Marne, Ardennes, Haute Marne, Meuse, Vosges, Meurthe, as well as the Fortress of Belfort, with its Territory, which shall serve as a pledge for the remaining 3,000,000,000 (3 milliards), and in which the number of the German Troops shall not exceed 50,000 men. His Majesty the Emperor will be willing to substitute for the Territorial Guarantee, consisting in the partial occupation of the French Territory, a Financial Guarantee, should it be offered by the French Government under conditions considered sufficient by His Majesty the Emperor and King for the interests of Germany. The 3,000,000,000 (3 milliards), the payment of which shall have been deferred, shall bear Interest at the rate of 5 per cent., beginning from the Ratification of the present Convention.

Maintenance of German Troops of Occupation.

ART. IV. The German Troops shall abstain from levying contributions either in money or in kind in the occupied Departments. On the other hand, the maintenance of the German Troops remaining in France shall be at the expense of the French Government in the manner decided upon by an Agreement with the German Military Administration.

Provisions to be made in favour of Inhabitants of ceded Territories.

ART. V. The interests of the Inhabitants of the Territories ceded by France, in everything relating to their Commerce and their Civil Rights shall be regulated in as favourable a manner as possible when the conditions of the Definitive Peace are settled. A certain time will be fixed, during which they will enjoy particular advantages for the disposal of their produce. The German Government will put no obstacle in the way of Free Emigration by the Inhabitants from the ceded Territories, and shall take no steps against them affecting their Persons or their Property.

Prisoners of War.

ART VI. The Prisoners of War who shall not have been already set at liberty by exchange shall be given up immediately after the Ratification of the present Preliminaries. In order to accelerate the transport of

French Prisoners, the French Government shall place at the disposal of the German Authorities in the interior of the German Territory a part of the rolling-stock of its Railways in such proportion as shall be determined by special arrangements, and at prices paid in France by the French Government for military transport.

Negotiations for Definitive Treaty of Peace.

ART. VII. The opening of negotiations for the Definitive Treaty of Peace to be concluded on the Basis of the present Preliminaries shall take place at Brussels, immediately after the Ratification of the latter by the National Assembly and by His Majesty the Emperor of Germany.

Administration of occupied Departments to be made over to French Authorities.

ART. VIII. After the conclusion and the Ratification of the Definitive Treaty of Peace, the Administration of the Departments which are still to remain occupied by the German Troops shall be made over to the French authorities. But the latter shall be bound to conform to the orders which the Commanders of the German troops may think necessary to give in the interests of the safety, maintenance, and distribution of the Troops.

Taxes in occupied Departments to be levied by and for the use of the French Government.

After the Ratification of the present Treaty, the Taxes in the occupied Departments shall be levied on account of the French Government, and by its own Officers.

German Military Authority not to extend to unoccupied Territory.

ART. IX. It is well understood that these stipulations do not give to the German Military Authority any right over the parts of Territory which it does not actually occupy.

Ratifications.

ART. X. The present Preliminary Treaty shall be immediately submitted to the Ratification of His Majesty the Emperor of Germany and to the French National Assembly sitting at Bordeaux.

In testimony whereof the Undersigned have signed the present Preliminary Treaty, and sealed it with the Seal of their Arms.

Done at Versailles, 26th February, 1871.

(L.S.) BISMARCK.   (L.S.) A. THIERS.

(L.S.) JULES FAVRE.

Accession of Baden, Bavaria, and Wurtemberg.

The Kingdoms of Bavaria and Wurtemberg, and the Grand Duchy of Baden, having taken part in the actual War as Allies of Prussia, and now forming part of the Germanic Empire, the Undersigned adhere to the present Convention in the name of their respective Sovereigns.

Versailles, 26th February, 1871.

CTE. DE BRAY-STEINBURG.　　MITTNACHT.
BN. DE WACHTER.　　　　　　JOLLY.

Conventions were concluded between France and Germany on the 21st May, and 12th October, 1871, on the 29th June, 1872, and on the 15th May, 1873, with reference to the payment of the War Indemnity of 5 Milliards = 5,000,000,000 Francs or £200,000,000. The last Instalment was paid by France on the 5th September, 1873, and the last German Troops passed the French Frontier on the 16th of the same Month.

97　TREATY OF LONDON

TREATY between Great Britain, Austria, France, Germany (Prussia), Italy, Russia, and Turkey, for the Revision of certain Stipulations of the Treaties of 30th March, 1856, relative to the Black Sea and Danube. Signed at London, 13th March, 1871. Ratifications exchanged, 15th May, 1871.

In the Name of Almighty God.

Reference to Treaty of 30th March, 1856.

HER Majesty the Queen of the United Kingdom of Great Britain and Ireland, His Majesty the Emperor of Germany, King of Prussia, His Majesty the Emperor of Austria, King of Bohemia, &c., and Apostolic King of Hungary, the Chief of the Executive Power of the French Republic, His Majesty the King of Italy, His Majesty the Emperor of All the Russias, and His Majesty the Emperor of the Ottomans, have judged it necessary to assemble their Representatives in Conference at London, in order to come to an understanding, in a spirit of concord, with regard to the revision of the stipulations of the Treaty concluded at Paris on the 30th March, 1856, relative to the navigation of the Black Sea, as well as to that of the Danube; being desirous, at the same time, to ensure in those regions new facilities for the development of the commercial activity of all nations, the High Contracting Parties have resolved to conclude a Treaty, and have for that purpose named as their Plenipotentiaries, that is to say:—

Her Majesty the Queen of the United Kingdom of Great Britain and Ireland, the Right Honourable Granville George Earl Granville, Lord Leveson, a Peer of the United Kingdom, a Member of Her Majesty's Privy Council, Lord Warden of the Cinque Ports and Constable of Dover Castle, Chancellor of the University of London, Her Majesty's Principal Secretary of State for Foreign Affairs, &c.;

His Majesty the Emperor of Germany, King of Prussia, the Sieur Albert, Count of Bernstorff-Stintenburg, his Minister of State and Chamberlain, Ambassador Extraordinary and Plenipotentiary of His Imperial and Royal Majesty to Her Britannic Majesty, &c.;

His Majesty the Emperor of Austria, King of Bohemia, &c., and Apostolic King of Hungary, the Sieur Rudolph Count Apponyi, Chamberlain, Privy Councillor of His Imperial and Royal Apostolic Majesty, his Ambassador Extraordinary to Her Britannic Majesty, &c.;

The Chief of the Executive Power of the French Republic, the Sieur James Victor Albert Duc de Broglie, Ambassador Extraordinary and Plenipotentiary of the Republic to Her Britannic Majesty, &c.;

His Majesty the King of Italy, the Chevalier Charles Cadorna, Minister of State, Senator of the Kingdom, his Envoy Extraordinary and Minister Plenipotentiary to Her Britannic Majesty, &c.;

His Majesty the Emperor of All the Russias, the Sieur Philip Baron de Brunnow, his Actual Privy Councillor, his Ambassador Extraordinary and Plenipotentiary to Her Britannic Majesty, &c.;

And His Majesty the Emperor of the Ottomans, Constantine Musurus Pasha, Muchir and Vizir of the Empire, his Ambassador Extraordinary and Plenipotentiary to Her Britannic Majesty, &c.;

Who, after having exchanged their Full Powers, found in good and due form, have agreed upon the following Articles:

Abrogation of Articles of Treaty of 30th March, 1856, and of Convention of 30th March, 1856.

ART. I. Articles XI, XIII, and XIV of the Treaty of Paris of the 30th March, 1856, as well as the special Convention concluded between Russia and the Sublime Porte, and annexed to the said Article XIV, are abrogated, and replaced by the following Article.

Closing of Straits of Dardanelles and Bosphorus, and power to open them to Vessels of War in time of Peace.

ART. II. The principle of the closing of the Straits of the Dardanelles and the Bosphorus, such as it has been established by the separate Convention of the 30th March, 1856, is maintained, with power to His Imperial Majesty the Sultan to open the said Straits in time of Peace to the Vessels of War of friendly and allied Powers, in case the Sublime

Porte should judge it necessary in order to secure the execution of the stipulations of the Treaty of Paris of the 30th March, 1856.

Black Sea open to Mercantile Marine of all Nations.

ART. III. The Black Sea remains open, as heretofore, to the Mercantile Marine of all Nations.

Extension of Term of Duration of Danube Commission to 24th April, 1883.

ART. IV. The Commission established by Article XVI of the Treaty of Paris, in which the Powers who joined in signing the Treaty are each represented by a delegate, and which was charged with the designation and execution of the works necessary below Isaktcha, to clear the Mouths of the Danube, as well as the neighbouring parts of the Black Sea, from the sands and other impediments which obstruct them, in order to put that part of the River and the said parts of the sea in the best state for navigation, is maintained in its present composition. The duration of that Commission is fixed for a further period of 12 years, counting from the 24th April, 1871, that is to say, till the 24th April, 1883, being the term of the Redemption of the Loan contracted by that Commission, under the Guarantee of Great Britain, Germany, Austria-Hungary, France, Italy, and Turkey.

Conditions of re-assembling of Riverain Commission.

ART. V. The conditions of the re-assembling of the Riverain Commission, established by Article XVII of the Treaty of Paris of the 30th March, 1856, shall be fixed by a previous understanding between the Riverain Powers, without prejudice to the clause relative to the 3 Danubian Principalities; and in so far as any modification of Article XVII of the said Treaty may be involved, this latter shall form the subject of a special Convention between the co-signatory Powers.

Provisional Tax on Vessels in the Danube, until extinction of Debt.

ART. VI. As the Powers which possess the shores of that part of the Danube where the Cataracts and the Iron Gates offer impediments to navigation reserve to themselves to come to an understanding with the view of removing those impediments, the High Contracting Parties recognise from the present moment their right to levy a Provisional Tax on Vessels of commerce of every flag which may henceforth benefit thereby, until the extinction of the Debt contracted for the execution of the Works; and they declare Article XV of the Treaty of Paris of 1856 to be inapplicable to that part of the River for a space of time necessary for the repayment of the debt in question.

Neutrality of Works and Establishments created by European Commission of the Danube.

ART. VII. All the Works and Establishments of every kind created by the European Commission in execution of the Treaty of Paris of 1856, or of the present Treaty, shall continue to enjoy the same Neutrality which has hitherto protected them, and which shall be equally respected for the future, under all circumstances, by the High Contracting Parties. The benefits of the immunities which result therefrom shall extend to the whole administrative and engineering staff of the Commission. It is, however, well understood that the provisions of this Article shall in no way affect the right of the Sublime Porte to send, as heretofore, its Vessels of War into the Danube in its character of Territorial Power.

Confirmation of Stipulations of Treaty of 30th March, 1856.

ART. VIII. The High Contracting Parties renew and confirm all the stipulations of the Treaty of the 30th March, 1856, as well as of its annexes, which are not annulled or modified by the present Treaty.

Ratifications.

ART. IX. The present Treaty shall be ratified, and the Ratifications shall be exchanged at London in the term of 6 weeks, or sooner if possible.

In witness whereof the respective Plenipotentiaries have signed the same, and have affixed thereto the Seal of their Arms.

Done at London, the 13th day of the month of March, in the year 1871.

(L.S.)   GRANVILLE.
(L.S.)   BERNSTORFF.
(L.S.)   APPONYI.
(L.S.)   BROGLIE.
(L.S.)   CADORNA.
(L.S.)   BRUNNOW.
(L.S.)   MUSURUS.

CONVENTION between Russia and Turkey, relative to the Black Sea. Signed at London, 13th March, 1871. Ratifications exchanged, 15th May, 1871.

[Communicated to the Conference on the 15th May, 1871, on the exchange of the Ratifications of the General Treaty of the 13th March.]

In the Name of Almighty God.

HIS Majesty the Emperor of All the Russias and His Imperial Majesty the Sultan, being mutually animated with the desire to consolidate the relations of Peace and good understanding happily existing between their Empires, have resolved to conclude for this purpose a Convention, and have named to that effect as their Plenipotentiaries, that is to say:

His Majesty the Emperor of All the Russias, the Sieur Philip Baron de Brunnow, his Actual Privy Councillor and his Ambassador Extraordinary and Plenipotentiary to Her Britannic Majesty, &c.;

And His Imperial Majesty the Sultan, Constantine Musurus Pasha, Muchir and Vizir of the Empire, his Ambassador Extraordinary and Plenipotentiary to Her Britannic Majesty, &c.;

Who, after having exchanged their Full Powers, found in good and due form, have agreed upon the following Articles:

Abrogation of Special Convention of 30th March, 1856, relative to the Black Sea.

ART. I. The Special Convention concluded at Paris between His Majesty the Emperor of All the Russias and His Imperial Majesty the Sultan, on the 18/30th March, in the year 1856, relative to the number and force of the Vessels of War of the two High Contracting Parties in the Black Sea, is and remains abrogated.

Ratifications.

ART. II. The present Convention shall be ratified, and the Ratifications thereof shall be exchanged at London in the space of 6 weeks, or sooner if possible.

In witness whereof, the respective Plenipotentiaries have signed the same, and have affixed thereto the Seal of their Arms.

Done at London, the 1st/13th day of the month of March, in the year 1871.

(L.S.)   BRUNNOW.
(L.S.)   MUSURUS.

A Convention between Turkey and Russia, *mutatis mutandis*, signed and ratified on the same days, was also communicated to the Conference at the same time.

98

CONVENTION between France and Germany, for the Delivery to the French Authorities of the Administration of the Departments occupied by German Troops. Signed at Rouen, 16th March, 1871.

BETWEEN M. Pouyer-Quertier, Minister of Finances; Baron de Ring, Delegate of the Minister for Foreign Affairs; and M. Casimir Fournier, Delegate of the Minister of the Interior, furnished with the Full Powers of the Government of the French Republic, on the one part; and, on the other part, Lieutenant-General de Fabrice, furnished with the Full Powers of His Majesty the Emperor of Germany, King of Prussia;

The Full Powers of the two Contracting Parties having been found in good and due form, it has been agreed as follows:

The Parties wishing to secure the easy and loyal execution of the Preliminary Treaty of Peace, signed at Versailles between the Empire of Germany and France, on the 26th February last, and to remove any possibility of a conflict between the German Army and the French Population, have agreed upon the following dispositions:

ART.

1. Departmental and Communal Administration of Departments occupied by *German* Troops, restored to *French* Authority on Ratification of Convention.
2. Re-establishment of *French* Prefects, &c. *German* Civil Commissioners to superintend *German* Interests. *French* Authorities to conform to measures of *German* Civil Commissioners.
3. *French* Tribunals, &c., to resume their functions. Reorganisation of Gendarmerie. Maintenance of state of Siege in Departments occupied by *Germans*.
4. *French* Administrative Authorities to conform to measures adopted by Commanders of *German* Troops.
5. Right of *German* Authorities to abrogate above Concessions in case their interests are compromised.
6. Ratifications.

Done at Rouen, 16th March, 1871.

(L.S.) FABRICE.   (L.S.)   POUYER-QUERTIER.
                         (L.S.)   N. DE RING.
                         (L.S.)   FOURNIER.

A Convention was signed on the same day relative to the payment of Taxes in arrear.

99

TREATY OF WASHINGTON between Great Britain and the United States. Concluded 8th May, 1871. Ratifications exchanged 17th June, 1871.

The United States of America and Her Britannic Majesty, being desirous to provide for an amicable settlement of all causes of difference between the two countries, have for that purpose appointed their respective Plenipotentiaries, that is to say: The President of the United States has appointed, on the part of the United States, as Commissioners in a Joint High Commission and Plenipotentiaries, Hamilton Fish, Secretary of State; Robert Cumming Schenck, Envoy Extraordinary and Minister Plenipotentiary to Great Britain; Samuel Nelson, an Associate Justice of the Supreme Court of the United States; Ebenezer Rockwood Hoar, of Massachusetts; and George Henry Williams, of Oregon; and Her Britannic Majesty, on her part, has appointed as her High Commissioners and Plenipotentiaries, the Right Honourable George Frederick Samuel, Earl de Grey and Earl of Ripon, Viscount Goderich, Baron Grantham, a Baronet, a Peer of the United Kingdom, Lord President of Her Majesty's Most Honourable Privy Council, Knight of the Most Noble Order of the Garter, etc., etc.; the Right Honourable Sir Stafford Henry Northcote, Baronet, one of Her Majesty's Most Honourable Privy Council, a Member of Parliament, a Companion of the Most Honourable Order of the Bath, etc., etc.; Sir Edward Thornton, Knight Commander of the Most Honourable Order of the Bath, Her Majesty's Envoy Extraordinary and Minister Plenipotentiary to the United States of America; Sir John Alexander Macdonald, Knight Commander of the Most Honourable Order of the Bath, a Member of Her Majesty's Privy Council for Canada, and Minister of Justice and Attorney General of Her Majesty's Dominion of Canada; and Mountague Bernard, Esquire, Chichele Professor of International Law in the University of Oxford.

And the said Plenipotentiaries, after having exchanged their full powers, which were found to be in due and proper form, have agreed to and concluded the following articles:

ART. I. Whereas differences have arisen between the Government of the United States and the Government of Her Britannic Majesty, and still exist, growing out of the acts committed by the several vessels which have given rise to the claims generically known as the "Alabama Claims: "

And whereas Her Britannic Majesty has authorized her High Commissioners and Plenipotentiaries to express, in a friendly spirit, the regret felt by Her Majesty's Government for the escape, under whatever circumstances, of the Alabama and other vessels from British ports, and for the depredations committed by those vessels:

Now, in order to remove and adjust all complaints and claims on the part of the United States, and to provide for the speedy settlement of such claims which are not admitted by Her Britannic Majesty's Government, the high contracting parties agree that all the said claims, growing out of acts committed by the aforesaid vessels, and generically known as the " Alabama Claims," shall be referred to a tribunal of arbitration to be composed of five Arbitrators, to be appointed in the following manner, that is to say: One shall be named by the President of the United States; one shall be named by Her Britannic Majesty; His Majesty the King of Italy shall be requested to name one; the President of the Swiss Confederation shall be requested to name one; and His Majesty the Emperor of Brazil shall be requested to name one.

In case of the death, absence, or incapacity to serve of any or either of the said Arbitrators, or, in the event of either of the said Arbitrators omitting or declining or ceasing to act as such, the President of the United States, or Her Britannic Majesty, or His Majesty the King of Italy, or the President of the Swiss Confederation, or His Majesty the Emperor of Brazil, as the case may be, may forthwith name another person to act as Arbitrator in the place and stead of the Arbitrator originally named by such head of a State.

And in the event of the refusal or omission for two months after receipt of the request from either of the high contracting parties of His Majesty the King of Italy, or the President of the Swiss Con-federation, or His Majesty the Emperor of Brazil, to name an Arbitrator either to fill the original appointment or in the place of one who may have died, be absent, or incapacitated, or who may omit, decline, or from any cause cease to act as such Arbitrator, His Majesty the King of Sweden and Norway shall be requested to name one or more persons, as the case may be, to act as such Arbitrator or Arbitrators.

ART. II. The Arbitrators shall meet at Geneva, in Switzerland, at the earliest convenient day after they shall have been named, and shall proceed impartially and carefully to examine and decide all questions that shall be laid before them on the part of the Governments of the United States and Her Britannic Majesty respectively. All questions considered by the tribunal, including the final award, shall be decided by a majority of all the Arbitrators.

Each of the high contracting parties shall also name one person to attend the tribunal as its Agent to represent it generally in all matters connected with the arbitration.

ART. III. The written or printed case of each of the two parties, accompanied by the documents, the official correspondence, and other evidence on which each relies, shall be delivered in duplicate to each of the Arbitrators and to the Agent of the other party as soon as may be after the organization of the tribunal, but within a period not exceeding six months from the date of the exchange of the ratifications of this treaty.

ART. IV. Within four months after the delivery on both sides of the written or printed case, either party may, in like manner, deliver in duplicate to each of the said Arbitrators, and to the Agent of the other party, a counter case and additional documents, correspondence, and evidence, in reply to the case, documents, correspondence, and evidence so presented by the other party.

The Arbitrators may, however, extend the time for delivering such counter case, documents, correspondence, and evidence, when, in their judgment, it becomes necessary, in consequence of the distance of the place from which the evidence to be presented is to be procured.

If in the case submitted to the Arbitrators either party shall have specified or alluded to any report or document in its own exclusive possession without annexing a copy, such party shall be bound, if the other party thinks proper to apply for it, to furnish that party with a copy thereof; and either party may call upon the other, through the Arbitrators, to produce the originals or certified copies of any papers adduced as evidence, giving in each instance such reasonable notice as the Arbitrators may require.

ART. V. It shall be the duty of the Agent of each party, within two months after the expiration of the time limited for the delivery of the counter case on both sides, to deliver in duplicate to each of the said Arbitrators and to the Agent of the other party a written or printed argument showing the points and referring to the evidence upon which his Government relies; and the Arbitrators may, if they desire further elucidation with regard to any point, require a written or printed statement or argument, or oral argument by counsel upon it; but in such case the other party shall be entitled to reply either orally or in writing, as the case may be.

ART. VI. In deciding the matters submitted to the Arbitrators, they shall be governed by the following three rules, which are agreed upon by the high contracting parties as rules to be taken as applicable to the case, and by such principles of international law not inconsistent therewith as the Arbitrators shall determine to have been applicable to the case.

RULES.

A neutral Government is bound—

First, to use due diligence to prevent the fitting out, arming, or equipping, within its jurisdiction, of any vessel which it has reasonable ground to believe is intended to cruise or to carry on war against a Power with which it is at peace; and also to use like diligence to prevent the departure from its jurisdiction of any vessel intended to cruise or carry on war as above, such vessel having been specially adapted, in whole or in part, within such jurisdiction, to warlike use.

Secondly, not to permit or suffer either belligerent to make use of its ports or waters as the base of naval operations against the other, or for the purpose of the renewal or augmentation of military supplies or arms, or the recruitment of men.

Thirdly, to exercise due diligence in its own ports and waters, and, as to all persons within its jurisdiction, to prevent any violation of the foregoing obligations and duties.

Her Britannic Majesty has commanded her High Commissioners and Plenipotentiaries to declare that Her Majesty's Government cannot assent to the foregoing rules as a statement of principles of international law which were in force at the time when the claims mentioned in Article I arose, but that Her Majesty's Government, in order to evince its desire of strengthening the friendly relations between the two countries and of making satisfactory provision for the future, agrees that in deciding the questions between the two countries arising out of those claims, the Arbitrators should assume that Her Majesty's Government had undertaken to act upon the principles set forth in these rules.

And the high contracting parties agree to observe these rules as between themselves in future, and to bring them to the knowledge of other maritime Powers, and to invite them to accede to them.

ART. VII. The decision of the tribunal shall, if possible, be made within three months from the close of the argument on both sides.

It shall be made in writing and dated, and shall be signed by the Arbitrators who may assent to it.

The said tribunal shall first determine as to each vessel separately whether Great Britain has, by any act or omission, failed to fulfil any of the duties set forth in the foregoing three rules, or recognized by the principles of international law not inconsistent with such rules, and shall certify such fact as to each of the said vessels. In case the tribunal find that Great Britain has failed to fulfil any duty or duties as aforesaid, it may, if it think proper, proceed to award a sum in gross to be paid by Great Britain to the United States for all the claims referred to it; and in such case the gross sum so awarded shall be paid in coin by the Government of Great Britain to the Government of the United States, at Washington, within twelve months after the date of the award.

The award shall be in duplicate, one copy whereof shall be delivered to the Agent of the United States for his Government, and the other copy shall be delivered to the Agent of Great Britain for his Government.

ART. VIII. Each Government shall pay its own Agent and provide for the proper remuneration of the counsel employed by it and of the Arbitrator appointed by it, and for the expense of preparing and submitting its case to the tribunal. All other expenses connected with the arbitration shall be defrayed by the two Governments in equal moieties.

ART. IX. The Arbitrators shall keep an accurate record of their proceedings, and may appoint and employ the necessary officers to assist them.

ART. X. In case the tribunal finds that Great Britain has failed to fulfil any duty or duties as aforesaid, and does not award a sum in gross, the high contracting parties agree that a board of assessors shall be appointed to ascertain and determine what claims are valid, and what amount or amounts shall be paid by Great Britain to the United States on account of the liability arising from such failure, as to each vessel, according to the extent of such liability as decided by the Arbitrators.

The board of assessors shall be constituted as follows: One member thereof shall be named by the President of the United States, one member thereof shall be named by Her Britannic Majesty, and one member thereof shall be named by the Representative at Washington of His Majesty the King of Italy; and in case of a vacancy happening from any cause, it shall be filled in the same manner in which the original appointment was made.

As soon as possible after such nominations the board of assessors shall be organized in Washington, with power to hold their sittings there, or in New York, or in Boston. The members thereof shall severally subscribe a solemn declaration that they will impartially and carefully examine and decide, to the best of their judgment and according to justice and equity, all matters submitted to them, and shall forthwith proceed, under such rules and regulations as they may prescribe, to the investigation of the claims which shall be presented to them by the Government of the United States, and shall examine and decide upon them in such order and manner as they may think proper, but upon such evidence or information only as shall be furnished by or on behalf of the Governments of the United States and of Great Britain, respectively. They shall be bound to hear on each separate claim, if required, one person on behalf of each Government, as counsel or agent. A majority of the Assessors in each case shall be sufficient for a decision.

The decision of the Assessors shall be given upon each claim in writing, and shall be signed by them respectively and dated.

Every claim shall be presented to the Assessors within six months from the day of their first meeting, but they may, for good cause shown, extend the time for the presentation of any claim to a further period not exceeding three months.

The Assessors shall report to each Government, at or before the expiration of one year from the date of their first meeting, the amount of claims decided by them up to the date of such report; if further claims then remain undecided, they shall make a further report at or before the expiration of two years from the date of such first meeting; and in case any claims remain undetermined at that time, they shall make a final report within a further period of six months.

The report or reports shall be made in duplicate, and one copy thereof shall be delivered to the Secretary of State of the United States, and one copy thereof to the Representative of Her Britannic Majesty at Washington.

All sums of money which may be awarded under this article shall be payable at Washington, in coin, within twelve months after the delivery of each report.

The board of assessors may employ such clerks as they shall think necessary.

The expenses of the board of assessors shall be borne equally by the two Governments, and paid from time to time, as may be found expedient, on the production of accounts certified by the board. The remuneration of the Assessors shall also be paid by the two Governments in equal moieties in a similar manner.

ART. XI. The high contracting parties engage to consider the result of the proceedings of the tribunal of arbitration and of the board of Assessors, should such board be appointed, as a full, perfect, and final settlement of all the claims hereinbefore referred to; and further engage that every such claim, whether the same may or may not have been presented to the notice of, made, preferred, or laid before the tribunal or board, shall, from and after the conclusion of the proceedings of the tribunal or board, be considered and treated as finally settled, barred, and thenceforth inadmissible.

ART. XII. The high contracting parties agree that all claims on the part of corporations, companies, or private individuals, citizens of the United States, upon the Government of Her Britannic Majesty, arising out of acts committed against the persons or property of citizens of the United States during the period between the thirteenth of April, eighteen hundred and sixty-one, and the ninth of April, eighteen hundred and sixty-five, inclusive, not being claims growing out of the acts of the vessels referred to in Article I of this treaty, and all claims, with the like exception, on the part of corporation, companies, or private individuals, subjects of Her Britannic Majesty, upon the Government of the United States, arising out of acts committed against the persons or property of subjects of Her Britannic Majesty during the same period, which may have been presented to either Government for its interposition with the other, and which yet remain unsettled, as well as any other such claims which may be presented within the time specified in Article XIV of this treaty, shall be referred to three Commissioners, to be appointed in the following manner, that is to say: One Commissioner shall be named by the President of the United States, one by Her Britannic Majesty, and a third by the President of the United States and Her Britannic Majesty conjointly; and in case the third Commissioner shall not have been so named within a period of three months from the date of the exchange of the ratifications of this treaty, then the third Commissioner shall be named by the Representative at Washington of His Majesty the King of Spain. In case of the death, absence, or incapacity of any Commissioner, or in the event of any Commissioner omitting or ceasing to act, the vacancy shall be filled in the manner hereinbefore provided for making the original appointment; the period of three months in case of such substitution being calculated from the date of the happening of the vacancy.

The Commissioners so named shall meet at Washington at the earliest convenient period after they have been respectively named; and shall, before proceeding to any business, make and subscribe a solemn declaration that they will impartially and carefully examine and decide, to the best of their judgment, and according to justice and equity, all such claims as shall be laid before them on the part of the Governments of the United States and of Her Britannic Majesty, respectively; and such declaration shall be entered on the record of their proceedings.

ART. XIII. The Commissioners shall then forthwith proceed to the investigation of the claims which shall be presented to them. They shall investigate and decide such claims in such order and such manner as they may think proper, but upon such evidence or information only as shall be furnished by or on behalf of the respective Governments. They shall be bound to receive and consider all written documents or statements which may be presented to them by or on behalf of the respective Governments in support of, or in answer to, any claim, and to hear, if required, one person on each side, on behalf of each Government, as counsel or agent for such Government, on each and every separate claim. A majority of the Commissioners shall be sufficient for an award in each case. The award shall be given upon each claim in writing, and shall be signed by the Commissioners assenting to it. It shall be competent for each Government to name one person to attend the Commissioners as its agent, to present and support claims on its behalf, and to answer claims made upon it, and to represent it generally in all matters connected with the investigation and decision thereof.

The high contracting parties hereby engage to consider the decision of the Commissioners as absolutely final and conclusive upon each claim decided upon by them, and to give full effect to such decisions without any objection, evasion, or delay whatsoever.

ART. XIV. Every claim shall be presented to the Commissioners within six months from the day of their first meeting, unless in any case where reasons for delay shall be established to the satisfaction of the Commissioners, and then, and in any such case, the period for presenting the claim may be extended by them to any time not exceeding three months longer.

The Commissioners shall be bound to examine and decide upon every claim within two years from the day of their first meeting. It shall be competent for the Commissioners to decide in each case whether any claim has or has not been duly made, preferred, and laid before them, either wholly or to any and what extent, according to the true intent and meaning of this treaty.

Art. XV. All sums of money which may be awarded by the Commissioners on account of any claim shall be paid by the one Government to the other, as the case may be, within twelve months after the date of the final award, without interest, and without any deduction save as specified in Article XVI of this treaty.

Art. XVI. The Commissioners shall keep an accurate record, and correct minutes or notes of all their proceedings, with the dates thereof, and may appoint and employ a secretary, and any other necessary officer, or officers, to assist them in the transaction of the business which may come before them.

Each Government shall pay its own Commissioner and Agent or Council. All other expenses shall be defrayed by the two Governments in equal moieties.

The whole expenses of the commission, including contingent expenses, shall be defrayed by a ratable deduction on the amount of the sums awarded by the Commissioners, provided always that such deduction shall not exceed the rate of five per cent. on the sums so awarded.

Art. XVII. The high contracting parties engage to consider the result of the proceedings of this commission as a full, perfect, and final settlement of all such claims as are mentioned in Article XII of this treaty upon either Government; and further engage that every such claim, whether or not the same may have been presented to the notice of, made, preferred, or laid before the said commission, shall, from and after the conclusion of the proceedings of the said commission, be considered and treated as finally settled, barred, and thenceforth inadmissible.

Art. XVIII. It is agreed by the high contracting parties that, in addition to the liberty secured to the United States fishermen by the convention between the United States and Great Britain, signed at London on the 20th day of October, 1818, of taking, curing, and drying fish on certain coasts of the British North American Colonies therein defined, the inhabitants of the United States shall have, in common with the subjects of Her Britannic Majesty, the liberty, for the term of years mentioned in Article XXXIII of this treaty, to take fish of every kind, except shell-fish, on the sea-coasts and shores, and in the bays, harbours, and creeks, of the provinces of Quebec, Nova Scotia, and New Brunswick, and the colony of Prince Edward's Island, and of the several islands thereunto adjacent, without being restricted to any distance from the shore, with permission to land upon the said coasts and shores and islands, and also upon the Magdalen Islands, for the purpose of drying their nets and curing their fish; provided that, in so doing, they do not interfere with the rights of private property, or with British fishermen, in the peaceable use of any part of the said coasts in their occupancy for the same purpose.

It is understood that the above-mentioned liberty applies solely to the sea fishery, and that the salmon and shad fisheries, and all other fisheries in rivers and the mouths of rivers, are hereby reserved exclusively for British fishermen.

ART. XIX. It is agreed by the high contracting parties that British subjects shall have, in common with the citizens of the United States, the liberty, for the term of years mentioned in Article XXXIII of this treaty, to take fish of every kind, except shell-fish, on the eastern sea coasts and shores of the United States north of the thirty-ninth parallel of north latitude, and on the shores of the several islands thereunto adjacent, and in the bays, harbours, and creeks of the said sea-coasts and shores of the United States and of the said islands, without being restricted to any distance from the shore, with permission to land upon the said coasts of the United States and of the islands aforesaid, for the purpose of drying their nets and curing their fish; provided that, in so doing, they do not interfere with the rights of private property, or with the fishermen of the United States in the peaceable use of any part of the said coasts in their occupancy for the same purpose.

It is understood that the above-mentioned liberty applies solely to the sea fishery, and that salmon and shad fisheries, and all other fisheries in rivers and mouths of rivers, are hereby reserved exclusively for fishermen of the United States.

ART. XX. It is agreed that the places designated by the Commissioners appointed under the first article of the treaty between the United States and Great Britain, concluded at Washington on the 5th of June, 1854, upon the coasts of Her Britannic Majesty's dominions and the United States, as places reserved from the common right of fishing under that treaty, shall be regarded as in like manner reserved from the common right of fishing under the preceding articles. In case any question should arise between the Governments of the United States and of Her Britannic Majesty as to the common right of fishing in places not thus designated as reserved, it is agreed that a commission shall be appointed to designate such places, and shall be constituted in the same manner, and have the same powers, duties, and authority as the commission appointed under the said first article of the treaty of the 5th of June, 1854.

ART. XXI. It is agreed that, for the term of years mentioned in Article XXXIII of this treaty, fish oil and fish of all kinds, (except fish of the inland lakes, and of the rivers falling into them, and except fish preserved in oil,) being the produce of the fisheries of the United States, or of the Dominion of Canada, or of Prince Edward's Island, shall be admitted into each country, respectively, free of duty.

ART. XXII. Inasmuch as it is asserted by the Government of Her Britannic Majesty that the privileges accorded to the citizens of the United States under Article XVIII of this treaty are of greater value than those accorded by Articles XIX and XXI of this treaty to the subjects of Her Britannic Majesty, and this assertion is not admitted by the Government of the United States, it is further agreed that Commissioners shall be appointed to determine, having regard to the privileges accorded by the United States to the subjects of Her Britannic Majesty, as stated in Articles XIX and XXI of this treaty, the amount of any compensation which, in their opinion, ought to be paid by the Government of the United States to the Government of Her Britannic Majesty in return for the privileges accorded to the citizens of the United States under Article XVIII of this treaty; and that any sum of money which the said Commissioners may so award shall be paid by the United States Government, in a gross sum, within twelve months after such award shall have been given.

ART. XXIII. The Commissioners referred to in the preceding article shall be appointed in the following manner, that is to say: One Commissioner shall be named by the President of the United States, one by Her Britannic Majesty, and a third by the President of the United States and Her Britannic Majesty conjointly; and in case the third Commissioner shall not have been so named within a period of three months from the date when this article shall take effect, then the third Commissioner shall be named by the Representative at London of His Majesty the Emperor of Austria and King of Hungary. In case of the death, absence, or incapacity of any Commissioner, or in the event of any Commissioner omitting or ceasing to act, the vacancy shall be filled in the manner hereinbefore provided for making the original appointment, the period of three months in case of such substitution being calculated from the date of the happening of the vacancy.

The Commissioners so named shall meet in the city of Halifax, in the province of Nova Scotia, at the earliest convenient period after they have been respectively named, and shall, before proceeding to any business, make and subscribe a solemn declaration that they will impartially and carefully examine and decide the matters referred to them to the best of their judgment, and according to justice and equity; and such declaration shall be entered on the record of their proceedings.

Each of the high contracting parties shall also name one person to attend the commission as its Agent, to represent it generally in all matters connected with the commission.

ART. XXIV. The proceedings shall be conducted in such order as the Commissioners appointed under Articles XXII and XXIII of this treaty shall determine. They shall be bound to receive such oral or written testimony as either Government may present. If either party shall offer oral testimony, the other party shall have the right of cross-examination, under such rules as the Commissioners shall prescribe.

If in the case submitted to the Commissioners either party shall have specified or alluded to any report or document in its own exclusive possession, without annexing a copy, such party shall be bound, if the other party thinks proper to apply for it, to furnish that party with a copy thereof; and either party may call upon the other, through the Commissioners, to produce the originals or certified copies of any papers adduced as evidence, giving in each instance such reasonable notice as the Commissioners may require.

The case on either side shall be closed within a period of six months from the date of the organization of the Commission, and the Commissioners shall be requested to give their award as soon as possible thereafter. The aforesaid period of six months may be extended for three months in case of a vacancy occurring among the Commissioners under the circumstances contemplated in Article XXIII of this treaty.

ART. XXV. The Commissioners shall keep an accurate record and correct minutes or notes of all their proceedings, with the dates thereof, and may appoint and employ a Secretary and any other necessary officer or officers to assist them in the transaction of the business which may come before them.

Each of the high contracting parties shall pay its own Commissioner and Agent or Counsel; all other expenses shall be defrayed by the two Governments in equal moieties.

ART. XXVI. The navigation of the river St. Lawrence, ascending and descending, from the forty-fifth parallel of north latitude, where it ceases to form the boundary between the two countries, from, to, and into the sea, shall forever remain free and open for the purposes of commerce to the citizens of the United States, subject to any laws and regulations of Great Britain, or of the Dominion of Canada, not inconsistent with such privilege of free navigation.

The navigation of the rivers Yukon, Porcupine, and Stikine, ascending and descending, from, to, and into the sea, shall forever remain free and open for the purposes of commerce to the subjects of Her Britannic Majesty and to the citizens of the United States, subject to any laws and regulations of either country within its own territory, not inconsistent with such privilege of free navigation.

ART. XXVII. The Government of Her Britannic Majesty engages to urge upon the Government of the Dominion of Canada to secure to the citizens of the United States the use of the Welland, St. Lawrence, and other canals in the Dominion on terms of equality with the inhabitants of the Dominion; and the Government of the United States engages that the subjects of Her Britannic Majesty shall enjoy the use of the St. Clair Flats canal on terms of equality with the inhabitants of the United States, and further engages to urge upon the State Governments to secure to the subjects of Her Britannic Majesty the use of the several State canals connected with the navigation of the lakes or rivers traversed by or contiguous to the boundary line between the possessions of the high contracting parties, on terms of equality with the inhabitants of the United States.

ART. XXVIII. The navigation of Lake Michigan shall also, for the term of years mentioned in Article XXXIII of this treaty, be free and open for the purposes of commerce to the subjects of Her Britannic Majesty, subject to any laws and regulations of the United States or of the States bordering thereon not inconsistent with such privilege of free navigation.

ART. XXIX. It is agreed that, for the term of years mentioned in Article XXXIII of this treaty, goods, wares, or merchandise arriving at the ports of New York, Boston, and Portland, and any other ports in the United States which have been or may, from time to time, be specially designated by the President of United States, and destined for Her Britannic Majesty's possessions in North America, may be entered at the proper custom-house and conveyed in transit, without the payment of duties, through the territory of the United States, under such rules, regulations, and conditions for the protection of the revenue as the Government of the United States may from time to time prescribe; and under like rules, regulations, and conditions, goods, wares, or merchandise may be conveyed in transit, without the payment of duties, from such possessions through the territory of the United States for export from the said ports of the United States.

It is further agreed that, for the like period, goods, wares, or merchandise arriving at any of the ports of Her Britannic Majesty's possessions in North America and destined for the United States may be entered at the proper custom-house and conveyed in transit, without the payment of duties, through the said possessions, under such rules and regulations, and conditions for the protection of the revenue, as the Governments of the said possessions may from time to time, prescribe; and under like rules, regulations, and conditions goods, wares, or merchandise may be conveyed in transit, without payment of duties, from the United States through the said possessions to other places in the United States, or for export from ports in the said possessions.

ART. XXX. It is agreed that, for the terms of years mentioned in Article XXXIII of this treaty, subjects of Her Britannic Majesty may carry in British vessels, without payment of duty, goods, wares, or merchandise from one port or place within the territory of the United States upon the St. Lawrence, the great lakes, and the rivers connecting the same, to another port or place within the territory of the United States as aforesaid: Provided, That a portion of such transportation is made through the Dominion of Canada by land carriage and in bond, under such rules and regulations as may be agreed upon between the Government of Her Britannic Majesty and the Government of the United States.

Citizens of the United States may for the like period carry in United States vessels, without payment of duty, goods, wares, or merchandise from one port or place within the possessions of Her Britannic Majesty in North America, to another port or place within the said possessions: Provided, That a portion of such transportation is made through the territory of the United States by land carriage and in bond, under such rules and regulations as may be agreed upon between the Government of the United States and the Government of Her Britannic Majesty.

The Government of the United States further engages not to impose any export duties on goods, wares, or merchandise carried under this article through the territory of the United States; and Her Majesty's Government engages to urge the Parliament of the Dominion of Canada and the Legislatures of the other colonies not to impose any export duties on goods, wares, or merchandise carried under this article; and the Government of the United States may, in case such export duties are imposed by the Dominion of Canada, suspend, during the period that such duties are imposed, the right of carrying granted under this article in favour of the subjects of Her Britannic Majesty.

The Government of the United States may suspend the right of carrying granted in favour of the subjects of Her Britannic Majesty under this article in case the Dominion of Canada should at any time deprive the citizens of the United States of the use of the canals of the said Dominion on terms of equality with the inhabitants of the Dominion, as provided in Article XXVII.

ART. XXXI. The Government of Her Britannic Majesty further

engages to urge upon the Parliament of the Dominion of Canada and the Legislature of New Brunswick, that no export duty, or other duty, shall be levied on lumber or timber of any kind cut on that portion of the American territory in the State of Maine watered by the river St. John and its tributaries, and floated down that river to the sea, when the same is shipped to the United States from the province of New Brunswick. And, in case any such export or other duty continues to be levied after the expiration of one year from the date of the exchange of the ratifications of this treaty, it is agreed that the Government of the United States may suspend the right of carrying hereinbefore granted under Article XXX of this treaty for such period as such export or other duty may be levied.

Art. XXXII. It is further agreed that the provisions and stipulations of Articles XVIII to XXV of this treaty, inclusive, shall extend to the colony of Newfoundland, so far as they are applicable. But if the Imperial Parliament, the Legislature of Newfoundland, or the Congress of the United States, shall not embrace the colony of Newfoundland in their laws enacted for carrying the foregoing articles into effect, then this article shall be of no effect; but the omission to make provision by law to give it effect, by either of the legislative bodies aforesaid, shall not in any way impair any other articles of this treaty.

Art. XXXIII. The foregoing Articles XVIII to XXV, inclusive, and Article XXX of this treaty shall take effect as soon as the laws required to carry them into operation shall have been passed by the Imperial Parliament of Great Britain, by the Parliament of Canada, and by the Legislature of Prince Edward's Island on the one hand, and by the Congress of the United States on the other. Such assent having been given, the said articles shall remain in force for the period of ten years from the date at which they may come into operation; and further until the expiration of two years after either of the high contracting parties shall have given notice to the other of its wish to terminate the same; each of the high contracting parties being at liberty to give such notice to the other at the end of the said period of ten years or at any time afterward.

Art. XXXIV. Whereas it was stipulated by Article I of the treaty concluded at Washington on the 15th of June, 1846, between the United States and Her Britannic Majesty, that the line of boundary between the territories of the United States and those of Her Britannic Majesty, from the point of the forty-ninth parallel of north latitude up to which it had already been ascertained, should be continued westward along the said parallel of north latitude "to the middle of the channel which separates the continent from Vancouver's Island, and thence southerly, through the middle of the said channel and of Fuca Straits, to the Pacific Ocean;"

and whereas the Commissioners appointed by the two high contracting parties to determine that portion of the boundary which runs southerly through the middle of the channel aforesaid, were unable to agree upon the same; and whereas the Government of Her Britannic Majesty claims that such boundary line should, under the terms of the treaty above recited, be run through the Rosario Straits, and the Government of the United States claims that it should be run through the Canal de Haro, it is agreed that the respective claims of the Government of the United States and of the Government of Her Britannic Majesty shall be submitted to the arbitration and award of His Majesty the Emperor of Germany, who, having regard to the above-mentioned article of the said treaty, shall decide thereupon, finally and without appeal, which of those claims is most in accordance with the true interpretation of the treaty of June 15, 1846.

ART. XXXV. The award of His Majesty the Emperor of Germany shall be considered as absolutely final and conclusive; and full effect shall be given to such award without any objection, evasion, or delay whatsoever. Such decision shall be given in writing and dated; it shall be in whatsoever form His Majesty may choose to adopt; it shall be delivered to the Representatives or other public Agents of the United States and of Great Britain, respectively, who may be actually at Berlin, and shall be considered as operative from the day of the date of the delivery thereof.

ART. XXXVI. The written or printed case of each of the two parties, accompanied by the evidence offered in support of the same, shall be laid before His Majesty the Emperor of Germany within six months from the date of the exchange of the ratifications of this treaty, and a copy of such case and evidence shall be communicated by each party to the other, through their respective Representatives at Berlin.

The high contracting parties may include in the evidence to be considered by the Arbitrator such documents, official correspondence, and other official or public statements bearing on the subject of the reference as they may consider necessary to the support of their respective cases.

After the written or printed case shall have been communicated by each party to the other, each party shall have the power of drawing up and laying before the Arbitrator a second and definitive statement, if it think fit to do so, in reply to the case of the other party so communicated, which definite statement shall be so laid before the Arbitrator, and also be mutually communicated in the same manner as aforesaid, by each party to the other, within six months from the date of laying the first statement of the case before the Arbitrator.

ART. XXXVII. If, in the case submitted to the Arbitrator, either party shall specify or allude to any report or document in its own exclusive possession without annexing a copy, such party shall be bound, if the other party thinks proper to apply for it, to furnish that party with a copy thereof, and either party may call upon the other, through the Arbitrator, to produce the originals or certified copies of any papers adduced as evidence, giving in each instance such reasonable notice as the Arbitrator may require. And if the Arbitrator should desire further elucidation or evidence with regard to any point contained in the statements laid before him, he shall be at liberty to require it from either party, and he shall be at liberty to hear one Counsel or Agent for each party, in relation to any matter, and at such time, and in such manner, as he may think fit.

ART. XXXVIII. The Representatives or other public Agents of the United States and of Great Britain at Berlin, respectively, shall be considered as the Agents of their respective Governments to conduct their cases before the Arbitrator, who shall be requested to address all his communications and give all his notices to such Representatives or other public Agents, who shall represent their respective Governments generally, in all matters connected with the arbitration.

ART. XXXIX. It shall be competent to the Arbitrator to proceed in the said arbitration, and all matters relating thereto, as and when he shall see fit, either in person, or by a person or persons named by him for that purpose, either in the presence or absence of either or both Agents, and either orally, or by written discussion or otherwise.

ART. XL. The Arbitrator may, if he think fit, appoint a Secretary, or Clerk, for the purposes of the proposed arbitration, at such rate of remuneration as he shall think proper. This, and all other expenses of and connected with the said arbitration, shall be provided for as hereinafter stipulated.

ART. XLI. The Arbitrator shall be requested to deliver, together with his award, an account of all the costs and expenses which he may have been put to, in relation to this matter, which shall forthwith be repaid by the two Governments in equal moieties.

ART. XLII. The Arbitrator shall be requested to give his award in writing as early as convenient after the whole case on each side shall have been laid before him, and to deliver one copy thereof to each of the said Agents.

ART. XLIII. The present treaty shall be duly ratified by the President of the United States of America, by and with the advice and consent of the Senate thereof, and by Her Britannic Majesty; and the ratifications shall be exchanged either at Washington or at London within six months from the date hereof, or earlier if possible.

In faith whereof, we, the respective Plenipotentiaries, have signed this treaty and have hereunto affixed our seals.

Done in duplicate at Washington the eighth day of May, in the year of our Lord one thousand eight hundred and seventy-one.

HAMILTON FISH.
ROBT. C. SCHENCK.
SAMUEL NELSON.
EBENEZER ROCKWOOD HOAR.
GEO. H. WILLIAMS.
DE GREY & RIPON.
STAFFORD H. NORTHCOTE.
EDWD. THORNTON.
JOHN A. MACDONALD.
MONTAGUE BERNARD.

AWARD OF THE EMPEROR OF GERMANY UNDER THE XXXIVth ARTICLE OF THE TREATY OF MAY 8, 1871; GIVING THE ISLAND OF SAN JUAN TO THE UNITED STATES.

We, William, by the grace of God, German Emperor, King of Prussia, &c., &c., &c.

After examination of the Treaty concluded at Washington on the 6th of May, 1871, between the Governments of Her Britannic Majesty and of the United States of America, according to which the said Governments have submitted to Our Arbitrament the question at issue between them, whether the boundary-line which, according to the Treaty of Washington of June 15, 1846, after being carried westward along the forty-ninth parallel of northern latitude to the middle of the channel which separates the continent from Vancouver's Island is thence to be drawn southerly through the middle of the said channel and of the Fuca Straits to the Pacific Ocean, should be drawn through the Rosario Channel as the Government of Her Britannic Majesty claims, or through the Haro Channel as the Government of the United States claims; to the end that We may finally and without appeal decide which of these claims is most in accordance with the true interpretation of the treaty of June 15, 1846.

After hearing the report made to Us by the experts and jurists summoned by Us upon the contents of the interchanged memorials and their appendices:—

Have decreed the following award:

Most in accordance with the true interpretations of the Treaty concluded on the 15th of June, 1846, between the Governments of Her Britannic Majesty and of the United States of America, is the claim of the Government of the United States that the boundary-line between the territories of Her Britannic Majesty and the United States should be drawn through the Haro Channel.

Authenticated by Our Autographic Signature and the impression of the imperial great seal.

Given at Berlin, October the 21st, 1872.

WILLIAM.

THE GENEVA AWARD UNDER ARTICLES I TO XI OF THE CONVENTION OF 1871 made by the tribunal of arbitration constituted by virtue of the first article of the treaty concluded at Washington the 8th of May 1871, between the United States and Great Britain.

The United States of America and Her Britannic Majesty having agreed by Article I. of the treaty concluded and signed at Washington the 8th of May 1871, to refer all the claims "generically known as the Alabama claims" to a tribunal of arbitration to be composed of five arbitrators named:

One by the President of the United States,
One by Her Britannic Majesty,
One by His Majesty the King of Italy,
One by the President of the Swiss Confederation,
One by his Majesty the Emperor of Brazil;

And the President of the United States, Her Britannic Majesty, His Majesty the King of Italy, the President of the Swiss Confederation, and His Majesty the Emperor of Brazil having respectively named their arbitrators, to wit:

The President of the United States, Charles Francis Adams, esquire;

Her Britannic Majesty, Sir Alexander James Edmund Cockburn, baronet, a member Her Majesty's privy council, lord chief justice of England;

His Majesty the King of Italy, His Excellency Count Frederick Sclopis of Salerno, a knight of the order of the Annunciata, minister of state, senator of the Kingdom of Italy;

The President of the Swiss Confederation, M. James Stampfli;

His Majesty the Emperor of Brazil, His Excellency Marcos Antonio d' Araujo, Viscount d' Itajuba, a grandee of the Empire of Brazil, member of the council of H. M. the Emperor of Brazil, and his envoy extraordinary and minister plenipotentiary in France.

And the five arbitrators above named having assembled at Geneva (In Switzerland) in one of the chambers of the Hotel de Ville on the 15th of December, 1871, in conformity with the terms of the second article of the treaty of Washington of the 8th of May of that year, and having proceeded to the inspection and verification of their respective powers, which were found duly authenticated, the tribunal of arbitration was declared duly organized.

The agents named by each of the high contracting parties, by virtue of the same article II. to wit:

For the United States of America, John C. Bancroft Davis, esquire;

And for Her Britannic Majesty, Charles Stuart Aubrey, Lord Tenterden, a peer of the United Kingdom, companion of the Most Honorable Order of the Bath, assistant under secretary of state for foreign affairs;

Whose powers were found likewise duly authenticated, then delivered to each of the arbitrators the printed case prepared by each of the two parties, accompanied by the documents, the official correspondence, and other evidence on which each relied, in conformity with the terms of the third article of the said treaty.

In virtue of the decision made by the tribunal at its first session, the counter case and additional documents, correspondence, and evidence referred to in article four of the said treaty were delivered by the respective agents of the two parties to the secretary of the tribunal on the 15th of April, 1872, at the chamber of conference, at the Hotel de Ville of Geneva.

The tribunal, in accordance with the vote of adjournment passed at their second session, held on the 16th of December, 1871, reassembled at Geneva on the 15th of June 1872; and the agent of each of the parties duly delivered to each of the arbitrators, and to the agent of the other party, the printed argument referred to in article V of the said treaty.

The tribunal having since fully taken into their consideration the treaty, and also the cases, counter cases, documents, evidence, and arguments, and likewise all other communications made to them by the two parties during the progress of their sittings and having impartially and carefully examined the same,

Has arrived at the decision embodied in the present award:

Whereas, having regard to the VIth and VIIth articles of the said treaty, the arbitrators are bound under the terms of the said VIth article, "in deciding the matters submitted to them, to be governed by the three rules therein specified and by such principles of international law, not inconsistent therewith, as the arbitrators shall determine to have been applicable to the case;"

And whereas the "due diligence" referred to in the first and third of the said rules ought to be exercised by neutral Governments in exact proportion to the risks to which either of the belligerents may be exposed, from a failure to fulfill the obligations of neutrality on their part;

And whereas the circumstances out of which the facts constituting the subject matter of the present controversy arose were of a nature to

call for the exercise on the part of Her Britannic Majesty's Government
of all possible solicitude for the observance of the rights and the duties
involved in the proclamation of neutrality issued by her Majesty on the
13th day of May 1861;

And whereas the effects of a violation of neutrality committed by
means of the construction, equipment and armament of a vessel are not
done away with by any commission which the Government of the belligerent power, benefited by the violation of neutrality, may afterwards
have granted to that vessel; and the ultimate step, by which the offence
is completed cannot be admissible as a ground for the absolution of the
offender, nor can the consummation of his fraud become the means of
establishing his innocence;

And whereas the privilege of extraterritoriality accorded to vessels of
war has been admitted into the law of Nations, not as an absolute right,
but solely as a proceeding founded on the principle of courtesy and
mutual deference between different nations, and therefore can never be
appealed to for the protection of acts done in violation of neutrality;

And whereas the absence of a previous notice cannot be regarded as a
failure in any consideration required by the law of nations in those cases
in which a vessel carries with its own condemnation;

And whereas in order to impart to any supplies of coal a character
inconsistent with the second rule prohibiting the use of neutral ports of
waters as a base of naval operations for a belligerent it is necessary that
the said supplies should be connected with special circumstances of time,
of persons, or of place, which may combine to give them such character;

And whereas with respect to the vessel called the Alabama, it clearly
results from all the facts relative to the construction of the ship at first
designated by the number "290" in the port of Liverpool and its equip-
ments and armament in the vicinity of Terceira through the agency of the
vessels called the "Agrippina" and the "Bahama", dispatch from Great
Britain to that end, that the British Government failed to use due
diligence in the performance of its neutral obligations; and especially
that it omitted, notwithstanding the warnings and official representations
made by the diplomatic agents of the United States during the construction of the said number "290", to take in due time any effective measures
of prevention, and that those orders which it did give at last, for the
detention of the vessel, were issued so late that their execution was not
practicable;

And whereas after the escape of that vessel, the measures taken for its
pursuit and its arrest were so imperfect as to lead to no result, and therefore cannot be considered sufficient to release Great Britain from the
responsibility already incurred;

And whereas, in spite of the violations of the neutrality of Great

Britain committed by the "290," this same vessel, later known as the confederate cruiser Alabama, was on several occasions freely admitted into the ports of colonies of Great Britain, instead of being proceeded against as it ought to have been in any and every port within British jurisdiction in which it might have been found;

And whereas the Government of Her Britannic Majesty cannot justify itself for a failure in due diligence on the plea of insufficiency of the legal means of action which it possessed:

For the arbitrators for the reasons above assigned and the fifth for the reasons separately signed by him,

Are of opinion—

That Great Britain has in this case failed by omission, to fulfil the duties prescribed in the first and the third of the rules, established by the VIth article of the treaty of Washington.

And whereas, with respect to the vessel called the "Florida" it results from all the facts relative to the construction of the "Oreto" in the port of Liverpool, and to its issue there from, which facts failed to induce the authorities in Great Britain to resort to measures adequate to prevent the violation of the neutrality of that nation, notwithstanding the warnings and repeated representations of the agents of the United States, that Her Majesty's Government has failed to use due diligence to fulfill the duties of neutrality;

And whereas it likewise results from all the facts relative to the stay of the "Oreto" at Nassau, to her issue from that port, to her enlistment of men, to her supplies, and to her armament, with the co-operation of the British vessel "Prince Alfred" at Green Cay, that there was negligence on the part of the British colonial authorities;

And whereas, notwithstanding the violation with Great Britain committed by the Oreto, this same vessel later known as the confederate cruiser Florida, was nevertheless on several occasions freely admitted into the ports of British colonies;

And whereas the judicial acquittal of the "Oreto" at Nassau cannot relieve Great Britain from the responsibility incurred by her under the principles of international law; nor can the fact of the entry of the Florida into the confederate port of Mobile, and of its stay there during four months extinguish the responsibility previously to that time incurred by Great Britain;

For these reasons,

The tribunal by a majority of four voices to one is of opinion—

That Great Britain has in this case failed by omission to fulfill the duties prescribed in the first, in the second, and in the third of the rules established by article VI. of the treaty of Washington.

And whereas, with respect to the vessel called the "Shenandoah," it results from all the facts relative to the departure from London of the merchant vessel "The Sea King" and to the transformation of that ship into a confederate cruiser under the name of the Shenandoah near the Island of Madeira, that the Government of Her Britannic Majesty is not chargeable with any failure, down to that date, in the use of all diligence to fulfill the duties of neutrality;

But whereas its results from all the facts connected with the stay of the Shenandoah at Melbourne, and especially with the augmentation which the British Government itself admits to have been clandestinely effected of her force, by the enlistment of men within that port, that there was negligence on the part of the authorities of that place:

For these reasons,

The tribunal is unanimously of opinion—

That Great Britain has not failed by any act or omission, "to fulfill any of the duties prescribed by the three rules of article VI in the treaty of Washington or by the principles of law not inconsistent therewith," in respect to the vessel called the Shenandoah, during the period of time anterior to her entry into the port of Melbourne;

And by a majority of three to two voices, the tribunal decided that Great Britain has failed, by omission to fulfill the duties prescribed by the second and third of rules aforesaid, in the case of this same vessel, from and after her entry into Hobson's Bay, and is therefore responsible for all acts committed by that vessel after her departure from Melbourne on the 18 day of February 1865.

And so far as relates to the vessels called—The Tuscaloosa, (tender to the Alabama), the Clarence, The Tacony, and The Archer, (tenders to the Florida),

The tribunal is unanimously of opinion—

That such tenders or auxiliary vessels, being properly regarded as accessories, must necessarily follow the lot of their principals, and be submitted to the same decision which applies to them respectively.

And so far as relates to the vessel called "Retribution,"

The tribunal by a majority of three to two voices is of opinion—

That Great Britain has not failed by any act or omission to fulfill any of the duties prescribed by the three rules of article VI in the treaty of Washington, or by the principles of international law not inconsistent therewith.

And so far as relates to the vessels called—The Georgia, The Sumter, The Nashville, The Tallahasse, and The Chickamauga, respectively,

The tribunal is unanimously of opinion—

That Great Britain has not failed, by any act or omission to fulfill any of the duties prescribed by the three rules of article VI. in the treaty of

Washington or by the principles of international law not inconsistent therewith.

And so far as relates to the vessels called—The Sallie, The Jefferson Davis, The Music, The Boston and the V. H. Joy, respectively,

The tribunal is unanimously of opinion—

That they ought to be excluded from consideration for want of evidence.

And whereas, so far as relates to the particulars of the indemnity claimed by the United States, the cost of pursuit of the confederate cruisers, are not, in the judgment of the tribunal, properly distinguishable from the general expenses of the war carried on by the United States.

The tribunal is therefore of opinion, by a majority of three to two voices—

That there is no ground for awarding to the United States any sum by way of indemnity under this head.

And whereas prospective earnings cannot properly be made the subject of compensation, inasmuch as they depend in their nature upon future and uncertain contingencies:

The tribunal is unanimously of opinion—

That there is no good ground for awarding to the United States any sum by way of indemnity under this head.

And whereas in order to arrive at an equitable compensation for the damages which have been sustained, it is necessary to set aside all double claims for the same losses, and all claims for "gross freights" so far as they exceed "net freights;"

And whereas it is just and reasonable to allow interest at a reasonable rate;

And whereas, in accordance with the spirit and letter of the treaty of Washington, it is preferable to adopt the form of adjudication of a sum in gross, rather than refer the subject of compensation for a further discussion and deliberation to a board of assessors, as provided by article X of the said treaty;

The tribunal, making use of the authority conferred upon it by article VII of the said treaty, by a majority of four voices to one awards to the United States a sum of $15,500,000 in gold as the indemnity to be paid by Great Britain to the United States, for the satisfaction of all the claims referred to the consideration of the tribunal, conformably to the provisions contained in article VII of the aforesaid treaty.

And, in accordance with the terms of article XI of the said treaty, the tribunal declares that "all the claims referred to in the treaty as submitted to the tribunal are hereby fully, perfectly, and finally settled".

Further it declares, that "each and every one of the said claims, whether the same may or may not have been presented to the notice of, or made, preferred, or laid before the tribunal, shall henceforth be considered and treated as finally settled, barred, and inadmissible."

In testimony whereof this present decision an award has been made in duplicate and signed by the arbitrators who have given their assent thereto, the whole being in exact conformity with the provisions of article VII of the said treaty of Washington.

Made and concluded at the Hotel de Ville of Geneva, in Switzerland, the 14th day of the month of September, in the year of our Lord, One thousand eight hundred and seventy-two.

CHAS. FRANCIS ADAMS.
FREDERICK SCLOPIS.
STAMPFLI.
VICOMTE D'ITAJUBA.

100 DEFINITIVE TREATY OF FRANKFORT

DEFINITIVE TREATY OF PEACE between France and Germany. Signed at Frankfort, 10th May, 1871. Ratifications exchanged at Frankfort, 20th May, 1871.

Reference to Preliminaries of Peace of 26th February, 1871.

M. JULES FAVRE, Minister for Foreign Affairs of the French Republic, M. Augustin Thomas Eugène de Pouyer-Quertier, Minister of Finances of the French Republic, and M. Marc Thomas Eugène Goulard, Member of the National Assembly, stipulating in the name of the French Republic, of the one part;

On the other, Prince Otho de Bismarck-Schœnhausen, Chancellor of the German Empire, Count Harry d'Arnim, Envoy Extraordinary and Minister Plenipotentiary of His Majesty the Emperor of Germany at the Papal Court, stipulating in the name of His Majesty the Emperor of Germany; having agreed to convert into a Definitive Treaty the Preliminaries of Peace of the 26th February of the present year modified as it is about to be by the following Dispositions, have agreed:

Line of Frontier round the Town and Fortifications of Belfort
to belong to France.

ART. I. The distance between the Town of Belfort and the Line of Frontier, such as it had been proposed during the negotiations of Versailles, and such as it is marked on the Map annexed to the Ratifications of the Preliminaries of the 26th February, is considered as describing the Radius which, by virtue of the Clause relating thereto in Article I of the Preliminaries, is to remain to France with the Town and Fortifications of Belfort.

Rectification of Frontier. Cession in favour of France.

The German Government is disposed to extend that Radius so as to include the Cantons of Belfort, Delle, the Giromagny, as well as the western part of the Canton of Fontaine, to the West of a line to be traced from the spot where the Canal from the Rhone to the Rhine leaves the Canton of Delle to the South of Montreux-Chateau, to the Northern Limits of the Canton between Bourg and Félon where that Line would join the Eastern Limit of the Canton of Giromagny.

Cessions in favour of Germany.

The German Government will, nevertheless, not cede the above Territories unless the French Republic agrees, on its part, to a rectification of Frontier along the Western Limits of the Cantons of Cattenom and Thionville which will give to Germany the Territory to the East of a Line starting from the Frontier of Luxemburg between Hussigny and Redingen, leaving to France the Villages of Thil and Villerupt, extending between Erronville and Aumetz between Beauvillers and Boulange, between Trieux and Lomeringen, and joining the ancient Line of Frontier between Avril and Moyeuvre.

International Boundary Commission.

The International Commission, mentioned in Article I of the Preliminaries, shall proceed to the spot immediately after the Ratifications of the present Treaty to execute the Works entrusted to them and to trace the new Frontier, in accordance with the preceding dispositions.

Choice of Nationality.

ART. II. French Subjects, Natives of the ceded Territories, actually domiciled on that Territory, who shall preserve their Nationality, shall up to the 1st October, 1872, and on their making a previous Declaration to that effect to the Competent Authority, be allowed to change their domicile into France and to remain there, that right in nowise infringing on the Laws on Military Service, in which case the title of French Citizen shall be maintained.

Retention of Immovable Property.

They shall be at liberty to preserve their Immovables situated in the Territory united to Germany.

Amnesty.

No Inhabitant of the ceded Territory shall be prosecuted, annoyed, or sought for, either in his person or his property, on account of his Political or Military Acts previous to the War.

Delivery of Archives and Documents.

ART. III. The French Government shall deliver over to the German Government the Archives, Documents, and Registers relating to the Civil, Military, and Judicial Administration of the ceded Territories. Should any of the Documents be found missing, they shall be restored by the French Government on the demand of the German Government.

Reimbursements to be made by French Government.

ART. IV. The French Government shall make over to the Government of the Empire of Germany within the term of 6 Months dating from the exchange of the Ratifications of this Treaty: 1. The amount of the sum deposited by the Departments, Communes, and Public Establishments of the ceded Territories. 2. The amount of the premium of Enlistment and Discharge belonging to Soldiers and Sailors natives of the ceded Territory who shall have chosen the German Nationality. 3. The Amount of Security of responsible Agents of the State. 4. The Amount of Sums deposited for Judicial Consignments on account of measures taken by the Administrative or Judicial Authorities in the ceded Territories.

Navigation of the Moselle and Canals.

ART. V. The two Nations shall enjoy equal privileges as far as regards the Navigation on the Moselle, the Canal of the Marne to the Rhine, the Canal of the Rhone to the Rhine, the Canal of the Sarre and the Navigable Waters communicating with those channels of Navigation. The Right of Floatage shall be maintained.

Religion.   Protestant and Jewish Dioceses.

ART. VI. The High Contracting Parties being of opinion that the Diocesan circumscriptions of the Territories ceded to the German Empire must agree with the new Frontier determined upon by Article I above, will consider, without delay, after the Ratification of the present Treaty, upon the measures to be taken in common on the subject.

The Communities belonging either to the Reformed Church or to the Augsburg Confession, established on the Territories ceded by France, shall cease to be under French Ecclesiastical Authority.

The Communities of the Church of the Augsburg Confession established in the French Territories shall cease to be under the Superior Consistories and of the Directors residing at Strasburg.

The Jewish Communities of the Territories situated to the East of the new Frontier shall cease to depend on the Central Jewish Consistory residing at Paris.

Payment of War Indemnity.

ART. VII. The payment of 500,000,000 ($\frac{1}{2}$ milliard) shall be made within 30 days after the re-establishment of the Authority of the French Government in the City of Paris. 1,000,000,000 (1 milliard) shall be paid in the course of the year, and 500,000,000 ($\frac{1}{2}$ milliard) on the 1st May, 1872. The last 3,000,000,000 (3 milliards) shall remain payable on the 2nd March, 1874, as stipulated in the Preliminary Treaty. From the 2nd March of the present year the Interest on those 3,000,000,000 francs (3 milliards) shall be paid each year on the 3rd March, at the rate of 5 per cent. per annum.

All sums paid in advance on the last 3,000,000,000 shall cease to bear Interest from the day on which the payment is made.

The payment can only be made in the principal German Commercial Towns, and shall be made in metal, Gold or Silver, in Prussian Bank Notes, in Netherlands Bank Notes, in Notes of the National Bank of Belgium, in first class Negotiable Bills to Order or Letters of Exchange, payable at sight.

Value of Prussian Thaler.

The German Government having fixed in France the value of a Prussian Thaler at 3 francs 75 centimes, the French Government accepts the conversion of the Moneys of both Countries at the rate above stated.

The French Government will inform the German Government, 3 months in advance, of all payments which it intends to make into the Treasury of the German Empire.

Conditions of Evacuation upon the payment of 2,000,000,000 (2 Milliards).

After the payment of the first 500,000,000 ($\frac{1}{2}$ milliard) and the Ratification of the Definitive Treaty of Peace, the Departments of the Somme, Seine Inférieure, and Eure shall be evacuated in so far as they shall be found to be still occupied by German Troops. The Evacuation of the Departments of the Oise, Seine-et-Oise, Seine-et-Marne, and Seine, as well as the Forts of Paris, shall take place so soon as the German Government shall consider the re-establishment of

Order, both in France and Germany, sufficient to ensure the execution of the Engagements contracted by France.

Under all circumstances, the Evacuation shall take place after the payment of the third 500,000,000 ($\frac{1}{2}$ milliard).

The German Troops, for their own security, shall have at their disposal the Neutral Zone between the German line of Demarcation and the Paris enclosure on the Right Bank of the Seine.

The stipulations of the Treaty of 26th February relative to the occupation of French Territories after the payment of the 2,000,000,000 (2 milliards), shall remain in force. None of the deductions which the French Government might have a right to make shall be made on the payment of the first 500,000,000 ($\frac{1}{2}$ milliard).

Contributions and Taxes.

ART. VIII. German Troops shall continue to abstain from levying contributions either in kind or money in the occupied Territories; that obligation on their part being correlative to the obligations contracted for their maintenance by the French Government, in case the French Government, notwithstanding the reiterated demands of the German Government, was behind-hand in the execution of the said obligations, the German Troops will have the right to procure what is necessary to their wants by levying Taxes and Contributions in the occupied Departments, and even outside of them, should their resources not be sufficient.

Maintenance of German Troops.

With reference to the Maintenance of the German Troops, the system actually in force shall be continued until the Evacuation of the Paris Forts.

In virtue of the Convention of Ferrières, of 11th March, 1871, the reductions pointed out by that Convention shall be put into force after the Evacuation of the Forts.

As soon as the effective of the German Army shall be reduced below the number of 500,000 men, account shall be taken of the reductions made below that number to establish a proportionate diminution in the price of the Maintenance of the Troops paid by the French Government.

Exceptional Treatment granted to the Produce of Industry of the ceded Territories.

ART. IX. The exceptional Treatment at present granted to the Produce of the Industry of the ceded Territories for Imports into France, shall be continued for 6 months, from the 1st March, under the conditions made with the Commissioners of Alsace.

Prisoners of War. Number of French Troops in and around Paris.

ART. X. The German Government shall continue to deliver up Prisoners of War, making arrangements with the French Government. The French Government shall send to their homes such of the Prisoners as can be discharged. As for those who shall not have completed their term of service, they shall be sent beyond the Loire. It is understood that the Army of Paris and Versailles, after the re-establishment of the authority of the French Government at Paris, and until the Evacuation of the Forts by German Troops, shall not exceed 80,000 men. Until that Evacuation, the French Government shall not concentrate Troops on the Right Bank of the Loire, but it shall provide Garrisons in the Towns within that circuit, according to the necessities for the maintenance of Public Order and Peace.

As the Evacuation shall proceed, the Commanders of Regiments shall agree together as to a Neutral Circuit between the Armies of the two Nations.

20,000 Prisoners shall be sent without delay to Lyons on condition that they are immediately sent to Algiers, after their organisation, to be employed in that Colony.

Commerce and Navigation. Most Favoured Nation Treatment.

ART. XI. The Treaties of Commerce with the different States of Germany having been annulled by the War, the French Government and the German Government will adopt as the basis of their Commercial Relations the system of reciprocal Treatment on the footing of the Most favoured Nation.

Are included therein Import and Export Duties, Transit Dues, Customs Formalities, the admission and treatment of both Nations as well as their Agents.

Shall nevertheless be excepted from the above Rule the favours which one of the Contracting Parties has granted or may grant, by Treaties of Commerce, to other States than the following: Great Britain, Belgium, Netherlands, Switzerland, Austria, Russia.

Renewal of Navigation, Railway, and Copyright Treaties, &c.

The Treaties of Navigation as well as the Convention relative to the International Service of Railways in its relation with the Cantons, and the Convention for the reciprocal Guarantee of Literary Works, shall be renewed.

Reservations of French Government.

The French Government nevertheless reserves to itself the right of levying Tonnage and Shipping Duties (*Droit de Pavillon*) on German

Vessels and their Cargoes, under the reservation that those Duties shall not be higher than those imposed on Vessels and Cargoes of the above-mentioned Nations.

Rights of Germans expelled from France.

ART. XII. All expelled Germans shall preserve the full and entire enjoyment of all Property which they may have acquired in France.

Such Germans who had obtained the authority required by French Laws to establish their Domicile in France shall be reinstated in all their Rights, and may consequently again establish their Domicile in French Territory.

Naturalisation.

The delay stipulated by French Laws to obtain Naturalisation shall be considered as not having been interrupted by the state of War for persons who shall take advantage of the above-mentioned facility of returning to France within 6 months after the exchange of the Ratifications of this Treaty, and the time which has elapsed between their expulsion and their return to the French Territory shall be taken into account, as if they had never ceased to reside in France.

The above conditions shall be applicable in perfect reciprocity to the French Subjects residing, or wishing to reside, in Germany.

Restoration of Maritime Prizes.

ART. XIII. German Vessels condemned by Prize Courts before the 2nd March, 1871, shall be considered as definitively condemned.

Those not condemned at the above-mentioned date shall be restored with the Cargoes in so far as it still exists. If the restoration of the Vessels and Cargo is no more possible, their value, fixed according to the price of the sale, shall be restored to their Owners.

Canalisation of the Moselle.

ART. XIV. Each of the two Parties shall continue on his Territory the Works undertaken for the Canalisation of the Moselle. The Common Interests of the separate parts of two Departments of the Meurthe and the Moselle shall be liquidated.

National Treatment to respective Subjects on account of events arising out of the War.

ART. XV. The High Contracting Parties mutually engage to extend to their respective Subjects the measures which they may consider necessary to adopt in favour of those of their Subjects who, in consequence of the events of the War, may have been prevented arriving in time for the safety or the preservation of their Rights.

Cemeteries.

ART. XVI. The two Governments, French and German, reciprocally engage to respect and preserve the Tombs of Soldiers buried in their respective Territories.

Additional Stipulations reserved for further Negotiations.

ART. XVII. The Regulation of additional Stipulations upon which an understanding is to be come to in consequence of this Treaty and the Preliminary Treaty, will be the object of further Negotiations which shall take place at Frankfort.

Ratifications.

ART. XVIII. The Ratification of the present Treaty by the National Assembly and by the Chief of the Executive of the French Republic, on the one part, and on the other by the Emperor of Germany, shall be exchanged at Frankfort, in the delay of 10 days, or sooner if possible.

In faith whereof the respective Plenipotentiaries have signed it and affixed thereto the Seal of their Arms.

Done at Frankfort, 10th May, 1871.

(L.S.) JULES FAVRE.   (L.S.) BISMARCK.
(L.S.) POUYER-QUERTIER.   (L.S.) ARNIM.
(L.S.) DE GOULARD.

ADDITIONAL ARTICLES. FRANKFORT, 10TH MAY, 1871.

ART. I. *Purchase of Railways of the East and Guillaume-Luxemburg.*

ART. II. *Purchase by Prussia of Rights and Property on Swiss Territory of Railways of the East.*

Rectification of Frontier near Belfort.

ART. III. The Cession of Territory near Belfort, offered by the German Government in Article I of the present Treaty in exchange for the rectification of the Frontier required to the West of Thionville, shall be increased by the Territories of the following Villages: Rougemont, Leval, Petite-Fontaine, Romagny, Félon, La-Chapelle-sous-Rougemont, Angeot, Vauthier-Mont, Rivière, Grasige, Reppe, Fontaine, Frais, Foussemagne, Cunelières, Montreux-Chateau, Brelagne, Chavannes-les-Grands, Chavanatte, and Suarce.

The Giromagny and Remiremont Road, thoroughfare to the Balloon of Alsace, shall remain to France throughout its whole extent, and shall serve as a Limit in so far as it is situated outside the Canton of Giromagny.

Done at Frankfort, 10th May, 1871.

(L.S.) JULES FAVRE.   (L.S.) BISMARCK.

(L.S.) POUYER-QUERTIER.   (L.S.) ARNIM.

(L.S.) DE GOULARD.

Accessions to the above Treaty.

Baden ....15th May, 1871.

Bavaria ....15th May, 1871.

Wurtemberg ...15th May, 1871.

1 0 1

ADDITIONAL CONVENTION to the Treaty of Peace of 10th May, 1871, between France and Germany. Signed at Frankfort, 11th December, 1871. Ratifications exchanged at Paris, 11th January, 1872.

Reference to Treaty of 10th May, 1871.

THE President of the French Republic, on the one part, and His Majesty the Emperor of Germany on the other part, having determined, in conformity with Article XVII of the Treaty of Peace concluded at Frankfort on the 10th May, 1871, to negotiate an Additional Convention to that Treaty, have to that effect appointed as their Plenipotentiaries, namely:

The President of the French Republic, M. Marc Thomas Eugène de Goulard, Member of the National Assembly, and M. Alexandre Johann Henry de Clercq, Minister Plenipotentiary of the First Class; and

His Majesty the Emperor of Germany, M. Weber, Councillor of State of His Majesty the King of Bavaria, and Count Uxkull, Intimate Councillor of Legation of His Majesty the King of Wurtemberg;

Who, after having communicated to each other their Full Powers, found in good and due form, have agreed upon the following Articles:

ARTS. I to VIII.

Diocesan Circumscriptions crossed by the New Frontier.

ART. IX. Until the conclusion of the arrangements alluded to in the first paragraph of Article VI of the Treaty of Peace of 10th May, 1871, it is agreed that the Bishops established in the Dioceses crossed by the New Frontier shall preserve, in their entirety, the spiritual authority actually vested in them, and shall remain free to provide for the religious necessities of the populations committed to their charge.

ARTS. X to XIII.

Payment by Germany of Expenses of Canals of the Sarre, Dieuse, and Colmar.

ART. XIV. The Canal of the Sarre, the Canal of the Salt Works of Dieuse, and the junction of Colmar, which forms the communication between that town and the Rhine, being entirely included within the Territories ceded to Germany, the latter takes upon herself the payment of the expenses of those 3 canals remaining due.

The Annuities still due on the sum advanced to the French State by the Town of Colmar, and by the manufacturers of the East, shall, dating from 1871, be payable by the German Government.

Payment of Annuities to Old Subscribers of the Canal of the Rhone to the Rhine.

The Canal of the Rhone to the Rhine being crossed by the New Frontier, it has been agreed that the 12 Annuities remaining to be paid to the old Subscribers on the purchase of their shares shall be divided between the High Contracting Parties in the proportion of the extent reverting to each of the two Countries.

Financial Mixed Commission to undertake the Accounts.

The Commission mentioned in Article XI shall be entrusted with the Accounts of the above mentioned Canals, as well as the liquidation of the Accounts relative to the canalisation of the Moselle, and of the common interests of the separate parts of the Departments of the Meurthe and the Moselle.

The French Government undertakes to furnish the Commission with all Contracts, Documents, &c., necessary for the fulfilment of their labours.

Mixed Commission relative to Canals from the Rhone to the Rhine, and from the Marne to the Rhine.

The High Contracting Parties shall appoint Commissioners, who shall be entrusted with the Regulation, in so far as regards the Canal from the Rhone to the Rhine, and the Canal from the Marne to the Rhine, of the supply of the dividing mill-courses.

(ARTS. XV to XVII. cover matters of minor importance).

Renewal of Treaties and Conventions between France and German States existing before the War.

ART. XVIII. Besides the International Arrangements mentioned in the Treaty of Peace of 10th May, 1871, the High Contracting Parties have agreed to renew the different Treaties between France and the German States existing previous to the War, with the reservation of the Declarations of Adhesion, to be supplied by the respective Governments at the time of the exchange of the Ratifications of the present Convention.

Exceptions.

The Special Conventions between France and Prussia, relative to the Canal of the Sarre being excepted.

Neither are the Stipulations of the present Article applicable to Postal relations, which are reserved for a subsequent arrangement between the two Governments.

Treaties provisionally Applicable to Alsace-Lorraine.

It is also agreed that the dispositions of the Convention between Baden and France, of the 16th April, 1846, relative to the execution of sentences of the Treaty of Extradition, concluded between France and Prussia, on the 21st July, 1845, and of the Copyright Convention between Bavaria and France, of the 24th March, 1865, shall be provisionally extended to Alsace-Lorraine, and that in matters to which they relate, these three arrangements shall serve as a rule for the relations between France and the ceded Territories.

Ratifications.

ART. XIX. The present Convention, drawn up in French and German, shall be ratified, on the one part by the President of the French Republic, after the approval of the National Assembly; and on the other part by His Majesty the Emperor of Germany, and the Ratifications thereof shall be exchanged in the delay of one month, or sooner, if possible.

In faith whereof the respective Plenipotentiaries have signed it, and have affixed thereto the Seal of their Arms.

Done at Frankfort, 11th December, 1871.

(L.S.)   E. DE GOULARD.   (L.S.)   WEBER.
(L.S.)   DE CLERCQ.   (L.S.)   UXKULL.

CLOSING PROTOCOL.

On proceeding to the signature of the Additional Convention to the Treaty of Peace of 10th May, 1871, concluded between them this day, the undersigned Plenipotentiaries made the following Declarations:

1. *French* Soldiers and Sailors to be liberated on making a Declaration of their Choice for *German* Nationality.

2. Reimbursement to *France* of Pensions paid by the *French* Treasury since the 2nd March, 1871.

3. Liquidation of Pension, Provident and other Funds in case one or more of their Members make Choice of *French* Nationality.

4. Judicial Offices.

5. Patents of Inventions.

6. Reimbursement of Funds belonging to Communes of ceded Territories deposited in the Coffers of *Colmar, Strasburg*, and *Metz*.

7. Reimbursement of Securities.

8. Recovery of Debts by *French* Government.

9. Liquidation by Branch Establishments of the Bank of *France* in the ceded Territories. Liquidator to complete his operations within 3 months after the Ratification of the Additional Convention. Withdrawal of Sequestration of Moneys belonging to Bank of *France*, and Restitution in Coin. Ratifications.

Frankfort, 11th December, 1871.

(L.S.)   E. DE GOULARD.   (L.S.)   WEBER.

(L.S.)   DE CLERCQ.   (L.S.)   UXKULL.

PROTOCOL OF SIGNATURE.

French Reservations relative to the Right of Felling Timber in the Forests of the States granted during the War on French Territory by the German Civil and Military Authorities. Declaration of German Plenipotentiaries, relative to the Railway from Nancy to Chateau-Salins and Vic.

Frankfort, 11th December, 1871.

(L.S.)   E. DE GOULARD.   (L.S.)   WEBER.

(L.S.)   DE CLERCQ.   (L.S.)   UXKULL.

PROCES-VERBAL ON THE EXCHANGE OF THE RATIFICATIONS.

Delivery of Adhesions of German States to Article XVIII of the Additional Convention of 11th December, 1871, relative to the Renewal of Treaties.

Declaration of German Ambassador, relative to Copyright Convention and Treaties of Navigation.

Paris, 11th January, 1872.

(L.S.)   REMUSAT.   (L.S.)   ARNIM.

Adhesions of German States to Article XVIII of the above Convention relative to the Renewal of Treaties.

Anhalt	.....................(No date)
Baden	.....................1st January, 1872
Bavaria	.................1st January, 1872
Bremen	....................2nd January, 1872
Hamburgh	...............8th January, 1872
Hesse-Darmstadt	......8th January, 1872
Lubeck	.................8th January, 1872
Mecklenburg-Schwerin	6th January, 1872
Mecklenburg-Strelitz	...8th January, 1872
Oldenburg	.................7th January, 1872
Prussia	....................6th January, 1872
Saxony	....................7th January, 1872
Saxe-Weimar	............6th January, 1872
Wurtemberg	............4th January, 1872

102   THE CONVENTION OF SCHÖNBRUNN

Agreement between the Emperor-King of Austria-Hungary and the Emperor of Russia. Signed at Schönbrunn, 25th May/ 6th June, 1873.

His Majesty the Emperor of Austria and King of Hungary and His Majesty the Emperor of All the Russias: desiring to give a practical form to the thought which presides over their intimate understanding, with the object of consolidating the state of peace which exists at present in Europe, and having at heart to reduce the chances of war which might disturb it—convinced that this object could not better be attained than by a direct and personal understanding between the Sovereigns, an understanding independent of the changes which might be made in their administrations, have come into agreement upon the following points:

1. Their Majesties mutually promise, even though the interests of their States should present some divergences respecting special questions, to take counsel together in order that these divergences may not be able to prevail over the considerations of a higher order which preoccupy them. Their Majesties are determined to prevent any one from succeeding in separating them in the field of the principles which they regard as alone capable of assuring, and, if necessary, of imposing

the maintenance of the peace of Europe against all subversions, from whatsoever quarter they may come.

2. In case an aggression coming from a third Power should threaten to compromise the peace of Europe, Their Majesties mutually engage to come to a preliminary understanding between themselves, without seeking or contracting new alliances, in order to agree as to the line of conduct to be followed in common.

3. If, as a result of this understanding, a military action should become necessary, it would be governed by a special convention to be concluded between Their Majesties.

4. If one of the High Contracting Parties, wishing to recover its independence of action, should desire to denounce the present Agreement, it must do so two years in advance, in order to give the other Party time to make whatever arrangements may be suitable.

Schönbrunn, May 25/June 6 1873.

FRANCIS JOSEPH.   ALEXANDER.

Accession of the Emperor of Germany.
[The whole text of the Agreement preceding.]

His Majesty the Emperor of Germany, having taken cognizance of the above understanding, drawn up and signed at Schönbrunn by Their Majesties the Emperor of Austria and King of Hungary and the Emperor of All the Russias, and finding the contents in conformity with the thought which has presided over the understanding signed at St. Petersburg between Their Majesties the Emperor William and the Emperor Alexander, accedes in every respect to the stipulations which are set forth therein.

Their Majesties the Emperor and King Francis Joseph and the Emperor and King William, in approving and in signing this Act of Accession, will bring it to the knowledge of His Majesty the Emperor Alexander.

Schönbrunn, October 22, 1873.

FRANCIS JOSEPH.   WILLIAM.

103

RESUME OF THE SECRET CONFERENCES OF REICHSTADT OF 8TH JULY, 1876.

The reasoning has been on two hypotheses: That of the Turks coming out of the struggle victorious and that of their being defeated.

In the event of the first, it was agreed not to let them obtain more than certain guaranties, which should not be excessive. Efforts were to be made to prevent the war from becoming a struggle for extermination; Serbia and Montenegro were to be maintained in the territorial limits which now circumscribe these two principalities, and the idea of a re-establishment of the Turkish fortresses in Serbia was to be opposed.

In the case of Serbia, the character of an independent state was not to be recognized; but agreement was reached to recognize it in the case of Montenegro, whatever might be the interpretation which other Powers might wish to give to the political position of the Black Mountain. As a consequence of this independence, the Austro-Hungarian Government has declared itself ready to close the two ports of Klek and of Cattaro to all importation of arms and of munitions for the opposing parties; although it foresees very grave objections on the part of the Turkish Government to the closing of the first of these ports.

Concerning the insurgents, it was agreed (always in the event of the victory of the Turks) to make common efforts to guarantee to them the liberties and the reforms which have been requested of the Porte and promised by it.

In all the eventualities abovementioned, there was to be no question of any territorial modification, either on one side or on the other.

In passing to the second hypothesis, that of a defeat of the Turks, the following are the ideas on which agreement was reached:

Austria-Hungary having declared that she can not permit that Serbia occupy and keep by right of conquest the enclave comprised between Dalmatia, Croatia, and Slavonia, as this would mean a danger to the provinces of the Monarchy, especially to its Dalmatian littoral, which, extending like a thin ribbon, would evidently have to be annexed to the new Serbia or else place the Imperial and Royal Government under the necessity of annexing Serbia herself, which is excluded from the programme; it was agreed that Serbia should obtain an extension of territory in the Drina region in Bosnia, at the same time as in that of Novi-Bazar in Old Serbia and in the direction of the Lim. On her side Montenegro should be rounded out by the annexation of a part of Herzegovina adjoining her territories; she should obtain the port of Spizza as well as an aggrandizement in the region of the Lim, in such a way that the tongue of land which now stretches between Serbia and Montenegro should be divided between the two principalities by the course of this river.

The rest of Bosnia and Herzegovina should be annexed to Austria-Hungary. Russia should resume her natural frontiers of before 1856 and might round herself off in the region of the Black Sea and in Turkey in Asia to the extent that this should be necessary for the establishment of better frontiers for herself in this direction and to serve as an equivalent for the slice of territory to be annexed to Austria-Hungary.

Bulgaria, Rumelia, and Albania might form autonomous states. Thessaly and the island of Crete should be annexed to Greece.

Constantinople, with a territory to be determined, should become a free city.

It was equally agreed that all these ideas should be kept secret between the two Emperors and their respective Ministers; that they should not be communicated to the other Powers, and more particularly not to the Serbians and Montenegrins, until the moment of their realization should arrive.

104

THE TREATY OF BUDAPEST between Austria-Hungary and Russia, 15th January, 1877.

His Majesty the Emperor of Austria, etc., and Apostolic King of Hungary, and His Majesty the Emperor of Russia, considering that in the pending diplomatic negotiations disagreements might arise of a nature to bring about a rupture between Russia and the Ottoman Empire, have decided, in conformity with the close friendship which binds them, and with the urgency of obviating the possibility of a collision between the interests of their respective States, to reach an understanding in contemplation of that eventuality.

For this purpose Their said Majesties have appointed as Their Plenipotentiaries: His Majesty the Emperor of Austria, King of Bohemia, etc., and Apostolic King of Hungary, the Sieur Julius Count Andrássy of Csik-Szent-Király and Kraszna-Horka, Grand Cross of His Order of St. Stephen, Chevalier of the Imperial Russian Order of St. Andrew, Grandee of Spain, etc., etc., His Privy Councillor, General in His Armies, His Minister of the Household and of Foreign Affairs;

and His Majesty the Emperor of All the Russias, His Privy Councillor the Sieur Eugene Novikow, His Ambassador Extraordinary and Plenipotentiary to His Majesty the Emperor of Austria, King of Bohemia, etc., and Apostolic King of Hungary, Chevalier of the Russian Orders of St. Alexander Nevsky, of the White Eagle, of St. Vladimir of the Second Class, of St. Anne of the First Class, and of St. Stanislas of the First Class; of the Austro-Hungarian Orders of St. Stephen, of Leopold, and of the Iron Crown of the First Class; and of several other foreign Orders:

Who, after having exchanged their full powers, found in good and due form, have agreed upon the following Articles:

ART. I. The High Contracting Parties, considering that the Christian and Mohammedan populations in Bosnia and in Herzegovina are too much intermingled for it to be permissible to expect from a mere autonomous organization a real amelioration of their lot, are agreed with one another to ask for these provinces in the conference of Constantinople only an autonomous regime not too greatly exceeding the measure fixed by the despatch of December 30, 1875, and the guaranties of the memorandum of Berlin. As Bulgaria is placed under more favourable conditions for the exercise of autonomous institutions, they mutually engage to demand for this province in the conference a larger autonomy, buttressed by substantial guaranties.

ART. II. In the case that the negotiations should not succeed, and should result in a rupture followed by war between Russia and Turkey, the Imperial and Royal Government formally pledges itself to observe an attitude of benevolent neutrality in the presence of the isolated action of Russia, and by its diplomatic action to paralyze, so far as this lies in its power, efforts at intervention or collective mediation which might be attempted by other Powers.

ART. III. If the Government of the Emperor and King is invited to assist in putting into force the treaty of April 15, 1856, it will, in the event foreseen by the present convention, refuse its co-operation, and, without contesting the validity of the said Treaty, it will proclaim its neutrality. Likewise it will not lend its active aid to effective action which might be proposed on the basis of Article VIII of the Treaty of March 30 of that same year.

ART. IV. Considering that the necessity for the Russian troops of crossing the Danube and the need to protect this crossing against the Turkish gunboats will oblige the Imperial Government of Russia to offer temporary hindrances to the navigation of a river placed under the guaranty of treaties, which may give rise to protests, the Austro-Hungarian Government, as a signatory of these treaties and the one principally interested in the freedom of the river, will regard this question as an incident of a temporary nature, inevitable in case of war, but not affecting the great principles whose maintenance is of interest to Europe. On its side, the Russian Government formally pledges itself to respect the principles of the freedom of navigation and of the neutrality of the Danube, and to put itself into agreement with the Government of His Majesty the Emperor and King to re-establish them as soon as may be.

ART. V. The Austro-Hungarian Government will lend, within the limits of the Convention of Geneva, its benevolent assistance to the organization of temporary Russian ambulances on the Cracow-Lemberg-Czernowitz lines of railroad (between Granicza and Suczava) with the Woloczysk and Brody branches, as well as to the movement on the abovementioned lines of the rolling stock necessary for these ambulances. It will admit into its civil and military hospitals along the abovementioned lines Russian sick and wounded, in return for payment according to the existing Austrian military tariff.

ART. VI. The Austro-Hungarian Government will not obstruct the commissioners and agents of the Russian Government in making in the limits of the Austro-Hungarian States purchases and contracts for objects indispensable to the Russian Army, with the exception of articles contraband of war prohibited by international laws. The Government of His Imperial and Royal Majesty, however, engages in the application and in the interpretation of these laws to show the broadest good will towards Russia.

ART. VII. His Majesty the Emperor of Austria, etc., and Apostolic King of Hungary reserves to himself the choice of the moment and of the mode of the occupation of Bosnia and of Herzegovina by his troops. It remains understood that this measure, without assuming a character of solidarity with the occupation of Bulgaria by the Russian Army, shall not present, either in its interpretation by the Government of His Imperial and Royal Majesty or in its execution, a character of hostility towards Russia. Likewise the intervention of the Russian Army in Turkey shall not present, either in its interpretation by the Imperial Government of Russia or in its execution, a character of hostility towards Austria-Hungary.

ART. VIII. The High Contracting Parties reciprocally engage not to extend the radius of their respective military action: His Majesty the Emperor of Austria, etc., and Apostolic King of Hungary, to Rumania, Serbia, Bulgaria, and Montenegro;

and His Majesty the Emperor of All the Russias to Bosnia, Herzegovina, Serbia, and Montenegro. Serbia, Montenegro, and the portion of Herzegovina which separates these two principalities are to form a continuous neutral zone, which the armies of the two Empires may not cross, and intended to preserve these latter from all immediate contact. It remains understood, however, that the Imperial and Royal Government will not oppose the combined action of Serbian and Montenegrin forces outside of their own countries with the Russian troops.

ART. IX. The consequences of war and the territorial modifications which would result from an eventual dissolution of the Ottoman Empire shall be regulated by a special and simultaneous convention.

ART. X. The High Contracting Parties mutually engage to keep secret the stipulations of the present Convention. It shall be ratified and ratifications thereof shall be exchanged within the period of four weeks, or sooner if may be.

In witness whereof the respective Plenipotentiaries have signed it and have affixed the seal of their arms.

Done at Budapest, the fifteenth day of the month of January in the year one thousand eight hundred and seventy-seven.

(L.S.)   ANDRÁSSY.

(L.S.)   NOVIKOW.

Additional Convention.

His Majesty the Emperor of Austria, etc., and King of Hungary on the one part, and His Majesty the Emperor of All the Russias on the other, in execution of Article IX of the secret Convention signed under today's date, have deemed it in conformity with the close friendship which binds them and with the urgency of obviating the possibility of a collision between the interests of their respective States, to reach an understanding respecting the consequences of the war, and to conclude for this purpose an Additional Convention designed to regulate in advance the territorial modifications which might result from the war or the dissolution of the Ottoman Empire. To this end Their said Majesties have appointed as Their Plenipotentiaries, to wit:

His Majesty the Emperor of Austria, King of Bohemia, etc., and Apostolic King of Hungary, the Sieur Julius Count Andrássy of Czik-Szent-Királyi, Grandee of Spain, His Actual Privy Councillor and Minister of Foreign Affairs, etc., etc.;

and His Majesty the Emperor of All the Russias, the Sieur Eugene Novikow, His Ambassador Extraordinary, etc., etc.:

Who, after having exchanged their full powers, found in good and due form, have agreed upon the following Articles:

ARTICLE 1. The two High Contracting Parties, having as their ultimate aim the amelioration of the lot of the Christians, and wishing to eliminate any project of annexation of a magnitude that might compromise peace or the European equilibrium, which is neither in their intentions nor in the interests of the two Empires, have come to an agreement to limit their eventual annexations to the following territories:

The Emperor of Austria, etc., and King of Hungary: to Bosnia and Herzegovina, with the exception of the portion comprised between Serbia and Montenegro, on the subject of which the two Governments reserve the right to reach an agreement when the moment for disposing of it arrives;

The Emperor of All the Russias: in Europe to the regions of Bessarabia which would re-establish the old frontiers of the Empire before 1856.

ARTICLE 2. The High Contracting Parties engage to lend each other mutual assistance in the diplomatic field, if the territorial modifications resulting from a war or from the dissolution of the Ottoman Empire should give rise to a collective deliberation of the Great Powers.

ARTICLE 3. His Majesty the Emperor of Austria, etc., and King of Hungary, and His Majesty the Emperor of All the Russias, in the interview which took place between them at Reichstadt, came to an agreement in principle on the following points: In case of a territorial modification or of a dissolution of the Ottoman Empire, the establishment of a great compact Slavic or other state is excluded; in compensation, Bulgaria, Albania, and the rest of Rumelia might be constituted into independent states; Thessaly, part of Epirus, and the island of Crete might be annexed to Greece; Constantinople, with a territory of which the limit remains to be determined, might become a free city. Their said Majesties record that they have nothing to change in these views, and declare anew that they wish to maintain them as bases of their subsequent political action.

ARTICLE 4. The High Contracting Parties engage to keep secret the stipulations of the present Convention, which shall be ratified and whose ratifications shall be exchanged at Vienna within the space of four weeks, or sooner if may be.

In witness whereof the respective Plenipotentiaries have signed it and have affixed thereto the seal of their arms.

Done at Budapest, the fifteenth day of the month of January in the year one thousand eight hundred and seventy-seven.

(L.S.)   ANDRÁSSY.   (L.S.)   NOVIKOW.

105

CONVENTION between Roumania and Russia, for regulating the passage of Russian Troops through Roumania. Signed at Bucharest, 16th April, 1877.

WORKING in accord with the other Great Powers for the amelioration of the conditions of existence of the Christians subject to the dominion of the Sultan, the Imperial Government of Russia drew the attention of the Guaranteeing Cabinets to the necessity of assuring in an efficacious manner the execution of the reforms demanded of the Porte.

As the excitement of the Mussulmans, and the visible weakness of the Ottoman Government, do not allow it to be hoped that serious measures will be taken for the execution on the part of the Turkish authorities, a military intervention from without may become necessary. In the case of the ulterior development of political affairs in the East forcing Russia to assume this task, and to direct her army into Turkey in Europe, the Imperial Government, desiring to respect the inviolability of the territory of the Roumanian State, has agreed to conclude with the Government of His Highness Prince Charles I a special Convention relative to the passage of the Russian troops through Roumania. Therefore were designated as Plenipotentiaries, on the part of His Imperial Majesty the Emperor of all the Russias, Baron D. Stuart, State Counsellor, Diplomatic Agent and Consul-General of Russia in Roumania, Chevalier of the Order of St. Vladimir, 3rd Class, St. Ann, 2nd Class, and Medjidie, 3rd Class, &c.; on the part of His Highness the Prince of Roumania, M. Cogalniceano, his Minister for Foreign Affairs, Grand Cross of the Order of St. Ann, 1st Class; Iron Cross, 1st Class; Medjidie, 1st Class, &c., who, after having exchanged their full powers, found in good and due form, have agreed to the following:—

Free Passage of Russian Army through Roumania.

Art. I. The Government of His Highness the Prince of Roumania, Charles I, assures to the Russian army, which will be called to go into Turkey, a free passage through Roumanian territory and the treatment reserved for friendly armies.

Russia to pay all Expenses.

All the expenses which may be occasioned for the necessities of the Russian army, for transport, and to satisfy all its requirements, fall naturally to the charge of the Imperial Government.

Russia to maintain Political Rights of Roumania, and to maintain and defend her Integrity.

Art. II. That no detriment nor danger may result to Roumania, from the fact of the passage of Russian troops on her territory, the Government of His Imperial Majesty of all the Russias undertakes to maintain and to cause to be respected the political rights of the Roumanian State, as resulting from internal laws and existing Treaties, as also to maintain and defend the actual integrity of Roumania.

Special Convention to be signed regulating the Details.

Art. III. All the details relative to the passage of Russian troops, their relations with the local authorities, as well as all arrangements which have to be made for this purpose, will form a Special Convention, which will be signed by the Delegates of both Governments, and ratified at the same time as the present, and will come immediately into operation.

Ratifications.

ART. IV. The Government of His Highness the Prince of Roumania undertakes to obtain for the present Convention, as also for that mentioned in the preceding Article, the ratification required by the Roumanian laws, and to render immediately executory the stipulations therein contained.

In faith of which the respective Plenipotentiaries have signed and sealed with their arms the present Convention.

Done in Bucharest 4/16th of April, in the year of Grace, 1877.

(L.S.) BARON DEMITRI STUART,
*Diplomatic Agent and Consul-General of
Russia in Roumania.*

(L.S.) M. COGALNICEANO,
Minister of Foreign Affairs of Roumania.

An Additional Convention between Roumania and Russia, regulating the details for facilitating the Passage of Russian Troops through Roumania was signed at Bucharest on the 4/16th April, 1877.

106

ADDITIONAL CONVENTION between Roumania and Russia, regulating the Details for facilitating the Passage of Russian Troops through Roumania. Signed at Bucharest, 16th April, 1877.

FOR the execution of Article III of the Convention signed this day, the undersigned Plenipotentiaries have met to regulate, by the present Special Convention, the agreements relative to the passage of the Imperial Russian troops, as also their relations with the local authorities.

ART. I. The Roumanian Government accords to the Russian army the use of the railways, rivers, roads, Roumanian posts and telegraphs, and places at its disposition the material resources of the country, in the way of provisions, forage, and transport, in the manner and under the conditions stipulated in the following Articles:—

ART. II. The relations of the Russian military authorities with the local authorities will be made by means of Special Roumanian Commissary Commissioners named to that effect. One Principal Commissioner will be delegated to the Commander-in-Chief of the Russian troops during the whole time of their passage through Roumania.

ART. III. The Roumanian Commissioner will be charged to give information relative to the material resources (such as forage, provisions, firing, &c.) which the country can furnish during the passage of the Russian troops along the railways, as also on the banks of the Pruth and the Danube, indicating the approximate prices of these articles at the places where they are to be delivered, the quantities which could be supplied, and the time when deliveries could be made.

ART. IV. The Russian military authorities, after informing themselves of the particulars mentioned in the previous Article, will decide on the quantities of the products which will be necessary for them, and on the places where they shall be delivered, and they will arrange with the Roumanian Commissioner as to the mode of delivery.

The furnishing of supplies will be made for account of the Russian army, either by the Roumanian authorities at agreed prices, or with the aid of the latter, by tender, on commission, or by direct purchase.

ART. V. A similar course will be adopted for all acquisitions necessary for encampments, bivouacking, the transport of troops, their baggage, material, and munition of war, as also for hospitals, ambulance, and hospital stores. Roumanian authorities will facilitate the supplying of these necessaries.

ART. VI. The Roumanian Government places at the disposition of the Russian army all the railways in the country for its transport, for that of its material, baggage, and stores which accompany it, as also of those things the transport of which may be necessary later. In respect of this transport the Imperial army will be entirely assimilated with the Roumanian army, and will be entitled to the same rights and prerogatives as the latter in all that concerns the obligations of the railway companies with reference to troops, and other conditions and details stipulated for the transport of soldiery by the Cahiers des Charges of the Companies, and by the laws and regulations in vigour in Roumania.

As to the cost of transport, the Roumanian Government undertakes *a priori* to reduce the ordinary tariff 40 per cent., and reserves to itself the arranging of this question by an ulterior understanding with the companies.

As to what concerns expenses and additional payments, such as registration, manipulation, &c., the same course will be adopted as that for the transport of Roumanian soldiery.

ART. VII. The Roumanian Ministry for Public Works will give, on the demand of the Russian Military Traffic Director, the necessary orders and instructions to the administrations of the Roumanian railways; so as to assure with the greatest possible success and celerity the transport of the Imperial Army with its material, baggage, supplies, &c., according to a plan to be agreed on beforehand as is below stipulated.

Military trains will have priority over all others, excepting the post-trains, and without prejudice to the transport of Roumanian troops.

In case of need, the number of ordinary passenger trains may be reduced, and the circulation of goods trains entirely stopped if necessary.

ART. VIII. For the transport of the Imperial troops and material on the Jassy-Ungheni line, which is of the same gauge as the Russian railways, a unity and continuity of the technical conditions of circulation will be established, after an understanding between both administrations, so as to avoid any delay or changing of carriages at the frontier.

ART. IX. So as to obtain the necessary unity of working on the Roumanian railways, to secure the most prompt and well-regulated transport of the Russian army, with its baggage, material, and munition of war of all descriptions, a Central Council will be instituted, under the direction of the Ministry of Public Works, composed of delegates from the different companies owning parts of the Roumanian railways. A Commissioner, named by the head of military communications of the Imperial army, will be delegated to the Ministry of Public Works to facilitate the business with the Russian military authorities.

The traffic service on all the Roumanian lines will be conducted provisionally under the immediate direction of the Central Council, the Minister of Public Works causing its working to agree with the wants and requirements which will be expressed by the chief of military communications concerning the transport in question.

ART. X. The superior direction and inspection of transport of the Imperial army will belong to the chief of military communications of the said army. So as to secure the continuous and regular service for this transport, it will be worked through a Roumanian Commissioner delegated *ad hoc*, and will suggest through him all the necessary measures to this effect.

ART. XI. The head of military communications will have the faculty of demanding, through the Roumanian Commissioner delegated to him, or through his delegate with the Central Council, the execution of all the works necessary for increasing and for the security of traffic, both on the lines and in the stations, the rolling stock, platforms, sidings, auxiliary embranchments, provisional stations, and the appropriation of goods-waggons and trucks for the transport of men, horses, material, &c. All the cost occasioned by these works will be at the charge of the Russian army; the manner of their being carried out will be regulated between the Minister of Public Works and the chief of the military communications of the Russian army.

ART. XII. In cases of urgency, the head of military communications will have the faculty, after a preliminary understanding with the Roumanian Commissioner, to replace, by the means at his disposal, everything that may be wanting or may threaten to impede the movement of the Russian army.

He may cause to be immediately suspended by the Roumanian Commissioner, and require of the Minister of Public Works, the dismissal of employés and subaltern agents who may show signs of insubordination.

ART. XIII. If the necessities of communications of the Russian armies make the construction of a section of branch railway necessary on Roumanian territory, the works will be executed by the Russian military authorities at the expense of the Imperial Government.

The Roumanian Government will facilitate these works, and take the required dispositions, so as to secure for the Russian army the right to enjoy temporarily the ground indispensable for the instalment of these railway sections or branch lines, on the basis adopted in Roumania for works of public utility.

When these lines become useless, the materials (" mobile ") used in their construction will be at the disposal of the Russian Government, but the works executed will become the property of the Roumanian Government without any remuneration.

ART. XIV. The working of the Roumanian lines will be carried on by the existing companies and administrations, under the direction of the Council mentioned in Article IX of the present Convention.

The companies will be indemnified for all transport effected under the tariff to be established in accordance with Article VI. These companies will also be repaid for all injuries which may accrue to their material through its use or abuse by Russian troops.

ART. XV. A plan for the transport of troops, lists of military trains, forms and details of requisitions for transport, documents of book-keeping and control, the terms and mode of payment, as also states during the time of transport, between Russian troops and the local agents of the Roumanian railways, will be regulated, immediately after the signing of the present Convention, by the Commissioner *ad hoc*.

The companies and the railway administrations must furnish him with all necessary documents and the materials to enable him to make this plan, the time-tables and details of service, and must afford him every assistance.

Every question of detail regulated by this Commissioner, and forming special instructions, which, being approved by the head of military communications of the Imperial army and by the Roumanian commissary delegated to him, will be obligatory both for the Russian troops and for the employés of the railways.

ART. XVI. During the passage of the Imperial army any crime or misdemeanour committed by railway employés, with the intention of hindering or stopping the transport of troops, or of putting military trains in danger, will be punished according to the existing Roumanian laws, and with the same rigour as if directed against the Roumanian army.

Art. XVII. The Roumanian Government accords to the Russian army the use of the State posts and telegraphs, and those of the railway companies, on the same footing as the Roumanian authorities whose expenses do not enter into the State Budget. Thus Russian official despatches will have priority over private correspondence.

So as not to impede the ordinary telegraph service, the Russian army will have the faculty, whenever it may be found necessary, to add for themselves an extra wire of their own to the telegraph posts of the State, and to those of the companies, and to fix their own apparatus for their especial use. Such wires will be guarded and looked after the same as Roumanian wires, and without any cost to the Russian army; repairs, however, will be charged for.

Art. XVIII. A line will be established in the rear of the Russian armies with places for storehouses, the town of Bucharest, where there will not be any Russian troops, being excepted.

It is well understood that the troops will not stop except where necessary for resting (or if they find obstacles independent of their will) and only the strict time needed for this purpose.

Along this line, as along the lines the troops move on—storehouses, magazines, and depôts for provisions, forage and food of all descriptions, may be made—as also bakeries for bread and biscuits—kitchens for the troops, &c. The sites with this purpose will be engaged by the Commissaries of the Russian army, with the concurrence of the Roumanian, on the same conditions as those for the requirements of the State. Similar measures will be taken for the acquisition of the materials necessary for the construction and insalment of the said establishments.

Art. XIX. The sick and wounded of the Russian army will be treated and cared for in sanitary establishments, organized for this purpose on the lines of communication, and those of the storehouses, and " étapes," wherever the Russian Commander-in-Chief may deem it necessary—excepting the town of Bucharest—and, as far as possible, away from the centres of population, excepting always hospitals for the wounded.

The Roumanian authorities will give their aid, and accord every facility for the installation of sanitary establishments, as also for the hiring of edifices necessary for such purposes. In places where there will be no Russian hospitals, the sick may be admitted provisionally, as far as possible, into Roumanian sanitary establishments, on payment of expenses for food, treatment, &c.

ART. XX. In localities where halts may be necessary during the passage of the Russian troops, under the conditions of Article XVIII— these troops will have facilities given them for lodging and encampment —which will be procured for them by the care of the local authorities. If from this cause payment become necessary, it will be regulated according to an understanding between the respective Commissioners.

ART. XXI. On the lines of communication of the Imperial army, in localities where military necessities demand the naming of Commanders of Russian Stations, these Commanders will communicate with the local authorities through the Roumanian Commissaries according to Article II.

ART. XXII. The Russian army will have the faculty of establishing bridges and river communications at points where it may be considered necessary, and to construct the works necessary for securing and protecting this passage. The Roumanian Government, for this object, will place barges and boats, &c., at the disposition of the Russian army, &c., *i.e.*, such as can be procured, and as far as the requirements of its own army allow, besides the quantity of wood necessary for construction and other materials, on equitable payment.

ART. XXIII. All payments to be effected, on the occasion of the passage of Russian troops through Roumania, whether to the Government, to the railway companies, or to private persons, will be calculated on the basis of the monetary unity, Roumanian or French.

These can be made either in money, or " bons," in due form emitted by the Commander of the Imperial army, and payable by the chest of said army, within two months at the outside. The form of these bills, their terms, mode, and place of payment, and control will be regulated and brought to the knowledge of the public, after an understanding between the Russian Commander-in-Chief and the Roumanian Commissary-General.

ART. XXIV. The Roumanian Government accords to the Russian Government for the term whilst the Imperial troops are in Roumania, and on this side of the Danube, the free importation into its territory, without duties, and the free transit of all articles and objects for the provisioning, and munition and war material, destined for the use of the Imperial army and even those things the entry of which is prohibited by Roumanian regulations.

ART. XXV. Should desertion take place of Russian troops during the passage through Roumania, the Roumanian authorities will assist to arrest the culprits, according to indications to be given by the Russian military authorities. Deserters arrested will be given over into the hands of the Russian Military Commanders nearest to the spot where the arrestations are made.

ART. XXVI. Any cases of differences which may occur on the occasion of the passage of Russian troops through Roumania, and which is not provided for by this Convention, shall be regulated by common accord by the Commissioners named *ad hoc* by the Chief Commander of the Russian forces and the Roumanian Commissioner-General.

In faith of which, the respective Plenipotentiaries have put their signatures and seals of their arms to this Supplementary Convention.

Made in duplicate in Bucharest, the 4/16th of April, in the year of Grace, 1877.

BARON D. STUART,
*Diplomatic Agent and Consul-General
of Russian in Roumania.*
M. COGALNICEANO,
Minister of Foreign Affairs in Roumania.

107   CONVENTION OF ADRIANOPLE

CONVENTION of Armistice between Russia, Servia and Roumania, and Turkey. Signed at Adrianople, 19th/31st January, 1878.

Reference to Bases of Peace.

IN consequence of the proposal of the Sublime Porte, and with the consent expressed by their Plenipotentiaries, their Excellencies Server Pasha and Namyk Pasha, to accept the Bases drawn up by Russia for the conclusion of Peace between the belligerent parties, the Commander-in-Chief of the Imperial Russian army declared himself ready to cause the cessation of military operations.

Plenipotentiaries for the conclusion of an Armistice have been appointed: on the part of his Imperial Highness the Commander-in-Chief, his Excellency the Aide-de-Camp General Népokoïtchitski, chief of the staff of the army in the field and his adjutant, the major-general of the staff of His Majesty the Emperor, Lavitski; and on the part of the Plenipotentiaries of the Sublime Porte, his Excellency the general of division of the staff, Nedjib Pasha, and the general of brigade of the staff, Osman Pasha.

These personages, in virtue of the full powers with which they are invested, have agreed to the following conditions:—

*Armistice between the Armies of Russia, Servia, and Roumania, and
Turkey.*

ART. I. An Armistice is concluded between the armed forces of Russia,

Servia, and Roumania on the one side, and those of Turkey on the other, during the whole time of the negotiations of peace until a favourable issue of the latter or of their rupture. In the latter alternative, and before the resumption of hostilities, each of the belligerent parties will be bound to denounce the Armistice three days beforehand, indicating the date and the hour at which hostilities may be resumed. The delay of three days shall begin from the time at which one of the respective parties shall have signified to the other on the spot the superior order he may have received on the subject.

Russia to invite Montenegro to adhere to Armistice.

The Russian Imperial Government will propose to Montenegro to cease military operations and to ahere to the conditions of the Armistice agreed upon between Russia and Turkey; the Sublime Porte will on her part cease operations against Montenegro.

Armistice to begin from date of Signature. Restoration of Booty taken after Signature of Armistice.

ART. II. The Armistice shall take effect from the moment that its conditions shall have been accepted and signed. The troops of either the one or the other party which, after that time, shall have infringed the line of demarcation specified above, shall retrace their steps, restoring the booty taken on the occasion.

Turkish Evacuation of Fortresses.

ART. III. Besides the evacuation of the fortresses of Widdin, Rustchuk, and Silistria, stipulated for in the Bases of Peace, the Imperial Ottoman troops will abandon Belgradjik, Razgrad, and Hadji-Oglou-Bazardjik.

Line of Demarcation between the Russian, Servian, and Roumanian, and Turkish Armies.

The line of demarcation to be established between the Russian, Servian, and Roumanian armies on the one side, and the Ottoman on the other, is traced as follows:—

The line of demarcation shall pass by Baltchik and Hadji-Oglou-Bazardjik in a straight line towards Razgrad, with a neutral zone of five kilomètres preceding that line. It shall continue from Razgrad in a straight line to Eski-Djouma; from Eski-Djouma to Osman-Bazar and Kotel (Kazan), which shall be occupied by Russian troops, and the neutral zone shall be traced beyond the line at five kilomètres distance.

Further on the line of demarcation shall run along the Medvan, Déli-Kamtchik, and Bogazdéré rivers, and through the villages of

Oglanloukeui and Hadjidéré, as far as Misservi; the neutral zone, of five kilomètres wide, following the two banks of those rivers as far as the sea, and along the coast as far as Lake Derkos. Nevertheless, the Russian troops shall only occupy Bourgas and Midia, on the coast of the Black Sea, for the purpose of facilitating the revictualling of the troops and for the exclusion of contraband of war.

From Lake Derkos the line of demarcation shall proceed by Tchekmedjik and Kardjali in a direct line, crossing the railway on the right bank of the Kara-sou, whose course it shall follow as far as the Sea of Marmora.

The Turkish troops shall evacuate the line of fortifications, as well as Derkos, Hademkeui and Bouyouk-Tchekmedjé. The line of demarcation on their side shall start from Kutchuk-Tchekmedjé in a direct line by Saint-George and Akbounar, on the coast of the Black Sea. The intermediate lands between the Turkish and Russian lines shall form a neutral zone in which no fortifications shall either be constructed or increased, nor repaired during the whole of the armistice.

From the Sea of Marmora the line of demarcation shall pass by the isthmus of Gallipoli, from Charkeui to Ourcha, and further on, along the Ægean Sea as far as Dédéagatch and Makri, the latter point included. From thence along the line where the tributary waters of the Maritsa (including the Arda) separate themselves, and of the rivers which flow into the Ægean Sea, as far as Djouma.

It shall continue on a line traced towards Kustendil, Vrania, Planina Goliak, the village of Meslitza, Grapachnitza Planina; the village of Loubtché, as far as the frontier of the Sandjak of Novi-Bazar, and by that frontier joining Servia, at a point called Kopaonik Planina. Djouma, Kustendil, Vrania, are occupied by Russian or Servian troops; Prichtina by Ottoman troops.

The tracing of the line of demarcation between the Imperial Ottoman troops and those of Montenegro shall be executed by a Special Commission of Turkish and Montenegrin Plenipotentiaries, with the assistance of a Russian Delegate. The settling on the spot of the limits of the zone of demarcation of the belligerent Imperial armies must take place without delay, immediately after the signature of these conditions, by means of a Commission of officers of both armies being empowered thereto, and chosen from corps and detachments nearest to the places to be traced. Where there are no troops in the vicinity, the zone of demarcation shall follow the direction, and be described by the above neutral limits, and which are brought to the knowledge of the two armies.

The zone of demarcation from Djouma by Vrania, as far as the frontier of the Sandjak of Novi-Bazar, shall be settled on the spot by a Commission of Delegates of the Imperial Ottoman troops on the one part, and of Servian troops on the other, assisted by a Russian Delegate.

Troops not within Line of Demarcation to fall back within Three Days.

ART. IV. The troops of both belligerent parties which, at the time of the signature of the present Act, shall be outside of the line stated, shall immediately fall back, and that not later than three days' delay.

Routes to be taken by Turkish Troops in evacuating Fortified Places, with their Arms, Ammunition, &c.

ART. V. In evacuating the fortified places mentioned in Article III, the Imperial Ottoman troops shall withdraw with their arms and munitions of war and accoutrements, as well as the stores which can be carried away, in the following directions:—

From Widdin and Belgradjik, by the St. Nicolas Pass, towards Ak-Palanka, Nisch, Leskovatz, and by Vrania or Prichtina, as it may be easiest to reach the railroad.

From Rustchuk, Silistria, Hadji-Oglou, Bazardjik, and Razgrad, towards Varna or Choumla, as may be decided on by the Ottoman Military Authorities.

The munitions of war and other stores of the fortresses, ships of war, or those belonging to the State, and everything belonging to them, may be taken away or left in the custody of the Russian military authority, who shall take measures for their preservation until the conclusion of peace, according to an inventory signed in duplicate by both parties. As to the stores which are from their nature perishable, they may be sold or ceded to the Russian military authority for an equivalent price to be agreed upon.

Private property remains intact.

The evacuation of the above-mentioned fortified places must be completed within seven days at latest, reckoning from the receipt of the order relating thereto by the local commander.

Ottoman Troops and Ships of War to leave Sulina within Three Days. Russia to open the Navigation of the Danube.

ART. VI. The Imperial Ottoman troops and ships of war shall also leave the Sulina within three days, should the ice put no impediment thereto. The Russian military authority, on his side, shall cause all obstacles to be removed from the Danube, and shall open the river to navigation, reserving to himself the superintendence thereof.

Ottoman Civil Authorities to remain and perform the Duties of their Office in Provinces occupied by Russian or Allied Troops.

Art. VII. In the provinces occupied by Russian or allied troops, in which at the time of the signature of these conditions Ottoman administrative authorities should still reside there, the latter must remain to continue to perform their duties and maintain tranquillity and order among the population; they will also have to fulfil, as far as possible, the requirements of the Russian military authorities.

Railway Traffic on the Lines occupied by the Ottoman and Russian Troops. Military Supervision.

Art. VIII. The railway lines within the radius occupied by Russian troops shall be respected in the same manner as every other private property, and their working shall be free throughout. To that end the Ottoman Government gives to the Companies the right of using their rolling stock throughout the whole extent of the line occupied, as well by the Ottoman armies as by Russian troops. Full liberty shall be granted to passenger and commercial traffic with the following exceptions: it shall be forbidden to carry munitions of war and troops throughout the line of demarcation. Throughout the radius occupied by the two armies the traffic shall take place under the supervision of the military authority of each of them.

Raising of Turkish Blockade of the Black Sea during the Armistice.

Art. IX. The Sublime Porte shall raise the Blockade of the ports of the Black Sea during the whole time of the Armistice, and shall not prevent the free entrance of vessels into those ports.

Sick and Wounded of Ottoman Army within the Lines occupied by Russian or Allied Troops.

Art. X. The sick and wounded belonging to the Imperial Ottoman army who may remain within the radius occupied by Russian troops or those of Servia and Montenegro, shall be taken under the care of the Russian and allied military authorities, but they shall be attended by an Ottoman medical staff, should such exist, on the spot. The sick and wounded shall not be considered as prisoners of war, but they shall not be allowed, without the special authority of the Russian and allied military chiefs, to be carried to other places.

The Armistice to commence from 31st January.

The Armistice shall date from the 19th/31st January, at seven o'clock in the evening. As to the other delays, they are stipulated for in the body of the Armistice.

Details of Armistice in Asia to be settled by Military Commissioners.

For the seat of war in Asia, the settlement of the details shall take place through the Plenipotentiaries appointed by the Commander-in-Chief of the Russian Army in Asia and those of the Ottoman Government.

Armistice to be telegraphed to Commander of Russian Army in Asia.

The commencement of the Armistice at the seat of the war in Europe shall be notified by telegraph to the Commander of the Russian army in Asia.

NEPOKOITCHITSKI.
LAVITSKI.
NEDJIB.
OSMAN.

On the 7th February, 1878, the British Ambassador at Constantinople (Mr. Layard), informed the Earl of Derby, by telegraph, that the Armistice commenced at 7 P.M. on the 31st January; that the Turks had commenced the withdrawal of guns from the Constantinople lines; and that the Turkish Commanders on the spot were to settle matters relating to the Armistice in Armenia.

108   PRELIMINARY TREATY OF SAN STEFANO

PRELIMINARY TREATY OF PEACE between Russia and Turkey. Signed at San Stefano, 19th February/3rd March, 1878. Ratifications exchanged at St. Petersburgh, 5th/17th March, 1878.

His Majesty the Emperor of Russia and His Majesty the Emperor of the Ottomans, inspired with the wish of restoring and securing the blessings of peace to their countries and people, as well as of preventing any fresh complication which might imperil the same, have named as their Plenipotentiaries, with a view to draw up, conclude, and sign the Preliminaries of Peace:—

His Majesty the Emperor of Russia on the one side, the Count Nicolas Ignatiew, Aide-de-Camp General of His Imperial Majesty, Lieutenant-General, Member of the Council of the Empire, &c.; and le Sieur Alexander Nelidow, Chamberlain of the Imperial Court, Conseiller d'Etat actuel, &c.;

And His Majesty the Emperor of the Ottomans on the other side,

Safvet Pasha, Minister for Foreign Affairs, &c.; and Sadoullah Bey, His Majesty's Ambassador at the Imperial Court of Germany, &c.;

Who, after having exchanged their full powers, which were found to be in good and proper form, have agreed to the following Articles:—

Montenegro. Rectification of Frontier.

ART. I. In order to put an end to the perpetual conflicts between Turkey and Montenegro, the frontier which separates the two countries will be rectified conformably to the Map hereto annexed, subject to the reserve hereinafter mentioned, in the following manner:—

From the mountain of Dobrostitza the frontier will follow the line indicated by the Conference of Constantinople as far as Korito by Bilek. Thence the new frontier will run to Gatzko (Metochia-Gatzko will belong to Montenegro), and towards the confluence of the Piva and the Tara, ascending towards the north by the Drina as far as its confluence with the Lim. The eastern frontier of the Principality will follow this last river as far as Prijepoljé, and will proceed by Roshaj to Sukha-Planina (leaving Bihor and Roshaj to Montenegro). Taking in Bugovo, Plava, and Gusinje, the frontier line will follow the chain of mountains by Shlieb, Paklen, and along the northern frontier of Albania by the crests of the Mountains Koprivnik, Babavik, Bor-vik, to the highest peak of Prokléti. From that point the frontier will proceed by the summit of Biskaschik, and will run in a straight line to the Lake of Tjiceni-hoti. Dividing Tjiceni-hoti and Tjiceni-kastrati, it will cross the Lake of Scutari to the Boyana, the thalweg of which it will follow as far as the sea. Nichsich, Gatzko, Spouje, Podgoritza, Zabliak, and Antivari will remain to Montenegro.

Montenegro. European Boundary Commission to be appointed.

A European Commission, on which the Sublime Porte and the Government of Montenegro shall be represented, will be charged with fixing the definitive limits of the Principality, making on the spot such modifications in the general tracing as it may think necessary and equitable, from the point of view of the respective interests and tranquillity of the two countries, to which it will accord in this respect the equivalents deemed necessary.

Montenegro. Navigation of the Boyana.

The navigation of the Boyana having always given rise to disputes between the Sublime Porte and Montenegro, will be the subject of a special regulation, which will be prepared by the same European Commission.

Montenegro. Independence recognized by the Porte. Character and Form of Relations between Turkey and Montenegro to be determined subsequently.

ART. II. The Sublime Porte recognizes definitively the Independence of the Principality of Montenegro.

An understanding between the Imperial Government of Russia, the Ottoman Government, and the Principality of Montenegro will determine subsequently the character and form of the relations between the Sublime Porte and the Principality as regards particularly the establishment of Montenegrin Agents at Constantinople, and in certain localities of the Ottoman Empire, where the necessity for such Agents shall be recognized, the extradition of fugitive criminals on the one territory or the other, and the subjection of Montenegrins travelling or sojourning in the Ottoman Empire to the Ottoman laws and authorities, according to the principles of international law and the established usages concerning the Montenegrins.

Montenegro. Convention to be concluded. Relations between Inhabitants on Confines; and Military Works.

A Convention will be concluded between the Sublime Porte and Montenegro to regulate the questions connected with the relations between the inhabitants of the confines of the two countries and with the military works on the same confines. The points upon which an understanding cannot be established will be settled by the arbitration of Russia and Austria-Hungary.

Montenegro. Disputes with Turkey. Arbitration of Russia and Austria-Hungary.

Henceforward, if there is any discussion or conflict, except as regards new territorial demands, Turkey and Montenegro will leave the settlement of their differences to Russia and Austria-Hungary, who will arbitrate in common.

Montenegro. Evacuation of Turkish Territory.

The troops of Montenegro will be bound to evacuate the territory not comprised within the limits indicated above within ten days from the signature of the Preliminaries of Peace.

Servia. Independence. Boundaries.

ART. III. Servia is recognized as independent. Its frontier, marked on the annexed Map, will follow the thalweg of the Drina, leaving Little Zwornik and Zakar to the Principality, and following the old limit as far as the sources of the stream Dezevo, near Stoilac. Thence the new line will follow the course of that stream as far as the River Raska, and then the course of the latter as far as Novi-Bazar.

From Novi-Bazar, ascending the stream which passes near the villages of Mekinje and Irgoviste, as far as its source, the frontier line will run by Bosur Planina, in the valley of the Ibar, and will then descend the stream which falls into this river, near the village of Ribanic.

The line will then follow the course of the Rivers Ibar, Sitnitza, and Lab, and of the brook Batintze to its source (upon the Grapachnitza Planina). Thence the frontier will follow the heights which separate the waters of the Kriva and the Veternitza, and will meet the latter river by the shortest route at the mouth of the stream Miovatzka, which it will ascend, crossing the Miovatzka Planina and redescending towards the Morava, near the village of Kalimanci.

From this point the frontier will descend to the Morava as far as the River Vlossina, near the village of Staïkovtzi. Reascending the latter river, as well as the Linberazda, and the brook Koukavitze, the line will pass by the Sukha Planina, will run along the stream Vrylo as far as the Nisawa, and will descend the said river as far as the village of Kronpatz, whence the line will rejoin by the shortest route the old Servian frontier to the south-east of Karaoul Baré, and will not leave it until it reaches the Danube.

Ada-Kale will be evacuated and razed.

Servia. *Appointment of a Boundary Commission.*

A Turco-Servian Commission, assisted by a Russian Commissioner, will, within three months, arrange upon the spot the definite frontier line, and will definitely settle the questions relating to the islands of the Drina. A Bulgarian delegate will be admitted to participate in the work of the Commission when it shall be engaged on the frontier between Servia and Bulgaria.

Servia. Right of Non-resident Mussulmans to hold Real Property. Turco-Servian Commission, assisted by Russian Commissioner, to be appointed.

ART. IV. The Mussulmans holding lands in the territories annexed to Servia, and who wish to reside out of the Principality, can preserve their real property by having them farmed out or administered by others. A Turco-Servian Commission, assisted by a Russian Commissioner, will be charged to decide absolutely, in the course of two years, all questions relating to the verification of real estate in which Mussulman interests are concerned.

Servia. Commission to settle Alienation of State Property, Religious Endowments (Vakoufs), and Private Interests. Rights of Servians travelling in Turkey.

This Commission will also be called upon to settle within three years the method of alienation of State property and of religious endowments (*Vakoufs*), as well as the questions relative to the interests of private persons which may be involved. Until a direct Treaty is concluded between Turkey and Servia determining the character of the relations between the Sublime Porte and the Principality, Servian subjects travelling or sojourning in the Ottoman Empire shall be treated according to the general principles of international law.

Servia. Evacuation of Turkish Territory by Servian Troops.

The Servian troops shall be bound to evacuate the territory not comprised within the above-mentioned limits within fifteen days from the signature of the Preliminaries of Peace.

Roumania. Independence. Indemnity to Roumania.

ART. V. The Sublime Porte recognises the Independence of Roumania, which will establish its right to an indemnity, to be discussed between the two countries.

Roumania. Rights of Roumanians in Turkey.

Until the conclusion of a direct Treaty between Turkey and Roumania, Roumanian subjects will enjoy in Turkey all the rights guaranteed to the subjects of other European Powers.

Bulgaria. An Autonomous Tributary Principality, with Christian Government and National Militia.

ART. VI. Bulgaria is constituted an autonomous tributary Principality, with a Christian Government and a national militia.

Bulgaria. Boundaries to be traced by Russo-Turkish Commission.

The definitive frontiers of the Bulgarian Principality will be traced by a special Russo-Turkish Commission before the evacuation of Roumelia by the Imperial Russian Army.

Bulgaria. Duties of Russo-Turkish Commission, Nationalities, &c.

This Commission will, in working out the modifications to be made on the spot in the general tracing, take into account the principle of the nationality of the majority of the inhabitants of the border districts, conformably to the Bases of Peace, and also the topographical necessities and practical interests of the intercommunication of the local population.

Bulgaria. Line of Boundary.

The extent of the Bulgarian Principality is laid down in general terms on the accompanying Map, which will serve as a basis for the definitive fixing of the limits. Leaving the new frontier of the Servian Principality, the line will follow the western limit of the Caza of Wrania as far as the chain of the Kara-dagh. Turning towards the west, the line will follow the western limits of the Cazas of Koumanovo, Kotchani, Kalkandelen, to Mount Korab; thence by the River Welestchitza as far as its junction with the black Drina. Turning towards the south by the Drina and afterwards by the western limit of the Caza of Ochride towards Mount Linas, the frontier will follow the western limits of the Cazas of Gortcha and Starovo as far as Mount Grammos. Then by the Lake of Kastoria, the frontier line will rejoin the River Moglénitza, and after having followed its course, and passed to the south of Yanitza (Wardar Yenidje), will go by the mouth of the Wardar and by the Galliko towards the villages of Parga and of Saraï-keui; thence through the middle of Lake Bechik-Guel to the mouth of the Rivers Strouma and Karassou, and by the sea coast as far as Buru-Guel; thence striking north-west towards Mount Tchaltépé by the chain of Rhodope as far as Mount Krouschowo, by the Black Balkans (Kara-Balkan), by the mountains Eschek-koulatchi, Tchepelion, Karakolas, and Tschiklar, as far as the River Arda.

Thence the line will be traced in the direction of the town of Tchirmen, and leaving the town of Adrianople to the south, by the villages of Sugutlion, Kara-Hamza, Arnaout-keui, Akardji, and Enidje, as far as the River Tékéderessi. Following the Rivers Tékéderessi and Tchorlouderessi as far as Loulé-Bourgaz, and thence, by the River Soudjak-déré as far as the village of Serguen, the frontier line will go by the heights straight towards Hakim-tabiassi, where it will strike the Black Sea. It will leave the sea coast near Mangalia, following the southern boundaries of the Sandjak of Toultcha, and will come out on the Danube above Rassova.

Bulgaria. Election of Prince. Exclusion of Dynasties of Great European Powers.

Art. VII. The Prince of Bulgaria shall be freely elected by the population and confirmed by the Sublime Porte, with the assent of the Powers. No member of the reigning dynasties of the great European Powers shall be capable of being elected Prince of Bulgaria.

Bulgaria. Election of Prince in case of Vacancy.

In the event of the dignity of Prince of Bulgaria being vacant, the election of the new Prince shall be made subject to the same conditions and forms.

Bulgaria. Assembly of Notables to draw up Organic Law previous to Election of Prince.

Before the election of the Prince, an Assembly of Bulgarian Notables, to be convoked at Philippopolis (Plowdiw) or Tyrnowo, shall draw up, under the superintendence of an Imperial Russian Commissioner, and in the presence of an Ottoman Commissioner, the organization of the future administration, in conformity with the precedent established in 1830 after the Peace of Adrianople, in the Danubian Principalities.

Bulgaria. Rights and Interests of different Populations.

In the localities where Bulgarians are mixed with Turks, Greeks, Wallachians (Koutzo-Vlachs), or others, proper account is to be taken of the rights and interests of these populations in the elections and in the preparation of the Organic Laws.

Bulgaria. Russian Commissioner to superintend New System for Two Years. Special European Delegates to be associated with Russian Commissioner after first Year.

The introduction of the new system into Bulgaria, and the superintendence of its working, will be entrusted for two years to an Imperial Russian Commissioner. At the expiration of the first year after the introduction of the new system, and if an understanding on this subject has been established between Russia, the Sublime Porte, and the Cabinets of Europe, they can, if it is deemed necessary, associate Special Delegates with the Imperial Russian Commissioner.

Bulgaria. Evacuation of, by Ottoman Troops. Fortresses to be razed. Disposal of Material of War by Turkey.

ART. VIII. The Ottoman army will no longer remain in Bulgaria, and all the ancient fortresses will be razed at the expense of the local government. The Sublime Porte will have the right to dispose, as it sees fit, of the war material and of the other property belonging to the Ottoman Government which may have been left in the Danubian fortresses already evacuated in accordance with the terms of the Armistice of the 19th/31st January, as well as of that in the strongholds of Schoumla and Varna.

Bulgaria. Russian Occupation until formation of Native Militia.

Until the complete formation of a native militia sufficient to preserve order, security, and tranquillity, and the strength of which will be fixed later on by an understanding between the Ottoman Government and the Imperial Russian Cabinet, Russian troops will occupy the country, and will give armed assistance to the Commissioner in case of need. This occupation will also be limited to a term approximating to two years.

Bulgaria. Strength of Army of Occupation. Expense to be borne by Bulgaria. Russian Communications, with necessary Depôts.

The strength of the Russian army of occupation, to be composed of six divisions of infantry and two of cavalry, which will remain in Bulgaria after the evacuation of Turkey by the Imperial army, shall not exceed 50,000 men. It will be maintained at the expense of the country occupied. The Russian troops of occupation in Bulgaria will maintain their communications with Russia, not only through Roumania, but also by the ports of the Black Sea, Varna and Bourgas, where they may organize, for the term of the occupation, the necessary depôts.

Bulgaria. Tribute to Turkey.

ART. IX. The amount of the annual tribute which Bulgaria is to pay the Suzerain Court, by transmitting it to a bank to be hereafter named by the Sublime Porte, will be determined by an agreement between Russia, the Ottoman Government, and the other Cabinets, at the end of the first year during which the new organization shall be in operation. This tribute will be calculated on the average revenue of all the territory which is to form part of the Principality.

Bulgaria. Agreement to be made with Turkey to undertake Obligations towards Rustchuck and Varna Railway Company, as well as with other Railway Companies.

Bulgaria will take upon itself the obligations of the Imperial Ottoman Government towards the Rustchuck and Varna Railway Company, after an agreement has been come to between the Sublime Porte, the Government of the Principality, and the Directors of this Company. The regulations as to the other railways (*voies ferrées*) which cross the Principality are also reserved for an agreement between the Sublime Porte, the Government established in Bulgaria, and the Directors of the Companies concerned.

Bulgaria. Transport of Turkish Troops, &c., through Bulgaria by fixed Routes. Special Regulation to lay down Conditions.

ART. X. The Sublime Porte shall have the right to make use of Bulgaria for the transport by fixed routes of its troops, munitions, and provisions to the provinces beyond the Principality, and *vice versâ*. In order to avoid difficulties and misunderstandings in the application of this right, while guaranteeing the military necessities of the Sublime Porte, a special regulation will lay down the conditions of it within three months after the ratification of the present Act by an understanding between the Sublime Porte and the Bulgarian Government.

Bulgaria. Irregular Troops, Bashi-Bazouks, and Circassians.

It is fully understood that this right is limited to the regular Ottoman troops, and that the irregulars, the Bashi-Bazouks, and the Circassians will be absolutely excluded from it.

Bulgaria. Right of Turkey to Postal and Telegraph Services.

The Sublime Porte also reserves to itself the right of sending its postal service through the Principality, and of maintaining telegraphic communication. These two points shall also be determined in the manner and within the period of time indicated above.

Bulgaria. Right of non-resident Mussulmans to hold Real Property. Turco-Bulgarian Commissions, under superintendence of Russian Commissioners, to be appointed.

ART. XI. The Mussulman proprietors or others who fix their personal residence outside the Principality may retain their estates by having them farmed or administered by others. Turco-Bulgarian Commissions shall sit in the principal centres of population, under the superintendence of Russian Commissioners, to decide absolutely in the course of two years all questions relative to the verification of real property in which either Mussulmans or others may be interested.

Bulgaria. Similar Commissions to settle Alienation, &c., of State Property and Religious Endowments (Vakoufs).

Similar Commissions will be charged with the duty of regulating within two years all questions relative to the mode of alienation, working, or use for the benefit of the Sublime Porte of the property of the State, and of the religious endowments (*Vakoufs*).

Bulgaria. Sale of unclaimed Properties.

At the expiration of the two years mentioned above, all properties which shall not have been claimed shall be sold by public auction, and the proceeds thereof shall be devoted to the support of the widows and orphans, Mussulman as well as Christian, victims of the recent events.

Danube. Fortresses to be razed. No Strongholds to exist on its Banks. Vessels of War not to navigate Waters of the Principalities. Exceptions.

ART. XII. All the Danubian fortresses shall be razed. There shall be no strongholds in future on the banks of this river, nor any men-of-war in the waters of the Principalities of Roumania, Servia, and Bulgaria, except the usual "stationnaires" and the small vessels intended for river-police and Custom-house purposes.

Damube.   Maintenance of Rights, &c., of International Commission of Lower Danube.

The rights, obligations, and prerogatives of the International Commission of the Lower Danube are maintained intact.

Danube.   Turkey to render passage of Soulina again navigable, and to indemnify Private Individuals.

ART. XIII. The Sublime Porte undertakes to render the passage of Soulina again navigable, and to indemnify the private individuals who have suffered loss by the war and the interruption of the navigation of the Danube, applying for this double charge a sum of 500,000 francs from the amount due to the Sublime Porte from the Danubian Commission.

Bosnia and Herzegovina.   Proposals of Conference at Constantinople to be introduced.

ART. XIV. The European proposals communicated to the Ottoman Plenipotentiaries at the first sitting of the Constantinople Conference, shall be immediately introduced into Bosnia and Herzegovina, with any modifications which may be agreed upon in common between the Sublime Porte, the Government of Russia, and that of Austria-Hungary.

Bosnia and Herzegovina.   Non-payment of Arrears of Taxes. Revenues to be applied to indemnify Families of Refugees and Inhabitants, and local needs.   Application of future Revenues.

The payment of arrears of taxes shall not be required, and the current revenues of those provinces until the 1st March, 1880, shall be exclusively applied to indemnify the families of refugees and inhabitants, victims of recent events, without distinction of race or creed, as well as to the local needs of the country. The sum to be received annually after this period by the Central Government shall be subsequently fixed by a special understanding between Turkey, Russia, and Austria-Hungary.

Crete.   Application of Organic Law of 1868.

ART. XV. The Sublime Porte engages to apply scrupulously in the Island of Crete the Organic Law of 1868 taking into account the previously expressed wishes of the native population.

Epirus, Thessaly, and other parts of Turkey in Europe.   Organic Laws.

An analogous law adapted to local requirements shall likewise be introduced into Epirus, Thessaly, and the other parts of Turkey in Europe, for which a special constitution is not provided by the present Act.

Organic Laws.   Special Commissions to settle Details.

Special Commissions, in which the native population will be largely represented, shall in each province be entrusted with the task of elaborating the details of the new organization, and the result of their labours shall be submitted to the Sublime Porte, who will consult the Imperial Government of Russia before carrying it into effect.

Armenia; Turkish Reforms and Improvements in, and in Provinces inhabited by Armenians. Security against Kurds and Circassians.

ART. XVI. As the evacuation by the Russian troops of the territory which they occupy in Armenia, and which is to be restored to Turkey, might give rise to conflicts and complications detrimental to the maintenance of good relations between the two countries, the Sublime Porte engages to carry into effect, without further delay, the improvements and reforms demanded by local requirements in the provinces inhabited by Armenians, and to guarantee their security from Kurds and Circassians.

Amnesty to Ottoman Subjects. Prisoners and Exiles to be restored to Liberty.

ART. XVII. A full and complete amnesty is granted by the Sublime Porte to all Ottoman subjects compromised by recent events, and all persons imprisoned on this account or sent into exile shall be immediately set at liberty.

Khotour. Possession of Town; and Delimitation of Turco-Persian Boundary.

ART. XVIII. The Sublime Porte will take into serious consideration the opinion expressed by the Commissioners of the Mediating Powers as regards the possession of the town of Khotour, and engages to have the works of the definitive delimitation of the Turco-Persian Boundary carried into effect.

War Indemnities, Pecuniary and Territorial, to be paid by Turkey to Russia.

ART. XIX. The war indemnity and the losses imposed on Russia which His Majesty the Emperor of Russia claims, and which the Sublime Porte has bound itself to reimburse to him, consist of—

(*a.*) 900,000,000 roubles for war expenses (maintenance of the army, replacing of war material, and war contracts).

(*b.*) 400,000,000 roubles on account of damage done to the south coast of Russia, to her export commerce, to her industries, and to her railways.

(*c.*) 100,000,000 roubles for injuries inflicted on the Caucasus by the invasion; and, (*d.*) 10,000,000 roubles for costs and damages of Russian subjects and establishments in Turkey.

Total 1,410,000,000 roubles.

Taking into consideration the financial embarrassments of Turkey, and in accordance with the wishes of His Majesty the Sultan, the Emperor of Russia consents to substitute for the payment of the greater part of the moneys enumerated in the above paragraph, the following territorial cessions:—

War Indemnities in Europe. Sandjak of Toultcha. Delta of the Danube, Island of Serpents, Bessarabia, &c.

(*a.*) The Sandjak of Toultcha, that is to say, the districts (Cazas) of Kilia, Soulina, Mahmoudié, Isaktcha, Toultcha, Matchine, Babadagh, Hirsowo, Kustendje, and Medjidie, as well as the Delta Islands and the Isle of Serpents.

Not wishing, however, to annex this territory and the Delta Islands, Russia reserves the right of exchanging them for the part of Bessarabia detached from her by the Treaty of 1856, and which is bounded on the south by the thalweg of the Kilia branch and the mouth of the Siary-Stamboul.

Waters and Fisheries.

The question of the apportionment of Waters and Fisheries shall be determined by a Russo-Roumanian Commission within a year after the ratification of the Treaty of Peace.

War Indemnities in Asia. Ardahan, Kars, Batoum, Bayazet, &c.

(*b.*) Ardahan, Kars, Batoum, Bayazet, and the territory as far as the Saganlough.

In its general outline, the frontier line, leaving the Black Sea coast, will follow the crest of the mountains which separate the affluents of the River Hopa from those of the River Tcharokh, and the chain of mountains to the south of the town of Artwin up to the River Tcharokh, near the villages of Alat and Bechaget; then the frontier will pass by the peaks of Mounts Dervenikghek, Hortchezor, and Bedjiguin-Dagh, by the crest which separates the affluents of the Rivers Tortoum-tchaï and the Tcharokh by the heights near Zaily-Vihine, coming down at the village Vihine-Kilissa to the River Tortoum-tchaï; thence it will follow the Sivridagh Chain to the pass (*col*) of the same name, passing south of the village of Noriman; then it will turn to the south-east and go to Zivine, whence the frontier, passing west of the road which leads from Zivine to the villages of Ardozt and Horassan, will turn south by the Saganlough Chain to the village of Gilitchman; then by the crest of the Charian-

Dagh it will arrive, ten versts south of Hamour, at the Mourad-tchai defile; then the line will follow the crest of the Alla-Dagh and the summits of the Hori and Tandourek, and, passing south of the Bayazet valley, will proceed to rejoin the old Turco-Persian frontier to the south of the lake of Kazligueul.

The definitive limits of the territory annexed to Russia, and indicated on the Map hereto appended, will be fixed by a Commission composed of Russian and Ottoman delegates.

This Commission in its labours will take into account the topography of localities, as well as considerations of good administration and other conditions calculated to insure the tranquillity of the country.

War Indemnities. Mode of Payment.

(c.) The territories mentioned in paragraphs (a) and (b) are ceded to Russia as an equivalent for the sum of one milliard and one hundred million (1,100,000,000) roubles. As for the rest of the indemnity, apart from the 10,000,000 of roubles intended to indemnify Russian interests and establishments in Turkey—namely, 300,000,000 of roubles—the mode of payment and guarantee of that sum shall be settled by an understanding between the Imperial Government of Russia and that of His Majesty the Sultan.

War Indemnities. Russian Subjects and Establishments.

(d.) The 10,000,000 roubles claimed as an indemnity for the Russian subjects and establishments in Turkey shall be paid as soon as the claims of those interested are examined by the Russian Embassy at Constantinople and handed to the Sublime Porte.

Lawsuits of Russian Subjects.

ART. XX. The Sublime Porte will take effective steps to put an amicable end to the lawsuits of Russian subjects pending for several years, to indemnify the latter if need be, and to carry into effect without delay all judgments passed.

Liberty to Inhabitants of Ceded Territories to leave and sell their Real Property.

ART. XXI. The inhabitants of the districts ceded to Russia who wish to take up their residence out of these territories will be free to retire on selling all their real property. For this purpose an interval of three years is granted to them, counting from the date of ratification of the present Act.

On the expiration of that time those of the inhabitants who shall not have sold their real property and left the country shall remain as Russian subjects.

Sale of State Property and Religious Establishments by Russo-Turkish Commission. Removal of War Material, &c., from Ceded Territories, not occupied by Russian Troops.

Real property belonging to the State, or to religious establishments situated out of the localities aforesaid, shall be sold within the same interval of three years, as shall be arranged by a special Russo-Turkish Commission. The same Commission shall be intrusted with determining how the Ottoman Government is to remove its war material, munitions, supplies, and other State property actually in the forts, towns, and localities ceded to Russia, and not at present occupied by Russian troops.

Rights of Russian Ecclesiastics, &c., travelling or residing in Turkey.

ART. XXII. Russian ecclesiastics, pilgrims, and monks travelling or sojourning in Turkey in Europe or in Asia shall enjoy the same rights, advantages, and privileges as the foreign ecclesiastics of any other nationality.

Russian Diplomatic and Consular Protection to Russian Ecclesiastics, their Possessions, &c., in Holy Places, and elsewhere.

The right of official protection by the Imperial Embassy and Russian Consulates in Turkey is recognised, both as regards the persons above-mentioned, and their possessions, religious houses, charitable institutions, &c., in the Holy Places and elsewhere.

Mount Athos. Rights and Privileges of Russian Monks.

The monks of Mount Athos, of Russian origin, shall be maintained in all their possessions and former privileges, and shall continue to enjoy in the three convents belonging to them and in the adjoining buildings the same rights and privileges as are assured to the other religious establishments and convents of Mount Athos.

Renewal of all Treaties of Commerce, Jurisdiction, &c., between Russia and Turkey, except clauses affected by present Act.

ART. XXIII. All the Treaties, Coventions, and agreements previously concluded between the two High Contracting Parties relative to commerce, jurisdiction, and the position of Russian subjects in Turkey, and which had been abrogated by the state of war, shall come into force again, with the exception of the clauses affected by the present Act. The two Governments will be placed again in the same relation to one another, with respect to all their engagements and commercial and other relations, as they were in before the declaration of war.

Bosphorus and Dardanelles. To remain open to Neutral Merchant Vessels in time of War. A Fictitious Blockade of Ports of Black Sea and Sea of Azow not to be renewed.

ART. XXIV. The Bosphorus and the Dardanelles shall remain open in time of war as in time of peace to the merchant vessels of neutral States arriving from or bound to Russian ports. The Sublime Porte consequently engages never henceforth to establish at the ports of the Black Sea and the Sea of Azow, a fictitious blockade (*blocus fictif,*) at variance with the spirit of the Declaration signed at Paris on the 4/16th of April, 1856.

Russian Evacuation of Turkey in Europe, except Bulgaria, after conclusion of Definitive Peace.

ART. XXV. The complete evacuation of Turkey in Europe, with the exception of Bulgaria, by the Russian army will take place within three months after the conclusion of the Definitive Peace between His Majesty the Emperor of Russia and His Majesty the Sultan.

Shipment of Russian Troops from ports of Black Sea and Sea of Marmora.

In order to save time, and to avoid the cost of the prolonged maintenance of the Russian troops in Turkey and Roumania, part of the Imperial army may proceed to the ports of the Black Sea and the Sea of Marmora, to be there shipped in vessels belonging to the Russian Government or chartered for the occasion.

Evacuation of Turkey in Asia, viâ Trebizond, after conclusion of Definitive Peace. Evacuation to commence after Exchange of Ratifications.

The evacuation of Turkey in Asia will be effected within the space of six months, dating from the conclusion of the definitive peace, and the Russian troops will be entitled to take ship at Trebizond, in order to return by the Caucasus or the Crimea.

The operations of the evacuation will begin immediately after the exchange of ratifications.

Russian Administration of occupied Localities until Evacuation. Turkey not to participate therein.

ART. XXVI. As long as the Imperial Russian troops remain in the localities which, in conformity with the present Act, will be restored to the Sublime Porte, the administration and order of affairs will continue in the same state as has existed since the occupation. The Sublime Porte will not participate therein during all that time, nor until the entire departure of all the troops.

Ottoman Authority not to be exercised until possession is handed over by Russia.

The Ottoman forces shall not enter the places to be restored to the Sublime Porte, and the Sublime Porte cannot begin to exercise its authority there until notice of each fortress and province having been evacuated by the Russian troops shall have been given by the Commander of these troops to the officer appointed for this purpose by the Sublime Porte.

Amnesty. Ottoman Subjects not to be punished for their Relations with Russia during the War. Liberty to Persons and their Families to leave with Russian Troops.

Art. XXVII. The Sublime Porte undertakes not to punish in any manner, or allow to be punished, those Ottoman subjects who may have been compromised by their relations with the Russian army during the war. In the event of any persons wishing to withdraw with their families when the Russian troops leave, the Ottoman authorities shall not oppose their departure.

Prisoners of War. Exchange of, on Ratification of Preliminaries of Peace.

Art. XXVIII. Immediately upon the ratification of the Preliminaries of Peace, the prisoners of war shall be reciprocally restored under the care of special Commissioners appointed on both sides, who for this purpose shall go to Odessa and Sebastopol. The Ottoman Government will pay all the expenses of the maintenance of the prisoners that are returned to them, in eighteen equal instalments in the space of six years, in accordance with the accounts that will be drawn up by the above-mentioned Commissioners.

The exchange of prisoners between the Ottoman Government and the Governments of Roumania, Servia, and Montenegro will be made on the same bases, deducting, however, in the account, the number of prisoners restored by the Ottoman Government from the number of prisoners that will have to be restored to that Government.

Ratifications.

Art. XXIX. The present Act shall be ratified by their Imperial Majesties the Emperor of Russia and the Emperor of the Ottomans, and the ratifications shall be exchanged in fifteen days, or sooner if possible, at St. Petersburgh, where likewise an agreement shall be come to as to the place and the time at which the stipulations of the present Act shall be invested with all the solemn forms usually observed in Treaties of Peace. It is, however, well understood that the High Contracting Parties consider themselves as formally bound by the present Act from the moment of its ratification.

In witness whereof the respective Plenipotentiaries have appended their signatures and seals to the present Act.

Done at San Stefano, the nineteenth February/third March, one thousand eight hundred and seventy-eight.

(L.S.)   Cte. N. IGNATIEW.
(L.S.)   NELIDOW.
(L.S.)   SAFVET.
(L.S.)   SADOULLAH.

Final Paragraph to Art. XI.

Bulgarians travelling or sojourning in Turkey to be subject to Turkish Laws and Authorities.

Final paragraph of Art. XI of the Act of the Preliminaries of Peace signed this day, February 19/March 3, 1878, which was omitted, and which should form an integral part of the said Article:—

The inhabitants of the Principality of Bulgaria when travelling or sojourning in the other parts of the Ottoman Empire shall be subject to the Ottoman laws and authorities.

(L.S.)   Cte. N. IGNATIEW.
(L.S.)   NELIDOW.
(L.S.)   SAFVET.
(L.S.)   SADOULLAH.

San Stefano, February 19/March 3, 1878.

Regulations for the Danubian Principalities, established in 1830.
REGULATIONS for the Reform of the Administration in the Principalities of Wallachia and Moldavia, comprised in nine chapters, viz.:—

Chapter I.—*The Election of Princes.*

They shall be elected by the Extraordinary General Assembly, convoked *ad hoc* by the Ordinary General Assembly, and without other functions than those of electing Princes. This Extraordinary General Assembly shall be comprised in the case of Wallachia of 192 members, viz.: of the Metropolitan Archbishop as President; of 3 Bishops; of 50 boyards of the first class; of 75 boyards of the second and third classes; of 36 Provincial Deputies elected by the notables of the districts; and of 27 Deputies of the Corporations of the towns.

In the case of Moldavia of 132 members, viz.: the Metropolitan Archbishop as President; 2 Bishops and 45 boyards of the first class; 30 of the second class; 32 Provincial Deputies; 21 Deputies of the Corporations of the towns; and one Deputy of the Academy.

Chapter II.—*The Ordinary General Assembly.*

It shall be composed, in the case of Wallachia, of 70 members, viz.: 3 Bishops, 4 Ministers (that is to say, of the Ministers of Finance, of Commerce, of the Interior, and of Justice), of 24 boyards of the first class, and 28 Deputies of the districts. The Metropolitan Archbishop will be President of this Assembly.

For Moldavia, of 40 members, viz.: 2 Bishops, 4 Ministers (that is to say, of the Ministers of Finance, of Commerce, of the Interior, and of Justice), of 14 boyards of the first class, and of 20 Deputies of the districts. This Assembly will also be presided over by the Metropolitan Archbishop.

This Assembly shall be convoked by the Prince every winter; he will also have the prerogative of dismissing it whenever he shall judge it expedient to do so.

The duties of the Assembly will be those of controlling the receipts and expenditure of the Administration, of voting the Budget, of enacting new laws, &c.

Chapter III.—*On Finance.*

All the former taxes, of whatever kind, shall be abolished, and will be replaced by new taxes, which, including the receipts from customs, salt mines, &c., are approximately estimated at a total sum of 11,605,000 Turkish piastres for Wallachia, and at that of 5,642,000 Turkish piastres for Moldavia.

The poll-tax imposed on the labouring class shall not vary from 24 piastres a head.

Chapter IV.—*The Administrative Council.*

This Council in each of the Principalities shall be composed of the Minister of the Interior as President, and of the Ministers of Finance and of Commerce.

Chapter V.—*On Commerce.*

There shall be free trade both by land and sea with all nations, without distinction as to preference or priority.

Chapter VI.—*On Sanitary Measures.*

A permanent sanitary line and quarantine stations shall be established on all the frontiers of the Principalities, and notably, for the present, on the left bank of the Danube.

Ships arriving at Galatz and Brahiloff from Constantinople, or other Turkish ports, shall always be subjected to a quarantine of four days when the plague does not exist on the near side of the Balkans, and of eight days when it exists between the mountains and the Danube.

Merchandize generally will undergo a quarantine of 16 days, but furs will remain in quarantine 24 days, and cotton and wool from Egypt 42 days.

Chapter VII.—*Of the Establishment of a Body of Gendarmerie.*
This force shall be composed, for the two Principalities, of 6,000 men both infantry and cavalry, namely, 4,460 for Wallachia, and 1,540 for Moldavia.

These troops shall be raised by recruitment, and not by conscription, except in case of urgent necessity. They shall be armed, equipped, fed, and paid by Government, and their families shall be exempted from taxation.

Chapter VIII.—*Of the Judicial Body.*
There shall be in every district a Court of First Instance, composed of seven Judges on active service, with six substitutes.

There shall also be Tribunals of Second Instance, each composed of seven Judges; a Judicial Divan composed of twelve members, seven of whom shall belong to the civil and five to the criminal section; and a High Court of Appeal.

Chapter IX and last.
This chapter contains general stipulations having reference to the administration of the property of the clergy, to public instruction, to promotions, to mortgages, and deeds of gift, and to the principle of nationality and co-citizenship between the inhabitants of the two Principalities.

(In this place the question of the advantages which would result from the reunion of the two Principalities under one Government is also touched upon.)

109

CONVENTION of Defensive Alliance between Great Britain and Turkey, with respect to the Asiatic Provinces of Turkey. Signed at Constantinople, 4th June, 1878.

HER Majesty the Queen of the United Kingdom of Great Britain and Ireland, Empress of India, and His Imperial Majesty the Sultan, being mutually animated with the sincere desire of extending and strengthening the relations of friendship happily existing between their two Empires, have resolved upon the conclusion of a Convention of Defensive Alliance with the object of securing for the future the territories in Asia of His Imperial Majesty the Sultan.

Their Majesties have accordingly chosen and named as their Plenipotentiaries, that is to say:—

Her Majesty the Queen of the United Kingdom of Great Britain and Ireland, Empress of India, the Right Honourable Austen Henry Layard, Her Majesty's Ambassador Extraordinary and Minister Plenipotentiary at the Sublime Porte;

And His Imperial Majesty the Sultan, his Excellency Safvet Pasha, Minister for Foreign Affairs of His Imperial Majesty;

Who, after having exchanged their full powers, found in due and good form, have agreed upon the following Articles:—

Engagement of Great Britain to join Turkey in event of Russia retaining Batoum, Ardahan, or Kars, and making any attempt to take further Territories in Asia.

ART. I. If Batoum, Ardahan, Kars, or any of them shall be retained by Russia, and if any attempt shall be made at any future time by Russia to take possession of any further territories of His Imperial Majesty the Sultan in Asia, as fixed by the Definitive Treaty of Peace, England engages to join His Imperial Majesty the Sultan in defending them by force of arms.

Engagement of Sultan, in return, to introduce Reforms in Government, and for Protection of Christian and other Subjects of the Porte, in Asia.

In return, His Imperial Majesty the Sultan promises to England to introduce necessary Reforms, to be agreed upon later between the two Powers, into the government, and for the protection of the Christian and other subjects of the Porte in these territories.

Occupation and Administration of Cyprus by Great Britain.

And in order to enable England to make necessary provision for executing her engagement, His Imperial Majesty the Sultan further consents to assign the Island of Cyprus to be occupied and administered by England.

Ratifications.

ART. II. The present Convention shall be ratified, and the ratifications thereof shall be exchanged, within the space of one month, or sooner if possible.

In witness whereof the respective Plenipotentiaries have signed the same, and have affixed thereto the seal of their arms.

Done at Constantinople, the fourth day of June, in the year one thousand eight hundred and seventy-eight.

        (L.S.) A. H. LAYARD.
        (L.S.) SAFVET.

110 CYPRUS CONVENTION

ANNEX TO CONVENTION of Defensive Alliance between Great Britain and Turkey, of 4th June, 1878. Conditions of British Occupation and Administration of Cyprus. Signed at Constantinople, 1st July, 1878.

THE Right Honourable Sir A. H. Layard, G.C.B., and his Highness Safvet Pasha, now the Grand Vizier of His Majesty the Sultan, have agreed to the following Annex to the Convention signed by them as Plenipotentiaries of their respective Governments on the 4th June, 1878.

Conditions of Occupation and Administration of Cyprus.

It is understood between the two High Contracting Parties that England agrees to the following conditions relating to her occupation and administration of the Island of Cyprus:—

Mussulman Religious Tribunal.

I. That a Mussulman religious Tribunal (Mehkéméi Shéri) shall continue to exist in the island, which will take exclusive cognizance of religious matters, and of no others, concerning the Mussulman population of the island.

Superintendence and Administration of Mussulman Schools and other Religious Establishments in Cyprus.

II. That a Mussulman resident in the island shall be named by the Board of Pious Foundations in Turkey (Evkraf) to superintend, in conjunction with a Delegate to be appointed by the British Authorities, the administration of the property, funds, and lands belonging to mosques, cemetries, Mussulman schools, and other religious establishments existing in Cyprus.

Excess of Revenue over Expenditure to be paid by England to Turkey.

III. That England will pay to the Porte whatever is the present excess of revenue over expenditure in the island; this excess to be calculated upon and determined by the average of the last five years, stated to be 22,936 purses, to be duly verified hereafter, and to the exclusion of the produce of State and Crown lands let or sold during that period.

Power reserved to Porte to Sell and Lease Lands and other Property of the Crown and State in Cyprus.

IV. That the Sublime Porte may freely sell and lease lands and other property in Cyprus belonging to the Ottoman Crown and State (Arazii Miriyé vé Emlaki Houmayoun) the produce of which does not form part of the revenue of the island referred to in Article III.

Purchase of Land by English Government.

V. That the English Government, through their competent authorities, may purchase compulsorily, at a fair price, land required for public improvements, or for other public purposes, and land which is not cultivated.

Conditions of Evacuation of Cyprus by Great Britain.

VI. That if Russia restores to Turkey Kars and the other conquests made by her in Armenia during the last war, the Island of Cyprus will be evacuated by England, and the Covention of the 4th of June, 1878, will be at an end

Done at Constantinople, the 1st day of July, 1878.

A. H. LAYARD.
SAFVET.

111

DECLARATIONS made by the British and Russian Plenipotentiaries at the Congress of Berlin, respecting the Straits of the Dardanelles and Bosphorus. 11th and 12th July, 1878.

I.
British Declaration.
Extract from Protocol, 11th July, 1878.

WITH regard to the paragraph relating to the Treaties of Paris and London, Lord Salisbury remarks that at first sight, at a preceding sitting, he had stated that he was not satisfied with the wording of this Article. These apprehensions are now partly set at rest by the explanations offered to the Congress: his Excellency confines himself to-day to asking that the following Declaration, which is binding only on his Government, may be inserted in the Protocol:—

"Considering that the Treaty of Berlin will modify an important part of the arrangements sanctioned by the Treaty of Paris of 1856, and that the interpretation of Article II of the Treaty of London, which is dependent on the Treaty of Paris, may thus become a matter of dispute;

"I declare on behalf of England that the obligations of Her Britannic Majesty relating to the closing of the Straits do not go further than an engagement with the Sultan to respect in this matter His Majesty's independent determinations in conformity with the spirit of existing Treaties."

Count Schouvaloff reserves the right of inserting in the Protocol a counter-declaration, if necessary.

2.
Russian Declaration.
Extract from Protocol 12th July, 1878.

Count Schouvaloff, referring to the Declaration made in the preceding sitting by Lord Salisbury, on the subject of the Straits, demands the insertion in the Protocol of a Declaration on the same subject presented by the Plenipotentiaries of Russia:—

"The Plenipotentiaries of Russia, without being able exactly to appreciate the meaning of the proposition of the Second Plenipotentiary of Great Britain, respecting the closing of the Straits, restrict themselves to demanding, on their part, the insertion in the Protocol of the observation: that, in their opinion, the principle of the closing of the Straits is an European principle, and that the stipulations concluded in this respect in 1841, 1856 and 1871, confirmed at present by the Treaty of Berlin, are binding on the part of all the Powers, in accordance with the spirit and letter of the existing Treaties, not only as regards the Sultan but also as regards all the Powers signatory to these transactions."

112

AGREEMENT signed by the Marquis of Salisbury and Count Schouvaloff respecting the tracing of the Line of the Alashkerd. Berlin, 12th July, 1878.

This Agreement was annexed to the Treaty of Berlin of 13th July, 1878.

Military Commission to trace the Line of the Alashkerd.
The more detailed tracing of the line of the Alashkerd shall be carried

out on the spot, in conformity with the Treaty of Berlin, by a Military Commission composed of a Russian officer, an Ottoman officer, and an English officer.

SALISBURY.
SCHOUVALOFF.

Berlin, July 12, 1878.

113   TREATY OF BERLIN

TREATY between Great Britain, Austria-Hungary, France, Germany, Italy, Russia, and Turkey, for the Settlement of the Affairs of the East. Signed at Berlin, 13th July, 1878.

In the name of Almighty God.

HER Majesty the Queen of the United Kingdom of Great Britain and Ireland, Empress of India, His Majesty the Emperor of Germany, King of Prussia, His Majesty the Emperor of Austria, King of Bohemia, &c., and King Apostolic of Hungary, the President of the French Republic, His Majesty the King of Italy, His Majesty the Emperor of all the Russias, and His Majesty the Emperor of the Ottomans, being desirous to regulate, with a view to European order, conformably to the stipulations of the Treaty of Paris of 30th March, 1856, the questions raised in the East by the events of late years and by the war terminated by the Preliminary Treaty of San Stefano, have been unanimously of opinion that the meeting of a Congress would offer the best means of facilitating an understanding.

Their said Majesties and the President of the French Republic have, in consequence, appointed as their Plenipotentiaries, that is to say:

Her Majesty the Queen of the United Kingdom of Great Britain and Ireland, Empress of India, the Right Honourable Benjamin Disraeli, Earl of Beaconsfield, Viscount Hughenden, a Peer of Parliament, Member of Her Majesty's Most Honourable Privy Council, First Lord of Her Majesty's Treasury, and Prime Minister of England; the Most Honourable Robert Arthur Talbot Gascoyne Cecil, Marquis of Salisbury, Earl of Salisbury, Viscount Cranborne, Baron Cecil, a Peer of Parliament, a Member of Her Majesty's Most Honourable Privy Council, Her Majesty's Principal Secretary of State for Foreign Affairs; and the Right Honourable Lord Odo William Leopold Russell, Member of Her Majesty's Most Honourable Privy Council, Her Ambassador Extraordinary and Plenipotentiary at the Court of His Majesty the Emperor of Germany, King of Prussia;

His Majesty the Emperor of Germany, King of Prussia, Otho, Prince Bismarck, His President of the Council of Ministers of Prussia, Chancellor of the Empire; Bernard Ernest de Bülow, His Minister of State and Secretary of State for Foreign Affairs; and Chlodwig Charles Victor, Prince of Hohenlohe-Schillingsfürst, Prince of Ratibor and Corvey, His Ambassador Extraordinary and Plenipotentiary to the French Republic, Great Chamberlain of the Crown of Bavaria.

His Majesty the Emperor of Austria, King of Bohemia, &c., and King Apostolic of Hungary, Jules, Count Andrassy of Csik Szent-Király and Krasna-Horka, Grandee of Spain of the First Class, Privy Councillor, His Minister of the Imperial Household and for Foreign Affairs, Lieutenant Field-Marshal in his Armies; Louis Count Károlyi of Nagy-Károlyi, Chamberlain and Privy Councillor, His Ambassador Extra-ordinary and Plenipotentiary at the Court of His Majesty the Emperor of Germany, King of Prussia; and Henri, Baron de Haymerle, Privy Councillor, His Ambassador Extraordinary and Plenipotentiary at the Court of His Majesty the King of Italy;

The President of the French Republic, William Henri Waddington, Senator, Member of the Institute, Minister Secretary of State for Foreign Affairs; Charles Raymond de la Croix de Chevrière, Count de Saint-Vallier, Senator, Ambassador Extraordinary and Plenipotentiary from France at the Court of His Majesty the Emperor of Germany, King of Prussia; and Félix Hippolyte Desprez, Councillor of State, Minister Plenipotentiary of the First Class, charged with the direction of Political Affairs at the Department for Foreign Affairs;

His Majesty the King of Italy, Louis, Count Corti, Senator, His Minister for Foreign Affairs; and Edward, Count de Launay, His Ambassador Extraordinary and Plenipotentiary at the Court of His Majesty the Emperor of Germany, King of Prussia;

His Majesty the Emperor of all the Russias, Alexander, Prince Gortchakow, His Chancellor of the Empire; Peter, Count de Schouvaloff, General of Cavalry, His Aide-de-Camp General, Member of the Council of the Empire, and His Ambassador Extraordinary and Plenipotentiary at the Court of Her Britannic Majesty; and Paul d'Oubril, His Ambassa-dor Extraordinary and Plenipotentiary at the Court of His Majesty the Emperor of Germany, King of Prussia;

And His Majesty the Emperor of the Ottomans, Alexander Cara-théodory Pasha, His Minister of Public Works; Mehemed Ali Pasha, Mushir of His Armies; and Sadoullah Bey, His Ambassador Extra-ordinary and Plenipotentiary at the Court of His Majesty the Emperor of Germany, King of Prussia;

Who, in accordance with the proposal of the Court of Austria-Hungary, and on the invitation of the Court of Germany, have met at Berlin furnished with full powers, which have been found in good and due form.

An understanding having been happily established between them, they have agreed to the following stipulations:—

Bulgaria. An Autonomous and Tributary Principality under Suzerainty of the Sultan. Christian Government. National Militia.
ART. I. Bulgaria is constituted an autonomous and tributary Principality under the suzerainty of His Imperial Majesty the Sultan; it will have a Christian Government and a national militia.

Bulgaria. Boundaries.
ART. II. The Principality of Bulgaria will include the following territories:—

Boundary between Bulgaria and Roumania. Silistria to Mangalia.
The frontier follows on the north the right bank of the Danube from the former frontier of Servia up to a point to be determined by a European Commission to the east of Silistria, and thence runs to the Black Sea to the south of Mangalia, which is included in Roumanian territory. The Black Sea forms the eastern boundary of Bulgaria.

Boundary between Bulgaria and Eastern Roumelia.
On the south the frontier follows upwards from its mouth the mid-channel of the brook near which are situated the villages of Hodžakiöj, Selam-Kiöj, Aivadšik, Kulibe, Sudžuluk; crosses obliquely the valley of the Deli-Kamčik, passes south of Belibe and Kemhalik and north of Hadžimahale after having crossed the Deli-Kamčik at 2 kilom. above Čengei; reaches the crest at a point situated between Tekenlik and Aidos-Bredza, and follows it by Karnabad Balkan, Prisevica Balkan, Kazan Balkan to the north of Kotel as far as Demir Kapu. It proceeds by the principal chain of the Great Balkan, the whole length of which it follows up to the summit of Kosica.

There it leaves the crest of the Balkan, descends southwards between the villages of Pirtop and Dužanci, the one being left to Bulgaria and the other to Eastern Roumelia, as far as the brook of Tuzlu Dere, follows that stream to its junction with the Topolnica, then the latter river until it meets the Smovskio Dere near the village of Petricevo, leaving to Eastern Roumelia a zone with a radius of 2 kilom. above that junction, ascends between the brooks of Smovskio Dere and the Kamenica, following the line of the watershed so as to turn to the south-west at the level of Voinjak and reach directly the point of 875 of the Austrian Staff map.

The frontier line cuts at right angles the upper basin of the brook of Ichtiman Dere, passes between Bogdina and Karaúla, so as to rejoin the line of the watershed separating the basins of the Isker and the Marica, between Camurli and Hadžilar, follows that line by the summits of Velina Mogila, the "col" 531, Zmailica Vrh, Sumnatica, and rejoins the administrative boundary of the Sandjak of Sofia between Sivri Taš and Čadir Tepe.

Boundary between Bulgaria and Turkey (Macedonia).

From Čadir Tepe, the frontier, taking a south-westerly direction, follows the watershed between the basins of the Mesta Karasu on the one side, and the Struma Karasu on the other, runs along the crests of the mountains of Rhodope called Demir Kapu, Iskoftepe, Kadimesar Balkan, and Aiji Gedük up to Kapetnik Balkan, and thus joins the former administrative frontier of the Sandjak of Sofia.

From Kapetnik Balkan the frontier is indicated by the water shed between the valleys of the Rilska reka and of the Bistrica reca, and follows the ridge called Vodenica Planina, descending into the valley of the Struma at the junction of this river with the Rilska reka, leaving the village of Barakli to Turkey. It ascends then south of the village of Jelešnica, and reaches by the shortest line the chain of Golema Planina at the summit of Gitka, and rejoins there the former administrative frontier of the Sandjak of Sofia, leaving, however, to Turkey the whole of the basin of the Suba reka.

From Mount Gitka the western frontier goes towards Mount Crni Vrh by the mountains of Karvena Jabuka, following the former administrative limit of the Sandjak of Sofia in the upper part of the basins of Egrisu and of the Lepnica, ascends with it the crests of Babina Polana, and reaches Mount Crni Vrh.

Boundary between Bulgaria and Servia.

From Mount Crni Vrh the frontier follows the watershed between the Struma and the Morava by the summits of the Strešer, Vilogolo, and Mešid Planina, rejoins by the Gačina, Crna Trava, Darkovska, and Drainica Plan, then the Deščani Kladanec, the watershed of the High Sukowa and of the Morava, goes straight to the Stol, and descends from it so as to cut the road from Sofia to Pirot, 1,000 metres north-west of the village of Seguša. It ascends in a straight line the Vidlic Planina and thence Mount Radočina in the chain of the Kodža Balkan, leaving to Servia the village of Doikinci and to Bulgaria that of Senakos.

From the summit of Mount Radočina the frontier follows towards the west the crest of the Balkans by Ciprovec Balkan and Stara Planina up to the former eastern frontier (*l'ancienne frontière orientale*) of the Principality of Servia, near to the Kula Smiljova Čuka, and thence that former frontier as far as the Danube, which it rejoins at Rakovitza.

Bulgaria. Delimitation by European Commission. Balkan Frontiers of Eastern Roumelia. Non-erection of Fortifications.

This delimitation shall be fixed on the spot by the European Commission, on which the Signatory Powers shall be represented. It is understood—

1. That this Commission will take into consideration the necessity for His Imperial Majesty the Sultan to be able to defend the Balkan frontiers of Eastern Roumelia.

2. That no fortifications may be erected within a radius of 10 kilom. from Samakow.

Bulgaria. Election of Prince. Exclusion of Members of Reigning Dynasties of Great European Powers.

ART. III. The Prince of Bulgaria shall be freely elected by the population and confirmed by the Sublime Porte, with the assent of the Powers. No member of the Reigning Dynasties of the Great European Powers may be elected Prince of Bulgaria.

Bulgaria. Election of Prince in case of a Vacancy.

In case of a vacancy in the princely dignity, the election of the new Prince shall take place under the same conditions and with the same forms.

Bulgaria. Assembly of Notables to draw up Organic Law at Tirnovo.

ART. IV. An Assembly of Notables of Bulgaria, convoked at Tirnovo, shall, before the election of the Prince, draw up the Organic Law of the Principality.

Rights and Interests of different Populations to be considered.

In the districts where Bulgarians are intermixed with Turkish, Roumanian, Greek, or other populations, the rights and interests of these populations shall be taken into consideration as regards the elections and the drawing up of the Organic Law.

Bulgaria. Basis of Public Law.

ART. V. The following points shall form the basis of the public law of Bulgaria:—

Bulgaria. Civil and Political Rights. Exercise of Professions and Industries by all, irrespective of Religious Creeds.

The difference of religious creeds and confessions shall not be alleged against any person as a ground for exclusion or incapacity in matters relating to the enjoyment of civil and political rights, admission to public employments, functions, and honours, or the exercise of the various professions and industries in any locality whatsoever.

Bulgaria.   Freedom of Religious Worship.

The freedom and outward exercise of all forms of worship are assured to all persons belonging to Bulgaria, as well as to foreigners, and no hindrance shall be offered either to the hierarchical organization of the different communions, or to their relations with their spiritual chiefs.

Bulgaria.   Provisional Administration by a Russian Commissary, assisted by a Turkish Commissary and by Consuls delegated by the Powers, until completion of Organic Law.

ART. VI. The provisional administration of Bulgaria shall be under the direction of an Imperial Russian Commissary until the completion of the Organic Law. An Imperial Turkish Commissary, as well as the Consuls delegated *ad hoc* by the other Powers, signatory of the present Treaty, shall be called to assist him so as to control the working of this provisional *régime*. In case of disagreement amongst the Consular Delegates, the vote of the majority shall be accepted, and in case of a divergence between the majority and the Imperial Russian Commissary or the Imperial Turkish Commissary, the Representatives of the Signatory Powers at Constantinople, assembled in Conference, shall give their decision.

Bulgaria.   Provisional Régime not to extend beyond Nine Months.

ART. VII. The provisional *régime* shall not be prolonged beyond a period of nine months from the exchange of the ratifications of the present Treaty.

Bulgaria.   Prince to be elected as soon as Organic Law is completed.

When the Organic Law is completed the election of the Prince of Bulgaria shall be proceeded with immediately. As soon as the Prince shall have been installed, the new organization shall be put into force, and the Principality shall enter into the full enjoyment of its autonomy.

Bulgaria.   Commercial Treaties, &c., between Foreign Powers and the Porte, to remain in force.

ART. VIII. The Treaties of Commerce and of Navigation as well as all the Conventions and arrangements concluded between Foreign Powers and the Porte, and now in force, are maintained in the Principality of Bulgaria, and no change shall be made in them with regard to any Power without its previous consent.

Bulgaria.   No Transit Duties to be levied.

No transit duties shall be levied in Bulgaria on goods passing through that Principality.

Bulgaria.   Equality of treatment for the Subjects, Citizens, and Commerce of all the Powers.

The subjects and citizens and commerce of all the Powers shall be treated in the Principality on a footing of strict equality.

Bulgaria.   Immunities and Privileges of Foreigners.   Consular Jurisdiction and Protection.

The immunities and privileges of foreigners, as well as the rights of Consular jurisdiction and protection as established by the Capitulations and usages, shall remain in full force so long as they shall not have been modified with the consent of the parties concerned.

Bulgaria.   Tribute to Suzerain Court.   Amount to be fixed by Signatory Powers.

ART. IX. The amount of the annual Tribute which the Principality of Bulgaria shall pay to the Suzerain Court—such amount being paid into whatever bank the Porte may hereafter designate—shall be fixed by an agreement between the Powers Signatory of the present Treaty at the close of the first year of the working of the new organization. This Tribute shall be calculated on the mean revenue of the territory of the Principality.

Bulgaria. Portion of Ottoman Public Debt to be paid by the Principality.

As Bulgaria is to bear a portion of the Public Debt of the Empire, when the Powers fix the Tribute, they shall take into consideration what portion of that Debt can, on the basis of a fair proportion, be assigned to the Principality.

Bulgaria. Acceptance of Obligations towards Rustchuck-Varna Railway Company.

ART. X. Bulgaria takes the place of the Imperial Ottoman Government in its undertakings and obligations towards the Rustchuck-Varna Railway Company, dating from the exchange of the ratifications of the present Treaty. The settlement of the previous accounts is reserved for an understanding between the Sublime Porte, the Government of the Principality, and the administration of this Company.

Bulgaria. Acceptance of Obligations in respect of other Railways of European Turkey in Principality.

The Principality of Bulgaria likewise, so far as it is concerned, takes the place of the Sublime Porte in the engagements which the latter has contracted, as well towards Austria-Hungary as towards the Company, for working the Railways of European Turkey in respect to the completion and connection, as well as the working of the Railways situated in its territory.

Bulgaria. Railway Conventions to be concluded with Austria-Hungary, the Porte, and Servia.

The Conventions necessary for the settlement of these questions shall be concluded between Austria-Hungary, the Porte, Servia, and the Principality of Bulgaria immediately after the conclusion of peace.

Bulgaria. Turkish Evacuation. Demolition of Fortresses.

ART. XI. The Ottoman army shall no longer remain in Bulgaria; all the old fortresses shall be razed at the expense of the Principality within one year or sooner if possible; the local Government shall immediately take steps for their demolition, and shall not construct fresh ones.

Bulgaria. Disposal of War Material, &c., in Fortresses of Danube, Shumla, and Varna.

The Sublime Porte shall have the right of disposing as it likes of the war material and other effects belonging to the Ottoman Government which may have remained in the fortresses of the Danube already evacuated in virtue of the Armistice of the 31st January, as well as of those in the strongholds of Shumla and Varna.

Bulgaria. Right of Non-resident Mussulman Proprietors and others to hold Real Property.

ART. XII. Mussulman proprietors or others who may take up their abode outside the Principality may continue to hold there their real property, by farming it out, or having it administered by third parties.

Bulgaria. State Property and Religious Foundations (Vakoufs).
Appointment of a Turco-Bulgarian Commission.

A Turco-Bulgarian Commission shall be appointed to settle, within a period of two years, all questions relative to the mode of alienation, working, or use on the account of the Sublime Porte, of property belonging to the State and religious foundations (vakoufs), as well as of the questions regarding the interests of private persons engaged therein.

Bulgarians travelling or dwelling in other parts of Turkey, subject to Ottoman Authorities and Laws.

Persons belonging to the Principality of Bulgaria, who shall travel or dwell in the other parts of the Ottoman Empire, shall be subject to the Ottoman authorities and laws.

Eastern Roumelia. Formation of Province under a Christian Governor-General.

Art. XIII. A province is formed south of the Balkans which will take the name of "Eastern Roumelia," and will remain under the direct political and military authority of His Imperial Majesty the Sultan, under conditions of administrative autonomy. It shall have a Christian Governor-General.

Eastern Roumelia. Boundaries.

Art. XIV. Eastern Roumelia is bounded on the north and north-west by Bulgaria, and comprises the territories included by the following line:—

Boundary between Eastern Roumelia and Bulgaria.

Starting from the Black Sea the frontier follows upwards from its mouth the mid-channel of the brook near which are situated the villages of Hodžakiöj, Selam-Kiöj, Aivadšik, Kulibe, Sudžuluk, crosses obliquely the Valley of the Deli Kamžik, passes south of Belibe and Kemhalik, and north of Hadžimahale, after having crossed the Deli-Kamžik at 2½ kilom. above Cengei; reaches the crest at a point situated between Tekenlik and Aidos-Bredza, and follows it by Karnabad Balkan, Prisevica Balkan, Kazan Balkan to the north of Kotel as far as Demir Kapu. It proceeds by the principal chain of the Great Balkan, the whole length of which it follows up to the summit of Kosica.

At this point the western frontier of Roumelia leaves the crest of the Balkan, descends southwards between the villages of Pirtop and Dužanci—the one being left to Bulgaria and the other to Eastern Roumelia, as far as the brook of Tuzlu Dere, follows that stream to its junction with the Topolnica, then the latter river until it meets the Smovskio Dere near the village of Petričevo, leaving to Eastern Roumelia a zone with a radius of 2 kilom. above that junction, ascends between the brooks of Smovskio Dere and the Kamenica, following the line of the watershed so as to turn to the south-west at the level of Voinjak and reach directly the point 875 of the Austrian Staff map.

The frontier line cuts at right angles the upper basin of the brook of Ichtiman Dere, passes between Bogdina and Karaúla, so as to rejoin

the line of the watershed separating the basins of the Isker and the
Marica, between Čamurli and Hadžilar, follows that line by the summits
of Velina Mogila, the " col " 531, Zmailica Vrh, Sumnatica, and rejoins
the administrative boundary of the Sandjak of Sofia between Sivri
Taš and Čadir Tepe.

Southern Boundary of Eastern Roumelia.

The frontier of Roumelia leaves that of Bulgaria at Mount Čadir
Tepe, following the line of the watershed between the basins of the
Marica and of its affluents on one side, and of the Mesta Karasu and
of its affluents on the other, and takes the direction south-east and then
south along the crest of the Despoto Dagh Mountains, towards Mount
Kruschowa (whence starts the frontier line of the Treaty of San Stefano).

From Mount Kruschowa the frontier is the same as the line laid down
by the Treaty of San Stefano, that is to say, the chain of the Black
Balkans (Kara Balkan), the mountains Kulaghy-Dagh, Eschek-
Tschepellü, Karakolas, and Ischiklar, from whence it descends due
south-east till it reaches the River Arda, and follows the mid-channel
of this river up to a point close to the village of Adacali, which remains
to Turkey.

From this point the frontier line ascends the crest of the Beštepe-
Dagh, which it follows, then descends and crosses the Maritza, at a
point situated 5 kilom. above the bridge of Mustafa Pasha; thence it
takes a northerly direction by the line of the watershed between Demir-
hanli Dere and the small affluents of the Maritza to Küdeler Baïr,
whence it runs east to Sakar Baïr; from this point it crosses the valley
of the Tundža in the direction of Büjük Derbend, which is left to the
north, as also is Soudzak. From Büjük Derbend it regains the line of the
watershed between the affluents of the Tundža on the north and those
of the Maritza on the south, up to the level of Kaibilar, which is included
in Eastern Roumelia, and passes to the south of V. Almali between the
basin of the Maritza to the south and the various streams which flow
straight into the Black Sea, between the villages of Belevrin and Alatli;
it follows to the north of Karanlik the crests of Vosna and Zuvak, the
line which separates the waters of the Duka and those of the Karagac-
Su, and rejoins the Black Sea between those two rivers.

Eastern Roumelia. Right of Sultan. Fortifications on Frontiers (Balkan Passes).

ART. XV. His Majesty the Sultan shall have the right of providing
for the defence of the land and sea frontiers of the province by erecting
fortifications on those frontiers, and maintaining troops there.

Eastern Roumelia. Maintenance of Internal Order. Irregular Troops, Bashi-Bazouks, and Circassians.

Internal order is maintained in Eastern Roumelia by a native gendarmerie assisted by a local militia.

In forming these corps, the officers of which are nominated by the Sultan, regard shall be paid in the different localities to the religion of the inhabitants.

His Imperial Majesty the Sultan undertakes not to employ irregular troops, such as Bashi-Bazouks and Circassians, in the garrisons of the frontiers. The regular troops detailed for this service must not in any case be billeted on the inhabitants. When they pass through the province they shall not make a stay there.

Eastern Roumelia. Right to summon Ottoman Troops in case of need. Powers to be informed.

ART. XVI. The Governor-General shall have the right of summoning the Ottoman troops in the event of the internal or external security of the province being threatened. In such an eventuality the Sublime Porte shall inform the Representatives of the Powers at Constantinople of such a decision, as well as of the exigencies which justify it.

Eastern Roumelia. Governor-General to be nominated by the Porte, with assent of Powers, for Five Years.

ART. XVII. The Governor-General of Eastern Roumelia shall be nominated by the Sublime Porte, with the assent of the Powers, for a term of five years.

Eastern Roumelia. Appointment of European Commission to arrange organization. Duties of Commission.

ART. XVIII. Immediately after the exchange of the ratifications of the present Treaty, a European Commission shall be formed to arrange, in concert with the Ottoman Porte, the organization of Eastern Roumelia. This Commission will have to determine, within three months, the powers and functions of the Governor-General, as well as the administrative, judicial, and financial system of the province, taking as its basis the various laws for the vilayets and the proposals made in the eighth sitting of the Conference of Constantinople.

Eastern Roumelia. Firman to be communicated to the Powers.

The whole of the arrangements determined on for Eastern Roumelia shall form the subject of an Imperial Firman, which will be issued by the Sublime Porte, and which it will communicate to the Powers.

Eastern Roumelia. European Commission to administer Finances of Province.

ART. XIX. The European Commission shall be charged to administer, in concert with the Sublime Porte, the financies of the province until the completion of the new organization.

Eastern Roumelia. Treaties, &c., between Foreign Powers and the Porte, to remain in force. Immunities and Privileges of Foreigners. Religious Liberty.

ART. XX. The Treaties, Conventions, and international arrangements of any kind whatsoever, concluded or to be concluded between the Porte and foreign Powers, shall apply in Eastern Roumelia as in the whole Ottoman Empire. The immunities and privileges acquired by foreigners, whatever their status, shall be respected in this province. The Sublime Porte undertakes to enforce there the general laws of the Empire on religious liberty in favour of all forms of worship.

Eastern Roumelia. Rights and Obligations of Turkey with regard to Railways.

ART. XXI. The rights and obligations of the Sublime Porte with regard to the Railways of Eastern Roumelia are maintained in their integrity.

Bulgaria and Eastern Roumelia. Russian Occupation.

ART. XXII. The strength of the Russian corps of occupation in Bulgaria and Eastern Roumelia, which shall be composed of six divisions of infantry and two divisions of cavalry, shall not exceed 50,000 men. It shall be maintained at the expense of the country occupied. The army of occupation will preserve its communications with Russia not only through Roumania, in accordance with arrangements to be concluded between the two States, but also through the ports of the Black Sea, Varna, and Bourgas, where it may, during the period of occupation, organize the necessary depôts.

Bulgaria and Eastern Roumelia. Period of Occupation.

The period of the occupation of Eastern Roumelia and Bulgaria by the Imperial Russian troops is fixed at nine months from the date of the exchange of the ratifications of the present Treaty.

Roumania. Period for Russian Evacuation.

The Imperial Russian Government undertakes that within a further period of three months the passage of its troops across Roumania shall cease, and that Principality shall be completely evacuated.

Crete. Application of Organic Law of 1868.

ART. XXIII. The Sublime Porte undertakes scrupulously to apply in the Island of Crete the Organic Law of 1868 with such modifications as may be considered equitable.

Organic Laws. Laws similar to Organic Law for Crete to be introduced into other parts of Turkey in Europe, except exemption from Taxation.

Similar laws adapted to local requirements, excepting as regards the exemption from taxation granted to Crete, shall also be introduced into the other parts of Turkey in Europe for which no special organization has been provided by the present Treaty.

Organic Laws. Special Commission to settle details of new Laws.

The Sublime Porte shall depute special Commissions, in which the native element shall be largely represented, to settle the details of the new laws in each province.

The schemes of organization resulting from these labours shall be submitted for examination to the Sublime Porte, which, before promulgating the Acts for putting them into force, shall consult the European Commission instituted for Eastern Roumelia.

Greece. Rectification of Frontier. Powers may offer Mediation in case of Disagreement between Turkey and Greece.

ART. XXIV. In the event of the Sublime Porte and Greece being unable to agree upon the rectification of frontier suggested in the 13th Protocol of the Congress of Berlin, Germany, Austria-Hungary, France, Great Britain, Italy, and Russia reserve to themselves to offer their mediation to the two parties to facilitate negotiations.

Bosnia and Herzegovina. To be occupied and administered by Austria-Hungary, Sandjak of Novi-Bazar excepted, with right of Austria-Hungary to keep Garrisons, and to have Military and Commercial Roads.

ART. XXV. The Provinces of Bosnia and Herzegovina shall be occupied and administered by Austria-Hungary. The Government of Austria-Hungary, not desiring to undertake the administration of the Sandjak of Novi-Bazar, which extends between Servia and Montenegro in a south-easterly direction to the other side of Mitrviotza, the Ottoman, Administration will continue to exercise its functions there. Nevertheless, in order to assure the maintenance of the new political state of affairs, as well as freedom and security of communications, Austria-Hungary reserves the right of keeping garrisons and having military and commercial roads in the whole of this part of the ancient Vilayet of Bosnia.

To this end the Governments of Austria-Hungary and Turkey reserve to themselves to come to an understanding on the details.

Montenegro.   Independence.

ART. XXVI. The independence of Montenegro is recognized by the Sublime Porte and by all those of the High Contracting Parties who had not hitherto admitted it.

Montenegro.   Conditions:—Civil and Political Rights, &c.   Exercise of Professions and Industries by all, irrespective of Religious Creeds.

ART. XXVII. The High Contracting Parties are agreed on the following conditions:—

In Montenegro the difference of religious creeds and confessions shall not be alleged against any person as a ground for exclusion or incapacity in matters relating to the enjoyment of civil and political rights, admission to public employments, functions, and honours, or the exercise of the various professions and industries in any locality whatsoever.

Montenegro.   Freedom of Religious Worship.

The freedom and outward exercise of all forms of worship shall be assured to all persons belonging to Montenegro, as well as to foreigners, and no hindrance shall be offered either to the hierarchical organization of the different communions, or to their relations with their spiritual chiefs.

Montenegro.   Boundaries.

ART. XXVIII. The new frontiers of Montenegro are fixed as follows:—

Starting at Ilino-brdo to the north of Klobuk, the line descends to the Trebinjčica towards Grančarevo, which remains to Herzegovina, then ascends the course of that river up to a point 1 kilom. below its confluence with the Čepelica, and from thence passes by the most direct line on to the heights which border the River Trebinjčica. It then proceeds in the direction of Pilatova, leaving that village to Montenegro, and continues along the heights in a northerly direction, maintaining as far as possible a distance of 6 kilom. from the Bilek-Korito-Gacko road, up to the " col " between the Somina Planina and Mount Čurilo, whence it proceeds in an easterly direction by Vratkoviči, leaving this village to Herzegovina, up to Mount Orline. Starting from this point the frontier, leaving Ravno to Montenegro, goes straight to the north-north-east, crossing the summits of the Leberšnik and of the Volujak, then descends by the shortest line on to the River Piva, which it crosses, and rejoins the River Tara, passing between Crkvica and Nedvina. From this point it ascends the Tara to Mojkovac, from which place it passes along the crest of the ridge as far as Siškojezero. Leaving this point, it coincides with the former frontier. as far as the village of Sekulare. From there the new frontier passes along the crests of the Mokra Planina, the village of Mokra remaining to Montenegro; it then reaches the point 2166 on the Austrian Staff Map, following the principal chain and the line of the watershed between the Lim on the one side, and the Drin as well as the Cievna (Zem) on the other.

It then coincides with the existing boundaries between the tribe of the Kuči-Drekaloviči on one side, and the Kučka-Krajna, as well as the tribes of the Klementi and Grudi, on the other, to the plain of Podgorica, from whence it proceeds towards Plavnica, leaving the Klementi, Grudi, and Hoti tribes to Albania.

Thence the new frontier crosses the lake near the Islet of Gorica-Topal, and, from Gorica-Topal, takes a straight line to the top of the crest, whence it follows the watershed between Megured and Kalimed, leaving Mrkovič to Montenegro, and reaching the Adriatic at V. Kruči.

On the north-west the frontier will be formed by a line passing from the coast between the villages of Sušana and Zubči, and terminating at the extreme south-east point of the existing frontier of Montenegro on the Vrsuta Planina.

Montenegro. Annexation of Antivari and its Sea-board. Conditions:—Dulcigno; Spizza; Navigation of the Boyana; Port of Antivari; No Ships of War; No Flag of War; Fortifications, Commerce, &c.

ART. XXIX. Antivari and its sea-board are annexed to Montenegro under the following conditions:—

The districts situated to the south of that territory, in accordance with the delimitation above laid down, as far as the Boyana, including Dulcigno, shall be restored to Turkey.

The Commune of Spiča, as far as the southernmost point of the territory indicated in the detailed description of the frontiers, shall be incorporated with Dalmatia.

Montenegro shall have full and complete freedom of navigation on the Boyana. No fortifications shall be constructed on the course of that river except such as may be necessary for the local defence of the stronghold of Scutari, and they shall not extend beyond a distance of 6 kilom. from that town.

Montenegro shall have neither ships of war nor flag of war.

The port of Antivari and all the waters of Montenegro shall remain closed to the ships of war of all nations.

The fortifications situated on Montenegrin territory between the lake and the coast shall be razed, and none shall be rebuilt within this zone.

The administration of the maritime and sanitary police, both at Antivari and along the coast of Montenegro, shall be carried out by Austria-Hungary by means of light coast-guard boats.

Montenegro shall adopt the maritime code in force in Dalmatia. On her side Austria-Hungary undertakes to grant Consular protection to the Montenegrin merchant flag.

Montenegro shall come to an understanding with Austria-Hungary on the right to construct and keep up across the new Montenegrin territory a road and a railway.

Absolute freedom of communication shall be guaranteed on these roads.

Montenegro. *Right of Non-resident Mussulmans and others to hold Real Property.*

ART. XXX. Mussulmans or others possessing property in the territories annexed to Montenegro, who may wish to take up their residence outside the Principality, can retain their real property either by farming it out, or by having it administered by third parties.

Montenegro. *Indemnity on Expropriation.*

No one shall be liable to be expropriated otherwise than by legal process for the public welfare, and with a previous indemnity.

Montenegro. *Turco-Montenegrin Commission to settle mode of Alienation.*

A Turco-Montenegrin Commission shall be appointed to settle, within a period of three years, all questions relative to the mode of alienation, working, or use, on the account of the Sublime Porte, of property belonging to the State and religious foundations (Vakoufs), as well as of the questions regarding the interests of private parties engaged therein.

Montenegro. *Appointment of Agents at Constantinople and other Places.*

ART. XXXI. The Principality of Montenegro shall come to a direct understanding with the Ottoman Porte with regard to the establishment of Montenegrin agents at Constantinople, and at certain places in the Ottoman Empire where the necessity for them shall be admitted.

Montenegrins travelling in Turkey to be subject to Ottoman Laws and Authorities.

Montenegrins travelling or residing in the Ottoman Empire shall be subject to the Ottoman laws and authorities, according to the general principles of international law, and the customs established with regard to Montenegrins.

Montengrin Troops to evacuate Turkish Territory.
ART. XXXII. The Montenegrin troops shall be bound to evacuate within twenty days from the date of the ratification of the present Treaty, or sooner if possible, the territory that they occupy at present beyond the new limits of the Principality.

Montenegrin Territories to be evacuated by Ottoman Troops.
The Ottoman Troops shall evacuate the territories ceded to Montenegro within the same period of twenty days. A supplementary period of fifteen days shall, however, be granted to them, as well for evacuating the fortresses and withdrawing the stores and material of war from them, as for drawing up inventories of the implements and articles which cannot be immediately removed.

Montenegro. Payment of portion of Ottoman Public Debt.
ART. XXXIII. As Montenegro is to bear a portion of the Ottoman public debt for the new territories assigned to her by the Treaty of Peace, the Representatives of the Powers at Constantinople shall determine the amount of the same in concert with the Sublime Porte on an equitable basis.

Servia. Conditional recognition of Independence.
ART. XXXIV. The High Contracting Parties recognise the independence of the Principality of Servia, subject to the conditions set forth in the following Article.

Servia. Civil and Political Rights. Exercise of Professions and Industries by all, irrespective of Religious Creeds.
ART. XXXV. In Servia the difference of religious creeds and confessions shall not be alleged against any person as a ground for exclusion or incapacity in matters relating to the enjoyment of civil and political rights, admission to public employments, functions, and honours, or the exercise of the various professions and industries, in any locality whatsoever.

Servia. Freedom of Religious Worship.
The freedom and outward exercise of all forms of worship shall be assured to all persons belonging to Servia, as well as to foreigners, and no hindrance shall be offered either to the hierarchical organization of the different communions, or to their relations with their spiritual chiefs.

Servia. Boundaries.

ART. XXXVI. Servia receives the territories included in the following delimitation:—

Boundary between Servia and Bosnia: Little Zwornik and Sakhar.

The new frontier follows the existing line ascending the mid-channel of the Drina from its confluence with the Save, leaving Mali Zwornik and Sakhar to the Principality, and continues to follow the former boundary of Servia as far as the Kopaonik, leaving it at the *summit of the Kanilug*. From that point it follows at first the western boundary of the Sandjak of Nisch by the *southern spur of the Kopaonik*, by the crests of the Marica and Mrdar Planina, which form the watershed between the basins of the Ibar and Sitnica on one side, and that of the Toplica on the other, leaving Prepolac to Turkey.

Boundary between Servia and Turkey (*Macedonia*).

It then turns to the south by the watershed between the Brvenica and the Medvedja, leaving the whole of the basin of the Medvedja to Servia; follows the crests of the Goljak Planina (which forms the watershed between the Kriva-Rjeka on one side, and the Poljanica, Veternica, and Morawa on the other), as far as the summit of the Poljanica. It then follows the spur of the Karpina Planina as far as the confluence of the Koinska and the Morawa, crosses this river, and ascends by the watershed between the Koinska brook and the stream which falls into the Morawa near Neradovce, to reach the Sv. Ilija Planina above Trgovište. Thence it follows the crest of the Sv. Ilija as far as Mount Kljuc, and passing by the points marked 1516 and 1547 on the map, and by the Babina Gora, it reaches Mount Crni-Vrh.

Boundary between Servia and Bulgaria.

From Mount Crni-Vrh the new delimitation coincides with that of Bulgaria, that is to say:—

The line of frontier follows the watershed between the Struma and the Morawa by the summits of Strešer, Vilogolo, and *Mešid Planina*, rejoins by the *Gačina, Crna Trava, Darkovska*, and *Drainica Plan*, then the Deščani Kladanec, the watershed of the High Sukowa and of the Morawa, goes straight to the Stol, and descends from it so as to cut the road from Sofia to Pirot, 1,000 metres north-west of the village of Seguša. It ascends in a straight line the Vidlič Planina, and thence *Mount Radočina* in the chain of the Kodža Balkan, leaving to Servia the village of Doikinci, and to Bulgaria that of Senakos.

From the summit of Mount Radočina the frontier follows towards the north-west the crest of the Balkans by Ciprovec Balkan and Stara

Planina up to the former eastern frontier (*l'ancienne frontière orientale*) of the Principality of Servia, near to the Kula Smiljova Čuka, and thence that former frontier as far as the Danube, which it joins at Rakovitza.

Servia. Commercial Intercourse with Foreign Countries.

ART. XXXVII. Until the conclusion of fresh arrangements no change shall be made in Servia in the actual conditions of the commercial intercourse of the Principality with foreign countries.

Servia. No Transit Duties to be levied.

No transit duties shall be levied on goods passing through Servia.

Servia. Immunities and Privileges of Foreigners. Consular Jurisdiction and Protection.

The immunities and privileges of foreign subjects, as well as the rights of Consular jurisdiction and protection, as at present existing, shall remain in full force so long as they shall not have been modified by mutual consent between the Principality and the Powers concerned.

Servia. Acceptance of Engagements of the Porte with regard to Railways in the Principality (Balkan Railways).

ART. XXXVIII. The Principality of Servia takes the place, so far as it is concerned, of the Sublime Porte in the engagements which the latter has contracted as well towards Austria-Hungary as towards the Company for the working of the Railways of Turkey in Europe, in respect to the completion and connection, as well as the working of the Railways to be constructed on the territory newly acquired by the Principality.

Servia. Conventions respecting Railways to be concluded with Austria-Hungary, the Porte, and Bulgaria.

The Conventions necessary for settling these questions shall be concluded, immediately after the signature of the present Treaty, between Austria-Hungary, the Porte, Servia, and, within the limits of its competency, the Principality of Bulgaria.

Servia. Right of Non-resident Mussulman Proprietors and others to hold Real Property.

ART. XXXIX. Mussulmans possessing property in the territories annexed to Servia, who may wish to reside outside the Principality, may retain their real property, either by farming it out or by having it administered by third parties.

Servia. Appointment of a Turco-Servian Commission. Religious Foundations, &c. (Vakoufs).

A Turco-Servian Commission shall be appointed to settle, within a period of three years, all questions relative to the mode of alienation, working, or use, on the account of the Sublime Porte of the property belonging to the State and religious foundations (Vakoufs), as well as of the questions regarding the interests of private persons engaged therein.

Servians travelling or residing in Turkey.

ART. XL. Until the conclusion of a Treaty between Turkey and Servia, Servian subjects travelling or residing in the Ottoman Empire shall be treated according to the general principles of international law.

Servian Troops to evacuate Turkish Territory.

ART. XLI. The Servian troops shall be bound to evacuate within fifteen days from the exchange of the ratifications of the present Treaty the territory not comprised within the new limits of the Principality.

Servia. Evacuation of Ceded Territories by Ottoman Troops.

The Ottoman troops shall evacuate the territories ceded to Servia within the same term of fifteen days. A supplementary term of an equal number of days shall, however, be granted to them as well for evacuating the fortresses and withdrawing the provisions and material of war as for drawing up the inventory of the implements and objects which cannot be removed at once.

Servia. Payment of portion of Ottoman Public Debt.

ART. XLII. As Servia is to bear a portion of the Ottoman Public Debt for the new territories assigned to her by the present Treaty, the Representatives at Constantinople shall fix the amount of it in concert with the Sublime Porte on an equitable basis.

Roumania. Conditional recognition of Independence.

ART. XLIII. The High Contracting Parties recognize the independence of Roumania, subject to the conditions set forth in the two following Articles.

Roumania. Civil and Political Rights. Exercise of Professions and Industries by all, irrespective of Religious Creeds.

ART. XLIV. In Roumania the difference of religous creeds and confessions shall not be alleged against any person as a ground for exclusion or incapacity in matters relating to the enjoyment of civil and political rights, admission to public employments, functions, and honours, or the exercise of the various professions and industries in any locality whatsoever.

Roumania.   Freedom of Religious Worship.

The freedom and outward exercise of all forms of worship shall be assured to all persons belonging to the Roumanian State, as well as to foreigners, and no hindrance shall be offered either to the hierarchical organization of the different communions, or to their relations with their spirititual chiefs.

Roumania.   Equal Treatment to Foreigners.

The subjects and citizens of all the Powers, traders or others, shall be treated in Roumania, without distinction of creed, on a footing of perfect equality.

Roumania.   Restoration to Russia of portion of Bessarabian Territory, detached from Russia in 1856.

ART. XLV. The Principality of Roumania restores to His Majesty the Emperor of Russia that portion of the Bessarabian territory detached from Russia by the Treaty of Paris of 1856, bounded on the west by the mid-channel of the Pruth, and on the south by the mid-channel of the Kilia Branch and the Stary-Stamboul mouth.

Roumania.   Acquisition of Islands forming Delta of the Danube; the Isle of Serpents; the Sandjak of Toultcha; and a portion of Territory to the South of the Dobroutcha.

ART. XLVI. The islands forming the Delta of the Danube, as well as the Isle of Serpents, the Sandjak of Toultcha, comprising the districts (cazas) of Kilia, Soulina, Mahmoudié, Isaktcha, Toultcha, Matchin, Babadagh, Hirsovo, Kustendje, Medjidié, are added to Roumania. The Principality receives in addition the territory situated to the south of the Dobroutcha as far as a line starting from the east of Silistria and terminating on the Black Sea, south of Mangalia.

Roumania.   Frontier to be determined by European Commission of Bulgaria.

The frontier line shall be determined on the spot by the European Commission appointed for the delimitation of Bulgaria.

Roumania.   Arbitration on Division of Waters and Fisheries.

ART. XLVII. The question of the division of the waters and the fisheries shall be submitted to the arbitration of the European Commission of the Danube.

Roumania.   No Transit Duties to be levied.

Art. XLVIII. No transit dues shall be levied in Roumania on goods passing through the Principality.

Roumania.   Conclusion of Consular Conventions with regard to Protection. Maintenance of existing Rights.

Art. XLIX. Roumania shall have power to make Conventions to determine the privileges and attributes of Consuls in regard to protection within the Principality. Existing rights shall remain in force so long as they shall not have been modified by the mutual consent of the Principality and the parties concerned.

Roumania.   Rights of respective Subjects travelling or residing in Turkey and in Roumania.

Art. L. Until the conclusion of a Treaty between Turkey and Roumania, fixing the privileges and attributes of Consuls, Roumanian subjects travelling or residing in the Ottoman Empire, and Ottoman subjects travelling or residing in Roumania, shall enjoy the rights guaranteed to the subjects of other European Powers.

Roumania.   Liability for Public Works and Enterprises in Ceded Territory.

Art. LI. With regard to public works and other enterprises of a like nature, Roumania shall be substituted for the Sublime Porte as regards its rights and obligations throughout the ceded territory.

Danube.   Fortresses and Fortifications to be razed.   Vessels of War not to navigate the River below the Iron Gates.   Exceptions.

Art. LII. In order to increase the guarantees which assure the freedom of navigation on the Danube which is recognized as of European interest, the High Contracting Parties determine that all the fortresses and fortifications existing on the course of the river from the Iron Gates to its mouths shall be razed, and no new ones erected. No vessel of war shall navigate the Danube below the Iron Gates with the exception of vessels of light tonnage in the service of the river police and Customs. The " stationnaires " of the Powers at the mouths of the Danube may, however, ascend the river as far as Galatz.

Danube.   European Commission to be maintained.   Roumania to be represented thereon.   Extension to Galatz.   Treaties, &c., confirmed.

Art. LIII. The European Commission of the Danube on which Roumania shall be represented is maintained in its functions, and shall exercise them henceforth as far as Galatz in complete independence of the territorial authorities. All the Treaties, arrangements, acts, and decisions relating to its rights, privileges, prerogatives, and obligations are confirmed.

Danube. Prolongation of Powers of European Commission.

ART. LIV. One year before the expiration of the term assigned for the duration of the European Commission (24th April, 1883) the Powers shall come to an understanding as to the prolongation of its powers, or the modifications which they may consider necessary to introduce.

Danube. Regulations respecting Navigation, &c., from Iron Gates to Galatz to be drawn up by European Commission and Delegates of Riverain States.

ART. LV. The regulations respecting navigation, river police, and supervision from the Iron Gates to Galatz shall be drawn up by an European Commission, assisted by Delegates of the Riverain States, and placed in harmony with those which have been or may be issued for the portion of the river below Galatz.

Danube Commission. Lighthouse on Isle of Serpents.

ART. LVI. The European Commission of the Danube shall come to an arrangement with the proper authorities to ensure the maintenance of the lighthouse on the Isle of Serpents.

Danube. Execution of Works at Iron Gates and Cataracts entrusted to Austria-Hungary.

ART. LVII. The execution of the works which have for their object the removal of the obstacles which the Iron Gates and the Cataracts place in the way of navigation is entrusted to Austria-Hungary. The Riverain States on this part of the river shall afford every facility which may be required in the interest of the works.

Danube. Provisional Tax maintained in favour of Austria-Hungary.

The provisions of the VIth Article of the Treaty of London of the 13th March, 1871, relating to the right of levying a provisional tax in order to cover the cost of these works, are maintained in favour of Austria-Hungary.

Asia. Cessions by Turkey to Russia. Ardahan, Kars, Batoum, &c. Frontier Line.

ART. LVIII. The Sublime Porte cedes to the Russian Empire in Asia the territories of Ardahan, Kars, and Batoum, together with the latter port, as well as all the territories comprised between the former Russo-Turkish frontier and the following line:—

The new frontier starting from the Black Sea, and coinciding with the line laid down by the Treaty of San Stefano as far as a point to the north-west of Khorda, and to the south of Artwin, continues in a straight line as far as the River Tchoroukh, crosses this river and passes to the east of Aschmichen, going in a straight line to the south so as to rejoin the Russian frontier indicated in the Treaty of San Stefano, at a point to the south of Nariman, leaving the town of Olti to Russia. From the point indicated near Nariman the frontier turns to the east, passes by Tebrenec, which remains to Russia, and continues as far as the Pennek Tschaï.

It follows this river as far as Bardouz, then turns towards the south, leaving Bardouz and Jönikioy to Russia. From a point to the west of the village of Karaougan, the frontier takes the direction of Medjingert, continues in a straight line towards the summit of the Mountain Kassadagh, and follows the line of the watershed between the affluents of the Araxes on the north and those of the Mourad Sou on the south, as far as the former frontier of Russia.

Asia. Batoum to be a Free Port.

Art. LIX. His Majesty the Emperor of Russia declares that it is his intention to constitute Batoum a free port, essentially commercial.

Asia. Valley of Alaschkerd and Town of Bayazid restored to Turkey.

Art. LX. The valley of Alaschkerd and the town of Bayazid, ceded to Russia by Article XIX of the Treaty of San Stefano, are restored to Turkey.

Asia. Cession of Khotour by Turkey to Persia.

The Sublime Porte cedes to Persia the town and territory of Khotour, as fixed by the mixed Anglo-Russian Commission for the delimitation of the frontiers of Turkey and of Persia.

Asia. Improvements and Reforms in favour of Armenians. Protection against Circassians and Kurds. The Powers to be kept periodically informed.

Art. LXI. The Sublime Porte undertakes to carry out, without further delay, the improvements and reforms demanded by local requirements in the provinces inhabited by the Armenians, and to guarantee their security against the Circassians and Kurds.

It will periodically make known the steps taken to this effect to the Powers, who will superintend their application.

Religious Liberty.

ART. LXII. The Sublime Porte having expressed the intention to maintain the principle of religious liberty, and give it the widest scope, the Contracting Parties take note of this spontaneous declaration.

Religion. Equal Civil and Political Rights.

In no part of the Ottoman Empire shall difference of religion be alleged against any person as a ground for exclusion or incapacity as regards the discharge of civil and political rights, admission to the public employments, functions and honours, or the exercise of the various professions and industries.

Religion. Evidence before Tribunals.

All persons shall be admitted, without distinction of religion, to give evidence before the tribunals.

Religious Worship.

The freedom and outward exercise of all forms of worship are assured to all, and no hindrance shall be offered either to the hierarchical organization of the various communions or to their relations with their spiritual chiefs.

Religion. Equal Rights to all Ecclesiastics, &c., travelling in Turkey

Ecclesiastics, pilgrims, and monks of all nationalities travelling in Turkey in Europe, or in Turkey in Asia, shall enjoy the same rights, advantages, and privileges.

Religion. Protection of Ecclesiastics, &c., by Diplomatic and Consular Agents of the Powers.

The right of official protection by the Diplomatic and Consular Agents of the Powers in Turkey is recognized both as regards the abovementioned persons and their religious, charitable, and other establishments in the Holy Places and elsewhere.

Religion. Rights of France and status quo in Holy Places.

The rights possessed by France are expressly reserved, and it is well understood that no alterations can be made in the status quo in the Holy Places.

Religion. Rights and Prerogatives of all Monks of Mount Athos.

The monks of Mount Athos, of whatever country they may be natives, shall be maintained in their former possessions and advantages, and shall enjoy, without any exception, complete equality of rights and prerogatives.

Maintenance of Treaties of 30 March, 1856, and 13 March, 1871
(Dardanelles and Bosphorus, &c.).

ART. LXIII. The Treaty of Paris of March 30, 1856, as well as the Treaty of London of March 13, 1871, are maintained in all such of their provisions as are not abrogated or modified by the preceding stipulations.

Ratifications.

ART. LXIV. The present Treaty shall be ratified, and the Ratifications exchanged at Berlin within three weeks, or sooner if possible.

In faith whereof the respective Plenipotentiaries have signed it, and affixed to it the seal of their arms.

Done at Berlin, the thirteenth day of the month of July, one thousand eight hundred and seventy-eight.

(L.S.)	BEACONSFIELD.
(L.S.)	SALISBURY.
(L.S.)	ODO RUSSELL.
(L.S.)	v. BISMARCK.
(L.S.)	BÜLOW.
(L.S.)	HOHENLOHE.
(L.S.)	ANDRÁSSY.
(L.S.)	KÁROLYI.
(L.S.)	HAYMERLE.
(L.S.)	WADDINGTON.
(L.S.)	SAINT-VALLIER.
(L.S.)	H. DESPREZ.
(L.S.)	L. CORTI.
(L.S.)	LAUNAY.
(L.S.)	GORTCHAKOW.
(L.S.)	SCHOUVALOFF.
(L.S.)	P. D'OUBRIL.
(L.S.)	AL. CARATHÉODORY.
(L.S.)	MEHEMED ALI.
(L.S.)	SADOULLAH.

Procès-Verbal. 3rd August, 1878.

Ratifications of Treaty of 13th July, 1878, exchanged between all the Powers.

THE Undersigned having met together for the purpose of exchanging the ratifications of the Treaty concluded at Berlin on the 13th July, 1878, the instruments of these ratifications confirming the said Treaty were produced by the Representatives of Her Majesty the Queen of the United Kingdom of Great Britain and Ireland, Empress of India, His

Majesty the German Emperor, King of Prussia, His Majesty the Emperor of Austria, King of Bohemia, &c., and Apostolic King of Hungary, His Excellency the President of the French Republic, His Majesty the King of Italy, and His Majesty the Emperor of all the Russias, and having, after examination, been found in good and due form, the exchange thereof took place.

Declaration by Turkish Ambassador that the Porte considers the Treaty valid, and that Ratifications will be sent.

The Ambassador of Turkey, while expressing the regret of the Sublime Porte that the Turkish instruments of ratification could not be despatched in time, announces that he is authorized to declare that His Majesty the Emperor of the Ottomans has likewise ratified the Treaty of the 13th July, 1878, and that he considers the same valid from this day's date.

Sadoullah Bey announces, moreover, that the exchange of the Turkish instruments of ratification will take place within fifteen days.

In witness whereof the Undersigned have drawn up the present *Procès-verbal*, to which they have affixed the seals of their arms.

Done at Berlin, the third day of the month of August, one thousand eight hundred and seventy-eight.

(L.S.) ODO RUSSELL.
(L.S.) RADOWITZ.
(L.S.) MOÜY.
(L.S.) LAUNAY.
(L.S.) ARAPOFF.
(L.S.) SADOULLAH.

114 CYPRUS AGREEMENT

AGREEMENT between Great Britain and Turkey, defining the Powers vested in Great Britain during the British Occupation of Cyprus. Signed at Therapia, 14th August, 1878.

The Right Honourable Sir A. Henry Layard, G.C.B., and his Highness Safvet Pasha, Grand Vizier and Minister for Foreign Affairs of His Imperial Majesty the Sultan, having met together this day, have, in virtue of their full powers, signed the following Additional Article to the Convention of the 4th June, 1878, signed by them as Plenipotentiaries of their respective Governments.

Powers vested in Great Britain during Occupation of Cyprus.
Laws, Conventions, Commercial and Consular Affairs.

It is understood between the High Contracting Parties, without prejudice to the express provisions of the Articles I, II, and IV of the Annex of the 1st July, 1878, that His Imperial Majesty the Sultan, in assigning the Island of Cyprus to be occupied and administered by England, has thereby transferred to and vested in Her Majesty the Queen, for the term of the occupation and no longer, full powers for making Laws and Conventions for the Government of the island in Her Majesty's name, and for the regulation of its Commercial and Consular relations and affairs free from the Porte's control.

Done at Constantinople, the 14th day of August, 1878.

A. H. LAYARD.
SAFVET.

115

TREATY OF PEACE between Russia and Turkey. Signed at Constantinople 27th January/8th February, 1879. Ratifications exchanged at St. Petersburgh, 9th/21st February, 1879.

In the Name of Almighty God.

His Majesty the Emperor of all the Russias, and His Majesty the Emperor of the Ottomans, wishing to perpetuate the restoration of Peace between the two Empires, and to settle permanently by a Treaty such Articles of the Preliminary Treaty of San Stefano as are to form the subjects of a direct understanding between the two States, have appointed for their Plenipotentiaries:

His Majesty the Emperor of all the Russias, on the one part, Prince Alexis Lobanow-Rostovsky, his Ambassador Extraordinary and Plenipotentiary to His Imperial Majesty the Sultan, Secretary of State, &c.;

And His Majesty the Emperor of the Ottomans, on the other part, Al. Carathéodory Pacha, his Minister for Foreign Affairs, &c., and Ali Pacha, his Minister Presiding over the Council of State, &c.;

Who, after having communicated to each other their full powers, found in good and due form, have agreed upon the following Articles:—

Peace and Friendship.

ART. I. Peace and friendship shall henceforth exist between the two Empires.

Substitution of Treaty of Berlin for Articles of Treaty of San Stefano altered by Berlin Congress.

ART. II. The two Powers agree in declaring that the stipulations of the Treaty concluded at Berlin by the seven Powers have been substituted for such Articles of the Preliminaries of Peace of San Stefano as have been abrogated or modified by the Congress.

Stipulations of Treaty of San Stefano not altered by Treaty of Berlin, permamently settled by present Treaty.

ART. III. The stipulations of the Treaty of San Stefano which have not been abrogated or modified by the Treaty of Berlin, are permanently settled by the following Articles of the present Treaty.

War Indemnity.

ART. IV. After deducting the value of the territories ceded by Turkey to Russia in conformity with the Treaty of Berlin the War Indemnity remains assessed at 802,500,000 francs.

Mode of Payment of War Indemnity.

The mode of payment of that sum, and also the securities by which it is to be guaranteed (save the declarations contained in the 11th Protocol of the Congress of Berlin with regard to the question of territories, and to the rights of creditors), will be settled by an understanding between the Governments of His Majesty the Emperor of all the Russias and His Majesty the Emperor of the Ottomans.

Compensation for Losses sustained by Russian Subjects during the War.

ART. V. The claims of Russian subjects and establishments ("*institutions*") in Turkey to compensation for losses sustained during the war shall be settled as soon as they shall have been inquired into by the Russian Embassy at Constantinople and transmitted to the Sublime Porte.

The total amount of those claims shall not, under any circumstances, exceed the sum of 26,750,000 francs.

The term of one year after the ratifications shall have been exchanged is assigned as the date from which claims can be presented to the Sublime Porte, and that of two years as the date after which claims shall no longer be admitted.

Expenses of Maintenance of Prisoners of War.

ART. VI. Special Commissioners shall be appointed by the Imperial Government of Russia and the Sublime Porte in order to draw up an account of the expenditure caused by the maintenance of Ottoman prisoners of war. This account shall be made up to the date of the signing of the Treaty of Berlin. From it shall be deducted the expenses incurred by the Ottoman Government for the maintenance of Russian prisoners, and the balance, once settled, shall be paid by the Sublime Porte in twenty-one equal instalments within the space of seven years.

Conditions under which Inhabitants of Localities ceded to Russia will be allowed to retire therefrom.

ART. VII. The inhabitants of the localities ceded to Russia who should wish to establish their residence beyond those territories, will be free to retire upon selling their real property. A delay of three years from the date of the ratification of the present Treaty will be granted to them for that purpose.

After that delay those inhabitants who should not have left the country and sold their immovable estates shall remain Russian subjects.

Russian or Ottoman Subjects compromised by Intercourse with either Army not to be molested. Persons wishing to retire after Withdrawal of Russians not to be opposed by Ottoman Authorities.

ART. VIII. Both parties pledge themselves not to molest or to allow to be molested in any manner those Russian or Ottoman subjects who might have become compromised in consequence of their intercourse with the armies of either Empire during the war. In case any persons should wish to retire with their families after the withdrawal of the Russian troops, the Ottoman authorities will not oppose their departure.

Amnesty to Ottoman Subjects.

ART. IX. A full and general amnesty is secured to all Ottoman subjects who shall have become compromised during the late events in the provinces of European Turkey, and all persons either detained on that account, or sent into exile or removed from their country, shall immediately be restored to the enjoyment of their liberty.

Treaties, &c., relating to Commerce, Jurisdiction, and the position of Russians in Turkey, to be the same as before the War.

ART. X. All Treaties, Conventions, and Engagements concluded between the two High Contracting Parties relating to commerce, jurisdiction, and the position of Russian subjects in Turkey, which had been suppressed in consequence of the state of war, shall be put in force again, and the two Governments will again be placed, with regard to all their commercial and other engagements and undertakings in the same position, in relation to one another, as they stood before the declaration of War, with the exception of such Articles as may have been altered by the present Treaty, or in virtue of the Treaty of Berlin.

Litigation of Russian Subjects to be terminated.

ART. XI. The Sublime Porte will take effective steps in order to terminate amicably all litigation of Russian subjects which have been pending for several years, to compensate the latter, should there be cause for it, and to cause the judgments given to be executed without delay.

Ratifications.

ART. XII. The present Treaty shall be ratified, and the ratifications shall be exchanged at St. Petersburgh within two weeks, or sooner, if possible.

In testimony whereof the Plenipotentiaries of Russia and Turkey have affixed to it their signatures and their seals.

Done at Constantinople, 27th January/8th February, 1879.

(L.S.)   LOBANOW.

(L.S.)   AL. CARATHÉODORY.

(L.S.)   ALI.

PROTOCOL *between Russia and Turkey respecting the Treaty of Peace of 27th January/8th February, 1879.   Signed at Constantinople, 27th January/8th February, 1879.*

THEIR Excellencies the Plenipotentiaries of Turkey and Russia, having met at the Ministry for Foreign Affairs, on the 27th January/ 8th February, 1879, in order to proceed to the signature of the Treaty negotiated by them, examine, Article by Article, the text of that Act, as well as the Draft Treaty previously communicated to the Sublime Porte by the Russian Plenipotentiary.

Treaties of San Stefano and Berlin.

With regard to Article II, the Ottoman Plenipotentiaries record the fact that it remains understood that that Article has only a declaratory character in the sense that the statements contained therein cannot bear any interpretation which may be in disagreement with the nature of the engagements entered into in the Treaty of Berlin. His Excellency Prince Lobanow, in accepting this declaration of the Ottoman Plenipotentiaries, records the fact that the Imperial Russian Government on its part has only in view the strict and faithful execution of the Treaty of Berlin in letter as well as in spirit.

Article V gives rise to the following explanation by the Russian Plenipotentiary:

Russia Claims for Losses during War.

His Excellency Prince Lobanow declares that the sum which is therein specified constitutes a maximum to which the total amount of claims will probably never reach; he adds that a Commission, *ad hoc*, will be established at the Russian Embassy for the careful examination of the claims which shall be laid before it, and that, according to the instructions of his Government, an Ottoman Delegate shall be allowed to take part in the examination of those claims. As to the term of one year fixed by this Article as the date from which the claims may be presented to the Sublime Porte, it is understood that an exception will be made in favour of the claim of the Russian Hospital, amounting to the sum of £11,200.

Roumania, Servia, and Montenegro.

With reference to the last part of paragraph (*c*) (Article IV) of the original draft, it is understood, without prejudice, that the Principalities of Roumania, Servia, and Montenegro, being now independent, those stipulations of the Treaty of San Stefano can find no place in the new Treaty unless the interested parties come to a direct understanding respecting them.

Interruption of Navigation of the Danube.

Paragraph (*d*) of the said draft being suppressed, the Russian Plenipotentiary refers to the declaration made on that subject by Count Schouvaloff, in the sitting of the 2nd of July, of the Congress of Berlin (Protocol 11), according to which no obligation could fall upon Russia through the interruption of the navigation of the Danube caused by the breaking out of war.

Eastern Roumelia.

Paragraph (*f*) of the Russian Draft is also eliminated; but to prevent any misunderstanding, His Excellency Prince Lobanow declares that this elimination can in no way be invoked against the administrative system existing in Eastern Roumelia, and that the *status quo* will be provisionally maintained there until the introduction of the new organisation elaborated by the European Commission.

On their side, the Ottoman Plenipotentiaries declare that they have demanded the suppression of that paragraph, precisely because they do not mean in any way to deal with Eastern Roumelia, the position of which is determined by the Treaty concluded between the Seven Powers at Berlin, and because they are neither qualified, nor is it their mission, to discuss the matter at the present time.

Evacuation of Territories.

Paragraph (*g*) of the same draft is also suppressed, and it is agreed that the Russian Ambassador shall address a note to the Sublime Porte declaring that the Imperial Government engages to give orders, immediately after the ratification of the Treaty of this day, for the evacuation of the territories occupied by the Russian troops outside the limits of Bulgaria and Eastern Roumelia. Moreover, the Russian Ambassador gives notice that he will call the attention of the Sublime Porte to the necessity of taking certain temporary measures for the maintenance of public order and tranquillity in the territories evacuated. The Ottoman Plenipotentiaries, on their part, affirm that their Government has always given its attention, in so far as it is concerned, to a change of administration in the territories evacuated by the Russian armies.

Amnesty.

With reference to Article IX, it is understood that the amnesty therein mentioned shall not hinder the local administration from taking such police measures, with regard to compromised persons, as may be rendered necessary by the exigencies of public order and tranquillity.

The signature of the Treaty is then proceeded with; His Excellency the Russian Ambassador hands in the note respecting the evacuation, and the Plenipotentiaries append their signatures to the present Protocol.

Constantinople, 27th January/8th February, 1879.

AL. CARATHÉODORY.   LOBANOW.
ALI.

116

CONVENTION between Austria-Hungary and Turkey, respecting the Occupation and Administration by Austria-Hungary of the Provinces of Bosnia and the Herzegovina. Constantinople, 21st April, 1879.

THE Governments of Austria-Hungary and Turkey, having reserved to themselves the right of coming to an understanding with regard to the details of the occupation stipulated for by Article XXV of the Treaty of Berlin, and the fact of the occupation of Bosnia and the Herzegovina in no way affecting the rights of Sovereignty of his Imperial Majesty the Sultan over these provinces, the two Governments have named for their Plenipotentiaries:

Austria-Hungary, on the one part, His Excellency M. le Comte F. Zichy, &c.; and Turkey, on the other part, His Excellency Al. Carathèodory Pasha, &c., and His Excellency Munif Effendi, &c.;

Who, after having exchanged their full powers, found in good and due form, have agreed upon the following Articles:—

Administration of Bosnia and the Herzegovina.

ART. I. The administration of Bosnia and the Herzegovina shall be carried on by Austria-Hungary, conformably to Article XXV of the Treaty of Berlin; the Austro-Hungarian Government, however, does not object to retain all those existing functionaries who may possess the necessary aptitude for the good administration of their departments. In filling up vacancies, preference will be given by the Austro-Hungarian Government to natives of these provinces.

Religious Liberty.

ART. II. The freedom and outward exercise of all existing religions shall be assured to persons residing or sojourning in Bosnia and the Herzegovina. Especially, entire freedom is assured to Mussulmans in their relations with their spiritual chiefs.

The commanders of the troops of His Majesty the Emperor and King, and the administrative authorities, shall continue to take the greatest care that no injury be done to the honour, to the customs, to the freedom of religion, to the security of the persons, or to the property, of Mussulmans. All aggression against Mussulmans, their property or their religion, shall be severely punished. The name of His Majesty the Sultan shall continue to be used in the public prayers of the Mussulmans as in times past.

Hoisting of Ottoman Flag on Minarets.

Wherever it shall have been the custom to hoist the Ottoman flag on the minarets, this custom shall be respected.

Administration of Revenues.

ART. III. The revenues of Bosnia and the Herzegovina shall be exclusively appropriated to the needs, to the administration of, and to the improvements deemed necessary in, those Provinces.

Current Ottoman Money.

ART. IV. The Ottoman currency shall continue to have free circulation in Bosnia and the Herzegovina.

Disposal of War Material, &c.

ART. V. The Sublime Porte shall dispose as it thinks fit of the arms, warlike stores, and other articles belonging to the Ottoman Government, and which were found in the fortified places or in the garrisons. For this purpose inventories shall be prepared with the intervention of Commissioners of the two Governments.

Treatment of Inhabitants when outside the Provinces.

ART. VI. The question of the treatment of the inhabitants of Bosnia and the Herzegovina sojourning or travelling outside these provinces, shall be regulated subsequently by a special arrangement.

Mode in which Article XXV of the Treaty of Berlin is to be carried out. Sandjak of Novi-Bazar.

ART. VII. To attain, in a common interest, the political and military object that Article XXV of the Treaty of Berlin has in view concerning the Sandjak of Novi-Bazar, the two Governments have resolved to regulate the mode in which it shall henceforward be carried into execution. For this purpose the Government of His Majesty the Emperor and King undertakes to give notice beforehand to the Government of His Majesty the Sultan of the time when the entrance of the Imperial and Royal troops shall take place.

In order to prevent all unnecessary delay, the two Governments, each in so far as it is itself concerned, undertakes, should occasion arise, to furnish their authorities and commanders, without delay, with the full powers necessary to settle directly among themselves the questions connected with the subsistence of the Imperial and Royal troops, as well as to their quartering, and other details relating thereto. Moreover it is understood that all expenses incurred under this head shall be borne by the Austro-Hungarian Government.

Presence of Troops in Sandjak of Novi-Bazar.

ART. VIII. The presence of the troops of His Majesty the Emperor and King in the Sandjak of Novi-Bazar, will not interfere with the functions of the Ottoman administrative authorities, judicial or financial, of every kind, which will continue to be exercised as in former times under the exclusive and direct orders of the Sublime Porte.

Maintenance of Troops in Garrisons and Positions of Sandjak of Novi-Bazar.

ART. IX. Should the Sublime Porte wish to maintain regular troops at the places in the Sandjak of Novi-Bazar where the Austro-Hungarian troops shall be garrisoned, no obstacles shall be raised to it. The troops of the two States shall be placed on a footing of perfect equality with regard to their number and military advantages, and the freedom of their movements.

Non-employment by Porte of Irregular Troops.

The Sublime Porte engages to maintain no irregular troops throughout the Sandjak of Novi-Bazar.

Power of Austria to maintain Troops in Garrison.

ART. X. It is nevertheless understood that the power of Austria-Hungary to maintain a sufficient number of troops, as circumstances may require, at the places where it is intended to keep garrisons, in conformity with the stipulations of Article VII, is not to be restricted by these arrangements.

In faith of which the Plenipotentiaries of Austria-Hungary and of Turkey, have signed the present Convention, and have affixed to it the seal of their arms.

Constantinople, 21st April, 1879.

(L.S.)   ZICHY.

(L.S.)   A. CARATHÉODORY.

(L.S.)   MUNIF.

ANNEX TO THE ABOVE CONVENTION.

Occupation of Positions by Austrian Troops.

It is understood that, under the present circumstances, the Government of Austria-Hungary, while reserving to itself all the rights secured to it by Article XXV of the Treaty of Berlin, only intends to place garrisons at three points situated on the Lim, between the frontiers of Servia and Montenegro; these points being Priboï, Priépoliyé, Biélopoliyé. The number of troops at present destined for the service of these garrisons will not exceed a total of between 4,000 and 5,000 men. If, in the course of events, the necessity should arise for placing garrisons at other points, it shall be carried out on both sides in accordance with the arrangements specified in Article VII, excepting that, should the Austrian Government have the intention of placing troops at points on the Balkan de Ragosna, it will be necessary to come to a direct understanding on that point with the Sublime Porte.

Constantinople, 21st April, 1879.

ZICHY.

AL. CARATHÉODORY.

MUNIF.

117   AUSTRO-GERMAN ALLIANCE OF 1879

Protocol between the Austro-Hungarian and German Governments describing the preliminary steps towards an Alliance. Vienna, 24th September, 1879. Ratifications exchanged, 21st October, 1879.

PROTOCOL.

The undersigned, Count Andrássy, Minister of the Imperial Household and of Foreign Affairs of Austria-Hungary, and Prince Bismarck, Chancellor of the German Empire, met at Vienna on the 24th day of September, 1879, to take counsel together as to what, according to their conscientious conviction, it might behoove their Exalted Sovereigns to devise and to do for the security and tranquillity of their peoples and for the preservation and consolidation of the peace of Europe.

The Chancellor of the German Empire declared on this occasion that he was empowered to present on behalf of His Majesty the German Emperor the proposal for an agreement, according to the terms of which both Powers should reciprocally engage to take further steps for the maintenance of peace and especially for the cultivation of their friendly relations with Russia; but, in case one of them should be attacked by one or more Powers, to repel this attack jointly.

Count Andrássy declared himself to be in agreement with the ideas underlying this proposal; on the other hand, however, he had serious doubts as to the conclusion of an agreement of such form and scope as that proposed by the German Imperial Chancellor: doubts which he was unable to repress, and which would not permit him to recommend to his Most Exalted Sovereign the acceptance of the proffered proposal in its abovementioned wording.

When Count Andrássy, even after the exhaustive exchange of opinions which was entered into concerning this matter, had declared that he was unable to overcome his doubts, he made, on his part, a proposal which defined in different form the fundamental ideas of an agreement equally of a purely defensive nature, and pledged himself to answer for its acceptance and faithful execution.

After mature consideration of this proposal, Prince Bismarck declared that the instructions which were in his possession did not empower him to proceed with the immediate binding conclusion of an agreement on this basis, but that he was ready to negotiate further on the principles laid down by Count Andrássy, in order that a wording might be found which would realize the fundamental ideas and the practical purposes of his original proposal in a form acceptable to both Parties.

As the result of exhaustive negotiations the undersigned later united on the appended draft of an Agreement, which they undertake to submit to their Exalted Sovereigns, and, in conformity with their convictions, to recommend to those Most Exalted Personages for Their most gracious approbation.

In witness whereof both have appended their signatures to this Protocol.

Done at Vienna, the 24th day of September, 1879.

ANDRÁSSY.　　　　　　　　　　　　　　v. BISMARCK.

(L.S.)　　　　　　　　　　　　　　　　(L.S.)

The words following should be stricken from the Agreement of the High Contracting Parties, in order that the Most Exalted sanction of the two Sovereigns be not anticipated.

ANDRÁSSY.　　　　　　　　　　　　　　v. BISMARCK.

Joint Memorandum signed by the Austro-Hungarian and the German Plenipotentiaries outlining the purposes of the Alliance. Vienna, September 24, 1879.

MEMORANDUM.

The Austro-Hungarian Minister of Foreign Affairs and the Chancellor of the German Empire have, on the occasion of their meeting in Vienna, taken counsel as to what actions, under the present conditions in Europe, it might behoove their Exalted Sovereigns to take for the benefit of Their Empires and for the consolidation of the peace of Europe.

Both Governments adhere firmly to the opinion that the maintenance and consolidation of the peace of Europe must be the main purpose of their policies.

They are resolved not to let themselves be diverted from this purpose by passing divergences with other Powers, and they are convinced that such differences of interest as may yet exist must be subordinated to the higher considerations of the world's peace.

The Governments believe that this purpose may be best attained if they once again promise one another to remain true to the settlements of the Congress of Berlin.

In order, however, to obviate every complication in the execution of this Treaty, both Cabinets shall, in regard to all provisions of the Treaty of Berlin which have not yet been executed, keep constantly before them their friendly attitude towards Russia. Without renouncing their independence of action in the field of diplomacy, or exacting such a renunciation from Russia, both Governments shall use their influence in a conciliatory sense as regards those questions of the Peace of Berlin concerning which it has not been possible to reach an understanding between Russia and the remaining Powers.

Both Governments agree in the view (and hope that the same view will be shared by Russia also) that none of the so far unsettled questions of the Peace of Berlin appears to be of sufficient importance to give occasion for violent measures or for a *casus belli* between the various Powers.

The two Governments for their part affirm it to be their common intention that neither of them shall take occasion, through the differences still pending regarding certain points of the Treaty of Berlin, to attack or to menace the Russian Empire, either by themselves or in alliance with other Powers. In this matter both Governments are acting on the presumption that the Russian Government also will be guided by the same aims.

As a proof of their reciprocally friendly sentiments, the two Cabinets intend to allow the beneficent effects of their close relations to be of still further profit to the peoples of both Empires through the especial cultivation of their neighborly trade relations as well as through the conclusion of new commercial treaties, as is shown by the fact that, independently of whether the most-favoured-nation treaty now in existence between them shall be prolonged or not, they are now already taking into consideration negotiations concerning further alleviation of tariff and trade difficulties.

It is their intention that Plenipotentiaries shall meet for this purpose in time to permit the result of their negotiations to be placed before the legislatures of both sides within the next year.

Done at Vienna, September 24, 1879.

ANDRÁSSY.   v. BISMARCK.

(L.S.)   (L.S.)

Treaty of Alliance between Austria-Hungary and Germany. October 7, 1879.

Inasmuch as Their Majesties the Emperor of Austria, King of Hungary, and the German Emperor, King of Prussia, must consider it Their imperative duty as Monarchs to provide for the security of Their Empires and the peace of Their subjects, under all circumstances;

inasmuch as the two Sovereigns, as was the case under the former existing relations of alliance, will be enabled by the close union of the two Empires to fulfil this duty more easily and more efficaciously;

inasmuch as, finally, an intimate co-operation of Germany and Austria-Hungary can menace no one, but is rather calculated to consolidate the peace of Europe as established by the stipulations of Berlin;

Their Majesties the Emperor of Austria, King of Hungary, and the Emperor of Germany, while solemnly promising each other never to allow Their purely defensive Agreement to develop an aggressive tendency in any direction, have determined to conclude an Alliance of peace and mutual defence.

For this purpose Their Most Exalted Majesties have designated as Their Plenipotentiaries:

His Most Exalted Majesty the Emperor of Austria, King of Hungary, His Actual Privy Councillor, Minister of the Imperial Household and of Foreign Affairs, Lieutenant-Fieldmarshal Count Julius Andrássy of Csik-Szent-Király and Kraszna-Horka, etc., etc.,

His Most Exalted Majesty the German Emperor, His Ambassador Extraordinary and Plenipotentiary, Lieutenant-General Prince Henry VII of Reuss, etc., etc.,

who have met this day at Vienna, and, after the exchange of their full powers, found in good and due form, have agreed upon the following Articles:

ART. I. Should, contrary to their hope, and against the loyal desire of the two High Contracting Parties, one of the two Empires be attacked by Russia, the High Contracting Parties are bound to come to the assistance one of the other with the whole war strength of their Empires, and accordingly only to conclude peace together and upon mutual agreement.

ART. II. Should one of the High Contracting Parties be attacked by another Power, the other High Contracting Party binds itself hereby, not only to support the aggressor against its high Ally, but to observe at least a benevolent neutral attitude towards its fellow Contracting Party.

Should, however, the attacking party in such a case be supported by Russia, either by an active co-operation or by military measures which constitute a menace to the Party attacked, then the obligation stipulated in Article I of this Treaty, for reciprocal assistance with the whole fighting force, becomes equally operative, and the conduct of the war by the two High Contracting Parties shall in this case also be in common until the conclusion of a common peace.

ART. III. The duration of this Treaty shall be provisionally fixed at five years from the day of ratification. One year before the expiration of this period the two High Contracting Parties shall consult together concerning the question whether the conditions serving as the basis of the Treaty still prevail, and reach an agreement in regard to the further continuance or possible modification of certain details. If in the course of the first month of the last year of the Treaty no invitation has been received from either side to open these negotiations, the Treaty shall be considered as renewed for a further period of three years.

ART. IV. This Treaty shall, in conformity with its peaceful character, and to avoid any misinterpretation, be kept secret by the two High Contracting Parties, and only communicated to a third Power upon a joint understanding between the two Parties, and according to the terms of a special Agreement.

The two High Contracting Parties venture to hope, after the sentiments expressed by the Emperor Alexander at the meeting at Alexandrovo, that the armaments of Russia will not in reality prove to be menacing to them, and have on that account no reason for making a communication at present; should, however, this hope, contrary to their expectations, prove to be erroneous, the two High Contracting Parties would consider it their loyal obligation to let the Emperor Alexander know, at least confidentially, that they must consider an attack on either of them as directed against both.

ART. V. This Treaty shall derive its validity from the approbation of the two Exalted Sovereigns and shall be ratified within fourteen days after this approbation has been granted by Their Most Exalted Majesties.

In witness whereof the Plenipotentiaries have signed this Treaty with their own hands and affixed their arms.

Done at Vienna, October 7, 1879.

ANDRÁSSY.   H. VII v. REUSS.
(L.S.)   (L.S.)

118

MINISTERIAL DECLARATION OF POLICY IN REGARD TO THE RELATION OF THE AUSTRO-GERMAN ALLIANCE TO THE LEAGUE OF THE THREE EMPERORS. 1881.

MINISTERIAL DECLARATION.

With regard to the negotiations which are to take place between His Majesty the German Emperor, King of Prussia, His Majesty the Emperor of Austria, King of Hungary, and His Majesty the Emperor of All the Russias concerning an Agreement for the safeguarding of the defensive position of their States, and for the elucidation of the relation which will exist between the aforementioned Agreement, if it should be concluded, and the defensive Alliance which was signed at Vienna on October 7, 1879, and ratified on the 21st day of the same month, between Their Majesties the German Emperor and His Apostolic Majesty, the Imperial German Government and the Imperial and Royal Austro-Hungarian Government have in this matter recorded the agreement of their conception and of their intention,

that the prospective Triple Agreement can under no circumstance prejudice their Treaty of Alliance of October 7, 1879; the latter, on the contrary, remains binding, as if the former did not exist, and shall be executed according to its contents and the intentions of the two treaty-making Powers;

that the Treaty of October 7, 1879, therefore continues to determine the relations of the two Powers without undergoing limitation or alteration in any point whatsoever through the prospective new Treaty with Russia.

In witness whereof the present Ministerial Declaration, which in accordance with the stipulation in Article IV of the Treaty of October 7, 1879, shall be kept secret, has been prepared, to be exchanged against a declaration of similar purport of the Imperial and Royal Ministry of Foreign Affairs.

Berlin, May 18, 1881.

(L.S.) THE IMPERIAL CHANCELLOR
v. BISMARCK.

119

CONVENTION between Her Majesty the Queen of the United Kingdom of Great Britain and Ireland, the German Emperor, the Emperor of Austria-Hungary, the President of the French Republic, the King of Italy, the Emperor of Russia, and the Sultan, for the Settlement of the Frontier between Greece and Turkey. Signed at Constantinople, 24th May, 1881.

HER Majesty the Queen of the United Kingdom of Great Britain and Ireland, Empress of India; His Majesty the German Emperor, King of Prussia; His Majesty the Emperor of Austria, King of Bohemia, &c., and Apostolic King of Hungary; the President of the French Republic; His Majesty the King of Italy; and His Majesty the Emperor of All the Russias, exercising the mediation contemplated by Article XXIV of the Treaty signed at Berlin on the 13th July, 1878, of the one part; and His

Majesty the Emperor of the Ottomans, of the other part; being equally animated by the desire to regulate, in the interest of European order, the questions relative to the rectification of the Turco-Greek frontiers, have determined to conclude a Convention destined to give a definite solution to this question.

Their said Majesties and the President of the French Republic have, to this effect, appointed as their Plenipotentiaries that is to say:

Her Majesty the Queen of the United Kingdom of Great Britain and Ireland, Empress of India: the Right Honourable George J. Goschen, Her Special Ambassador Extraordinary and Plenipotentiary at the Court of His Majesty the Emperor of the Ottomans;

His Majesty the German Emperor, King of Prussia: Paul, Count de Hatzfeldt Wildenburg, His Ambassador Extraordinary and Plenipotentiary at the Court of His Majesty the Emperor of the Ottomans;

His Majesty the Emperor of Austria, King of Bohemia, &c., and Apostolic King of Hungary: Henry, Baron Calice, His Ambassador Extraordinary and Plenipotentiary at the Court of His Majesty the Emperor of the Ottomans;

The President of the French Republic: Charles Tissot, Ambassador of the French Republic at the Court of His Majesty the Emperor of the Ottomans;

His Majesty the King of Italy: Louis, Count Corti, His Ambassador Extraordinary and Plenipotentiary at the Court of His Majesty the Emperor of the Ottomans;

His Majesty the Emperor of All the Russias: Eugène Novikow, His Ambassador Extraordinary and Plenipotentiary at the Court of His Majesty the Emperor of the Ottomans;

And His Majesty the Emperor of the Ottomans: Mahmoud Server Pasha, President of His Council of State; the Mushir Ghazi Ahmed Moukhtar Pasha, President of the Commission of Inspection of Military Reforms; the Mushir Aly Nyzami Pasha; Artin Effendi Dadian, Under-Secretary of State in the Department for Foreign Affairs;

Who, furnished with the necessary powers, have agreed to the following Articles:—

New Frontiers.

ART. I. The new frontiers of Turkey and Greece are fixed as follows:—
The new frontier line starting from a point near the defile of Karalik-Dervend, between the mouth of the Salamvrias and Platamona, about 4 kilom. to the south of the latter point, follows in a westerly direction the crest of the mountains, passes first between Krania and Avarnitza, then between Nezeros and Analipsis, arrives at the summit of Mount Godaman, then descends towards the south, following the crest of

Olympus, reaches the summit of Kokkinopetra, and, taking a westerly direction from this point without leaving the same crest, passes between Ligara and Derveni-Melona, and arrives at the summit of Mount Kritiri. Thence turning towards the south the line gains the right bank of the Xeraghis, and, following the line of watershed towards the south-west, gains the summit of the heights situated to the north of the village of Zarko, then turns to the north-west in the direction of Diminitza and keeps to the line of watershed, leaving to Turkey the village of Elevtherokhorion. Before reaching Diminitza, at a distance of about 18 kilom. from that place, the frontier-line turns towards the west, still on the line of watershed, and passes by the villages of Flamouristi, Gavronon, and Georgitza to the summit of Mount Kratchovo. Then turning southwards by the crest, it passes by the summits of Mounts Zygos, Dokini, and Peristeri, and gains the River Arta, following the stream which carries off by the shortest way the rainfall from the summit of Mount Peristeri to this river, and passing near the villages of Kalarrhytes and Mikalitzi. Beyond these last points the line follows the thalweg of the River Arta to its mouth.

Boundary Commission.   Mode of Voting.

This delimitation will be fixed on the spot by a Commission composed of the Delegates of the Six Powers and of the two parties interested.

The Delimitation Commission will pass their Resolutions by a majority of votes, each Power having but one vote.

It should meet within eight days after the ratification of the present Convention, or sooner if possible, so as to commence its labours.

Cession of Punta to Greece.

ART. II. Punta and its territory, as it was determined by the first Article of the Act signed at Constantinople on the 21st July, 1832, will be ceded to Greece.

Gulf of Arta; Disarmament of Fortifications; Free Navigation.

All the fortifications commanding the entrance to the Gulf of Arta, both on the side of Prevesa as well as on that of Punta, will be disarmed within three months after the signature of this Convention, and will remain disarmed in time of peace between the two States.

The navigation of the Gulf of Arta will be free.

Inhabitants of Ceded Territories.

ART. III. The lives, property, honour, religion, and customs of those of the inhabitants of the localities ceded to Greece who shall remain under the Hellenic administration will be scrupulously respected. They will enjoy exactly the same civil and political rights as Hellenic subjects of origin.

Rights of Property.

ART. IV. The rights of property on the farms, as well as on the pasturages, meadows, grazing grounds ("kechlak"), forests, and every kind of lands or other real estate, held by private individuals and communes in virtue of firmans, hodjets, tapous, and other titles, or else by the Ottoman law, in the districts ceded to Greece, will be recognized by the Hellenic Government.

The titles of property called vakoufs, which serve to keep up the mosques, colleges, schools, and other pious or charitable institutions, will be equally recognized.

Estates of the Sultan.

ART. V. His Majesty the Sultan shall be enabled, as in the past, to dispose of the Imperial estates, the revenues of which are collected on behalf of His Majesty or of the Imperial family.

In the case of the nature and destination of these properties being contested, the question shall be submitted to the examination of the Commission of which the appointment is contemplated by Article IX of the present Convention, and, eventually, according to the terms of the said Article, to the decision of the Mediating Powers.

Land Owners.

ART. VI. No one may be deprived of his property except for some object of public utility, duly established, in the cases and in the manner provided by law, and in exchange for a fair and prepaid compensation.

No landlord shall be obliged to sell his goods to the cultivators of the soil or to third parties, nor to hand over any portion of them; nor shall any alteration be introduced into the relations between landlords and the cultivators of the soil, except by a general law, applicable to the whole Kingdom.

Land owners settled outside the Kingdom, and possessing real property in the ceded territories, may let their lands under a lease, or have them administered through third parties.

Pasture Lands.

ART. VII. The inhabitants of the provinces bordering on the territories ceded to Greece, who have been for a long time in the habit of sending their flocks to the meadows and pasture lands, as well as on the farms situated within those territories, shall continue to enjoy these privileges as in the past.

Religious Freedom in Territories ceded to Greece.

ART. VIII. Freedom of religion and of public worship is secured to Mussulmans in the territories ceded to Greece.

No interference shall take place with the autonomy or hierarchial organization of Mussulman religious bodies now existing, or which may hereafter be formed; nor with the management of the funds and real property belonging to them.

No obstacle shall be placed in the way of the relations of these bodies with their spiritual heads in matters of religion.

Local Courts of the Chéri.

The local Courts of the Chéri shall continue to exercise their jurisdiction in matters purely religious.

Settlement of Disputes: State Property: Private Interests.

ART. IX. A Turco-Hellenic Commission shall be entrusted with the settlement, within two years, of all matters concerning the property of the State, as well as of questions relating to the interests of private individuals, who may happen to be connected with them.

Indemnity to be paid by Greece for Ottoman Government Lands.

This Commission will have to decide on the indemnity which Greece is to pay to Turkey from the lands, which shall be admitted to belong *bonâ fide* to the Ottoman Government, and to fix the annual revenue to be paid on them.

Those questions on which an understanding cannot be come to shall be submitted to the decision of the Mediating Powers.

Greece: Share of Ottoman Debt.   Ceded Territories.

ART. X. Greece shall bear a part of the Ottoman Public Debt proportionate to the revenues of the ceded territories. This portion shall be determined ultimately between the Sublime Porte and the Representatives of the Mediating Powers at Constantinople.

Disarmament.

ART. XI. No exclusive and exceptional measure of disarmament shall be taken with regard to Mussulmans.

Brigandage.

ART. XII. The Hellenic Government shall propose to the Chamber a Law for the renewal of the Convention of 1856 (A.H. 1272), relating to the suppression of brigandage.

Emigration.

ART. XIII. The natives of the territories ceded to Greece, or persons actually domiciled in these provinces, who intend to retain Ottoman nationality, shall, for the space of three years from the exchange of the ratifications, and by a preliminary declaration made before a competent authority, enjoy the right of transferring their residence into the Ottoman Empire, and of establishing themselves there, in which case they shall retain their character of Ottoman subjects.

Those persons emigrating within the above-mentioned period of three years shall continue to enjoy the privilege stipulated for in the third paragraph of Article VI of the present Convention in favour of proprietors settled outside the limits of the Kingdom.

Military Service.

During the same period of three years Mussulmans shall not be liable to military service.

Arrears of Taxes.

ART. XIV. The Commission created in virtue of Article IX of the present Convention is entrusted with the settlement, within the shortest period possible, of the questions relating to arrears of taxes due to the Ottoman Government in the ceded territories, as well as those which might arise from the collection of the taxes during the current year.

Evacuation.

ART. XV. The details of the evacuation and transfer of the ceded territories are settled in a separate Act, which is, and remains, annexed to the present Convention, and will have the same force and value as if it formed part of it.

The Imperial Ottoman troops are bound to evacuate the ceded territories within the period fixed by this Act.

The Imperial Ottoman Government will, however, endeavour to shorten that period as far as possible.

Technical Commissioners.

ART. XVI. It is understood that the Mediating Powers reserve to themselves the power to appoint Technical Commissioners for the purpose of superintending the operations connected with the cession of the territories.

Amnesty.

ART. XVII. A full and entire amnesty shall be granted by Turkey and Greece to all persons implicated or compromised in political events anterior to the present Convention, and relating to the question which is settled by it.

Conclusion of a Similar Convention between Greece and Turkey.

ART. XVIII. The Convention concluded this day between Her Majesty the Queen of the United Kingdom of Great Britain and Ireland, Empress of India; His Majesty the German Emperor, King of Prussia; His Majesty the Emperor of Austria, King of Bohemia, &c., Apostolic King of Hungary; the President of the French Republic; His Majesty the King of Italy; His Majesty the Emperor of All the Russias; and His Majesty the Emperor of the Ottomans shall be immediately followed by the stipulation of a Convention, containing the same provisions, between His Majesty the Emperor of the Ottomans and His Majesty the King of the Hellenes.

Ratifications.

ART. XIX. The present Convention shall be ratified and its ratifications exchanged at Constantinople within three weeks, or sooner, if possible.

In witness whereof the respective Plenipotentiaries have signed it, and have affixed thereto the seal of their arms.

Done at Constantinople, the 24th day of May, in the year 1881.

(L.S.)   GEORGE J. GOSCHEN.
(L.S.)   v. HATZFELDT.
(L.S.)   CALICE.
(L.S.)   TISSOT.
(L.S.)   L. CORTI.
(L.S.)   NOVIKOW.
(L.S.)   SERVER.
(L.S.)   MOUKHTAR.
(L.S.)   ALY.
(L.S.)   ARTIN DADIAN.

ANNEX.

SEPARATE ACT, *settling details for Turkish Evacuation of Territories ceded to Greece. Constantinople, 24th May, 1881.*

HER Majesty the Queen of the United Kingdom of Great Britain and Ireland, Empress of India; His Majesty the German Emperor, King of Prussia; His Majesty the Emperor of Austria, King of Bohemia, &c., Apostolic King of Hungary; the President of the French Republic; His Majesty the King of Italy; His Majesty the Emperor of All the Russias; and His Majesty the Emperor of the Ottomans, being desirous of settling the details and the mode of evacuation, and of the taking possession of the territories ceded to Greece in virtue of the Convention signed this day, have resolved with this view to sign a separate Act in accordance with the terms of Article XV of the said Convention, and have to this effect appointed:—

Her Majesty the Queen of Great Britain and Ireland, Empress of India: the Right Honourable George J. Goschen, Her Special Ambassador Extraordinary and Plenipotentiary at the Court of His Majesty the Emperor of the Ottomans;

His Majesty the German Emperor, King of Prussia: Paul, Count de Hatzfeldt Wildenburg, His Ambassador Extraordinary and Plenipotentiary at the Court of His Majesty the Emperor of the Ottomans;

His Majesty the Emperor of Austria, King of Bohemia, &c., Apostolic King of Hungary: Henry, Baron Calice, His Ambassador Extraordinary and Plenipotentiary at the Court of His Majesty the Emperor of the Ottomans;

The President of the French Republic: Charles Tissot, Ambassador of the French Republic at the Court of His Majesty the Emperor of the Ottomans;

His Majesty the King of Italy: Louis, Count Corti, His Ambassador Extraordinary and Plenipotentiary at the Court of His Majesty the Emperor of the Ottomans;

His Majesty the Emperor of All the Russias: Eugène Novikow, His Ambassador Extraordinary and Plenipotentiary at the Court of His Majesty the Emperor of the Ottomans;

And His Majesty the Emperor of the Ottomans: Mahmoud Server Pasha, President of His Council of State; the Mushir Ghazi Ahmed Moukhtar Pasha, President of the Commission of Inspection of Military Reforms; the Mushir Aly Nyzami Pasha; Artin Effendi Dadian, Under Secretary of State in the Department of Foreign Affairs;

Who, furnished with the necessary powers, have agreed to the following Articles:—

Map of Territories ceded to Greece.

ART. I. The territories to be ceded to Greece are divided into six sections, in accordance with the indications marked upon the annexed map.

Evacuation of Territories by Sections.

ART. II. The evacuation of one of these sections shall take place within three weeks from the date fixed for the exchange of the ratifications of the Convention signed this day.

Four other sections shall be completely evacuated within three months from the same date.

The sixth section, which comprises Volo, and constitutes the only means of exit by which the Ottoman Government can remove its war material, shall be evacuated during the two following months, that is to say, within the whole period of five months from the date fixed for the exchange of the ratifications of the Convention.

It is understood that these various periods shall be abridged if possible.

War Material.

The Ottoman authorities will draw up an inventory of that portion of the war material which cannot be removed during the said period of five months.

Commission to be composed of Military Delegates.

ART. III. The Mediating Powers will name Military Delegates, who will constitute a Commission, destined to act as intermediary, for the evacuation by the Ottoman authorities, and the taking over by the Hellenic authorities of the ceded territories.

This Commission will exercise a general supervision over the evacuation and occupation of the ceded territories. It will intervene for the purpose of establishing an agreement between the Commanders on both sides, both as regards the military movements on either side, the fixing the distance which must always divide the troops of the two Powers, and the period which must elapse between the evacuation and the taking over of the different points to be ceded.

Aid and Protection to be afforded to Military Commission.

ART. IV. It will be the duty of the Ottoman and Greek authorities to afford aid and protection to this Commission during the accomplishment of its mission.

This Act to form an Integral Part of the Convention signed the same day.

ART. V. The present Act forms an integral part of the Convention signed this day at Constantinople, and will have the same force and value. In witness whereof the respective Plenipotentiaries have signed it, and have affixed thereto the seal of their arms.

Done at Constantinople, the 24th day of the month of May, 1881.

(L.S.) GEORGE J. GOSCHEN.
(L.S.) v. HATZFELDT.
(L.S.) CALICE.
(L.S.) TISSOT.
(L.S.) L. CORTI.
(L.S.) NOVIKOW.

(L.S.) SERVER.
(L.S.) MOUKHTAR.
(L.S.) ALY.
(L.S.) ARTIN DADIAN.

120

TREATY of Alliance between Austria-Hungary and Serbia. Belgrade, 16th/28th June, 1881. Ratifications exchanged 29th June/11th July, 1881.

His Majesty the Emperor of Austria, King of Bohemia, etc., and Apostolic King of Hungary, and

His Highness the Prince of Serbia, animated by the desire to maintain peace in the Orient and to guarantee against all eventualities the relations of perfect friendship which exist between Their Governments, have resolved to conclude to this end a Treaty and have appointed as Their Plenipotentiaries, to wit:

His Imperial and Royal Apostolic Majesty:

the Sieur Gabriel Baron von Herbert-Rathkeal, His Chamberlain, Minister Resident in Serbia, etc.,

His Highness the Prince of Serbia:

the Sieur Chedomille Mijatovich, His Minister of Foreign Affairs, etc., etc.,

who, after having communicated to one another their full powers, found in good and due form, have agreed upon the following Articles:—

Art. I. There shall be stable peace and friendship between Austria-Hungary and Serbia. The two Governments engage to follow mutually a friendly policy.

Art. II. Serbia will not tolerate political, religious, or other intrigues, which, taking her territory as a point of departure, might be directed against the Austro-Hungarian Monarchy, including therein Bosnia, Herzegovina, and the Sanjak of Novibazar.

Austria-Hungary assumes the same obligation with regard to Serbia and her dynasty, the maintenance and strengthening of which she will support with all her influence.

Art. III. If the Prince of Serbia should deem it necessary, in the interest of His dynasty and of His country, to take in behalf of Himself and of His descendants the title of King, Austria-Hungary will recognize this title as soon as its proclamation shall have been made in legal form, and will use her influence to secure recognition for it on the part of the other Powers.

ART. IV. Austria-Hungary will use her influence with the other European Cabinets to second the interests of Serbia.

Without a previous understanding with Austria-Hungary, Serbia will neither negotiate nor conclude any political treaty with another Government, and will not admit to her territory a foreign armed force, regular or irregular, even as volunteers.

ART. V. If Austria-Hungary should be threatened with war or find herself at war with one or more other Powers, Serbia will observe a friendly neutrality towards the Austro-Hungarian Monarchy, including therein Bosnia, Herzegovina and the Sanjak of Novibazar, and will accord to it all possible facilities, in conformity with their close friendship and the spirit of this Treaty.

Austria-Hungary assumes the same obligation towards Serbia, in case the latter should be threatened with war or find herself at war.

ART. VI. In any case where military co-operation is considered necessary by the two Contracting Parties, the questions touching this co-operation, especially those of the superior command and of the contingent passage of troops through the respective territories, shall be regulated by a military convention.

ART. VII. If, as a result of a combination of circumstances whose development is not to be foreseen at present, Serbia were in a position to make territorial acquisitions in the direction of her southern frontiers (with the exception of the Sanjak of Novibazar), Austria-Hungary will not oppose herself thereto, and will use her influence with the other Powers for the purpose of winning them over to an attitude favourable to Serbia.

ART. VIII. The present Treaty shall remain in force for a period of ten years, dating from the day of the exchange of ratifications. Six months before its expiration the Contracting Parties shall, if there is occasion, take counsel together in regard to its prolongation or to the modifications which the circumstances of the moment may render desirable.

ART. IX. The Contracting Parties undertake to keep the present Treaty secret, and not to communicate either its existence or its tenor to any other Government without a previous understanding.

ART. X. The ratifications of the present Treaty shall be exchanged at Belgrade within a period of a fortnight, or sooner if may be.

In witness whereof the respective Plenipotentiaries have signed it and have affixed to it the seal of their arms.

Done at Belgrade, in duplicate, the twenty-eighth/sixteenth of June of the year 1881.

BARON DE HERBERT.   CH. MIJATOVICH.
        (L.S.)   (L.S.)

121 THE LEAGUE OF THE THREE EMPERORS

CONVENTION between Austria-Hungary, the German Empire, and Russia. Berlin, 18th June, 1881. Ratifications exchanged 27th June, 1881.

The Courts of Austria-Hungary, of Germany, and of Russia, animated by an equal desire to consolidate the general peace by an understanding intended to assure the defensive position of their respective States, have come into agreement on certain questions which more especially concern their reciprocal interests.

With this purpose the three Courts have appointed:

His Majesty the Emperor of Austria, King of Bohemia, etc., and Apostolic King of Hungary, the Sieur Emeric Count Széchényi, His Ambassador Extraordinary and Plenipotentiary to His Majesty the Emperor of Germany, King of Prussia,

His Majesty the Emperor of Germany, King of Prussia, the Sieur Otto Prince Bismarck, His President of the Council of Ministers of Prussia, Chancellor of the Empire,

His Majesty the Emperor of All the Russias, the Sieur Peter Sabouroff, Privy Councillor, His Ambassador Extraordinary and Plenipotentiary to His Majesty the Emperor of Germany, King of Prussia,

who, furnished with full powers, which have been found in good and due form, have agreed upon the following Articles:—

ART. I. In case one of the High Contracting Parties should find itself at war with a fourth Great Power, the two others shall maintain towards it a benevolent neutrality and shall devote their efforts to the localization of the conflict.

This stipulation shall apply likewise to a war between one of the three Powers and Turkey, but only in the case where a previous agreement shall have been reached between the three Courts as to the results of this war.

In the special case where one of them should obtain a more positive support from one of its two Allies, the obligatory value of the present Article shall remain in all its force for the third.

ART. II. Russia, in agreement with Germany, declares her firm resolution to respect the interests arising from the new position assured to Austria-Hungary by the Treaty of Berlin.

The three Courts, desirous of avoiding all discord between them, engage to take account of their respective interests in the Balkan Peninsula. They further promise one another that any new modifications in the territorial status quo of Turkey in Europe can be accomplished only in virtue of a common agreement between them.

In order to facilitate the agreement contemplated by the present Article, an agreement of which it is impossible to foresee all the conditions, the three Courts from the present moment record in the Protocol annexed to this Treaty the points on which an understanding has already been established in principle.

ART. III. The three Courts recognize the European and mutually obligatory character of the principle of the closing of the Straits of the Bosphorus and of the Dardanelles, founded on international law, confirmed by treaties, and summed up in the declaration of the second Plenipotentiary of Russia at the session of July 12 of the Congress of Berlin (Protocol 19).

They will take care in common that Turkey shall make no exception to this rule in favour of the interests of any Government whatsoever, by lending to warlike operations of a belligerent Power the portion of its Empire constituted by the Straits.

In case of infringement, or to prevent it if such infringement should be in prospect, the three Courts will inform Turkey that they would regard her, in that event, as putting herself in a state of war towards the injured Party, and as having deprived herself thenceforth of the benefits of the security assured to her territorial status quo by the Treaty of Berlin.

ART. IV. The present Treaty shall be in force during a period of three years, dating from the day of the exchange of ratifications.

ART. V. The High Contracting Parties mutually promise secrecy as to the contents and the existence of the present Treaty, as well as of the Protocol annexed thereto.

ART. VI. The secret Conventions concluded between Austria-Hungary and Russia and between Germany and Russia in 1873 are replaced by the present Treaty.

ART. VII. The ratifications of the present Treaty and of the Protocol annexed thereto shall be exchanged at Berlin within a fortnight, or sooner if may be.

In witness whereof the respective Plenipotentiaries have signed the present Treaty and have affixed thereto the seal of their arms.

Done at Berlin, the eighteenth day of the month of June, one thousand eight hundred and eighty-one.

(L.S.)   SZÉCHÉNYI.
(L.S.)   v. BISMARCK.
(L.S.)   SABOUROFF.

Separate Protocol on the same date to the Convention of Berlin. June 18, 1881.

The undersigned Plenipotentiaries of His Majesty the Emperor of Austria, King of Bohemia, etc., and Apostolic King of Hungary,

His Majesty the Emperor of Germany, King of Prussia, and

His Majesty the Emperor of All the Russias,

having recorded in accordance with Article II of the secret Treaty concluded today the points affecting the interests of the three Courts of Austria-Hungary, Germany, and Russia in the Balkan Peninsula upon which an understanding has already been reached among them, have agreed to the following Protocol:

1. BOSNIA AND HERZEGOVINA.

Austria-Hungary reserves the right to annex these provinces at whatever moment she shall deem opportune.

2. SANJAK OF NOVIBAZAR.

The Declaration exchanged between the Austro-Hungarian Plenipotentiaries and the Russian Plenipotentiaries at the Congress of Berlin under date of July 13/1, 1878, remains in force.

3. EASTERN RUMELIA.

The three Powers agree in regarding the eventuality of an occupation either of Eastern Rumelia or of the Balkans as full of perils for the general peace. In case this should occur, they will employ their efforts to dissuade the Porte from such an enterprise, it being well understood that Bulgaria and Eastern Rumelia on their part are to abstain from provoking the Porte by attacks emanating from their territories against the other provinces of the Ottoman Empire.

4. BULGARIA.

The three Powers will not oppose the eventual reunion of Bulgaria and Eastern Rumelia within the territorial limits asssigned to them by the Treaty of Berlin, if this question should come up by the force of circumstances. They agree to dissuade the Bulgarians from all aggression against the neighbouring provinces, particularly Macedonia; and to inform them that in such a case they would be acting at their own risk and peril.

5. ATTITUDE OF AGENTS IN THE EAST.

In order to avoid collisions of interests in the local questions which may arise, the three Courts will furnish their representatives and agents in the Orient with a general instruction, directing them to endeavour to smooth out their divergences by friendly explanations between themselves in each special case; and, in the cases where they do not succeed in doing so, to refer the matters to their Governments.

6.

The present Protocol forms an integral part of the secret Treaty signed on this day at Berlin, and shall have the same force and validity.

In witness whereof the respective Plenipotentiaries have signed it and have affixed thereto the seal of their arms.

Done at Berlin, June 18, 1881.

(L.S.)	SZÉCHÉNYI.
(L.S.)	v. BISMARCK.
(L.S.)	SABOUROFF.

Additional Protocol to the Convention of June 18, 1881. *Berlin, June* 27, 1881.

In order to define still more precisely Paragraph 5 of the Protocol annexed to the secret Treaty of June 18, 1881, the undersigned Plenipotentiaries of His Majesty the Emperor of Austria, King of Hungary, and of His Majesty the Emperor of All the Russias declare that the 'local questions' mentioned in the said paragraph do not comprise affairs specially and exclusively interesting either Austria-Hungary or Russia, such as the protection of the respective nationals, commercial questions, claims, rights derived from treaties, etc.

It is understood that friendly co-operation, without being obligatory, may also be asked and accorded reciprocally by the agents of the two States in questions which do not fall under Paragraph 5 of the Protocol.

Berlin, June 27, 1881.

SZÉCHÉNYI.   SABOUROFF.

Procès-verbal of the exchange of ratifications of the Convention of June 18, 1871. *Berlin, June* 27, 1881.

PROCÈS-VERBAL.

On June 27, 1881, the undersigned met together at the Ministry of Foreign Affairs at Berlin for the purpose of proceeding with the exchange of ratifications of the secret Treaty and of the Protocol thereto annexed, signed at Berlin, June 18, 1881, by the Plenipotentiaries of His Majesty the Emperor of Austria, King of Bohemia, and Apostolic King of Hungary, of His Majesty the Emperor of Germany, King of Prussia, and of His Majesty the Emperor of All the Russias. The six instruments having been produced, the undersigned have found the following errata:

1. In the German copy intended for Russia, the alternat has not been observed.

2. In the Austrian copy intended for Germany, the word "between" has been omitted at the end of the first line of the second paragraph of Article I of the Treaty.

3. In the German copy intended for Russia, the word "divergence" in Article V of the Protocol is written "divergeance".

4. In the Austrian copy intended for Russia, in the second line of the preamble of the Treaty ,the word "animated" is written in the masculine.

In other respects, the undersigned after examination have found the instruments in good and due form and have effected the exchange.

In witness whereof the undersigned have drawn up the present Procès-verbal and have affixed their signatures and the seal of their arms.

Done at the Ministry of Foreign Affairs at Berlin, June 27, 1881.

(L.S.)	SZÉCHÉNYI.
(L.S.)	BUSCH.
(L.S.)	SABOUROFF.

122

CONVENTION between Greece and Turkey, for the Settlement of the Frontier. Signed at Constantinople, 2nd July, 1881.

IN execution of Article XVIII of the Convention concluded the 24th May, 1881, between the Sublime Porte and the Representatives of the Powers co-signataries of the Treaty of Berlin, their Majesties the King of the Hellenes and the Emperor of the Ottomans having agreed to conclude an Act reproducing textually the said Convention, have nominated for that purpose:—

His Majesty the King of the Hellenes, le Sieur A. G. Coundourioti, his Envoy Extraordinary and Minister Plenipotentiary near His Majesty the Emperor of the Ottomans; and

His Majesty the Emperor of the Ottomans, Mahmoud Server Pacha, President of his Council of State;

Who, furnished with the necessary Powers, have agreed upon the following:

[Here follows the Convention with the Annex, which Documents are substantially the same as those which were signed at Constantinople on the 24th May, 1881, between Great Britain, Austria-Hungary, France, Germany, Italy, Russia, and Turkey.

Done at Constantinople, the 2nd day of July (N.S.), 1881.

(L.S.)	A. G. COUNDOURIOTI.
(L.S.)	SERVER.

123

CONVENTION between Russia and Turkey, for the Settlement of the Russian War Indemnity. Signed at Constantinople, 14th May, 1882. Ratifications exchanged at St. Petersburgh, 30th June/12th July, 1882.

HIS Majesty the Emperor of the Ottomans, and His Majesty the Emperor of All the Russias wishing, in execution of Article IV of the Treaty signed between Turkey and Russia on the 27th January/8th February, 1879, to regulate definitively by a Convention the mode of payment of the Russian War indemnity, and the guarantee to be assigned to it, have named for their Plenipotentiaries:

His Majesty the Emperor of the Ottomans, on the one part, Mehemmed Assim Pasha, his Muchir, &c.; and Mahmoud Server Pasha, his Muchir, &c.;

His Majesty the Emperor of All the Russias, on the other part, le Sieur Eugène Novikow, his Ambassador Extraordinary and Plenipotentiary to his Imperial Majesty the Sultan, Privy Councillor, &c.; and le Sieur Theodore de Thœrner, Member of the Council and of the Ministry of Finance, and Director of the Department of the Treasury of the Empire, Privy Councillor, &c.; who, after having communicated to each other their Powers, have agreed upon the following Articles:—

ART. I. The sum of 802,500,000 fr. which, according to Article IV of the said Treaty, constitutes the amount of the indemnity of the Russian War, shall be paid by the Ottoman Government by means of annual instalments of £T.350,000. It is agreed that this sum of £T.350,000 shall be entirely appropriated to the reduction of the capital of the War Indemnity.

In compliance with the wish of the Ottoman Government, the Russian Government, at the same time, consents not to claim interest upon the said capital.

ART. II. The Ottoman Government declares that the stipulated annuity of £T.350,000 shall be specially derived from the tithe and sheep tax.

ART. III. The tithes and the sheep tax appropriated to the payment of the War Indemnity shall be assigned on those vilayets or mutessarifliks in which the Imperial Ottoman Bank possesses branches or agents.

ART. IV. The sums thus assigned to the payment of the War Indemnity in each vilayet or mutessariflik should be 25 per cent. less than the total of the produce of the said taxes in the said localities.

ART. V. The produce of the net total of the said taxes in the vilayets and mutessarifliks alluded to, that is to say, the sum which shall remain after the deduction of the expenses of the collection of the taxes, shall be deposited directly and in full by the local authority charged with the collection of the taxes in the said vilayets or mutessarifliks into the *caisses* of the Imperial Ottoman Bank, or to the agent of the said bank, in virtue of a special and permanent order sanctioned by Imperial Iradé. Nevertheless, if the revenues derived from the sheep and tithe taxes appropriated to the War Indemnity should happen to produce a surplus over and above the 25 per cent. granted, in that case the Imperial Ottoman Bank shall be compelled to hand over to the Ministry of Finance of the cazas, the revenues of which derived from the sheep tax and the tithe ought to be equal, the eventual surplus mentioned above.

If, on the other hand, these said revenues should suffer so great a falling off that the surplus of 25 per cent, could not be realized, then the Ottoman Minister of Finance engages to assign to the Imperial Ottoman Bank new cazas, the revenues of which derived from the tithes and sheep taxes shall suffice to complete the deficit in question.

ART. VI. The Imperial Ottoman Bank shall be bound to make a special arrangement with the Imperial Russian Bank for the operations of the Ottoman Bank at Constantinople respecting the payment of the War Indemnity.

ART. VII. The Director of the Imperial Ottoman Bank shall be obliged, after the signature of the Convention, to retain immediately, in proportion to the receipts from the sheep tax and tithes, the sum assigned for the Russian War indemnity; and he shall hold immediately at the disposal of the local administration the whole surplus of each vilayet, after the part which is due for payment for the War Indemnity shall have been deducted and put aside to be placed to the account of the Imperial Russian Bank.

ART. VIII. The Imperial Ottoman Government engages itself to prohibit its Minister of Finance, as well as the administration of the vilayets or of the mutessarifliks, to issue "havales," cheques, or other orders for payment on the sheep tax and on the tithes thus assigned in the localities indicated.

ART. IX. According to the arrangement thus entered into, the share of the sheep tax and of the titles assigned to the payment of the Russian Indemnity, shall only appear in the Ottoman Budget under the title of Receipts and Expenses ("Irad masraf").

ART. X. In consequence of Articles III and IV of the present Convention, the revenues indicated below of the vilayets of Aleppo, Konich, Castamouni, Adana, and Sivas shall be assigned for the payment of the stipulated annuities from which revenues the expenses attending the collection of taxes have already been deducted.

Net Revenues.

	Sheep Tax.	Tithes.	Total.
	£T.	£T.	£T.
Aleppo	40,000	..	40,000
Konich	..	138,000	138,000
Castamouni	..	110,000	110,000
Adana	..	70,000	70,000
Sivas:— £T.			
Sandjak of Sivas .. 55,000			
Sandjak of Tokad .. 20,000			
Sandjak of Kara Hissar Charki:—			
Caza de Kara Hissar ⎫			
Caza de Sou Chekri ⎭ 4,500	..	79,500	79,500
79,500			
	40,000	397,500	437,500

Of this total £T.350,000 represents the amount of the annual payment, and the remainder the supplementary guarantee of 25 per cent., in accordance with Articles V and VIII of the present Convention.

ART. XI. The Imperial Ottoman Government reserves to itself the right to substitute, in case of necessity, other localities for the localities designated, after a previous understanding with the Imperial Ottoman Bank, upon the securities for the same payments.

Official announcement shall immediately be given to the Imperial Russian Government.

ART. XII. The present Act shall be ratified, and the ratifications shall be exchanged at St. Petersburg in the space of two weeks, or sooner if possible.

In faith of which the Plenipotentiaries of Turkey and Russia have affixed their signatures and the seal of their arms.

Done at Constantinople, the 25th Dzemazi-ul-Akhiré, 1299, 2/14th May, 1882.

(L.S.) M. ASSIM.   (L.S.) NOVIKOW.

(L.S.) SERVER.   (L.S.) THŒRNER.

124

First Treaty of Triple Alliance between Austria-Hungary, Germany, and Italy. Vienna, 20th May, 1882. Ratifications exchanged, 30th May, 1882.

Their Majesties the Emperor of Austria, King of Bohemia, etc., and Apostolic King of Hungary, the Emperor of Germany, King of Prussia, and the King of Italy, animated by the desire to increase the guaranties of the general peace, to fortify the monarchical principle and thereby to assure the unimpaired maintenance of the social and political order in Their respective States, have agreed to conclude a Treaty which, by its essentially conservative and defensive nature, pursues only the aim of forestalling the dangers which might threaten the security of Their States and the peace of Europe.

To this end Their Majesties have appointed, to wit, His Majesty the Emperor of Austria, King of Bohemia, etc., and Apostolic King of Hungary,

Count Gustavus Kálnoky, General, His Minister of the Imperial Household and of Foreign Affairs:

His Majesty the Emperor of Germany, King of Prussia,

Prince Henry VII of Reuss, Aide-de-Camp General, His Ambassador Extraordinary and Plenipotentiary to His Imperial and Royal Apostolic Majesty,

His Majesty the King of Italy,

Count Charles Felix Nicolis de Robilant, Lieutenant-General, His Ambassador Extraordinary and Plenipotentiary to His Imperial and Royal Apostolic Majesty,

who, furnished with full powers, which have been found in good and due form, have agreed upon the following Articles:

ART. I. The High Contracting Parties mutually promise peace and friendship, and will enter into no alliance or engagement directed against any one of their States.

They engage to proceed to an exchange of ideas on political and economic questions of a general nature which may arise, and they further promise one another mutual support within the limits of their own interests.

ART. II. In case Italy, without direct provocation on her part, should be attacked by France for any reason whatsoever, the two other Contracting Parties shall be bound to lend help and assistance with all their forces to the Party attacked.

This same obligation shall devolve upon Italy in case of any aggression without direct provocation by France against Germany.

ART. III. If one, or two, of the High Contracting Parties, without direct provocation on their part, should chance to be attacked and to be engaged in a war with two or more Great Powers nonsignatory to the present Treaty, the *casus foederis* will arise simultaneously for all the High Contracting Parties.

ART. IV. In case a Great Power nonsignatory to the present Treaty should threaten the security of the states of one of the High Contracting Parties, and the threatened Party should find itself forced on that account to make war against it, the two others bind themselves to observe towards their Ally a benevolent neutrality. Each of them reserves to itself, in this case, the right to take part in the war, if it should see fit, to make common cause with its Ally.

ART. V. If the peace of any of the High Contracting Parties should chance to be threatened under the circumstances foreseen by the preceding Articles, the High Contracting Parties shall take counsel together in ample time as to the military measures to be taken with a view to eventual co-operation.

They engage henceforward, in all cases of common participation in a war, to conclude neither armistice, nor peace, nor treaty, except by common agreement among themselves.

ART. VI. The High Contracting Parties mutually promise secrecy as to the contents and existence of the present Treaty.

ART. VII. The present Treaty shall remain in force during the space of five years, dating from the day of the exchange of ratifications.

ART. VIII. The ratifications of the present Treaty shall be exchanged at Vienna within three weeks, or sooner if may be.

In witness whereof the respective Plenipotentiaries have signed the present Treaty and have affixed thereto the seal of their arms.

Done at Vienna, the twentieth day of the month of May of the year one thousand eight hundred and eighty-two.

KÁLNOKY.	H. VII OF REUSS.	C. ROBILANT.
(L.S.)	(L.S.)	(L.S.)

Additional Declaration of Italy that the provisions of the Alliance could not be regarded as directed against England. Rome, May 22, 1882.

MINISTERIAL DECLARATION.

The Royal Italian Government declares that the provisions of the secret Treaty concluded May 20, 1882, between Italy, Austria-Hungary, and Germany, cannot, as has been previously agreed, in any case be regarded as being directed against England.

In witness whereof the present ministerial Declaration, which equally must remain secret, has been drawn up to be exchanged against identic Declarations of the Imperial and Royal Government of Austria-Hungary and of the Imperial Government of Germany.

Rome, May 22, 1882.

The Royal Minister of Foreign Affairs.
(L.S.) MANCINI.

Declaration of Austria-Hungary similar to the Italian one.
Vienna, May 28, 1882.

MINISTERIAL DECLARATION.

The Imperial and Royal Government declares that the provisions of the secret Treaty concluded May 20, 1882, between Austria-Hungary, Germany, and Italy, cannot, as has been previously agreed, in any case be regarded as being directed against England.

In witness whereof the present ministerial Declaration, which equally must remain secret, has been drawn up to be exchanged against identic Declarations of the Imperial Government of Germany and of the Royal Government of Italy.

The Imperial and Royal Minister of Foreign Affairs.

Vienna, May 28, 1882.   (L.S.) KÁLNOKY.

Declaration of Germany similar to the Italian one. Berlin, May 28,
1882.

MINISTERIAL DECLARATION.

The Imperial Government declares that the provisions of the secret Treaty concluded May 20, 1882, between Germany, Austria-Hungary, and Italy, cannot, as has been previously agreed, in any case be regarded as being directed against England.

In witness whereof the present ministerial Declaration, which equally must remain secret, has been drawn up to be exchanged against identic Declarations of the Imperial and Royal Government of Austria-Hungary and of the Royal Government of Italy.

Berlin, May 28, 1882.

The Chancellor of the Empire.
(L.S.) V. BISMARCK.

125

SELF-DENYING PROTOCOL signed by the Representatives of Great Britain, Austria-Hungary, France, Germany, Italy, and Russia, with reference to the Affairs of Egypt. Therapia, 25th June, 1882.

THE Governments represented by the Undersigned engage themselves in any arrangement which may be made in consequence of their concerted action for the regulation of the affairs of Egypt, not to seek any territorial advantage, nor any concession of any exclusive privilege, nor any commercial advantage for their subjects other than those which any other nation can equally obtain.

DUFFERIN.
HIRSCHFELDT.
CALICE.
MARQUIS DE NOAILLES.
L. CORTI.
ONOU.

Therapia, June 25th, 1882.

126   TREATY OF LONDON

TREATY between Great Britain, Austria-Hungary, France, Germany, Italy, Russia, and Turkey, relative to the Navigation of the Danube. Signed at London, 10th March, 1883. Ratifications exchanged 21st and 24th August, and 25th October, 1883.

In the Name of Almighty God!

THE Signatory Powers of the Treaty of Berlin, having deemed it necessary to assemble their Plenipotentiaries in Conference at London, in order to come to an understanding as to the decisions to be taken in virtue of Article LIV of the Treaty of Berlin of the 13th July, 1878, and in respect of the execution of Article LV of the same Treaty, concerning the navigation of the Danube from the Iron Gates to its mouths, have appointed as their Plenipotentiaries, that is to say:

Her Majesty the Queen of the United Kingdom of Great Britain and Ireland, the Right Honourable Granville George, Earl Granville, K.G.; Her Majesty's Principal Secretary of State for Foreign Affairs, &c., &c.; and Lord Edmond George Petty Fitzmaurice, Member of Parliament of the United Kingdom, Under-Secretary of State for Foreign Affairs, &c., &c.;

His Majesty the Emperor of Germany, King of Prussia, George Herbert, Count Münster, his Ambassador Extraordinary and Plenipotentiary to Her Britannic Majesty;

His Majesty the Emperor of Austria, King of Bohemia, &c., and Apostolic King of Hungary, Louis, Count Károlyi of Nagy-Károly, his Ambassador Extraordinary to Her Britannic Majesty, &c., &c.;

The President of the French Republic, Charles Tissot, Ambassador of the French Republic to Her Britannic Majesty, &c., &c.; and Camille Barrère, Minister Plenipotentiary of the second class, French Delegate on the Danube Commission, &c.; &c.;

His Majesty the King of Italy, Count Constantine Nigra, his Ambassador Extraordinary and Plenipotentiary to Her Britannic Majesty, &c., &c.;

His Majesty the Emperor of All the Russias, Arthur, Baron Mohrenheim, his Ambassador Extraordinary and Plenipotentiary to Her Britannic Majesty, &c., &c.;

His Majesty the Emperor of the Ottomans, Constantine Musurus Pasha, Muchir and Vizier of the Empire, his Ambassador and Plenipotentiary to Her Britannic Majesty, &c., &c.;

Who, after exchanging their full powers, found in good and due form, have agreed on the following Articles:—

Extension of European Commission to Ibraïla.

Art. I. The jurisdiction of the European Commission of the Danube is extended from Galatz to Ibraïla.

Prolongation of Powers of European Commission.

Art. II. The powers of the European Commission are prolonged for a period of 21 years, dating from the 24th April, 1883.

Duration of European Commission.

At the expiration of the said period, the powers of the said Commission shall continue in force by tacit prolongation ("tacite réconduction") for successive terms of three years, unless one of the High Contracting Parties should notify, one year before the expiration of one of these terms of three years, the intention of proposing modifications in the constitution or in the powers of the Commission.

Non-control of Commission over certain Portions of Kilia Branch.

Art. III. The European Commission shall exercise no effective control over those portions of the Kilia branch of which both banks belong to one of the Riverain States of that branch.

Kilia Branch, between Russia and Roumania. Regulations for Management.

Art. IV. With regard to that portion of the Kilia branch which flows between Russian and Roumanian territory, and in order to insure uniformity in the management of the Lower Danube, the regulations in force on the Sulina branch shall be applied under the superintendence of the Russian and Roumanian Delegates of the European Commission.

Kilia Branch.   Works undertaken by Russia or Roumania.

ART. V. In case Russia or Roumania should undertake works in the Kilia branch, either in the part which divides their respective territories, or that which flows exclusively within the territories of either of them, the competent authority shall communicate the plans of these works to the European Commission with the sole view of establishing that they do not interfere in any way with the navigable state of the other branches.

Tchatal of Ismaïl.

The works which have already been carried out at the Tchatal of Ismaïl, remain at the charge and under the control of the European Commission of the Danube.

Plans of New Works.

Should there be a difference of opinion between the Russian or Roumanian authorities and the European Commission respecting the plans of works to be undertaken in the Kilia branch, or a difference of opinion in that Commission respecting any extension that it might be advisable to make in the works at the Tchatal of Ismaïl, the case shall be submitted directly to the Powers.

Understanding with Russia as to Tolls to be levied on Sulina or Kilia Branch.

ART. VI. It is understood that there shall be no restriction upon the right of Russia to levy tolls intended to cover the expenses of the works undertaken by her.

Nevertheless, with the view of providing a safeguard for the reciprocal interests of the navigation on the Sulina branch and on the Kilia branch, the Russian Government shall put the Governments represented in the European Commission in possession of the Regulations respecting the tolls which they may think it advisable to introduce, so as to insure an understanding on the subject.

Regulations for Navigation, Police, &c., between Iron Gates and Ibraïla.

ART. VII. The Regulations for navigation, river police, and superintendence drawn up on the 2nd June, 1882, by the European Commission of the Danube, assisted by the Delegates of Servia and Bulgaria, are adopted in the form annexed to the present Treaty, and declared applicable to that part of the Danube which is situated between the Iron Gates and Ibraïla.

Confirmations of former Treaties and Acts.

ART. VIII. All the Treaties, Conventions, Acts, and arrangements relating to the Danube and its mouths are maintained in all such of their provisions as are not abrogated or modified by the preceding stipulations.

Ratifications.

ART. IX. The present Treaty shall be ratified, and the ratifications exchanged at London, within the space of six months, or sooner if possible.

A Declaration was signed on the 23rd April, 1883, for the maintenance of the European Commission of the Danube between the 24th April, 1883, and the date of the exchange of the ratifications of this Treaty.

In faith whereof the respective Plenipotentiaries have signed it, and affixed to it the seal of their arms.

Done at London, the 10th day of March, 1883.

(L.S.) GRANVILLE.

E. FITZMAURICE.

(L.S.) MÜNSTER.

(L.S.) KÁROLYI.

(L.S.) CH. TISSOT.

(L.S.) C. BARRÈRE.

(L.S.) NIGRA.

(L.S.) MOHRENHEIM.

(L.S.) MUSURUS.

ANNEX TO TREATY OF 10TH MARCH, 1883.

Regulations for the Navigation, River Police, and Superintendence, applicable to that part of the Danube which is situated between the Iron Gates and Ibraïla.

I.—GENERAL ADMINISTRATION OF THE NAVIGATION.

Free Navigation between Ibraïla and the Iron Gates.

ART. I. The navigation shall continue to be entirely free on the whole portion of the Danube, comprised between Ibraïla and the Iron Gates. Merchant vessels of all nations shall freely carry on there, as in the past, the transport of passengers and goods, and towage, under the conditions of perfect equality stipulated for by the XVIth Article of the treaty of Paris.

Tolls and Dues.

ART. II. No toll shall be levied on the Danube based solely on the fact of the navigation of the river, nor any dues on goods, so long as they remain on board vessels, transports, or rafts.

Port Dues.

ART. III. The Riverain States have a right to levy in their respective ports, dues in respect of quays, cranes, scales, magazine, and discharging, on account of existing establishments and of such as may be formed in future.

Nevertheless, these dues must be levied without distinction, in accordance with fixed and published rates, irrespective of the places from which the vessels and their cargoes arrive, and only so far as the vessels subject to these dues shall have made use of the said establishments.

It is well understood that the tariffs of these dues are not to form a source of revenue, but that they shall produce only a sum sufficient for the payment of the interest and sinking fund of the capital expended, and for the maintenance of these establishments. As soon as the capital sum has been paid off, the dues shall only be sufficient to cover the expenses of maintenance.

ART. IV. *Construction of Bridges.*

ART. V. *Mills, Fishing Establishments and Irrigation Wheels.*

Customs Limits.

ART. VI. The Customs limits follow throughout the banks of the river, without ever crossing it. Accordingly, vessels, transports, rafts, &c., so long as they are navigating or at anchor in the bed of the river, without carrying on any commercial operation with the bank, are entirely outside the action of custom-houses.

Customs Dues on Goods Discharged on Banks.

Consequently, the Riverain States can only levy customs dues in respect of goods discharged on the banks, and this prohibition applies also to vessels, transports, or rafts traversing the sections of a river where both banks belong to the same State.

Free Transit of Goods.   Custom-House Officers.

ART. VII. Transit is absolutely free for the goods of all nations, whatever be their origin or destination. When a vessel, transport, or raft traverses a section of the river where both banks belong to the same

State, the captains or masters cannot be subjected to other formalities, as regards goods in transit, than the affixing of seals or the superintendence of a Custom-house officer, up to the point where the two banks, or one of them, cease to belong to that State. The Custom-house officer, during the time he remains on board, has a right to food, firing, and lighting on the same footing as the crew, but to no other remuneration whatever. The vessel shall be bound to give a free passage to the said Custom-house officer, without food or other expenses, at least as far as the last national port at which it shall touch on its return journey.

Ships' Papers.

ART. VIII. Sea-going vessels cannot be called upon to produce other documents than their ship's papers. River boats or transports must be furnished with the documents granted by the authority to whom they are subordinated, and necessary to prove the name, nationality, and capacity of the boat or transport and the identity of the captain or master and of the crew.

Coasting and Port to Port Trades.

It is understood that no other modification shall be introduced into the conditions under which the coasting and port to port trades are now carried on without distinction of flag.

Small Craft and Fishing Boats.

Small craft and fishing boats are not obliged to take out the documents mentioned in the present Article; the masters and crews of these boats are bound to provide themselves merely with the documents necessary to prove their identity when they wish to come alongside a bank lying in a foreign country. But it must be understood that this provision does not affect the laws and regulations relative to the exercise of fishing rights in each of the Riverain States.

Towing-Paths.

ART. IX. No mill or other establishment, no new building nor reservoir, shall be constructed in such a manner as to interrupt the circulation on existing towing-paths, and those paths shall be kept in proper order.

The same rules shall be applied to towing-paths newly constructed and to prolongations of those which now exist.

Quarantine. Bills of Health.

ART. X. The Regulations respecting quarantine shall be framed in such a manner as to conciliate the guarantees in respect of health with the requirements of maritime and river trade.

It is expressly understood that these measures shall be exclusively applicable to vessels and passengers with foul bills of health, and in ports which the contagion has not reached, and that all exceptional and restrictive measures shall be suppressed in respect of intercourse between the ports of the river so soon as an epidemic has become general along its banks.

As a general rule, so long as it is not established that an epidemic prevails, either above the Iron Gates or below Ibraïla, vessels shall be free from all sanitary control while navigating between Ibraïla and the Iron Gates, whether they be ascending or descending the river.

If an epidemic break out in a maritime port, every vessel arriving from the sea, and which has obtained a clean bill of health at Sulina, at Kilia, or at St. George, shall be free of all formalities except the visit of the sanitary officers, and of all quarantine for purposes of observation, in respect of the whole course of its voyage up the river as far as the Iron Gates.

If an epidemic were to break out on the banks of the river, above the Iron Gates or below Ibraïla, a clean bill of health obtained by vessels in the course of navigation, at the first uncontaminated river port at which they shall have touched between the Iron Gates and Ibraïla, shall be sufficient to insure them free access to all the other ports situated on this part of the river.

Finally, if an epidemic were to break out on the banks of this same portion of the river, sea-going vessels, as well as river boats, shall continue to carry on their operations in full liberty, so long as they have not touched at any of the contaminated ports. They shall simply be bound to produce their bill of health in the ports where they cast anchor.

River Police.

In order to facilitate the maintenance of the river police during an epidemic, the Inspector of the Navigation, the Sub-Inspectors, and the other officers set over the police, shall continue to move about freely for the requirements of their service, on the sole condition that, in case of suspicion, they submit to the measures provided by the Regulations to which the Health Officers are subject.

II.—POLICE.
Chapter I.—*General Provisions.*

ART. XI. *Merchant Steamers. Duty towards Inspectors, &c.*

Service Boats. Flag.
ART. XII. The service-boats of the authority intrusted with the execution of the Regulations shall carry a flag identical with that of the

European Commission, with the exception of the letters on the blue band of this flag, which letters shall be determined hereafter.

ART. XIII. *Duty of Captains and Crews towards Inspectors, &c.*

ART. XIV. *Measurement of rise and fall of Waters in the River.*

ART. XV. *Jurisdiction in respect of Differences between Captains and Crews.*

ART. XVI. *Stranding of Vessels. Wrecks and Salvage.*

ART. XVII. *Marking of Places, &c., at which Vessels are forbidden to anchor.*

ART. XVIII. *Vessels anchored or moored to the Bank. Dangers to Navigation.*

Chapter 2.—*Rules for Vessels crossing or passing one another. Tugs, &c.*
ARTS. XIX—XXVII.

Chapter 3.—*Rules relative to Tracking from the Banks.*
ARTS. XXVIII—XXX.

Chapter 4.—*Rules for Navigation at Night or in a Fog.*
ARTS. XXXI—XXXIII.

Chapter 5.—*Rules for Vessels at Anchor.*
ARTS. XXXIV—XXXIX.

Chapter 6.—*Rules in respect of cases of Stranding and Shipwreck.*
ARTS. XL—XLV.

Chapter 7.—*Rules for the Discharge of Ballast.*
ARTS. XLVI—XLVII.

Chapter 8.—*On the Lighterage of the River Trade.*
ART. XLVIII.

Chapter 9.—*On Towage.*
ARTS. XLIX—LII.

Chapter 10.—*On the Police of the Ports.*
ARTS. LIII—LXV.

Chapter 11.—*On Pilotage in the River.*
ARTS. LXVI—LXXI.

Chapter 12.—*Of Offences.*
SECTION (A).—ASSESSMENT OF FINES.
1. *Offences against the General Administration of the Navigation.*
ART. LXXII.

2. *Offences in respect of the River Police.*
ARTS. LXXIII—LXXX.

3. *Offences in respect of the Police of the Ports.*
ARTS. LXXXI—LXXXV.

4. *Offences committed by Licensed Pilots.*
ART. LXXXVI.

5. *Abusive Language and Assaults.*
ART. LXXXVII.

SECTION (B).—RULES FOR THE INFLICTION OF FINES.

ARTS. LXXXVIII—XCV.

III.—EXECUTION AND SUPERINTENDENCE OF THE REGULATIONS BY "MIXED COMMISSION OF THE DANUBE."

Constitution of Mixed Austro-Hungarian, Bulgarian, Roumanian, and Servian Commission.
ART. XCVI. The execution of the present Regulations is placed under the authority of a Commission called the "Mixed Commission of the Danube," in which Austria-Hungary, Bulgaria, Roumania, and Servia shall each be represented by one Delegate.

Presidency.
The presidency of this Commission shall devolve on the Delegate of Austria-Hungary.

Participation of a Member of the European Commission in Work of Mixed Commission.
A member of the European Commission of the Danube, appointed for a period of six months, according to the alphabetical order of the States, shall take part in the work of the Mixed Commission, and shall enjoy, during this time, all the rights that appertain to the other members of the Commission.

The States that are already represented on the Mixed Commission shall not be included in the alphabetical roster above alluded to.

In order that the member of the European Commission may be in a position to take part in the deliberations of the Mixed Commission, the latter shall send him a statement of the proposed work one month before the opening of each session.

The European Commission may, when they consider it advisable, require, through the medium of their member, information from the Mixed Commission respecting such of the decisions of that Commission as may affect liberty of navigation.

Powers of Mixed Commission.

ART. XCVII. The powers of the Mixed Commission shall have a duration equal to those of the European Commission, and the constitution and powers of the Mixed Commission shall, in case of need, be modified in any way that may become necessary with the reservation of the coexistence of the two Commissions.

Sittings of Mixed Commission.

ART. XCVIII. The Mixed Commission shall hold two ordinary sessions every year, the dates of which shall be fixed in such a manner as to avoid the Mixed Commission and the European Commission meeting simultaneously.

Decisions by a Majority.

Their decisions shall be arrived at by a majority of votes.

They shall themselves decide upon the interior Regulations regarding the order of their work; as also upon the special instructions to be addressed to their officers in respect of the working of the present Regulations on such points as have not been determined by the Regulations themselves. The Commission shall in their first session proceed to appoint the officers mentioned in Article CI under the Nos. 1, 2, and 4.

Nevertheless, the interior Regulations and the instructions of a general character and of the nature of Regulations (such, for instance, as those treated in Article IX of the Public Act of the 2nd November, 1865, relative to the navigation at the mouths of the Danube) shall be previously communicated to the European Commission, and shall not be put in force till that Commission is satisfied that they are framed in accordance with the principles which have formed the basis of the present Regulations.

Cost of Administration.

ART. XCIX. The cost of administration shall be at the charge of the

States represented in the Mixed Commission. They shall contribute in the following proportions:—

Austria-Hungary, four-tenths; Roumania, four-tenths; Bulgaria and Servia, each one-tenth.

At the second ordinary meeting the Mixed Commission will fix its budget for the following year.

The contributions of the different States shall be made half-yearly in advance. Fines levied in respect of offences against the present Regulations shall go into the cash-chest of the Mixed Commission, to be applied to the requirements of the service.

Officers.

ART. C. The officers mentioned below shall perform their duties, each within the limits assigned to him, under the orders of the Mixed Commission, that is to say:—

1. An Inspector.

2. Sub-Inspectors.

3. Harbour-masters, in so far as their duties are connected with the river-way.

4. A Secretary and subordinate officers.

ART. CI. The officers mentioned in the preceding Article shall be chosen from among competent persons. They shall be appointed and paid as follows:—

The Inspector, as well as the Secretary and subordinate officers, shall be appointed and paid by the Mixed Commission.

The Sub-Inspectors and Harbour-masters shall be appointed and paid by the respective Riverain States, who will inform the Mixed Commission of their appointment or of their being replaced.

The above-mentioned officers, with the exception of the Sub-Inspectors and Harbour-masters, may be dismissed by the Mixed Commission.

ART. CII. The Inspector, being in charge of the management, must see that the provisions of the present Regulations are strictly observed, and that they are uniformly applied.

In this respect he is considered as the immediate superior of the Sub-Inspectors and Harbour-masters.

Division of the River between Iron Gates and Ibraïla into Sections.

ART. CIII. The left bank of the Danube between the Iron Gates and Ibraïla shall be divided into four sections for the purposes of inspection.

The first shall extend from the Iron Gates to Beket inclusive.

The second from Beket to Simnitza inclusive.

The third from Simnitza to Calarash-Silistria.

The fourth, which includes both banks of the river, from Calarash-Silistria to Ibraïla, exclusive of this last port.

The right bank shall be divided into three sections, of which—

The first shall extend from the Iron Gates to the mouth of the Timok;

The second, from the Timok to Nicopolis, inclusive;

The third, from Nicopolis to Silistria, inclusive.

The residence of each of the Sub-Inspectors shall at a future date be fixed by the Riverain States, in concert with the Mixed Commission.

ART. CIV. The Riverain States will give the Mixed Commission and its officers all the assistance they may require in the execution of their task.

Ports or Trading Places.

ART. CV. The ports or trading places which are situated within the limits of each of the sections of the river, and for which the Riverain States shall have appointed Harbour-masters, in conformity with the provisions of the present Regulations, shall not be comprised within the jurisdiction of the Sub-Inspectors of the section. These ports or trading places shall be placed under the superintendence of the Harbour-masters, who, in so far as their action on the river way is concerned, are subordinate to the Inspector, and must obey his instructions.

For the purposes of the present Regulations, the word "port" shall be held to apply to all that part of the river which is comprised between two straight lines drawn at right angles to the bank at the upper and lower boundaries of the said ports or trading places and carried out to the mid-channel.

If the opposite bank belongs to the same State, the port shall be held to comprise also that part of the river situated beyond the mid-channel, between two lines carried across to the said bank, always provided that on the said bank there is not a port or trading place for which a separate Harbour-master has been appointed.

Vessels traversing the waters of a port in the course of navigation without stopping at this port, are not subject to the jurisdiction of the Harbour-masters; the Inspector and the Sub-Inspectors are alone competent to take action in respect of such vessels.

Judicial Police.

ART. CVI. The special prerogatives of the judicial police of the river shall be exercised by the Sub-Inspectors and the Harbour-masters, each within the district assigned to him for superintendence, and appeals shall lie to the Mixed Commission, whose decisions are final.

If, in the exercise of their duties, Sub-Inspectors become aware of offences committed beyond the limits of their district, they shall take note of these offences and report them to the competent Sub-Inspector.

Meetings to be held at Giurgevo.
ART. CVII. The Mixed Commission shall sit at Giurgevo.

Modification of Articles.
ART. CVIII. Articles I, II, III, VI, VII, VIII, IX, and X, as well as Articles XCVI to CVIII inclusive, can only be modified by Agreement between the Powers interested. The other Articles cannot be modified by the Mixed Commission without the consent of the European Commission of the Danube.

PROTOCOL. *Exchange of Ratifications. Great Britain and Germany, &c. London, 21st August,* 1883.
THE Signatory Powers of the Treaty signed at London the 10th March, 1883, relative to the navigation of the Danube, having agreed that the exchange of the ratifications of the said Treaty should be effected at London by means of a single instrument by each Power, the Undersigned, duly authorized to that effect, met at the Foreign Office to deposit the said ratifications.

The said ratifications were produced by the Representatives of Her Majesty the Queen of the United Kingdom of Great Britain and Ireland, &c., and of His Majesty the German Emperor, King of Prussia, &c.

And having been examined and found in good and due form and correct, the deposition of these instruments was duly recorded.

In faith whereof the Undersigned have signed the present Protocol, and have affixed thereto the Seal of their Arms.

Done at London, the 21st August, 1883.

           (L.S.)   GRANVILLE.
                     EDMOND FITZMAURICE.
           (L.S.)   L. PLESSEN.

PROTOCOL. *Exchange of Ratifications. Great Britain and Russia. Russian Reservation;—Relations between Bulgaria and Turkey. London, 24th August,* 1883.
THE Signatory Powers of the Treaty signed at London the 10th March, 1883, relative to the navigation of the Danube, having agreed that the exchange of the ratifications of the said Treaty should be effected at London by means of a single instrument by each Power, the Undersigned, duly authorised to that effect, met at the Foreign Office to deposit the said ratifications.

The said ratifications were produced by the Representatives of

Her Majesty the Queen of the United Kingdom of Great Britain and Ireland, &c., and of His Majesty the Emperor of All the Russias, &c.

And having been examined and found in due form and correct, the deposition of these instruments was duly recorded.

Before proceeding to the exchange of ratifications, the Representative of His Majesty, the Emperor of All the Russias, made the following declaration:—

"Considering that the question treated by the Conference at its meeting of the 7th March, concerning the relations between the Principality of Bulgaria and the Suzerain Power, does not come within the programme of the three points which alone were brought before that Assembly, and of which alone it was called upon to take cognizance, the Imperial Government of Russia cannot recognise as obligatory the conclusions which the Conference has thought itself enabled to draw up in this respect beyond the limits of its legal competence; and the Russian Government continues, in consequence, to regard the question as an open one, reserving explicitly to itself full and entire liberty of opinion upon the principle involved therein."

The Representative of Her Majesty the Queen of the United Kingdom of Great Britain and Ireland, President of the Conference, whilst stating that he had nothing to add upon this subject to the observations made by him at the meeting of the 7th March, took note of the Reserve expressed by the Representative of Russia, which is inserted in the present Protocol, engaging to bring it to the knowledge of the other Signatory Powers of the Treaty.

In faith whereof the Undersigned have signed the present Protocol, and have affixed thereto the Seal of their Arms.

Done at London, the 24th August, 1883.

(L.S.)   GRANVILLE.
        EDMOND FITZMAURICE.

(L.S.)   MOHRENHEIM.

PROTOCOL. *Exchange of Ratifications. Great Britain and Turkey. Turkish Reservation;—Nomination of Bulgarian Delegate to Mixed Commission. London, 25th October, 1883.*

THE Signatory Powers of the Treaty signed at London the 10th March, 1883, relative to the navigation of the Danube, having agreed that the exchange of the ratifications of the said Treaty should be effected at London by means of a single instrument by each Power, the Undersigned, duly authorized to that effect, met at the Foreign Office to deposit the said ratifications.

The said ratifications were produced by the Representatives of Her

Majesty the Queen of the United Kingdom of Great Britain and Ireland, &c., and of His Majesty the Emperor of the Ottomans, &c.

And having been examined and found in good and due form and correct, the deposition of these instruments was duly recorded.

Before proceeding to the exchange of the ratifications, the Representative of His Majesty the Emperor of the Ottomans made the following declaration:—

"Considering that the Conference lately assembled at London was competent to pronounce upon the Reserves of the Sublime Porte concerning the nomination of the Bulgarian Delegate to the Mixed Commission, from the fact that that question, inseparable from the Regulations drawn up at Galatz, and which instituted the said Commission, came within the programme of the three points of which the Commission was called upon to take cognizance, and of which the second had for its object the confirmation of the aforesaid Regulations; considering, consequently, that the opinion of the Imperial Government of Russia, expressed in the Declaration inserted in the Protocol of the 24th August last, recording the exchange of the ratifications of the Treaty of the 10th March between Great Britain and Russia, cannot in anywise invalidate the competence of the Conference in this respect, the Sublime Porte declares that it understands that the ratification of the said Treaty by the High Contracting Parties implies that of the right, recognised as appertaining to the Sublime Porte by the Conference at its meeting of the 7th March, of approving the nomination of the Bulgarian Delegate to the Mixed Commission, a right the insertion of which in the Protocol of that meeting has, according to the unanimous declaration of the Conference, the same efficacy as if it formed part of the Treaty itself; and that thenceforward the Sublime Porte maintains, as a consequence of the sanction given to that Treaty by His Imperial Majesty the Sultan, that the Bulgarian Delegate, whose nomination will be approved by the Sublime Porte, shall represent the Ottoman Empire upon the Mixed Commission, and shall duly keep the Imperial Government informed of the acts and deliberations of that Commission, his vote being decisive only in so far as it is in conformity with the instructions, and meets with the approbation of the Sublime Porte."

The Representative of Her Majesty the Queen of the United Kingdom of Great Britain and Ireland, President of the Conference, whilst stating that he had nothing to add upon this subject to the observations made by him at the meeting of the 7th March, took note of the Reserve expressed by the Representative of His Majesty the Emperor of the Ottomans, which is inserted in the present Protocol, engaging to bring it to the knowledge of the other Signatory Powers of the Treaty.

In faith whereof the Undersigned have signed the present Protocol, and have affixed thereto the Seal of their Arms.

Done at London, the 25th October, 1883.

(L.S.) GRANVILLE.

EDMOND FITZMAURICE.

(L.S.) MUSURUS.

127

PROTOCOL between Austria-Hungary and Germany in regard to the prolongation of the Austro-German Alliance of 1879. Vienna, 22nd March, 1883. Ratifications exchanged 1st April, 1883.

PROTOCOL.

The undersigned, Count Kálnoky of Körös-Patak, Minister of the Imperial Household and of Foreign Affairs of His Imperial and Royal Apostolic Majesty, and Prince Henry VII of Reuss, Ambassador Extraordinary and Plenipotentiary of His Majesty the German Emperor, have, by virtue of Most Exalted authorization, met this day in Vienna to take counsel concerning the prolongation of the secret Treaty, signed in the same place on October 7, 1879, and ratified on the 21st day of the same month, between Their Majesties the Emperor of Austria, King of Hungary, and the German Emperor, King of Prussia, and, by plenipotentiary authority from Their Majesties, have agreed upon the following:

1. The Treaty designated above shall be prolonged for five years, dating from October 21, 1884, to October 21, 1889.

2. Article III shall moreover be so modified that the two High Contracting Parties are to enter into negotiations not one year, but two years, before October 21, 1889, with regard to the question whether the conditions serving as a basis to the Treaty still prevail, and that the Treaty shall be considered as renewed for a further period of three years if, in the course of the first month of the next to last year of the Treaty, no invitation has been received from either side to open these negotiations.

3. This Protocol shall be submitted and recommended to both the Exalted Sovereigns for ratification, and the exchange of the instruments of ratification shall take place here within three weeks.

In witness whereof this Protocol has been drawn up in two copies, signed, and sealed.

Done at Vienna, on the twenty-second day of March in the year of grace one thousand eight hundred and eighty-three.

KÁLNOKY.   H. VII. REUSS.
(L.S.)   (L.S.)

128

TREATY of Alliance between Austria-Hungary and Rumania. Vienna, 30th October, 1883. Ratifications exchanged 15th November, 1883.

His Majesty the Emperor of Austria, King of Bohemia, etc., and Apostolic King of Hungary, and

His Majesty the King of Rumania, animated by an equal desire to maintain the general peace, in conformity with the aim pursued by the Austro-Hungarian and German Alliance, to assure the political order, and to guarantee against all eventualities the perfect friendship which binds Them together, have determined to conclude to this end a Treaty which by its essentially conservative and defensive nature pursues only the aim of forestalling the dangers which might menace the peace of Their States.

For this purpose Their said Majesties have named as Their Plenipotentiaries, to wit:

His Majesty the Emperor of Austria, King of Bohemia, etc., and Apostolic King of Hungary: the Sieur Gustavus Kálnoky of Körös-Patak, Chamberlain and Actual Privy Councillor, His Minister of the Imperial Household and of Foreign Affairs, General in His Armies,

His Majesty the King of Rumania: the Sieur Demetrius A. Stourdza, His Minister of Foreign Affairs, who, after having communicated to each other their full powers, found in good and due form, have agreed upon the following Articles:

ART. 1. The High Contracting Parties promise one another peace and friendship, and will enter into no alliance or engagement directed against any one of their States. They engage to follow a friendly policy and to lend one another mutual support within the limits of their interests.

ART. 2. If Rumania, without any provocation on her part, should be attacked, Austria-Hungary is bound to bring her in ample time help and assistance against the aggressor. If Austria-Hungary be attacked under the same circumstances in a portion of her states bordering on Rumania, the *casus foederis* will immediately arise for the latter.

ART. 3. If one of the High Contracting Parties should find itself threatened by an aggression under the abovementioned conditions, the respective Governments shall put themselves in agreement as to the measures to be taken with a view to co-operation of their armies. These military questions, especially that of the unity of operations and of passage through the respective territories, shall be regulated by a military convention.

ART. 4. If, contrary to their desire and hope, the High Contracting Parties are forced into a common war under the circumstances foreseen by the preceding Articles, they engage neither to negotiate nor to conclude peace separately.

ART. 5. The present Treaty shall remain in force for a period of five years, dating from the day of the exchange of ratifications. If the present Treaty is not denounced one year before its expiration, or if its revision is not demanded by either of the High Contracting Parties, it shall be regarded as prolonged for a period of three years more.

ART. 6. The High Contracting Parties mutually promise secrecy as to the contents of the present Treaty.

ART. 7. The present Treaty shall be ratified and the ratifications shall be exchanged within a period of three weeks, or sooner if may be.

In witness whereof the respective Plenipotentiaries have signed it and have affixed thereto the seal of their arms.

Done at Vienna, the thirtieth day of the month of October in the year of grace one thousand eight hundred and eighty-three.

KÁLNOKY.
(L.S.)
D. STOURDZA.
(L.S.)

Treaty providing for the Accession of Germany. Vienna, October 30, 1883. Ratifications exchanged, November 19, 1883.

His Majesty the Emperor of Austria, Apostolic King of Hungary, and His Majesty the King of Rumania having concluded the Treaty of friendship and alliance which follows:

[*Articles 1-7 of the Austro-Hungarian-Rumanian Treaty follow.*]

have invited His Majesty the Emperor of Germany, King of Prussia, to accede to the provisions of the aforesaid Treaty.

Consequently His Majesty the Emperor of Germany, King of Prussia, has furnished with His full powers for this purpose His Representative at Vienna, Counsellor of Legation Count Max von Berchem, to adhere formerly to the provisions contained in the abovementioned Treaty. In virtue of this Act of Accession His Majesty the Emperor of Germany, King of Prussia, takes in the name of the German Empire towards Their Majesties the Emperor of Austria, Apostolic King of Hungary, and the King of Rumania, and at the same time Their Majesties the Emperor of Austria, Apostolic King of Hungary, and the King of Rumania take towards His Majesty the Emperor of Germany, King of Prussia, the same engagements by which the High Contracting Parties have mutually bound themselves according to the stipulations of the said Treaty inserted above.

The present Act of Accession shall be ratified and the ratifications shall be exchanged within a period of three weeks, or sooner if may be. In witness whereof the respective Plenipotentiaries have signed the present Act of Accession and have affixed thereto the seal of their arms.

Done at Vienna, the thirtieth day of the month of October in the year one thousand eight hundred and eighty-three.

KÁLNOKY.
(L.S.)
BERCHEM.
(L.S.)
D. STOURDZA.
(L.S.)

Treaty providing for the Accession of Italy. Vienna, May 15, 1888. Ratifications exchanged June 2, 1888.

His Majesty the Emperor of Austria, King of Bohemia, etc., and Apostolic King of Hungary, and

His Majesty the King of Rumania, having concluded on October 30, 1883, a Treaty of friendship and alliance, now in force, the tenor of which Treaty follows:

[The text of the Treaty as above follows.]

This Treaty having received on the same date the Accession of His Majesty the Emperor of Germany, King of Prussia,

and having been then communicated by the abovementioned High Contracting Parties to His Majesty the King of Italy, with an invitation to accede thereto,

His Majesty the King of Italy, approving the purpose for which this Treaty has been concluded, and which is the preservation of the general peace and of the existing order, has authorized the undersigned, Sieur Constantine Count de Nigra, His Ambassador Extraordinary and

Plenipotentiary to His Majesty the Emperor of Austria, Apostolic King of Hungary, to declare in His name that He accedes to the said Treaty within the limits indicated below so far as concerns the provisions of Articles 2 and 3, to wit:

If eventualities that could give rise to the *casus foederis*, as it is foreseen in Articles 2 and 3, should chance to occur, Their Majesties the Emperor of Austria, Apostolic King of Hungary, the King of Italy, and the King of Rumania assume a mutual engagement to take counsel together in ample time as to common action, the detailed procedure of which shall be regulated by a special convention.

The present Accession shall be in force for five years, dating from the day of signature; but if the principal Treaty of October 30, 1883, happen to expire before this period, it shall be considered as having expired at the same time.

This Act of Accession shall be kept secret, and cannot be revealed without the consent of each of the High Contracting Parties.

His Majesty the Emperor of Austria, King of Bohemia, etc., and Apostolic King of Hungary has for his part authorized the undersigned, Sieur Gustavus Count Kálnoky of Körös-Patak, Chamberlain and Actual Privy Councillor, His Minister of the Imperial Household and of Foreign Affairs, Lieutenant-Fieldmarshal in His Armies, to declare in His name that He accepts in the terms above stated, and with the same mutual obligations, the Accession of His Majesty the King of Italy to the Treaty of October 30, 1883.

The present Act of Accession and of acceptance shall be ratified by His Majesty the Emperor of Austria, King of Bohemia, etc., and Apostolic King of Hungary, and by His Majesty the King of Italy, and the ratifications shall be exchanged as soon as possible.

In witness whereof the undersigned,

the Sieur Gustavus Count Kálnoky of Körös-Patak, Chamberlain and Actual Privy Councillor, Minister of the Imperial Household and of Foreign Affairs of His Majesty the Emperor of Austria, King of Bohemia, etc., and Apostolic King of Hungary, Lieutenant-Fieldmarshal, and the Sieur Constantine Count de Nigra, Ambassador Extraordinary and Plenipotentiary of His Majesty the King of Italy to His Majesty the Emperor of Austria, King of Bohemia, etc., and Apostolic King of Hungary,

have signed the present Act and have affixed thereto the seal of their arms.

Done at Vienna, the fifteenth day of the month of May in the year of grace one thousand eight hundred and eighty-eight.

KÁLNOKY.   NIGRA.
  (L.S.)   (L.S.)

129

TREATY of 1884 between Austria-Hungary, Germany, and Russia, concerning the prolongation of their Treaty of 1881. Ratifications exchanged 15th April, 1884.

Their Majesties the Emperor of Austria, Apostolic King of Hungary, the Emperor of Germany, King of Prussia, the Emperor of All the Russias, having resolved to prolong for three years the duration of the Treaty concluded between Them June 18, 1881, have appointed for this purpose:

His Majesty the Emperor of Austria, King of Bohemia, etc., and Apostolic King of Hungary, the Sieur Emeric Count Széchényi, His Ambassador Extraordinary and Plenipotentiary to His Majesty the Emperor of Germany, King of Prussia,

His Majesty the Emperor of Germany, King of Prussia, the Sieur Otto Prince Bismarck, His President of the Council of Ministers, Chancellor of the Empire,

His Majesty the Emperor of All the Russias, the Sieur Nicholas Prince Orloff, His Aide-de-Camp General, General of Cavalry, His Ambassador Extraordinary and Plenipotentiary to His Majesty the Emperor of Germany, King of Prussia.

The said Plenipotentiaries, assembled together this day at the Ministry of Foreign Affairs at Berlin, after having produced and verified their full powers, declare, in the name of their August Sovereigns, that Their Majesties are agreed upon prolonging for three years, dating from June 18 of the current year, the duration of the secret Treaty concluded between them, June 18, 1881, the text of which is to be found affixed to this Protocol, after it has undergone the two following modifications, upon which the undersigned, in the name of their Sovereigns, have come to an agreement.

1. The third paragraph of the first Article, worded in these terms:

" In the special case where one of them should obtain a more positive support from one of its two Allies, the obligatory value of the present Article shall remain in all its force for the third."

is suppressed.

2. In the second paragraph of the second Article the words:

" of Turkey in Europe " are replaced by the words:

" of the said peninsula."

The ratifications of the present Protocol shall be exchanged at Berlin within a period of three weeks, or sooner if may be.

In witness whereof the undersigned have drawn up the present

Protocol, prepared in three copies, to which they have affixed their signatures and the seals of their arms.

Done at Berlin, the twenty-seventh day of the month of March, one thousand eight hundred and eighty-four.

SZÉCHÉNYI.
(L.S.)
v. BISMARCK.
(L.S.)
ORLOFF.
(L.S.)

130

MEDITERRANEAN AGREEMENT OF GREAT BRITAIN, ITALY, AND AUSTRIA-HUNGARY IN 1887.

Italian Note to the British Government in regard to a Mediterranean Agreement. London, February 12, 1887.

DESPATCH OF COUNT CORTI TO LORD SALISBURY.

February 12, 1887.

The undersigned, Ambassador Extraordinary and Plenipotentiary of His Majesty the King of Italy, has received from his Government instructions to bring to the attention of His Excellency the Marquess of Salisbury, Principal Secretary of State of Her Britannic Majesty for Foreign Affairs, the following:

The Government of His Majesty the King, animated by the desire of establishing with that of Her Majesty the Queen an understanding upon various questions concerning their interests, is of the opinion that this object could be attained by the adoption of the following bases:

I. The status quo in the Mediterranean as well as in the Adriatic, the Aegean Sea, and the Black Sea shall be maintained so far as possible. Care must be taken in consequence to watch, and, if need be, to prevent any change, which, under form of annexation, occupation, protectorate, or in any other manner whatsoever, would affect the present situation to the detriment of the two Powers.

II. If the maintenance of the status quo becomes impossible, they shall so act that no modification whatsoever shall occur except after a previous agreement between the two Powers.

III. Italy is entirely ready to support the work of Great Britain in Egypt. Great Britain in her turn is disposed, in case of encroachments on the part of a third Power, to support the action of Italy at every other point whatsoever of the North African coast districts, and especially in Tripolitania and Cyrenaica.

IV. In general, and to the extent that circumstances shall permit, Italy and England promise one another mutual support in the Mediterranean in every difference which may arise between one of them and a third Power.

In expressing the confidence that these bases will receive the assent of the Government of Her Britannic Majesty the Queen, the undersigned avails himself, etc.

British Note to the Italian Government in regard to a Mediterranean Agreement. London, February 12, 1887.
NOTE OF LORD SALISBURY TO COUNT CORTI.

Secret.

The statement of Italian policy which is contained in your Exc.'s dispatch of the 12th of February has been received by H. M.'s Government with great satisfaction, as it enables them to reciprocate cordially Count Robilant's friendly sentiments and to express their own desire to co-operate generally with the Government of Italy in matters of common interest to the two countries. The character of that co-operation must be decided by them, when the occasion for it arises, according to the circumstances of the case.

In the interest of peace and of the independence of the territories adjacent to the Mediterranean sea, Her Majesty's Government wish to act in the closest concert and agreement with that of Italy. Both powers desire that the shores of the Euxine, the Aegean, the Adriatic and the northern coast of Africa shall remain in the same hands as now. If, owing to some calamitous events, it becomes impossible to maintain the absolute status quo, both powers desire that there shall be no extension of the domination of any other Great Power over any portion of those coasts. It will be the earnest desire of H. M.'s Government to give their best co-operation, as hereinbefore expressed, to the Government of Italy in maintaining these cardinal principles of policy.

Accession of Austria-Hungary to the Agreement. London, March 24, 1887.
NOTE OF COUNT KÁROLYI TO THE MARQUESS OF SALISBURY.

March 24, 1887.

I have the honour, by order of my Government, to address to Your Excellency the following communication:

It is with a lively satisfaction that the Cabinet of Vienna has taken cognizance of the understanding reached between the British Cabinet and that of Italy on the bases of a common policy to be followed in the questions of the Mediterranean and of the adjacent seas.

I am charged with expressing to Your Excellency the deepest thanks of the Imperial and Royal Government for having been apprised without loss of time of this important and eminently conservative agreement.

Animated, above all things, by the desire to contribute so far as possible to the maintenance of European public law and of peace, the Austro-Hungarian Government is happy to be able to note that the fundamental principles and the political objects which are established by this understanding conform to those which guide the policy of Austria-Hungary.

Moved by the conviction that these objects would best be assured by our co-operation, the Government of His Imperial and Royal Apostolic Majesty is ready to adhere to the declarations of friendship and of identity of political views such as are recorded in the notes exchanged between Your Excellency and Count Corti under date of February 12 of the current year.

In announcing this adhesion, the Austro-Hungarian Government congratulates itself particularly on the political rapprochement between England and Austria-Hungary and on the resulting consolidation of reciprocal relations. These relations will thereby be distinctly placed on a common basis looking to the pursuit of identical aims and the defence of common interests.

Although the questions of the Mediterranean in general do not primarily affect the interests of Austria-Hungary, my Government has the conviction that England and Austria-Hungary have the same interests so far as concerns the Eastern Question as a whole, and therefore the same need of maintaining the status quo in the Orient, so far as possible, of preventing the aggrandizement of one Power to the detriment of others, and consequently of acting in concert in order to insure these cardinal principles of their policy.

In expressing the confidence that these declarations will receive the cordial assent of the Government of Her Majesty the Queen, I avail myself, etc.

Italian acknowledgment of the accession of Austria-Hungary.
London, March 24, 1887.

To His Excellency Count Károlyi, Ambassador of Austria-Hungary, London.

London, March 24, 1887.
Mr. Ambassador,

I have had the honour to receive the communication of Your Excellency of today by which you have been good enough to inform me that the Government of His Majesty the Emperor, animated by the desire to contribute to the maintenance of European public law and of peace, and believing that the understanding reached between the Governments of Italy and of England, and formulated in the notes exchanged February 12 last between the Marquess of Salisbury and myself, conforms to the policy of Austria-Hungary, adheres thereto.

In conformity with the orders which I have received from my Government I have the honour to express to Your Excellency the sincere satisfaction which the Government of His Majesty the King has shown on learning that the Government of His Imperial and Royal Apostolic Majesty was animated by these intentions, which can only make ever firmer the relations of good friendship existing between the two States; and I hasten to accept in the name of the Government of His Majesty the King the adhesion of that of His Majesty the Emperor to the Italo-English understanding, as this adhesion has been formulated in the above-mentioned communication of Your Excellency.

I avail myself of this occasion to tender you, Mr. Ambassador, the assurance of my highest consideration.

L. CORTI
Ambassador of Italy.

British acknowledgment of the accession of Austria-Hungary.
London, March 24, 1887.
His Excellency the Count Károlyi, etc. etc. etc.
Foreign Office, March 24, 1887.
Mr. Ambassador,

It is a matter of the liveliest satisfaction to H. M$^{y's}$ Government that the exchange of views which has passed between England and Italy, and which has been communicated to the Cabinet of Vienna, has met with their approbation, and has been recognized by them as tending to the preservation of European peace and the maintenance of public right.

H. M$^{y's}$ Government received with no less gratification the intimation that the Austro-Hungarian Government are prepared to adhere to those declarations of friendship and of identity in political views which are embodied in the communications between England and Italy; and they concur in the belief that the cordial relations, based on a similarity of interests and policy, which have long subsisted between the two countries, will be strengthened and established by the present proceeding.

They are fully convinced that, in respect to the political future of the territories which are washed by the Mediterranean and the adjacent seas, the interests of Austria-Hungary are closely related to those of Great Britain and Italy. It is rather, however, with the Euxine and the

Aegean than with the western portion of the Mediterranean that the policy of Austria is engaged.

But in respect to the territories bordering on those seas whose political status more specially affects the interests of the Austro-Hungarian Empire, the objects of English and Austrian policy are the same, and the principles which ought to guide it are clearly indicated in the communications to which Count Kálnoky has expressed his willingness to adhere.

Without determining beforehand the character which the co-operation of the two Powers ought in any particular contingency to take, the efforts of H. M$^{y's}$ Government in harmony with those of the Austro-Hungarian Government will be constantly directed to secure in these regions the maintenance, so long as it shall be possible, of the status quo, and, should that unhappily cease to be possible, the prevention of the growth of any novel domination hostile to the interests of the two countries.

I have the honour to be, with the highest consideration, Mr. l'ambassadeur, your Exc. most obedient, humble servant

SALISBURY.

131

SECOND TREATY of the Triple Alliance between Austria-Hungary, the German Empire, and Italy. Berlin, 20th February, 1887. Ratifications exchanged 10th March, 1887.

Their Majesties
the Emperor of Austria, King of Bohemia, etc., and Apostolic King of Hungary,
the Emperor of Germany, King of Prussia,
and the King of Italy,
animated by the desire of maintaining the bonds established between Their States and Their Governments by the Treaty concluded at Vienna on May 20, 1882, have resolved to prolong its duration by means of an Additional Treaty, and for this purpose have appointed as Their Plenipotentiaries, to wit:

His Majesty the Emperor of Austria, King of Bohemia, etc., and Apostolic King of Hungary, the Sieur Emeric Count Széchényi of Sárvári Felsö-Vidék, Chamberlain and Actual Privy Councillor, His Ambassador Extraordinary and Plenipotentiary to His Majesty the Emperor of Germany, King of Prussia,

His Majesty the Emperor of Germany, King of Prussia, the Sieur Otto Prince Bismarck, His President of the Council of Ministers of Prussia, Chancellor of the Empire,

His Majesty the King of Italy, the Sieur Edward Count de Launay, His Ambassador Extraordinary and Plenipotentiary to His Majesty the Emperor of Germany, King of Prussia,

who, furnished with full powers, which have been found in good and due form, have agreed upon the following Articles:

ART. I. The Treaty of Alliance concluded at Vienna on May 20, 1882, between the Powers signatory to the present Additional Treaty, is confirmed and kept in force in its whole extent until May 30, 1892.

ART. II. The present Treaty shall be ratified and the ratifications shall be exchanged at Berlin within a period of a fortnight, or sooner if may be.

In witness whereof the respective Plenipotentiaries have signed the present Additional Treaty and have affixed thereto their seal.

Done at Berlin, the twentieth day of the month of February, one thousand eight hundred and eighty-seven.

(L.S.)   SZÉCHÉNYI.

(L.S.)   v. BISMARCK.

(L.S.)   LAUNAY.

Separate Treaty between Austria-Hungary and Italy. Berlin, February 20, 1887.

Their Majesties

the Emperor of Austria, King of Bohemia, etc., and Apostolic King of Hungary,

and the King of Italy,

deeming it opportune to give some development to the Treaty of Alliance signed at Vienna on May 20, 1882, the prolongation of which has been stipulated today by an Additional Act, have resolved to conclude a Separate Treaty which shall take ever better account of the reciprocal interests of Their States and of Their Governments, and have for this purpose appointed as Their Plenipotentiaries, to wit:

His Majesty the Emperor of Austria, King of Bohemia, etc., and Apostolic King of Hungary, the Sieur Emeric Count Széchényi of Sárvári Felsö-Vidék, Chamberlain and Actual Privy Councillor, His Ambassador Extraordinary and Plenipotentiary to His Majesty the Emperor of Germany, King of Prussia,

His Majesty the King of Italy, the Sieur Edward Count de Launay, His Ambassador Extraordinary and Plenipotentiary to His Majesty the Emperor of Germany, King of Prussia,

who, furnished with full powers found in good and due form, have agreed upon the following Articles:

ART. I. The High Contracting Parties, having in mind only the maintenance, so far as possible, of the territorial status quo in the Orient, engage to use their influence to forestall any territorial modification which might be injurious to one or the other of the Powers signatory to the present Treaty. They shall communicate to one another all information of a nature to enlighten each other mutually concerning their own dispositions, as well as those of other Powers.

However, if, in the course of events, the maintenance of the status quo in the regions of the Balkans or of the Ottoman coasts and islands in the Adriatic and in the Aegean Sea should become impossible, and if, whether in consequence of the action of a third Power or otherwise, Austria-Hungary or Italy should find themselves under the necessity of modifying it by a temporary or permanent occupation on their part, this occupation shall take place only after a previous agreement between the two Powers aforesaid, based upon the principle of a reciprocal compensation for every advantage, territorial or other, which each of them might obtain beyond the present status quo, and giving satisfaction to the interests and well founded claims of the two Parties.

ART. II. The High Contracting Parties mutually promise secrecy as to the contents of the present Treaty.

ART. III. The present Treaty shall enter into force from the day of the exchange of ratifications and shall remain so until May 30, 1892.

ART. IV. The ratifications shall be exchanged at Berlin within a period of a fortnight, or sooner if may be.

In witness whereof the respective Plenipotentiaries have signed the present Treaty and have affixed thereto their seal.

Done at Berlin, the twentieth day of the month of February, one thousand eight hundred and eighty-seven.

(L.S.)   SZÉCHÉNYI.
(L.S.)   LAUNAY.

Separate Treaty between the German Empire and Italy. Berlin, February, 20, 1887.

Their Majesties the King of Italy and the Emperor of Germany, King of Prussia, wishing, in a spirit of mutual good understanding, to strengthen more and more the bonds already established between Their States and Their Governments by the Treaty of Alliance concluded at Vienna on May 20, 1882, the prolongation of which has just been signed today, have resolved to enact a Separate Treaty which shall be more and more in keeping with the present circumstances, and have for this purpose appointed as Their Plenipotentiaries, to wit: His Majesty the Emperor of Germany, King of Prussia; the Sieur Otto Prince Bismarck, His President of the Council of Ministers of Prussia, Chancellor of the

Empire; and His Majesty the King of Italy, the Sieur Edward, Count of Launay, His Ambassador Extraordinary and Plenipotentiary to His Majesty, the Emperor of Germany, King of Prussia; who, furnished with full powers, which have been found in good and due form, have agreed upon the following Articles.

ART. I. The High Contracting Parties, having in mind only the maintenance, so far as possible, of the territorial status quo in the Orient, engage to use their influence to forestall, on the Ottoman coasts and islands in the Adriatic and the Aegean Seas, any territorial modification which might be injurious to one or the other of the Powers signatory to the present Treaty. To this end they shall communicate to one another all information of a nature to enlighten each other mutually concerning their own dispositions, as well as those of other Powers.

ART. II. The stipulations of Article I apply in no way to the Egyptian question, with regard to which the High Contracting Parties preserve respectively their freedom of action, regard being always paid to the principles upon which rest the present Treaty and that of May 20, 1882.

ART. III. If it were to happen that France should make a move to extend her occupation, or even her protectorate or her sovereignty, under any form whatsoever in the North African territories, whether of the Vilayet of Tripoli or of the Moroccan Empire, and that in consequence thereof Italy, in order to safeguard her position in the Mediterranean, should feel that she must herself undertake action in the said North African territories, or even have recourse to extreme measures in French territory in Europe, the state of war which would thereby ensue between Italy and France would constitute *ipso facto*, on the demand of Italy and at the common charge of the two Allies, the *casus foederis* with all the effects foreseen by Articles II and V of the aforesaid Treaty of May 20, 1882, as if such an eventuality were expressly contemplated therein.

ART. IV. If the fortunes of any war undertaken in common against France should lead Italy to seek for territorial guaranties with respect to France for the security of the frontiers of the Kingdom and of her maritime position, as well as with a view to the stability of peace, Germany will present no obstacle thereto; and, if need be, and in a measure compatible with circumstances, will apply herself to facilitating the means of attaining such a purpose.

ART. V. The High Contracting Parties mutually promise secrecy as to the contents of the present Treaty.

ART. VI. The present Treaty shall enter into force from the day of the exchange of ratifications and shall remain in force until May 30, 1892.

ART. VII. The ratifications shall be exchanged at Berlin within a period of a fortnight, or sooner if may be.

In witness whereof, etc. [Berlin, February 20, 1887.]

(L.S.)   v. BISMARCK.
(L.S.)   LAUNAY.

Final Protocol between Austria-Hungary, the German Empire, and Italy. February 20, 1887.

The undersigned have just proceeded to the signing of an Additional Treaty prolonging the duration of the Treaty of Alliance concluded at Vienna, May 20, 1882.

There has been signed at the same time a Separate Treaty between Austria-Hungary and Italy and a Separate Treaty between Germany and Italy. These last two Acts, although distinct, respond none the less to the general spirit of the aforementioned agreement of 1882; because today, as then, the three Monarchies are aiming essentially at the maintenance of peace.

The simultaneity of the signatures affixed to the Treaties under date of this day demonstrates this uniformity of understanding between the respective Governments, and the undersigned are pleased to testify thereto by signing the present and single Procès-verbal.

Done at Berlin, February 20, 1887.

SZÉCHÉNYI.
v. BISMARCK.
LAUNAY.

132

MEDITERRANEAN AGREEMENT BETWEEN ITALY AND SPAIN.   1887.

Spanish Note to Italy proposing a Mediterranean Agreement. Madrid, May 4, 1887.

Ministry of State.

Madrid, May 4, 1887.

The undersigned, Minister of Foreign Affairs of Spain, has the honour to bring the following to the knowledge of Marquis Maffei, Envoy Extraordinary and Minister Plenipotentiary of His Majesty the King of Italy:

The Government of Her Majesty the Queen Regent, animated by the desire to seek an understanding with the Government of His Majesty the King of Italy for the purpose of fortifying more and more the monarchical principle and of contributing to the strengthening of the peace, declares itself from the present time in favour of the acceptance of the following provisions:

1. Spain will not lend herself as regards France, in so far as the North African territories among others are concerned, to any treaty or

political arrangement whatsoever which would be aimed directly or indirectly against Italy, Germany, and Austria, or against any one of these Powers.

2. Abstention from all unprovoked attack, as well as from all provocation.

3. In view of the interests involved in the Mediterranean, and for the principal purpose of maintaining there the present status quo, Spain and Italy will keep in communication with one another on this subject, by conveying to each other all information of a kind to enlighten each other concerning their respective dispositions, as well as those of other Powers.

In expressing the hope that these present and secret proposals will obtain the assent of the Government of His Majesty the King of Italy, the undersigned avails himself of this occasion to renew to Marquis Maffei the assurances of his most distinguished consideration.

Madrid, the fourth of May, one thousand eight hundred and eighty-seven.

(signed) MORET.

For copy true to the original:
Madrid, May 8, 1887.

(L.S.)   MORET.

Italian reply to Spanish Note.   Madrid, May 4, 1887.
Royal Legation of Italy.

Madrid, May 4, 1887.

The undersigned, Envoy Extraordinary and Minister Plenipotentiary of His Majesty the King of Italy, has received the Note which His Excellency the Minister of Foreign Affairs of Spain has done him the honour to address to him under today's date, and he is authorized to respond thereto in the following terms:

The Government of the King gives its assent to the provisions enunciated in the aforesaid Note and pledges itself to reciprocity.

At the same time, it reserves to itself to examine, in full agreement with the Governments of Their Majesties the Emperor of Germany, King of Prussia, and the Emperor of Austria, King of Hungary, whether and to what extent there may be need, according to circumstances, to enter into further concert with the Cabinet of Madrid in order the better to assure the purpose which it too has in view.

In the meantime, the Government of His Majesty takes note of the abovementioned communication and regards the secret agreement established by the present exchange of Notes as entering into force from today, and for a period of four years.

The undersigned avails himself of this occasion to renew to His Excellency the Minister of Foreign Affairs of Spain the assurances of his most distinguished consideration.

Madrid, the fourth of May, one thousand eight hundred and eighty-seven.

(signed) MAFFEI.

For copy true to the original:
Madrid, May 8, 1887.

(L.S.)   MAFFEI.

For certified copy true to the authentic copy of the two Notes filed in the Archive of the Royal Ministry of Foreign Affairs.

Rome, May 16, 1887.

The President of the Council and Minister Secretary of State for Foreign Affairs.

(L.S.)   DEPRETIS.

For certification of the signature of His Excellency Signor Depretis, President of the Council and Minister Secretary of State for Foreign Affairs, of His Majesty the King of Italy.

The Ambassador of His Majesty the King of Italy at Vienna.

(L.S.)   NIGRA.

Vienna, May 20, 1887.

Accession of Austria-Hungary. May 21, 1887.
To Count Nigra.

Vienna, May 21, 1887.

The undersigned has received the Note which His Excellency the Ambassador of Italy has done him the honour to address to him under date of the 21st instant as well as the two annexes, and hastens to notify the accession of the Imperial Government to the Notes exchanged at Madrid the 4th of the same month between the Representative of His Majesty the King of Italy and His Excellency the Minister of State of Her Majesty the Queen Regent.

The undersigned expresses his satisfaction that the negotiations have led to a result of a nature to assure the co-operation of Spain in the realization of the programme of peace and of conservation with which the Governments of Austria-Hungary and of Italy are inspired.

At the same time he avails himself of this occasion, etc., etc.

(signed)   KÁLNOKY.

133   THE 'REINSURANCE TREATY' OF 1887

TREATY between Germany and Russia. Berlin, 18th June, 1887.

The Imperial Courts of Germany and of Russia, animated by an equal desire to strengthen the general peace by an understanding destined to assure the defensive position of their respective States, have resolved to confirm the agreement established between them by a special arrangement, in view of the expiration on June 15/27, 1887, of the validity of the secret Treaty and Protocol, signed in 1881 and renewed in 1884 by the three Courts of Germany, Russia, and Austria-Hungary.

To this end the two Courts have named as Plenipotentiaries:

His Majesty the Emperor of Germany, King of Prussia, the Sieur Herbert Count of Bismarck-Schoenhausen, His Secretary of State in the Department of Foreign Affairs;

His Majesty the Emperor of All the Russias, the Sieur Paul Count Schouvaloff, His Ambassador Extraordinary and Plenipotentiary to his Majesty the Emperor of Germany, King of Prussia,

who, being furnished with full powers, which have been found in good and due form, have agreed upon the following Articles:

ART. I. In case one of the High Contracting Parties should find itself at war with a third great Power, the other would maintain a benevolent neutrality towards it, and would devote its efforts to the localization of the conflict. This provision would not apply to a war against Austria or France in case this war should result from an attack directed against one of these two latter Powers by one of the High Contracting Parties.

ART. II. Germany recognizes the rights historically acquired by Russia in the Balkan Peninsula, and particularly the legitimacy of her preponderant and decisive influence in Bulgaria and in Eastern Rumelia. The two Courts engage to admit no modification of the territorial status quo of the said peninsula without a previous agreement between them, and to oppose, as occasion arises, every attempt to disturb this status quo or to modify it without their consent.

ART. III. The two Courts recognize the European and mutually obligatory character of the principle of the closing of the Straits of the Bosphorus and of the Dardanelles, founded on international law, confirmed by treaties, and summed up in the declaration of the second Plenipotentiary of Russia at the session of July 12 of the Congress of Berlin (Protocol 19).

They will take care in common that Turkey shall make no exception to this rule in favour of the interests of any Government whatsoever, by lending to warlike operations of a belligerent power the portion of its Empire constituted by the Straits. In case of infringement, or to prevent it if such infringement should be in prospect, the two Courts will inform Turkey that they would regard her, in that event, as putting herself in a state of war towards the injured Party, and as depriving herself thenceforth of the benefits of the security assured to her territorial status quo by the Treaty of Berlin.

ART. IV. The present Treaty shall remain in force for the space of three years, dating from the day of the exchange of ratifications.

ART. V. The High Contracting Parties mutually promise secrecy as to the contents and the existence of the present Treaty and of the Protocol annexed thereto.

ART. VI. The present Treaty shall be ratified and ratifications shall be exchanged at Berlin within a period of a fortnight, or sooner if may be.

In witness whereof the respective Plenipotentiaries have signed the present Treaty and have affixed thereto the seal of their arms.

Done at Berlin, the eighteenth day of the month of June, one thousand eight hundred and eighty-seven.

(L.S.)   COUNT BISMARCK.
(L.S.)   COUNT PAUL SCHOUVALOFF.

Additional Protocol. Berlin, June 18, 1887.
ADDITIONAL AND VERY SECRET PROTOCOL.

In order to complete the stipulations of Articles II and III of the secret Treaty concluded on this same date, the two Courts have come to an agreement upon the following points:

1.

Germany, as in the past, will lend her assistance to Russia in order to re-establish a regular and legal government in Bulgaria. She promises in no case to give her consent to the restoration of the Prince of Battenberg.

2.

In case His Majesty the Emperor of Russia should find himself under the necessity of assuming the task of defending the entrance of the Black Sea in order to safeguard the interests of Russia, Germany engages to accord her benevolent neutrality and her moral and diplomatic support to the measures which His Majesty may deem it necessary to take to guard the key of His Empire.

3.

The present Protocol forms an integral part of the secret Treaty signed on this day at Berlin, and shall have the same force and validity.

In witness whereof the respective Plenipotentiaries have signed it and have affixed thereto the seal of their arms.

Done at Berlin, the eighteenth day of the month of June, one thousand eight hundred and eighty-seven.

(L.S.)   COUNT BISMARCK.
(L.S.)   COUNT PAUL SCHOUVALOFF.

134

SECOND MEDITERRANEAN AGREEMENT BETWEEN GREAT BRITAIN, AUSTRIA-HUNGARY, AND ITALY. 1887.

Austrian Note to Great Britain proposing a further Agreement in the Mediterranean. London, December 12, 1887.

To His Excellency the Marquis of Salisbury.

As a result of the understanding reached between the governments of His Majesty the Emperor of Austria and King of Hungary, Her Majesty the Queen of the United Kingdom of Great Britain and Ireland, and the King of Italy by the exchange of Notes in the month of March 1887, the government of Austria-Hungary has come to an agreement with the government of Italy to propose to the British government the adoption of the following points, intended to confirm the principles established by the aforementioned exchange of Notes, and to define the common attitude of the three Powers in prospect of the eventualities which might occur in the Orient.

1. The maintenance of peace and the exclusion of all policy of aggression.

2. The maintenance of the status quo in the Orient, based on treaties, to the exclusion of all policy of compensation.

3. The maintenance of the local autonomies established by these said treaties.

4. The independence of Turkey, as guardian of important European interests (independence of the Caliphate, the freedom of the Straits, etc.), of all foreign preponderating influence.

5. Consequently, Turkey can neither cede nor delegate suzerain rights over Bulgaria to any other power, nor intervene in order to establish a foreign administration there, nor tolerate acts of coercion undertaken with this latter object, under the form either of a military occupation or of the despatch of volunteers. Likewise Turkey, constituted by the treaties guardian of the Straits, can neither cede any portion of her sovereign rights, nor delegate her authority to any other Power in Asia Minor.

6. The desire of the three Powers to be associated with Turkey for the common defence of these principles.

7. In case of Turkey resisting any illegal enterprises such as are indicated in Article 5, the three Powers will immediately come to an agreement as to the measures to be taken for causing to be respected

the independence of the Ottoman Empire and the integrity of its territory, as secured by previous treaties.

8. Should the conduct of the Porte, however, in the opinion of the three Powers, assume the character of complicity with or connivance at any such illegal enterprise, the three Powers will consider themselves justified by existing treaties in proceeding, either jointly or separately, to the provisional occupation by their forces, military or naval, of such points of Ottoman territory as they may agree to consider it necessary to occupy in order to secure the objects determined by previous treaties.

9. The existence and the contents of the present Agreement between the three Powers shall not be revealed, either to Turkey or to any other Powers who have not yet been informed of it, without the previous consent of all and each of the three Powers aforesaid.

The undersigned Ambassador Extraordinary and Minister Plenipotentiary of His Imperial and Royal Apostolic Majesty has been instructed by his Government to sign the present Note and to exchange it against a similar Note of the Government of Her Britannic Majesty.

The undersigned takes this occasion to renew to His Excellency the Marquess of Salisbury, Principal Secretary of State for Foreign Affairs of Her Majesty the Queen, the expression of his highest consideration.

Signed: KÁROLYI

British reply to Austrian Note. London, December 12, 1887.

H. M$^{y's}$ Government have considered the points commended to their acceptance by the identic note of the Austro-Hungarian and Italian Governments.

The three Powers have already communicated to each other their conviction that it is their common interest to uphold the existing state of things upon the shores of the Mediterranean and the adjoining seas. The four first points recited in the note are in strict conformity with this understanding, as well as with the policy which has always been pursued by the Government of Great Britain.

The fifth, sixth, and seventh points refer to certain special dangers by which the state of things established by treaties and the interests of the three Powers in the East may be menaced, and to the course which should be pursued if those dangers should arise. The illegal enterprises anticipated by the fifth article would affect especially the preservation of the Straits from the domination of any other Power but Turkey and the independent liberties of the Christian communities on the northern border of the Turkish Empire established by the Treaty of Berlin. H. M$^{y's}$ Government recognise that the protection of the Straits and the liberties of these communities are objects of supreme importance and are to Europe among the most valuable results of the treaty; and they cordially concur with the Austro-Hungarian and Italian Governments in taking special precautions to secure them.

The eighth point provides against a contingency which, without technical illegality, may frustrate the object of the treaties altogether. It is necessary, however, to avoid a premature publicity which might precipitate the lapse of Turkey into that state of vassalage from which it is the aim of the three Powers to protect her. In view of these considerations, the undersigned, H. M$^{y's}$ Secretary of State for Foreign Affairs, is charged by H. M$^{y's}$ Government to communicate to the Austro-Hungarian Government their entire adhesion to the nine points recited in the identic note of the two powers, that is to say:

1. The maintenance of peace to the exclusion of all policy of aggression.

2. The maintenance of the status quo in the East, based on the treaties, to the exclusion of all policy of compensation.

3. The maintenance of the local autonomies established by these same treaties.

4. The independence of Turkey as guardian of important European interests (the Caliphate, the freedom of the Straits, etc.) to be independent (*sic*) of all foreign preponderating influence.

5. Consequently, Turkey can neither cede nor delegate her rights over Bulgaria to any other Power, nor intervene in order to establish a foreign administration there, nor tolerate acts of coercion undertaken with this latter object, under the form either of a military occupation or of the despatch of volunteers; neither will Turkey, who has by the treaties been constituted guardian of the Straits, be able to cede any portion of her sovereign rights, nor delegate her authority to any other power in Asia Minor.

6. The desire of the three Powers to be associated with Turkey for the common defence of these principles.

7. In case of Turkey resisting any illegal enterprises such as are indicated in Article 5, the three Powers will immediately come to an agreement as to the measures to be taken for causing to be respected the independence of the Ottoman Empire and the integrity of its territory as secured by previous treaties.

8. Should the conduct of the Porte, however, in the opinion of the three Powers, assume the character of complicity with or connivance at any such illegal enterprise, the three Powers will consider themselves justified by existing treaties in proceeding either jointly or separately to the provisional occupation by their forces, military or naval, of such points of Ottoman territory as they may agree to consider it necessary to occupy in order to secure the objects determined by previous treaties.

9. The existence and the contents of the present agreement between

the three Powers shall not be revealed either to Turkey or to any other Powers who have not yet been informed of it without the previous consent of all and each of the three Powers aforesaid.

Foreign Office. December 12, 1887.

SALISBURY.

Italian confirmation of the Agreement.

As a result of the understanding reached between the Governments of His Majesty the King of Italy and of Their Majesties the Emperor of Austria, King of Hungary, and the Queen of the United Kingdom of Great Britain and Ireland by the exchange of Notes effected at London in the month of March, 1887, the Government of His Majesty the King of Italy has come to an agreement with the Governments of Austria-Hungary and Great Britain as to the adoption of the following points, intended to confirm the principles established by the aforementioned exchange of Notes, and to define the common attitude of the three Powers in prospect of the eventualities which might occur in the Orient.

[*Articles* 1-9 *of the Austrian Note are repeated here*]

The undersigned Ambassador of His Majesty the King of Italy has been instructed to sign the present Note and to exchange it against an identic Note of the Government of His Majesty the Emperor of Austria, King of Hungary.

Vienna, December 16, 1887.

NIGRA.

135

TREATY between Austria-Hungary and Serbia prolonging the Treaty of 1881. Belgrade, 28th January/9th February, 1889. Ratifications exchanged 5th/17th February, 1889.

His Majesty the Emperor of Austria, King of Bohemia, etc., and Apostolic King of Hungary, and

His Majesty the King of Serbia,

animated by the desire, not only to maintain, but to develop and to consolidate the relations of perfect friendship which exist between Their Governments and to guarantee them against every eventuality, have resolved to prolong the Treaty concluded between them on June 23, 1881, and to define the meaning of some of its Articles. For this purpose, They have appointed as Their Plenipotentiaries, to wit:

His Imperial and Royal Apostolic Majesty: the Sieur Ladislas Hengelmüller of Hengervár, His Envoy Extraordinary and Minister Plenipotentiary to His Majesty the King of Serbia, etc.,

His Majesty the King of Serbia: the Sieur Chedomille Mijatovich, His Minister of Foreign Affairs, etc., etc.,

who, after having communicated to each other their full powers, found in good and due form, have agreed upon the following Additional Articles:

ART. 1. The Treaty of June 23, 1881, with the Declaration annexed thereto, shall remain in force until January 1/13, 1895. Three months before its expiration the High Contracting Parties shall, if there is cause therefor, take counsel together as to its prolongation or as to the modifications which circumstances might render desirable.

By the present Article the provisions of Article VIII of the Treaty of June 23, 1881, are abolished.

ART. 2. With a view to better defining the meaning of Article II of the Treaty of June 23, 1881, by which the two High Contracting Parties reciprocally engage not to tolerate in their countries political, religious, or other intrigues directed against either of them, and by which Austria-Hungary assumes the engagement to support the maintenance and the strengthening of the Obrenovitch dynasty, the Imperial Government declares that, should the occasion arise, it will take all measures to prevent by every means, and even by armed force, every hostile incursion which might be directed from Montenegro against Serbia and her royal dynasty through the territory placed under the administration of the Imperial and Royal authorities.

Austria-Hungary will also, if need be, exercise her good offices with the Sublime Porte, to the end that the Ottoman authorities observe on their territory an analogous attitude with regard to Montenegrin incursions directed against Serbia and the dynasty of Obrenovitch.

ART. 3. The contingencies of Article VI of the Treaty of June 23, 1881, shall not be put in force except in conformity with the provisions of the Constitution of the Kingdom of Serbia dated December 22, 1888/January 3, 1889 (Articles 52 and 200).

ART. 4. If the circumstances foreseen by Article VII of the Treaty of June 23, 1881, should chance to occur while this Treaty remains in force and while Serbia has faithfully observed its stipulations, it is understood that Austria-Hungary will recognize, and support with other Powers, the recognition in favour of the Kingdom of Serbia of the territorial extension foreseen by Article VII above-mentioned, which extension may be carried in the direction of the valley of the Vardar as far as the circumstances will permit.

ART. 5. In order to respond to a desire expressed by His Majesty King Milan I and in conformity with the spirit of perfect friendship in which the Treaty of June 23, 1881, and the present Additional Act have been concluded, the Imperial and Royal Government declares its willingness to aid, so far as possible, in the consolidation of the economic and financial condition of the Kingdom of Serbia, and engages, with that in view, as soon as the request shall have been made to it, to enter into negotiations with the Serbian Government in regard to certain modifications of the Treaty of Commerce in force between Austria-Hungary and Serbia relative to duties and imposts on foodstuffs.

ART. 6. The present Additional Act, which the High Parties equally engage to keep secret, shall form an integral part of the Treaty of June 23, 1881; it shall be ratified and the ratifications shall be exchanged at Belgrade within a period of a fortnight, or sooner if may be.

In witness whereof the respective Plenipotentiaries have signed it and affixed thereto the seal of their arms.

Done at Belgrade, in duplicate, February 9/January 28 of the year 1889.

(L.S.) v. HENGELMÜLLER. (L.S.) CH. MIJATOVICH.

Declaration of the Serbian Regents recognizing the Treaties of 1881 *and* 1889. *Belgrade, March* 7/19, 1889.
To His Excellency Mr. Hengelmüller, Envoy Extraordinary and Minister Plenipotentiary of Austria-Hungary at Belgrade.
Very Confidential.   Belgrade, March 7/19, 1889.
Mr. Minister,

We have received the Note which Your Excellency, by order of your Government, has done us the honour to address to us in order to call our attention to the secret Treaty concluded between Serbia and Austria-Hungary June 28 (*sic*), 1881, and the Additional Act constituting a part thereof dated February 9 of the current year.

Although the Imperial and Royal Government does not doubt the fidelity with which the Royal Regency will fulfil the international obligations of Serbia contracted in good and due form under the preceding reign, or the care that it will take to see to their scrupulous observance, it desires nevertheless, in view of the high importance of the abovementioned Acts, to obtain official and explicit information as to the point of view which the Royal Regency intends to adopt with regard to them.

Having taken cognizance of the abovementioned Treaties and examined their contents with care, we hasten to inform Your Excellency that we have found them concluded in good and due form and in full and entire conformity with the sovereign rights granted to the King of Serbia by the old Constitution of 1899 and the new Constitution of the Kingdom promulgated on December 22, 1888.

The legal validity of the secret Treaty of June 28 (*sic*), 1881, as well as of its Additional Act of February 9 of the current year consequently not being contestable for a single instant, we do not hesitate to declare to you, Mr. Minister, that the Royal Regency has no scruples in adopting the point of view of strict and faithful observance of these international stipulations.

This task will be the easier for us since we ourselves attach the greatest value to seeking all the means suitable to assure the development of the good and cordial relations which so happily exist between Serbia and the powerful neighbouring Monarchy.

We like to hope that Your Excellency will be good enough to lend his friendly support to the attainment of this purpose; and we pray you, Mr. Minister, to accept the assurances of our highest consideration.

The Regents of the Kingdom:

DR. J. RISTITCH.
GENERAL K. S. PROTITCH.
GENERAL BELIMARKOVIC.

136   HELIGOLAND AGREEMENT

AGREEMENT between Great Britain and Germany, for the Cession of the Island of Heligoland to Germany. Signed at Berlin, 1st July, 1890. This formed part of a wider arrangement, Articles I—XI of which dealt with Africa. For these see Appendix I.

ART. XII. 1. Subject to the assent of the British Parliament, the sovereignty over the Island of Heligoland, together with its dependencies, is ceded by Her Britannic Majesty to His Majesty the Emperor of Germany.

Nationality.
2. The German Government will allow to all persons, natives of the territory thus ceded, the right of opting for British Nationality by means of a declaration to be made by themselves, and, in the case of children under age, by their parents or guardians, which must be sent in before the 1st of January, 1892.

Military and Naval Service.
3. All persons, natives of the territory thus ceded, and their children born before the date of the signature of the present agreement, are free from the obligation of service in the military and naval forces of Germany.

Native Laws and Customs.

4. Native laws and customs now existing will, as far as possible, remain undisturbed.

Customs Tariff.

5. The German Government binds itself not to increase the Customs Tariff at present in force in the territory thus ceded until the 1st January, 1910.

Property of Private Persons and Corporations. Lloyd's Right of Signalling.

6. All rights to property which private persons or existing Corporations have acquired in Heligoland, in connection with the British Government, are maintained; obligations resulting from them are transferred to His Majesty the Emperor of Germany. It is understood that the above term, " rights to property," includes the right of signalling now enjoyed by Lloyd's.

British Fishermen.

7. The rights of British fishermen with regard to anchorage in all weathers, to taking in provisions and water, to making repairs, to transshipment of goods, to the sale of fish, and to the landing and drying of nets, remain undisturbed.

Berlin, 1st July, 1890.

> EDWARD B. MALET.
> H. PERCY ANDERSON.
> v. CAPRIVI.
> K. KRAUEL.

137

PROLONGATION OF THE MEDITERRANEAN AGREEMENT BETWEEN SPAIN AND ITALY. 1891.

Italian-Spanish Protocol relating to the prolongation of the Agreement. Madrid, May 4, 1891.

PROTOCOL.

The Government of His Majesty the King of Italy and the Government of Her Majesty the Queen Regent of Spain, animated by the desire to fortify the monarchical principle ever further and to contribute to the strengthening of peace, have decided to renew the secret Agreement of

1887 and in the same terms which were drawn up between the two Governments by the exchange of Notes of May 4 of the said year, to wit:

ART. I. Italy and Spain will not lend themselves as regards France, in so far as the North African territories among others are concerned, to any treaty or political arrangement whatsoever which should be aimed directly or indirectly against Italy, Spain, Germany, and Austria-Hungary, or against any one of these Powers.

ART. II. Abstention from all unprovoked attack, as well as from all provocation.

ART. III. In view of the interests involved in the Mediterranean, and for the principal purpose of maintaining there the present status quo, Italy and Spain will keep in communication with one another on this subject, by conveying to one another all information of a kind to enlighten each other concerning their respective dispositions, as well as those of other Powers.

The preceding provisions, which are the reproduction of the Agreement of 1887, enter into force anew, dating from today, for a period of four years, and shall continue to be kept secret.

The Italian Government engages as in 1887 to present the above stated clauses for the adhesion of the Governments of His Majesty the Emperor of Germany, King of Prussia, and of His Majesty the Emperor of Austria, King of Hungary.

In witness whereof Their Excellencies the Marquis Maffei, Ambassador Extraordinary and Plenipotentiary of His Majesty the King of Italy, and the Duke of Tetuan, Minister of Foreign Affairs of Spain, duly authorized, have signed this Protocol in duplicate originals.

Done at Madrid, the fourth of May, one thousand eight hundred and ninety-one.

(Signed) MAFFEI.   (Signed) THE DUKE OF TETUAN.

For copy true to the original:

(L.S.)   MAFFEI.

Madrid, May 4, 1891.

Spanish Note to Italy regarding Morocco. May 4, 1891.

Royal Embassy of Italy.

Copy of the Note addressed by His Excellency the Duke of Tetuan, Minister of Foreign Affairs of Spain, to His Excellency the Marquis Maffei, Ambassador of Italy.

Madrid, May 4, 1891.

Mr. Ambassador: Referring to the secret Agreement which I have today had the honour of signing with Your Excellency in the name of our respective Governments, I deem it my duty to formulate the following reserve on the subject matter of clause 3 of the said Agreement so far as it concerns Morocco: The Government of Her Majesty the Queen Regent declares that the status quo to the preservation of which the Agreement looks must be considered not only in relation to the *de facto* situation existing in Morocco, but also in relation to the *de jure* situation of Spain according to the Treaty of Wad Ras and without impairing her freedom of action for maintaining the security of the frontier line of the Spanish possessions in the territory of Morocco. In bringing the preceding to the knowledge of Your Excellency, I beg you to be kind enough to acknowledge receipt thereof in the name of your Government and to give notice of it as well to Their Excellencies the Ambassadors of Germany and of Austria-Hungary, inviting them to take note thereof in the name of their respective Governments. Pray accept the assurance of my high consideration.

(Signed) THE DUKE OF TETUAN.

To His Excellency Marquis Maffei, Ambassador of His Majesty the King of Italy.

For copy true to the original:

(L.S.)   MAFFEI.

Madrid, May 4, 1891.

Accession of Austria-Hungary to the Protocol and Note.
Madrid, May 4, 1891.

Madrid, May 4, 1891.

By his Note of today His Excellency the Ambassador of His Majesty the King of Italy has been good enough to send to the undersigned a certified true copy of the Protocol which he signed this morning with His Excellency the Duke of Tetuan, Minister of State, for the renewal of the secret Agreement of May 4, 1887, as well as the certified true copy of the Notes relative to the reserves formulated by the Spanish Government on the subject of Morocco.

The undersigned hastens, by order of his Government, to announce the accession of the latter to the said Protocol and to the Notes exchanged at Madrid today, the 4th instant, between the Representative of His Majesty the King of Italy and His Excellency the Minister of State of Her Majesty the Queen Regent.

The undersigned avails himself of this occasion to renew to His Excellency the Marquis Maffei the assurance of his high consideration.

The Ambassador of Austria-Hungary.

(Signed) DUBSKY.

138   THIRD TREATY OF
THE TRIPLE ALLIANCE

TREATY of Alliance between Austria-Hungary, the German Empire, and Italy. Berlin, 6th May, 1891. Ratifications exchanged 17th May, 1891.

Their Majesties the Emperor of Austria, King of Bohemia, etc., and Apostolic King of Hungary, the Emperor of Germany, King of Prussia, and the King of Italy, firmly resolved to assure to Their States the continuation of the benefits which the maintenance of the Triple Alliance guarantees to them, from the political point of view as well as from the monarchical and social point of view, and wishing with this purpose to prolong the duration of this Alliance, concluded on May 20, 1882, and already renewed a first time by the Treaties of February 20, 1887, whose expiration was fixed for May 30, 1892, have, for this purpose, appointed as Their Plenipotentiaries, to wit:

His Majesty the Emperor of Austria, King of Bohemia, etc., and Apostolic King of Hungary: the Sieur Emeric Count Széchényi of Sárvári Felsö-Vidék, Chamberlain and Actual Privy Councillor, His Ambassador Extraordinary and Plenipotentiary to His Majesty the Emperor of Germany, King of Prussia,

His Majesty the Emperor of Germany, King of Prussia: the Sieur Leo von Caprivi, General of Infantry, Chancellor of the Empire, His President of the Council of Ministers of Prussia,

His Majesty the King of Italy: the Sieur Edward Count de Launay, His Ambassador Extraordinary and Plenipotentiary to His Majesty the Emperor of Germany, King of Prussia,

who, after exchange of their full powers, found in good and due form, have agreed upon the following Articles:

ART. I. The High Contracting Parties mutually promise peace and friendship, and will enter into no alliance or engagement directed against any one of their States.

They engage to proceed to an exchange of ideas on political and economic questions of a general nature which may arise, and they further promise one another mutual support within the limits of their own interests.

ART. II. In case Italy, without direct provocation on her part, should be attacked by France for any reason whatsoever, the two other

Contracting Parties shall be bound to lend help and assistance with all their forces to the Party attacked.

This same obligation shall devolve upon Italy in case of any aggression without direct provocation by France against Germany.

ART III. If one, or two, of the High Contracting Parties, without direct provocation on their part, should chance to be attacked and to be engaged in a war with two or more Great Powers nonsignatory to the present Treaty, the *casus foederis* will arise simultaneously for all the High Contracting Parties.

ART. IV. In case a Great Power nonsignatory to the present Treaty should threaten the security of the states of one of the High Contracting Parties, and the threatened Party should find itself forced on that account to make war against it, the two others bind themselves to observe towards their Ally a benevolent neutrality. Each of them reserves to itself, in this case, the right to take part in the war, if it should see fit, to make common cause with its Ally.

ART. V. If the peace of one of the High Contracting Parties should chance to be threatened under the circumstances foreseen by the preceding Articles, the High Contracting Parties shall take counsel together in ample time as to the military measures to be taken with a view to eventual co-operation.

They engage henceforward, in all cases of common participation in a war, to conclude neither armistice, nor peace, nor treaty, except by common agreement among themselves.

ART. VI. Germany and Italy, having in mind only the maintenance, so far as possible, of the territorial status quo in the Orient, engage to use their influence to forestall, on the Ottoman coasts and islands in the Adriatic and the Aegean Seas, any territorial modification which might be injurious to one or the other of the Powers signatory to the present Treaty. To this end, they will communicate to one another all information of a nature to enlighten each other mutually concerning their own dispositions, as well as those of other Powers.

ART. VII. Austria-Hungary and Italy, having in mind only the maintenance, so far as possible, of the territorial status quo in the Orient, engage to use their influence to forestall any territorial modification which might be injurious to one or the other of the Powers signatory to the present Treaty. To this end, they shall communicate to one another all information of a nature to enlighten each other mutually concerning their own dispositions, as well as those of other Powers.

However, if, in the course of events, the maintenance of the status quo in the regions of the Balkans or of the Ottoman coasts and islands in the Adriatic and in the Aegean Sea should become impossible, and if, whether in consequence of the action of a third Power or otherwise,

Austria-Hungary or Italy should find themselves under the necessity of modifying it by a temporary or permanent occupation on their part, this occupation shall take place only after a previous agreement between the two Powers, based upon the principle of a reciprocal compensation for every advantage, territorial or other, which each of them might obtain beyond the present status quo, and giving satisfaction to the interests and well founded claims of the two Parties.

ART. VIII. The stipulations of Articles VI and VII shall apply in no way to the Egyptian question, with regard to which the High Contracting Parties preserve respectively their freedom of action, regard being always paid to the principles upon which the present Treaty rests.

ART. IX. Germany and Italy engage to exert themselves for the maintenance of the territorial status quo in the North African regions on the Mediterranean, to wit, Cyrenaica, Tripolitania, and Tunisia. The Representatives of the two Powers in these regions shall be instructed to put themselves into the closest intimacy of mutual communication and assistance.

If unfortunately, as a result of a mature examination of the situation, Germany and Italy should both recognize that the maintenance of the status quo has become impossible, Germany engages, after a formal and previous agreement, to support Italy in any action in the form of occupation or other taking of guaranty which the latter should undertake in these same regions with a view to an interest of equilibrium and of legitimate compensation.

It is understood that in such an eventuality the two Powers would seek to place themselves likewise in agreement with England.

ART. X. If it were to happen that France should make a move to extend her occupation, or even her protectorate or her sovereignty, under any form whatsoever, in the North African territories, and that in consequence thereof Italy, in order to safeguard her position in the Mediterranean, should feel that she must herself undertake action in the said North African territories, or even have recourse to extreme measures in French territory in Europe, the state of war which would thereby ensue between Italy and France would constitute *ipso facto*, on the demand of Italy, and at the common charge of Germany and Italy, the *casus foederis* foreseen by Articles II and V of the present Treaty, as if such an eventuality were expressly contemplated therein.

ART. XI. If the fortunes of any war undertaken in common against France by the two powers should lead Italy to seek for territorial guaranties with respect to France for the security of the frontiers of the Kingdom and of her maritime position, as well as with a view to the stability of peace, Germany will present no obstacle thereto, and, if need be, and in a measure compatible with circumstances, will apply herself to facilitating the means of attaining such a purpose.

ART. XII. The High Contracting Parties mutually promise secrecy as to the contents of the present Treaty.

ART. XIII. The Signatory Powers reserve the right of subsequently introducing, in the form of a protocol and of a common agreement, the modifications of which the utility should be demonstrated by circumstances.

ART. XIV. The present Treaty shall remain force for the space of six years, dating from the exchange of ratifications; but if it has not been denounced one year in advance by one or another of the High Contracting Parties, it shall remain in force for the same duration of six more years.

ART. XV. The ratifications of the present Treaty shall be exchanged at Berlin within a period of a fortnight, or sooner if may be.

In witness whereof the respective Plenipotentiaries have signed the present Treaty and have affixed thereto the seal of their arms.

Done at Berlin, in triplicate, the sixth day of the month of May, one thousand eight hundred and ninety-one.

(L.S.)	SZÉCHÉNYI.
(L.S.)	v. CAPRIVI.
(L.S.)	LAUNAY.

(b)

Final Protocol to the Treaty.

PROTOCOL.

At the moment of proceeding to the signing of the Treaty of this day between Austria-Hungary, Germany, and Italy, the undersigned Plenipotentiaries of these three Powers, thereto duly authorized, mutually declare themselves as follows:

1. Under reserve of parliamentary approval for the executory stipulations proceeding from the present declaration of principle, the High Contracting Parties promise each other, from this moment, in economic matters (finances, customs, railroads), in addition to most-favoured-nation treatment, all of the facilities and special advantages which would be compatible with the requirements of each of the three States and with their respective engagements with third Powers.

2. The accession of England being already acquired, in principle, to the stipulations of the Treaty of this day which concern the Orient, properly so-called, to wit, the territories of the Ottoman Empire, the High Contracting Parties shall exert themselves at the opportune

moment, and to the extent that circumstances may permit it, to bring about an analogous accession with regard to the North African territories of the central and western part of the Mediterranean, including Morocco. This accession might be realized by an acceptance, on the part of England, of the programme established by Articles IX and X of the Treaty of this day.

In witness whereof the three Plenipotentiaries have signed the present Protocol in triplicate.

Done at Berlin, the sixth day of the month of May, one thousand eight hundred and ninety-one.

SZÉCHÉNYI.

v. CAPRIVI.

LAUNAY.

139

UNDERSTANDING BETWEEN FRANCE AND RUSSIA.

M. de Mohrenheim, Ambassador of Russia at Paris, to M. Ribot, Minister of Foreign Affairs of France, communicating the instructions of M. de Giers, Russian Minister of Foreign Affairs.

Paris, August 15/27, 1891.

During my recent sojourn in St. Petersburg, whither I was ordered by my August Sovereign, it pleased the Emperor to provide me with special instructions, set forth in the letter, sub-joined in copy, which His Excellency, M. de Giers, Minister of Foreign Affairs, addressed to me, and which His Majesty has deigned to direct me to communicate to the Government of the Republic.

In excution of this Supreme order, I am making it my pressing duty to bring this document to the knowledge of Your Excellency, in the firm hope that its contents, previously concerted and formulated by common agreement between our two Cabinets, will meet with the full approbation of the French Government; and that you will be kind enough, Mr. Minister, in conformity with the wish expressed by M. de Giers, to honour me with a reply testifying to the perfect agreement fortunately established from this time on between our two Governments.

The ulterior developments, of which the two points thus agreed upon not only are susceptible, but which will form their necessary comple-ment, may be made the subject of confidential and intimate conferences at the moment judged opportune by either Cabinet, when they believe they can proceed to it at a good time.

Holding myself for this purpose at the entire disposition of Your Excellency, I am happy to be able to take advantage of such an occasion to ask you to be kind enough to accept the renewed homage of my highest consideration and of my most unalterable devotion.

MOHRENHEIM.

ANNEX.

Letter of M. de Giers, Minister of Foreign Affairs of Russia,
to M. de Mohrenheim, Ambassador of Russia at Paris.

Petersburg, August 9/21, 1891.

The situation created in Europe by the open renewal of the Triple Alliance and the more or less probable adhesion of Great Britain to the political aims which that alliance pursues, has, during the recent sojourn here of M. de Laboulaye, prompted an exchange of ideas between the former Ambassador of France and myself, tending to define the attitude which, as things now stand and in the presence of certain eventualities, might best suit our respective Governments, which, having kept out of any league, are none the less sincerely desirous of surrounding the maintenance of peace with the most efficacious guaranties.

It is thus that we have been led to formulate the two points below:

1. In order to define and consecrate the cordial understanding which unites them, and desirous of contributing in common agreement to the maintenenace of the peace which forms the object of their sincerest aspirations, the two Governments declare that they will take counsel together upon every question of a nature to jeopardize the general peace;

2. In case that peace should be actually in danger, and especially if one of the two parties should be threatened with an aggression, the two parties undertake to reach an understanding on the measures whose immediate and simultaneous adoption would be imposed upon the two Governments by the realization of this eventuality.

Having submitted to the Emperor the fact of this exchange of ideas as well as the text of the conclusions resulting therefrom, I have the honour to inform you today that His Majesty has deigned to approve completely these principles of agreement, and would view with favour their adoption by the two Governments.

In informing you of these Sovereign dispositions, I beg that you be kind enough to bring to the knowledge of the French Government and to communicate to me the decisions which it may take on its side.

GIERS.

M. Ribot, French Minister of Foreign Affairs, to M. de Mohrenheim,
Russian Ambassador at Paris, in reply to the preceding.

Paris, August 27, 1891.

You have been kind enough, by order of your Government, to communicate to me the text of the letter of the Minister of Foreign Affairs of the Empire, wherein are set forth the special instructions with which the Emperor Alexander decided to provide you in pursuance of the last exchange of ideas to which the general situation of Europe had given rise between M. de Giers and the Ambassador of the French Republic at St. Petersburg.

Your Excellency was instructed to express at the same time the hope that the contents of this document, previously concerted and formulated in common agreement between the two Cabinets, would meet with the full assent of the French Government.

I hasten to thank Your Excellency for this communication.

The Government of the Republic can only take the same view as does the Imperial Government of the situation created in Europe by the conditions under which the renewal of the Triple Alliance has come to pass, and believes with it that the moment has arrived to define the attitude which, as things now stand and in the presence of certain eventualities, might seem best to the two Governments, equally desirous of assuring the guaranties for the maintenance of peace which result from the European balance of power.

I am, therefore, happy to inform Your Excellency that the Government of the Republic gives its entire adhesion to the two points which form the subject of the communication of M. de Giers and which are formulated as follows:

1. In order to define and consecrate the cordial understanding which unites them, and desirous of contributing in common agreement to the maintenance of the peace which forms the object of their sincerest aspirations, the two Governments declare that they will take counsel together upon every question of a nature to jeopardize the general peace;

2. In case that peace should be actually in danger, and especially if one of the two parties should be threatened with an agression, the two parties undertake to reach an understanding on the measures whose immediate and simultaneous adoption would be imposed upon the two Governments by the realization of this eventuality.

I furthermore hold myself at your disposal for the examination of all questions which, under present political conditions, make more particular demand upon the attention of the two Governments.

Conversely, the Imperial Government will doubtless appreciate, as do we, the importance of confiding to special delegates, who should be designated as soon as possible, the practical study of measures designed to meet the eventualities foreseen by the second point of the agreement.

In begging you to bring the reply of the French Government to the knowledge of the Government of His Majesty, I wish to emphasize how much I cherish the opportunity to participate in the consecration of an understanding which has been the constant object of our common efforts.

RIBOT.

140

SECOND TREATY of Alliance between Austria-Hungary and Roumania. Sinaia, 13th/25th July, 1892. Ratifications exchanged 25th July/4th August, 1892.

His Majesty the Emperor of Austria, King of Bohemia, etc., and Apostolic King of Hungary, and

His Majesty the King of Roumania,

animated by an equal desire to maintain the general peace, in conformity with the purpose pursued by the Austro-Hungarian and German Alliance, to assure the political order, and to guarantee against all eventualities the perfect friendship which binds Them together, have resolved to conclude to this end a Treaty which by its essentially conservative and defensive nature pursues only the aim of forestalling the dangers which might menace the peace of Their States.

For this purpose Their said Majesties have named as Their Plenipotentiaries, to wit:

His Majesty the Emperor of Austria, King of Bohemia, etc., and Apostolic King of Hungary: the Sieur Agenor Count Goluchowski, Imperial and Royal Chamberlain, His Envoy Extraordinary and Minister Plenipotentiary to His Majesty the King of Roumania,

His Majesty the King of Roumania: the Sieur Alexander N. Lahovary, His Minister, Secretary of State for Foreign Affairs,

who, after having communicated to each other their full powers, found in good and due form, have agreed upon the following Articles:

ART. 1. The High Contracting Parties promise one another peace and friendship, and will enter into no alliance or engagement directed against any one of their States. They engage to follow a friendly policy, and to lend one another mutual support within the limits of their interests.

ART. 2. If Roumania, without any provocation on her part, should be attacked, Austria-Hungary is bound to bring her in ample time help and assistance against the aggressor. If Austria-Hungary be attacked under the same circumstances in a portion of her states bordering on Roumania, the *casus foederis* will immediately arise for the latter.

ART. 3. If one of the High Contracting Parties should find itself threatened by an aggression under the abovementioned conditions, the respective Governments shall put themselves in agreement as to the measures to be taken with a view to co-operation of their armies. These military questions, especially that of the unity of operations and of passage through the respective territories, shall be regulated by a military convention.

ART. 4. If, contrary to their desire and hope, the High Contracting Parties be forced into a common war under the circumstances foreseen by the preceding Articles, they engage neither to negotiate nor to conclude peace separately.

ART. 5. The present Treaty shall remain in force for a period of four years, dating from the day of the exchange of ratifications. If the present Treaty is not denounced one year before its expiration, or if its revision is not demanded by either of the High Contracting Parties, it shall be regarded as prolonged for a period of three more years.

ART. 6. The High Contracting Parties mutually promise secrecy as to the contents of the present Treaty.

ART. 7. The present Treaty shall be ratified and the ratifications shall be exchanged within a period of three weeks, or sooner if may be.

In witness whereof the respective Plenipotentiaries have signed it and have affixed thereto the seal of their arms.

Done at Sinaia, the twenty-fifth/thirteenth day of the month of July of the year of grace one thousand eight hundred and ninety-two.

    AGENOR COUNT GOLUCHOWSKI.   AL. LAHOVARI.
        (L.S.)   (L.S.)

Treaty between Austria-Hungary, Germany, and Roumania
providing for the accession of Germany to the Alliance. Bucharest,
November 11/12, 1892. Ratifications exchanged December 1/13, 1892.

His Majesty the Emperor of Austria, King of Bohemia, etc., and Apostolic King of Hungary, and

His Majesty the King of Roumania, having concluded at Sinaia on July 25/13 of the current year the Treaty of friendship and alliance which follows:

    [*Articles 1–7 of the Treaty of July 25, 1892, follow.*]

have invited His Majesty the Emperor of Germany, King of Prussia, to accede to the provisions of the aforesaid Treaty.

Consequently His Majesty the Emperor of Germany, King of Prussia, has furnished with His full powers for this purpose His Representative at Bucharest, Counsellor of Legation Bernhard von Bülow, to adhere formally to the provisions contained in the above-mentioned Treaty. In virtue of this Act of Accession His Majesty the Emperor of Germany, King of Prussia, takes in the name of the German Empire towards Their Majesties the Emperor of Austria, King of Bohemia, etc., and Apostolic King of Hungary, and the King of Roumania, and at the same time Their Majesties the Emperor of Austria, King of Bohemia, etc., and Apostolic King of Hungary, and the King of Roumania take towards His Majesty the Emperor of Germany, King of Prussia, the same engagements by which the High Contracting Parties have mutually bound themselves according to the stipulations of the said Treaty inserted above.

The present Act of Accession shall be ratified and the ratifications shall be exchanged within a period of three weeks, or sooner if may be.

In witness whereof the respective Plenipotentiaries have signed the present Act of Accession and have affixed thereto the seal of their arms.

Done at Bucharest, the twenty-third/eleventh day of the month of November of the year of grace one thousand eight hundred and ninety-two.

(L.S.)	A. GOLUCHOWSKI.
(L.S.)	AL. LAHOVARI.
(L.S.)	BERN. BÜLOW.

Treaty between Austria-Hungary and Italy providing for the accession of Italy to the Alliance. November 28, 1892.
Ratifications exchanged, December 24, 1892.

His Majesty the Emperor of Austria, Apostolic King of Hungary, and His Majesty the King of Roumania, having concluded on July 25/13, 1892, a Treaty of friendship and alliance, now in force, the tenor of which Treaty follows:

[The text of the Treaty as above follows.]

This Treaty having received on November 23, 1892, the Accession of His Majesty the Emperor of Germany, King of Prussia, and having been then communicated by the High Contracting Parties above-mentioned to His Majesty the King of Italy with an invitation to accede thereto, His Majesty the King of Italy, approving the purpose for which this Treaty has been concluded, and which is the preservation of the general peace and of the existing order, has authorized the undersigned Sieur Francis dei marchesi Curtopassi, His Envoy Extraordinary and Minister Plenipotentiary to His Majesty the King of Roumania, to declare in His name that He accedes to the said Treaty within the limits indicated below, so far as concerns the stipulations of Articles 2 and 3, to wit:

If eventualities that could give rise to the *casus foederis* as it is foreseen in Articles 2 and 3 should chance to occur, Their Majesties the Emperor of Austria, Apostolic King of Hungary, the King of Italy, and the King of Roumania assume a mutual engagement to take counsel together in ample time as to common action, the detailed procedure of which shall be regulated by a special convention.

The present Accession shall be in force, dating from the day of signature, for the whole duration of the principal Treaty of July 25/13, 1892.

This Act of Accession shall be kept secret, and cannot be revealed without the consent of each of the High Contracting Parties.

His Majesty the Emperor of Austria, Apostolic King of Hungary, has for his part authorized the undersigned Sieur Agenor Count Goluchowski, Imperial and Royal Chamberlain, His Envoy Extraordinary and Minister Plenipotentiary to His Majesty the King of Roumania, to declare in His name that He accepts in the terms above stated, and with the same mutual obligations, the Accession of His Majesty the King of Italy to the Treaty of July 25/13, 1892.

The present Act of Accession and of acceptance shall be ratified by His Majesty the Emperor of Austria, Apostolic King of Hungary, and by His Majesty the King of Italy, and the ratifications shall be exchanged as soon as possible.

In witness whereof the respective Plenipotentiaries have signed the present Act of Accession and have affixed thereto the seal of their arms.

Done at Bucharest, the twenty-eighth day of the month of November, one thousand eight hundred and ninety-two.

(L.S.)   AGENOR COUNT GOLUCHOWSKI.
(L.S.)   FRANCESCO CURTOPASSI.

141

DRAFT of Military Convention between France and Russia, 1892.

France and Russia, being animated by an equal desire to preserve peace, and having no other object than to meet the necessities of a defensive war, provoked by an attack of the forces of the Triple Alliance against the one or the other of them, have agreed upon the following provisions:

1. If France is attacked by Germany, or by Italy supported by Germany, Russia shall employ all her available forces to attack Germany.

If Russia is attacked by Germany, or by Austria supported by Germany, France shall employ all her available forces to fight Germany.

2. In case the forces of the Triple Alliance, or of one of the Powers composing it, should mobilize, France and Russia, at the first news of the event and without the necessity of any previous concert, shall mobilize immediately and simultaneously the whole of their forces and shall move them as close as possible to their frontiers.

3.   The available forces to be employed against Germany shall be, on the part of France, 1,300,000 men, on the part of Russia, 700,000 or 800,000 men.

These forces shall engage to the full, with all speed, in order that Germany may have to fight at the same time on the East and on the West.

4. The General Staffs of the Armies of the two countries shall co-operate with each other at all times in the preparation and facilitation of the execution of the measures above foreseen.

They shall communicate to each other, while there is still peace, all information relative to the armies of the Triple Alliance which is or shall be within their knowledge.

Ways and means of corresponding in times of war shall be studied and arranged in advance.

5. France and Russia shall not conclude peace separately.

6. The present Convention shall have the same duration as the Triple Alliance.

7. All the clauses above enumerated shall be kept rigorously secret.

Signature of the Minister:
Signature of the Minister:

General Aide-de-Camp,
   Chief of the General Staff,
Signed: OBRUCHEFF.

General of Division,
   Councillor of State,
Sub-Chief of the General
Staff of the Army,
Signed: BOISDEFFRE.

Approval of the Convention.

M. de Giers, Russian Minister of Foreign Affairs, to M. de Montbello, French Ambassador at St. Petersburg.

St. Petersburg, December 15/27, 1893.

Very secret.

After having examined by Supreme order the draft of a military convention drawn up by the Russian and French General Staffs, in August, 1892, and after having submitted my estimate thereof to the Emperor, I esteem it my duty to inform Your Excellency that the text of this arrangement, as approved in principle by His Majesty and signed by Aide-de-Camp General Obrucheff and General of Division de Boisdeffre, may be regarded henceforth as having been definitively adopted in its existing form.—The two General Staffs will thus have the faculty of taking counsel together at any time and of reciprocally communicating any information which might be useful to them.

GIERS.

142

TREATY of Alliance between Korea and Japan, signed at Seoul, 26th August, 1894.

"In view of the fact that on the 25th of July 1894, the Korean Government entrusted His Imperial Majesty's Envoy Extraordinary and Minister Plenipotentiary at Sôul, Korea, with the expulsion, on their behalf, of Chinese soldiers from Korean territory, the Governments of Japan and Korea have been placed in a situation to give mutual assistance both offensive and defensive. Consequently the undersigned Plenipotentiaries, duly authorized by their respective Governments, have, with a view of defining the fact and of securing in the premises concerted action on the part of the two countries, agreed to the following Articles:—

"ARTICLE I.—The object of the alliance is to maintain the independence of Korea on a firm footing and to promote the respective interests of both Japan and Korea by expelling Chinese soldiers from Korean territory.

"ARTICLE II.—Japan will undertake all warlike operations against China, both offensive and defensive, while Korea will undertake to give every possible facility to Japanese soldiers regarding their movements and supply of provisions.

"ARTICLE III.—This treaty shall cease and determine at the conclusion of a treaty of peace with China.

"In witness whereof the Plenipotentiaries of the two countries have signed the treaty and hereunto affixed their seals.

"Done at Sôul this 26th day of August, 1894.

"KEISUKE OTORI,

"*H. I. J. M.'s Envoy Extraordinary and Minister Plenipotentiary.*

"KIM IN SHIOUKU,

"*H. K. M.'s Minister for Foreign Affairs.*"

143   TREATY OF SHIMONOSEKI

TREATY of peace between Japan and China (with separate articles and Convention to prolong Armistice), 17th April, 1895. Ratifications exchanged at Chefoo, 8th May, 1895.

His Majesty the Emperor of China and His Majesty the Emperor of Japan, desiring to restore the blessings of peace to their countries and subjects and to remove all cause for future complications, have named as their Plenipotentiaries for the purpose of concluding a Treaty of peace; that is to say, His Majesty the Emperor of China, Li Hung-chang, Senior Tutor to the Heir Apparent, Senior Grand Secretary of State, Minister Superintendent of Trade for the Northern Ports of China, Viceroy of the Province of Chihli, and Earl of the First Rank, and Li Ching-fong, Ex-Minister of the Diplomatic Service, of the Second Official Rank;

And His Majesty the Emperor of Japan, Count Ito Hirobumi, Junii, Grand Cross of the Imperial Order of Paullownia, Minister President of State, and Viscount Mutsu Munemitsu, Junii, First Class of the Imperial Order of the Sacred Treasure, Minister of State for Foreign Affairs;

Who, after having exchanged their full powers, which were found to be in good and proper form, have agreed to the following Articles:—

Independence of Korea.

ART. I. China recognizes definitely the full and complete independence and autonomy of Korea, and in consequence the payment of tribute and the performance of ceremonies and formalities by Korea to China, in derogation of such independence and autonomy, shall wholly cease for the future.

Cession of part of Fêngtien Province.

ART. II. China cedes to Japan in perpetuity and full sovereignty the following territories, together with all fortifications, arsenals, and public property thereon:

(a) The southern portion of the province of Fêngtien, within the following boundaries:—

The line of demarcation begins at the mouth of the River Yalu and ascends that stream to the mouth of the River An-ping; from thence the line runs to Fêng-huang; from thence to Haicheng; from thence to Ying-kow, forming a line which describes the southern portion of the territory. The places above named are included in the ceded territory. When the line reaches the River Liao at Ying-kow, it follows the course of that stream to its mouth where it terminates. The mid-channel of the River Liao shall be taken as the line of demarcation.

This cession also includes all islands appertaining or belonging to the province of Fêngtien, situated in the eastern portion of the Bay of Liao-tung and in the northern part of the Yellow Sea.

(b) The island of Formosa, together with all islands appertaining or belonging to said island of Formosa.

(*c*) The Pescadores Group, that is to say, all islands lying between the 119th and 120th degrees of longitude east of Greenwich and the 23rd and 24th degrees of north latitude.

Delimitation of ceded territory.

ART. III. The alignments of the frontiers described in the preceding Article and shown on the annexed map, shall be subject to the verification and demarcation on the spot, by a Joint Commission of Delimitation consisting of two or more Chinese and two or more Japanese Delegates to be appointed immediately after the exchange of the ratifications of this Act. In case the boundaries laid down in this act are found to be defective at any point, either on account of topography or in consideration of good administration, it shall also be the duty of the Delimitation Commission to rectify the same.

The Delimitation Commission will enter upon its duties as soon as possible and will bring its labours to a conclusion within the period of one year after appointment.

The alignments laid down in this Act shall, however, be maintained until the rectifications of the Delimitation Commission, if any are made, shall have received the approval of the Governments of China and Japan.

War Indemnity to Japan.

ART. IV. China agrees to pay to Japan as a war indemnity the sum of 200,000,000 Kuping Taels. The said sum is to be paid in eight instalments. The first instalment of 50,000,000 Taels to be paid within six months, and the second instalment of 50,000,000 Taels to be paid within twelve months after the exchange of the ratifications of this Act. The remaining sum to be paid in six equal annual instalments, as follows: The first of such equal annual instalments to be paid within two years; the second within three years; the third within four years; the fourth within five years; the fifth within six years, and the sixth within seven years, after the exchange of the ratifications of this Act. Interest at the rate of 5 *per centum per annum* shall begin to run on all unpaid portions of the said indemnity from the date the first instalment falls due.

China shall, however, have the right to pay by anticipation at any time any or all of said instalments. In case the whole amount of the said indemnity is paid within three years after the exchange of the ratifications of the present Act, all interest shall be waived and the interest for two years and a half or for any less period if then already paid, shall be included as a part of the principal amount of the indemnity.

Inhabitants of Ceded Territory.

ART. V. The inhabitants of the territory ceded to Japan, who wish to take up their residence outside the ceded districts shall be at liberty to sell their real property and retire.

For this purpose a period of two years from the date of the exchange of the ratifications of the present Act, shall be granted. At the expiration of that period those of the inhabitants who shall not have left such territories shall at the option of Japan, be deemed to be Japanese subjects.

Each of the two Governments shall immediately upon the exchange of the ratifications of the present Act, send one or more Commissioners to Formosa to effect a final transfer of that Province and within the space of two months after the exchange of the ratifications of this Act, such transfer shall be completed.

Treaty of Commerce and Navigation to be Negotiated.

ART. VI. All treaties between China and Japan having come to an end in consequence of war, China engages immediately upon the exchange of the ratifications of this Act, to appoint Plenipotentiaries to conclude, with the Japanese Plenipotentiaries, a Treaty of Commerce and Navigation and a Convention to regulate Frontier Intercourse and Trade. The Treaties, Conventions, and Regulations now subsisting between China and European Powers shall serve as a basis for the said Treaty and Convention between China and Japan. From the date of the exchange of the ratifications of this Act until the said Treaty and Convention are brought into actual operation, the Japanese Government; its officials; commerce; navigation; frontier intercourse and trade; industries; ships, and subjects, shall, in every respect, be accorded by China most-favoured-nation treatment.

China makes in addition the following concessions, to take effect six months after the date of the present Act:

Opening of New Localities in China to Trade.

1st. The following cities, towns, and ports, in addition to those already opened, shall be opened to the trade, residence, industries, and manufactures of Japanese subjects, under the same conditions and with the same privileges and facilities as exist at the present open cities, towns, and ports of China.

(1) Shashih, in the province of Hupeh.

(2) Chungking, in the province of Szechuan.

(3) Suchow, in the province of Kiangsu.

(4) Hang-chow, in the province of Chekiang.

The Japanese Government shall have the right to station Consuls at any or all of the above-named places.

Navigation on Chinese Inland Waters.

2nd. Steam navigation for vessels under the Japanese flag for the conveyance of passengers and cargo shall be extended to the following places:

(1) On the upper Yangtsze River, from I-chang to Chung-king.

(2) On the Woo-sung River and the Canal, from Shanghai to Su-chow and Hang-chow. The Rules and Regulations which now govern the navigation of the inland waters of China by foreign vessels shall, so far as applicable, be enforced in respect of the above-named routes until new Rules and Regulations are conjointly agreed to.

Renting Warehouses.

3rd. Japanese subjects purchasing goods or produce in the interior of China or transporting imported merchandise into the interior of China, shall have the right temporarily to rent or hire warehouses for the storage of the articles so purchased or transported, without the payment of any taxes or exactions whatever.

Right to Manufacture in Open Localities.

4th. Japanese subjects shall be free to engage in all kinds of manufacturing industries in all the open cities, towns, and ports of China, and shall be at liberty to import into China all kinds of machinery paying only the stipulated duties thereon.

All articles manufactured by Japanese subjects in China, shall in respect of inland transit and internal taxes, duties, charges and exactions of all kinds and also in respect of warehousing and storage facilities in the interior of China, stand upon the same footing and enjoy the same privileges and exemptions as merchandise imported by Japanese subjects into China.

In the event additional Rules and Regulations are necessary in connection with these concessions, they shall be embodied in the Treaty of Commerce and Navigation provided for by this Article.

Evacuation of China.

ART. VII. Subject to the provisions of the next succeeding Article, the evacuation of China by the armies of Japan, shall be completely effected within three months after the exchange of the ratifications of the present Act.

Temporary Military Occupation of Wei-hai-wei. Its Evacuation.

ART. VIII. As a guarantee of the faithful performance of the stipulations of this Act, China consents to the temporary occupation by the military forces of Japan, of Wei-hai-wei in the Province of Shantung.

Upon the payment of the first two instalments of the war indemnity herein stipulated for and the exchange of the ratifications of the Treaty of Commerce and Navigation, the said place shall be evacuated by the Japanese forces, provided the Chinese Government consent to pledge, under suitable and sufficient arrangements, the Customs Revenue of China as a security for the payment of the principal and interest of the remaining instalments of said indemnity. In the event no such arrangements are concluded, such evacuation shall only take place upon the payment of the final instalment of said indemnity.

It is, however, expressly understood that no such evacuation shall take place until after the exchange of the ratifications of the Treaty of Commerce and Navigation.

Prisoners of War.

ART. IX. Immediately upon the exchange of the ratifications of this Act, all prisoners of war then held shall be restored and China undertakes not to ill-treat or punish prisoners of war so restored to her by Japan. China also engages to at once release all Japanese subjects accused of being military spies or charged with any other military offenses. China further engages not to punish in any manner nor to allow to be punished, those Chinese subjects who have in any manner been compromised in their relations with the Japanese army during the war.

Cessation of Military Operations.

ART. X. All offensive military operations shall cease upon the exchange of the ratifications of this Act.

ART. XI. The present Act shall be ratified by their Majesties the Emperor of China and the Emperor of Japan, and the ratifications shall be exchanged at Chefoo, on the 14th day of the 4th month of the 21st year of Kwang Hsü, corresponding to the 8th day of the 5th month of the 28th year of Meiji. (May 8th, 1895.)

In witness whereof, the respective Plenipotentiaries have signed the same and have affixed thereto the seal of their arms.

Done at Shimonoseki, in duplicate, this 23d day of the 3d month of the 21st year of Kwang Hsü, corresponding to the 17th day of the 4th month of the 28th year of Meiji. (April 17th, 1895.)

(L. S.)   LI HUNG CHANG.

Plenipotentiary of His Majesty the Emperor of China, Senior Tutor of the Heir Apparent, Senior Grand Secretary of State, Minister Superintendent of Trade for the North Ports of China, Viceroy of the Province of Chihli, and Earl of the First Rank.

LI CHING FONG.
Plenipotentiary of His Majesty the Emperor of China, Ex-Minister of the Diplomatic Service, of the Second Official Rank.

(L. S.) COUNT ITO HIROBUMI.
Junii, Grand Cross of the Imperial Order of Paullownia, Minister President of State, Plenipotentiary of His Majesty the Emperor of Japan.

(L. S.) VISCOUNT MUTSU MUNEMITSU.
Junii, First Class of the Imperial Order of the Sacred Treasure, Minister of State for Foreign Affairs, Plenipotentiary of His Majesty the Emperor of Japan.

SEPARATE ARTICLES.

Military Force to Occupy Wei-hai-wei.

ART. I. The Japanese military forces which are, under Article VIII of the treaty of peace signed this day, to temporarily occupy Wei-hai-wei, shall not exceed one Brigade and from the date of the exchange of the ratifications of the said treaty of peace, China shall pay annually, one-fourth of the amount of the expenses of such temporary occupation that is to say, at the rate of 500,000 Kuping Taels per annum.

Territory Occupied at Wei-hai-wei.

ART. II. The territory temporarily occupied at Wei-hai-wei shall comprise the island of Liu-kung and a belt of land 5 Japanese Ri wide along the entire coast line of the Bay of Wei-hai-wei.

No Chinese troops shall be permitted to approach or occupy any place within a zone of 5 Japanese Ri wide beyond the boundaries of the occupied territory.

Chinese to Retain Civil Administration.

ART. III. The civil administration of the occupied territory shall remain in the hands of the Chinese Authorities. But such Authorities shall at all times be obliged to conform to the orders which the Commander of the Japanese Army of occupation may deem it necessary to give in the interest of the health, maintenance, safety, distribution or discipline of the Troops.

All military offences committed within the occupied territory shall be subject to the jurisdiction of the Japanese Military Authorities.

The foregoing Separate Articles shall have the same force, value and effect as if they had been, word for word, inserted in the Treaty of Peace signed this day.

In witness whereof, the respective Plenipotentiaries have signed the same and have affixed thereto the seal of their arms.

Done at Shimonoseki, in duplicate, this 23rd day of the third month of the 21st year of Kuang Hsü, corresponding to the 17th day of the 4th month of the 28th year of Meiji. (April 17th, 1895.)

(Signatures (4) and titles, same as in Treaty.)

CONVENTION TO PROLONG ARMISTICE

The undersigned (insert here names and titles of the 2 Chinese Plenipotentiaries, as in Preamble of Treaty) Plenipotentiaries of His Majesty the Emperor of China, and (insert here names and titles of 2 Japanese Plenipotentiaries as in preamble of Treaty) Plenipotentiaries of His Majesty the Emperor of Japan, having concluded a Treaty of Peace, have, in order to provide for the peaceful exchange of the ratifications of said Treaty, agreed upon and signed the following Articles:

Armistice.

I. The Convention of Armistice concluded on the 5th day of the 3rd month of the 21st year of Kwang Hsü, corresponding to the 30th day of the 3rd month of the 28th year of Meiji, is prolonged for the period of 21 days from this date.

II. The armistice, which is prolonged by this Convention, shall terminate, without notice on either side, at midnight on the 14th day of the 4th month of the 21st year of Kwang Hsü, corresponding to the 8th day of the 5th month of the 28th year of Meiji. The rejection in the meantime, however, of the said Treaty of Peace, by either High Contracting Party, shall have the effect of at once terminating this Armistice without previous notice.

In witness whereof the Plenipotentiaries of China and Japan have hereunto set their hands and affixed their seal.

Done at Shimonoseki, this 23rd day of the 3rd month of the 21st year of Kuang Hsü, corresponding to the 17th day of the 4th month of the 28th year of Meiji. (April 17th, 1895.)

(Signatures (4) and titles, same as in Treaty.)

144   CONVENTION OF PEKING

CONVENTION for the retrocession by Japan to China of the southern portion of the Province of Fêng-Tien (i.e., the Liaotung Peninsula), 8th November, 1895. Ratifications exchanged at Peking, 29th November, 1895.

His Majesty the Emperor of Japan and His Majesty the Emperor of China, desiring to conclude a Convention for the retrocession by Japan of all the southern portion of the province of Fêng-Tien to the sovereignty of China, have for that purpose named as Their Plenipotentiaries, that is to say:

His Majesty the Emperor of Japan—Baron Hayashi Tadasu, Shoshii, Grand Cross of the Imperial Order of the Sacred Treasure, Grand Officer of the Imperial Order of the Rising Sun, Minister Plenipotentiary and Envoy Extraordinary.

and His Majesty the Emperor of China—Li Hung-Chang, Minister Plenipotentiary, Senior Tutor of the Heir-Apparent, Senior Grand Secretary of State and Earl of the First Rank,

Who, after having communicated to each other their full powers, which were found to be in good and proper form, have agreed upon the following Articles:

Territory Retroceded.

ART. I. Japan retrocedes to China in perpetuity and full sovereignty the southern portion of the Province of Fêng-Tien, which was ceded to Japan under Article II of the Treaty of Shimonoseki of the 17th day of the 4th month of the 28th year of Meiji, corresponding to the 23rd day of the 3d month of the 21st year of Kuang Hsü, together with all fortifications, arsenals and public property thereon at the time the retroceded territory is completely evacuated by the Japanese forces in accordance with the provisions of Article III of this Convention, that is to say, the southern portion of the Province of Fêng-Tien from the mouth of the River Yalu to the mouth of the River An-ping, thence to Feng Huang Ch'êng, thence to Haicheng, and thence to Ying-kow; also all cities and towns to the south of this boundary and all islands appertaining or belonging to the Province of Fêng-Tien situated in the eastern portion of the Bay of Liao-Tung and in the northern part of the Yellow Sea. Article III of the said Treaty of Shimonoseki is in consequence suppressed, as are also the provisions in the same Treaty with reference to the conclusion of a Convention to regulate frontier intercourse and trade.

Compensation in Lieu of Territory.

ART. II. As compensation for the retrocession of the southern portion of the Province of Feng-Tien, the Chinese Government engage to pay to the Japanese Government 30,000,000 Kuping taels on or before the 16th day of the 11th month of the 28th year of Meiji, corresponding to the 30th day of the 9th month of the 21st year of Kuang Hsü.

Mode of Payment.

ART. III. Within three months from the day on which China shall have paid to Japan the compensatory indemnity of 30,000,000 Kuping taels provided for in Article II of this Convention, the retroceded territory shall be completely evacuated by the Japanese forces.

Immunity to Inhabitants.

ART. IV. China engages not to punish in any manner nor to allow to be punished those Chinese subjects who have in any manner been compromised in connection with the occupation by the Japanese forces of the retroceded territory.

English Text Authoritative.

ART. V. The present Convention is signed in duplicate, in the Japanese, Chinese, and English languages. All these texts have the same meaning and intention, but in case of any differences of interpretation between the Japanese and Chinese texts, such differences shall be decided by reference to the English text.

ART. VI. The present Convention shall be ratified by His Majesty the Emperor of Japan and His Majesty the Emperor of China, and the ratifications thereof shall be exchanged at Peking within twenty-one days from the present date.

In witness whereof the respective Plenipotentiaries have signed the same and have affixed thereto the seal of their arms.

Done at Peking, this 8th day of the 11th month of the 28th year of Meiji, corresponding to the 22nd day of the 9th month of the 21st year of Kuang Hsü.

(L. S.)   HAYASHI TADASU.
(L. S.)   LI HUNG-CHANG.

PROTOCOL.

In view of the insufficiency of time to effect a formal exchange of the ratifications of the Convention between Japan and China signed this day respecting the retrocession of the Peninsula of Fêng-Tien, before the date named in the said Convention for certain stipulations thereof to take effect, the Government of His Majesty the Emperor of Japan and the Government of His Majesty the Emperor of China, in order to prevent the possibility of delay in putting into execution the several provisions of the said Convention, have, through their respective Plenipotentiaries, agreed upon the following stipulations:

The Governments of Japan and China shall, within the period of five days after the date of this Protocol, announce to each other through the undersigned, their respective Plenipotentiaries, that the said Convention has received the approval of His Majesty the Emperor of Japan and His Majesty the Emperor of China, respectively, and thereupon the said Convention in all its parts shall come into operation as fully and effectually as if the ratifications thereof had actually been exchanged.

In witness whereof the respective Plenipotentiaries have signed the same, and have affixed thereto the seal of their arms.

Done at Peking, this 8th day of the 11th month of the 28th year of Meiji, corresponding to the 22nd day of the 9th month of the 21st year of Kuang Hsü.

(L. S.)   HAYASHI TADASU.
(L. S.)   LI HUNG-CHANG.

145

PROTOCOL between Austria-Hungary and Roumania regarding the prolongation of the Alliance. Sinaia, 30th September, 1896.

The undersigned, furnished with full powers by their Sovereigns, found in good and due form, taking into consideration the stipulations of the Treaty of Alliance, signed on July 25, 1892, between Roumania and Austria-Hungary, and desirous to record once more the intimate understanding established in prospect of certain eventualities mentioned in this Treaty, have come into agreement upon the following:

Although the Treaty, of which the duration had first been fixed for four years, continues, in virtue of Article 5, tacitly to keep its validity until July 25, 1899, the undersigned have to declare in a formal manner that the engagements assumed on both sides shall remain fully and entirely in force during the entire period of seven years foreseen by the said Treaty.

Convinced of the good results obtained by this understanding for the interests of the two Contracting Parties, and wishing to make sure of its benefits for a prolonged period, the undersigned assume the engagement that the Treaty in question shall remain in force in all its parts and in all its tenor until July 25, 1903.

It is well understood that the present Protocol, drawn up in conformity with the full powers granted by Their Majesties the King of Roumania and the Emperor of Austria, Apostolic King of Hungary, forms an integral part of the Treaty of Alliance of July 25, 1892.

Done at Sinaia, the eighteenth/thirtieth day of the month of September of the year of grace one thousand eight hundred and ninety-six.

D. STURDZA.   GOLUCHOWSKI.
(L. S.)   (L. S.)

Accession of the German Empire to the Protocol. Berlin, May 7, 1899.

NOTE VERBALE.

The duration of the secret Treaty concluded between Austria-Hungary and Roumania in the year 1892 and prolonged in the year 1896 is determined in Article 5 of this Treaty. The last paragraph of this Article reads:

" If the present Treaty is not denounced one year before its expiration, or if its revision is not demanded by either of the High Contracting Parties, it shall be considered as prolonged for a period of three more years."

On the basis of this wording of the Article, and in conformity with the generally accepted principles of the interpretation of treaties, the Imperial Government, which adhered to the secret Treaty in November, 1892, is of the opinion that the Treaty automatically continues as regards every Signatory Party which has not given notice of its withdrawal one year before the expiration of the said Treaty. Since no notice was given by the Government of His Majesty in the course of this year, the said Government considers itself bound, as previously, by the stipulations of the Treaty.

The Imperial Government, in reply to an inquiry of the Roumanian Minister of Berlin, was as early as December of last year in a position to inform him in writing concerning the abovementioned conception of the duration of the Treaty, and in this statement met with the approval and the complete satisfaction of His Majesty King Charles.

Berlin, May 7, 1899.

Acknowledgment by Austria-Hungary of the German accession to the Protocol. Berlin, May 15, 1899.

Secret.

Excellency:

It is with the most sincere thanks that I have had the honour to receive the Note Verbale which Your Excellency was good enough to transmit to me, together with the secret Memorandum of May 7 last.

In these documents, which I have not failed to lay before my Government, Your Excellency defines the position which the Imperial German Government takes with regard to the duration of the obligations which are incumbent on it through its participation in the Treaty concluded between Austria-Hungary and Roumania.

Your Excellency has formulated the opinion of the Imperial German Government in this matter, that by virtue of the wording of Article 5 of the secret Treaty which was concluded with Roumania in 1892 and prolonged in 1896, and in conformity with the generally accepted principles of the interpretation of treaties, the Treaty in question is automatically prolonged as regards each Signatory Party which has not given notice of its withdrawal one year before the expiration of the said Treaty; and that therefore, as no notice was given by the Government of His Majesty the German Emperor in the course of this year, the said Government considers itself bound, as previously, by the stipulations of the Treaty.

Your Excellency had the further kindness to state that the Imperial German Government, in reply to an inquiry of the Roumanian Minister in Berlin, was as early as December of the previous year in a position to inform him in writing concerning the abovementioned opinion of the duration of its treaty obligations, and that in this statement it met with the approval and complete satisfaction of His Majesty King Charles.

By the direction and in the name of the Imperial and Royal Government I have the honour to make known most respectfully to Your Excellency that it sees in the above declaration of Your Excellency the written adhesion on its part foreshadowed already in November, 1896, by the Imperial German Government, to the Treaty prolongation stipulated between Austria-Hungary and Roumania in September of that year.

I am further charged to bring to Your Excellency's gracious attention that the Imperial and Royal Government takes note of the communication of the Imperial German Government just referred to, and intends forthwith to impart it to the Royal Italian Government, so that the latter may be in a position to become acquainted on its part with the German interpretation, and to adhere to it through a similar declaration.

I avail myself at the same time of this occasion to renew to Your Excellency the assurance of my distinguished consideration.

VON SZÖGYÉNY, M. P.

Accession of Italy to the Protocol. Rome, June 5, 1899.
Ministry of Foreign Affairs.

Rome, June 5, 1899.

Mr. Ambassador.

By order of your Government, Your Excellency has done me the honour to inform me of an exchange of Notes which took place, on May 7 and 15 last, between the Secretary of State of the German Empire for Foreign Affairs and the Ambassador of Austria-Hungary at Berlin on the subject of the secret Treaty between Austria-Hungary and Roumania. It is evident from these documents that the German Government regards itself, in virtue of Article 5 of this Treaty, and in conformity with the generally admitted rules of the interpretation of treaties, as engaged still and for the future by its accession to the said Treaty until the expiration of a new triennial period.

The Government of the King, so far as it is concerned, does not hesitate to associate itself with the opinion expressed by the Imperial Government of Germany. The accession of Italy and of Germany to the secret Treaty between Austria-Hungary and Roumania applying to Article 5 as well as to all the other Articles, it is not doubtful that the secret Treaty, by the fact that it was not denounced in sufficient time by any of the interested Parties, is found prolonged in full force for a further period of three years, and that the obligations contracted by the two Powers which have acceded thereto remain likewise in force for the same period.

In begging Your Excellency to be good enough to bring the above to the notice of the Imperial and Royal Government, in reply to the query which it has addressed to us through your kind services, I avail myself of the occasion to renew to you the assurance of my very high consideration.

VISCONTI VENOSTA.

To His Excellency Baron Pasetti, Ambassador of Austria-Hungary, Rome.

146

AGREEMENT between Austria-Hungary and Russia on the Affairs of the Balkans. 1897.

*Despatch from the Austrian Government to the Ambassador in
St. Petersburg containing the Agreement reached between
Austria-Hungary and Russia in regard to Balkan affairs.
Vienna, May 8, 1897.*

Copy

of a secret despatch to Prince Liechtenstein at St. Petersburg, dated
Vienna, May 8, 1897.

On my return from St. Petersburg it seems to me useful to set down
in a short summary the cardinal points of the understanding which has
so happily resulted from the exchange of views and ideas which I have
had with Count Mouravieff and of which the conclusions have been
ratified by Their Majesties the Emperor and King, our August Master,
and the Emperor Nicholas.

The conference which the two Sovereigns, accompanied by Their
Ministers of Foreign Affairs, held at the Winter Palace has had for its
practical result the establishment of a common line of conduct in the
affairs of the Orient, which, while taking account of the security and of
the vital interests of the two Empires, and while eliminating the danger
of a rivalry disastrous to the peace of Europe on the seething soil of the
Balkan Peninsula, permits us now and henceforward to view with more
calm and quiet the political complications which, at a given moment,
may present themselves in our immediate neighbourhood.

Based on a principle of reciprocal confidence and loyalty, this understanding includes all the elements necessary to an efficacious
co-operation; and thus understood, as I have every reason to believe it is,
by the two Cabinets, it offers at the same time solid guaranties for the
pacific solution of the Oriental problem.

This established, I wish to bring to notice, in the first place, that,
having come to an agreement as to the *necessity of maintaining* the
present status quo as long as circumstances will permit, we, Count
Mouravieff and I, were pleased to record that there existed between
Austria-Hungary and Russia no divergence of principle of a nature to
preclude the possibility of an understanding between our two countries
to guard against eventualities which, in a perhaps near future, might,
even against our inclination, occur in the Balkan Peninsula. Quite the
contrary. After having maturely examined the question in all its details,
we had no difficulty in convincing ourselves that it would be easy to
reconcile the interests of the two great Empires, on the condition,
however, of dissipating all spirit of mistrust in our relations and of
explaining to one another in perfect frankness and loyalty the principles
which are to regulate our conduct henceforth.

Imbued with these sentiments, we thenceforth applied ourselves to
establishing the bases of an agreement between the Cabinets of Vienna
and of St. Petersburg, which, approved without restriction by our
August Sovereigns, is found in summary in the following points:

1. It was agreed that, in case the maintenance of the present status
quo becomes impossible, Austria-Hungary and Russia discard in

advance all idea of conquest in the Balkan Peninsula, and that they are decided to make this principle respected by every other Power which might manifest designs on the above-mentioned territory.

2. It was equally recognized that the question of Constantinople and of the adjacent territory as well as that of the Straits (Dardanelles and Bosphorus), having an eminently European character, is not of a nature to be made the object of a separate understanding between Austria-Hungary and Russia.

Count Mouravieff did not hesitate to declare in this connection that, far from striving for any modification of the present state of things, sanctioned by the Treaty of Paris and the Convention of London, the Imperial Government held, on the contrary, to the complete maintenance of the provisions relative thereto, which gave full and entire satisfaction to Russia in prohibiting, by the closing of the Straits, access to the Black Sea to foreign war vessels.

In its inability to admit of concession on this point, the Cabinet of St. Petersburg was only guided by a principle of legitimate security, a principle the recognition of which was accorded by us from the outset.

3. On the other hand, the establishment of a new order of things in the Balkan Peninsula, outside Constantinople and the Straits, would, in case it should occur, give rise to a special stipulation between Austria-Hungary and Russia, who, being chiefly interested in the settlement of this question, declare themselves disposed to act in common accord in fixing henceforth the bases of their understanding, to wit:

a. The territorial advantages, accorded to Austria-Hungary by the Treaty of Berlin, are and remain acquired by her. In consequence, the possession of Bosnia, of Herzegovina, and of the Sanjak of Novibazar may not be made the object of any discussion whatsoever, the Government of His Imperial and Royal Apostolic Majesty reserving to itself the right of substituting, when the moment arrives, for the present status of occupation and of right of garrisoning that of annexation.

b. The part comprised between Janina to the south and the Lake of Scutari to the north, with a sufficient extension on the east side, shall form an independent state under the name of the principality of Albania, to the exclusion of every foreign domination.

c. The rest of the territory to be disposed of shall be the object of an equitable partition between the different small existing Balkan States, a partition on the subject of which Austria-Hungary and Russia reserve the right of being heard in good time. While inclined to take into consideration as far as possible the legitimate interests of the participants, they are resolved, on the other hand, to safeguard the principle of the present equilibrium, and, if need be by means of rectifications of frontiers, to exclude every combination which would favour the establishment of a marked preponderance of any particular Balkan principality to the detriment of the others.

d. Having finally recorded that our two Cabinets have no other objective in the Balkan Peninsula than the maintenance, the consolidation, and the pacific development of the small States established there, we agreed to pursue in future in this field a policy of perfect harmony, and to avoid in consequence everything which might engender between us the elements of conflict or of mistrust.

Such is, Prince, the summary of the conferences of St. Petersburg, which I believe I have reproduced as faithfully as possible.

I do not doubt for a moment that Count Mouravieff will confirm its exactness to you; and it is for that reason that I ask you to let him read my present despatch, a copy of which you should leave in his hands with the request that he acknowledge its receipt.

Accept, etc.

Note of the Russian Government to the Austrian Ambassador in St. Petersburg in regard to the Balkan Agreement.

St. Petersburg, May 5 (17), 1897.

Mr. Ambassador,

The secret despatch which Count Goluchowski addressed to Your Highness under date of Vienna, May 8 instant, and a copy of which you have been kind enough to send me, summarizes, in general terms, the exchange of views and of ideas to which the recent stay in Russia of His Majesty the Emperor-King Francis Joseph and of his Minister of Foreign Affairs gave rise.

I feel that I ought to reply to this kind communication by a succinct statement of the impressions which I received from it, in order to eliminate any possibility of a misunderstanding in our conceptions.

As Count Goluchowski states, we " came to an agreement as to the necessity of maintaining the present status quo in the Balkan Peninsula, as long as circumstances will permit," and we recognized that there exists between Russia and Austria-Hungary no divergence of principle, nor the least reason for distrust. Therefore, it seemed evident to us " that the interests of the two Empires could always be reconciled by means of frank and loyal explanations."

It was agreed that, in case, in spite of all our efforts, the present status quo of the Balkan Peninsula can no longer be maintained, " Russia and Austria-Hungary discard in advance all idea of conquest; and they are decided to make this principle respected by every other Power which should manifest contrary designs."

As Russia is unable to admit the least infringement of the provisions relative to the closing of the Straits of the Bosphorus and of the

Dardanelles, as sanctioned by existing treaties, Austria-Hungary " recognizes from the outset the perfect legitimacy of this principle."

On the other hand, " the establishment of a new order of things in the Balkan Peninsula, in case it should occur, would give rise to a special stipulation between Austria-Hungary and Russia."

Count Goluchowski, in his note of May 8, fixed, henceforth, as a basis of such an understanding, the four following points:

a. " The advantages accorded to Austria-Hungary by the Treaty of Berlin are and remain acquired by her."

In subscribing to this principle, we deem it necessary to observe that the Treaty of Berlin assures to Austria-Hungary the right of military occupation of Bosnia and Herzegovina. The annexation of these two provinces would raise a more extensive question, which would require special scrutiny at the proper times and places. As to the Sanjak of Novibazar, there would also be the necessity to specify its boundaries, which, indeed, have never been sufficiently defined.

It seems to us that points *b* and *c*, having regard to the eventual formation of a principality of Albania and to the equitable partition of all the territory to be disposed of between the different small Balkan States, touch upon questions of the future which it would be premature and very difficult to decide at present.

As to point *d*, providing: " having finally recorded that our two Cabinets have no other objective in the Balkan Peninsula than the maintenance, the consolidation, and the pacific development of the small States established there, we agreed to pursue in future in this field a policy of perfect harmony, and to avoid in consequence everything which might engender between us elements of conflict or of mistrust "— this point answers entirely to the views of the Emperor, my August Master.

I beg Your Highness to be kind enough to bring all the above to the knowledge of Count Goluchowski; who, I trust, will remark, in spite of some slight differences of interpretation which I have felt it my duty to call to your attention, the perfect conformity in our way of looking at things, so far as regards the broad political lines so happily laid down during our recent interview.

Accept, Mr. Ambassador, the assurance of my high consideration.

COUNT MOURAVIEFF.

His Most Serene Highness the Prince of Liechtenstein, etc., etc., etc.

147

CONVENTION between Great Britain and China respecting an Extension of Hong Kong Territory. Signed at Peking, 9th June, 1898. Ratifications exchanged at London, 6th August, 1898.

WHEREAS it has for many years past been recognized that an extension of Hong Kong territory is necessary for the proper defence and protection of the Colony.

Enlargement of British Territory, under Lease.

It has now been agreed between the Governments of Great Britain and China that the limits of British territory shall be enlarged under lease to the extent indicated generally on the annexed map. The exact boundaries shall be hereafter fixed when proper surveys have been made by officials appointed by the two Governments. The term of this lease shall be ninety-nine years.

Jurisdiction.

It is at the same time agreed that within the city of Kowloon the Chinese officials now stationed there shall continue to exercise jurisdiction except so far as may be inconsistent with the military requirements for the defence of Hong Kong. Within the remainder of the newly-leased territory Great Britain shall have sole jurisdiction. Chinese officials and people shall be allowed as heretofore to use the road from Kowloon to Hsinan.

Use of Landing Place, near Kowloon, by Chinese.

It is further agreed that the existing landing-place near Kowloon city shall be reserved for the convenience of Chinese men-of-war, merchant and passenger vessels, which may come and go and lie there at their pleasure; and for the convenience of movement of the officials and people within the city.

Railway.

When hereafter China constructs a railway to the boundary of the Kowloon territory under British control, arrangements shall be discussed.

No Expropriation or Expulsion of Natives.

It is further understood that there will be no expropriation or expulsion of the inhabitants of the district included within the extension, and that if land is required for public offices, fortifications, or the like official purposes, it shall be bought at a fair price.

Extradition.

If cases of extradition of criminals occur, they shall be dealt with in accordance with the existing Treaties between Great Britain and China and the Hong Kong Regulations.

Use of Mirs Bay and Deep Bay by Chinese Ships of War.

The area leased to Great Britain, as shown on the annexed map, includes the waters of Mirs Bay and Deep Bay, but it is agreed that Chinese vessels of war, whether neutral or otherwise, shall retain the right to use those waters.

Ratifications.

This Convention shall come into force on the 1st day of July, 1898, being the 13th day of the 5th moon of the 24th year of Kuang Hsü. It shall be ratified by the Sovereigns of the two countries, and the ratifications shall be exchanged in London as soon as possible.

In witness whereof the Undersigned, duly authorized thereto by their respective Governments, have signed the present Agreement.

Done at Peking in quadruplicate (four copies in English and four in Chinese) the 9th day of June, in the year of our Lord 1898, being the 21st day of the 4th moon of the 24th year of Kuang Hsü.

(L.S.)   CLAUDE M. MacDONALD.
(L.S.)   [Seal of Chinese Plenipotentiary.]

148

CONVENTION between Great Britain and Germany regarding Angola, Mozambique and Portuguese Timor. Signed 30th August, 1898.

In view of the possibility that Portugal may require financial assistance from some foreign Power or Powers, and in order to obviate the international complications which such a condition of things may produce, and to preserve her integrity and independence, the Undersigned, duly authorised by their respective Sovereigns, have agreed as follows:—

I. Whenever either the British or the German Government is of opinion that it is expedient to accede to a request for an advance of money to Portugal on the security of the Customs revenues or other revenues of Mozambique, Angola, and the Portuguese part of the Island of Timor, it shall communicate the fact to the other Government, and the other Government shall have the right to advance a portion of the total sum required.

In the event of the other Government signifying its intention to exercise this right, the two Governments shall consult as to the terms of the two loans, and these loans shall be issued on the security of the Customs revenues of Mozambique, Angola, and Portuguese Timor as near as possible simultaneously. The loans shall bear as near as possible the same proportion to each other as the amounts of the Customs revenues respectively assigned as their security.

The loans shall be issued on terms as favourable to Portugal as the condition of the money market and the security of the loans permit, and shall in other respects be subject as near as possible to similar conditions.

II. Of the Customs revenues, referred to in Article I, those of the Province of Mozambique south of the Zambezi, and of the part of that province lying on the left bank of the Zambezi above its confluence with the Shiré, and those of the portions of the Province of Angola, as hereinafter described, shall be assigned to the British loan. The Customs revenues of the remaining parts of the Provinces of Mozambique and Angola and the Customs revenues of Portuguese Timor shall be assigned to the German loan.

The portion of the Province of Angola, of which the Customs revenues shall be assigned to the British loan, is comprised within the following limits: the northern frontier shall run from the coast along the 8th parallel of south latitude to the 16th degree of longitude east of Greenwich, thence it shall descend that degree to the 9th parallel of latitude, and shall follow that parallel eastwards as far as the frontier of the Congo Free State. The southern frontier shall start from a point on the coast 5 English miles north of Egito, and shall run thence due east to the eastern frontier of the Province of Angola. The western frontier shall be the sea; the eastern frontier shall be the eastern limit of the Province of Angola.

III. Any Delegates sent by Great Britain or Germany to take note of the collection of the revenues which are the security for their respective loans shall have only rights of inspection, but no rights of administration, interference, or control, so long as there is no default in the payment of interest or sinking fund.

IV. In case of default in the payment of the interest or sinking fund of either loan, the administration of the various custom-houses in the two provinces and in Portuguese Timor shall be handed over by Portugal; those assigned for the German loan to Germany, those assigned for the British loan to Great Britain.

V. It is well understood that all rights, whether British or German, acquired in the provinces affected before the date of this Convention, shall be fully safeguarded, provided they are of a purely private character, and convey neither political rights nor territorial or administrative jurisdiction.

It is also understood that no influence will be used in the future, either by the British or the German Governments, to obtain fresh Concessions, except in those portions of the provinces of which the customs revenues are assigned to their respective loans.

VI. The present Convention shall be ratified, and the ratifications thereof shall be exchanged as soon as possible. The Convention shall come into force immediately after the exchange of ratifications.

In witness whereof the Undersigned, duly authorised, have signed the same, and have affixed thereto their seals.

Done in duplicate, at London, the 30th day of August, 1898.

(L. S.)   ARTHUR JAMES BALFOUR.

(L. S.)   P. HATZFELDT.

Secret Convention between Great Britain and Germany. Signed 30th August, 1898.

Whereas, notwithstanding the provisions of the preceding Convention of this day's date, it may unfortunately not be found possible to maintain the integrity of the African possessions of Portugal south of the Equator, as well as of those in Timor, the Undersigned, duly authorised by their respective Sovereigns, have further agreed as follows:—

I. Great Britain and Germany agree jointly to oppose the intervention of any third Power in the Provinces of Mozambique, Angola and in Portuguese Timor, either by way of loan to Portugal on the security of the revenues of those provinces, or by way of acquisition of territory, by grant, cession, purchase, lease, or otherwise.

II. It is understood that, from the conclusion of the Conventions of this day's date, Great Britain will abstain from advancing any claim of whatsoever kind to the possession, occupation, control, or exercise of political influence in or over those portions of the Portuguese provinces in which the Customs revenues have been assigned to Germany, and that Germany will in like manner abstain from advancing any claim of whatsoever kind to the possession, occupation, control, or exercise of political influence, in or over those portions of those Portuguese provinces in which the Customs revenues have been assigned to Great Britain.

III. In case Portugal renounces her sovereign rights over Mozambique, Angola, and Portuguese Timor, or loses these territories in any other manner, it is understood that the subjects of, and natives of the Protectorates of, one Contracting Party, together with their goods and ships, and also the produce and the manufactures of its dominions, possessions, Colonies and Protectorates, shall, in such portions of the territories comprised in the present Convention as may fall to the other Contracting Party, participate in all the prerogatives, exemptions and privileges with regard to trade, commerce, taxation and navigation which are there enjoyed by the subjects of, and natives of the Protectorates of, the other Contracting Party.

IV. With regard to the Vth Article of the Convention of to-day's date, which refers to private rights of British or German subjects in the Provinces of Mozambique, Angola, and Portuguese Timor, it is well understood between the two Governments that this Article applies, among others, to the so-called Katembe Concession, and, further, that the Government of Great Britain will adopt a friendly attitude in respect to the confirmation of this Concession by the Portuguese Government in case such a confirmation should be applied for.

V. The present Convention shall be ratified, and the ratifications thereof shall be exchanged as soon as possible. The Convention shall come into force immediately after the exchange of ratifications.

In witness whereof the Undersigned, duly authorised, have signed the same, and have affixed thereto their seals.

Done in duplicate, at London, the 30th day of August, 1898.

(L. S.)　　ARTHUR JAMES BALFOUR.
(L. S.)　　P. HATZFELDT.

Secret Note exchanged between Great Britain and Germany,
30th August, 1898.

In order to make clear the intention of the two Conventions of this day's date, it is further understood between the two Governments as follows:—

In the event of one of the two Governments obtaining from the Portuguese Government before the contingency contemplated in Article III of the Secret Convention a cession of territory, or the concession of special privileges not of an occasional character, in those portions of the Portuguese Provinces of Mozambique, Angola, or Timor, the customs revenues of which have been assigned to it, it is well understood between the two Governments that such cessions of territory, or concessions of privileges, shall not become operative until analogous grants as near as possible of equal value have been accorded to the other Government in those portions of the provinces, the customs revenues of which have been assigned to it by the present arrangement.

In case either Government applies for special privileges of an occasional character, it shall immediately inform the other Government, and if these privileges are granted, and if the other Government should desire it, shall use its influence to obtain for the other Government similar special privileges of an occasional character and of equal value.

And whereas, owing to the imperfect surveys which alone are at present available, the IInd Article of the Convention of this day's date may not exactly carry out the intentions of the Contracting Parties, it is understood between them that in any case the port and town of Ambriz shall be included in the security assigned to Germany.

In case, therefore, that the port and town of Ambriz should be found to lie to the south of the 8th parallel of south latitude, the line of demarcation shall start from a point on the coast 5 English miles south of the port of Ambriz, and be continued thence due east until it reaches the 16th degree of longitude east of Greenwich.

From the intersection of the line, which may be determined as the line of demarcation, with the 16th degree of longitude aforesaid, the line shall, if necessary, be extended along that degree of longitude so far south of the 9th parallel of south latitude as will secure to Germany a strip of territory not less than a geographical degree in width between the southern extremity of the Congo Free State in the region of Lunda and the northern frontier of the portion of Angola of which the customs revenues are assigned to Great Britain.

Done in duplicate, at London, the 30th day of August, 1898.

(L. S.)   ARTHUR JAMES BALFOUR.
(L. S.)   P. HATZFELDT.

Secret Declaration between Great Britain and Portugal. Signed, 14th, October 1899.

The Government of Her Majesty the Queen of the United Kingdom of Great Britain and Ireland, Empress of India, and the Government of His Most Faithful Majesty the King of Portugal and the Algarves, considering as of full force and effect the ancient treaties of alliance, amity and guarantee which subsist between the two Crowns, specifically confirm on this occasion Article 1 of the Treaty of the 29th January, 1642, which runs as follows:—

" It is concluded and accorded that there is, and shall be for ever, a good true and firm peace and amity between the most renowned Kings, Charles King of Great Britain and John the Fourth King of Portugal, their heirs and successors, and their Kingdoms, Countries, Dominions, Lands, People, Leigemen, Vassals and Subjects whomsoever, present and to come, of whatsoever condition, dignity or degree they may be, as well by land as by sea and fresh waters, so as the said Vassals and Subjects are each of them to favour the other and to use one another with friendly offices and true affection, and that neither of the said most renowned Kings, their heirs and successors, by himself or by any other, shall do or attempt anything against each other, or their Kingdoms, by land or by sea, nor shall consent nor adhere unto any war, counsel, or Treaty, in prejudice of the other."

They equally confirm the final Article of the Treaty of the 23rd June, 1661, of which the first part runs as follows:—

"Over and above all and singular agreed and concluded in the Treaty of Marriage between the Most Serene and Most Powerful Charles, the Second of that name, King of Great Britain and the Most Virtuous and Serene Lady Catherine, Infanta of Portugal, it is by the Secret Article concluded and accorded, that His Majesty of Great Britain, in regard of the great advantages and increase of dominion he hath purchased by the above-mentioned Treaty of Marriage shall promise and oblige himself as by this present Article he doth, to defend and protect all conquests or colonies belonging to the Crown of Portugal against all his enemies, as well future as present."

The Government of His Most Faithful Majesty undertakes not to permit, after the declaration of war between Great Britain and the South African Republic, or during the continuance of the war, the importation and passage of arms, and of munitions of war destined for the latter.

The Government of His Most Faithful Majesty will not proclaim neutrality in the war between Great Britain and the South African Republic.

Done, in duplicate, at London, this 14th day of October, 1899.

(L.S.)   SALISBURY.

(L.S.)   LUIZ DE SOVERAL.

149

CONVENTION between Great Britain and China respecting Weihaiwei. Signed at Peking, 1st July, 1898. Ratifications exchanged at London, 5th October, 1898.

In order to provide Great Britain with a suitable naval harbour in North China, and for the better protection of British commerce in the neighbouring seas, the Government of His Majesty the Emperor of China agree to lease to the Government of Her Majesty the Queen of Great Britain and Ireland Weihaiwei, in the Province of Shantung, and the adjacent waters, for so long a period as Port Arthur shall remain in the occupation of Russia.

Extent of Leased Territory. Jurisdiction.

The territory leased shall comprise the Island of Liu Kung, and all the Islands in the Bay of Weihaiwei, and a belt of land 10 English miles wide along the entire coast-line of the Bay of Weihaiwei. Within the above-mentioned territory leased Great Britain shall have sole jurisdiction.

Right to Erect Fortifications, &c.

Great Britain shall have in addition the right to erect fortifications, station troops, or take any other measures necessary for defensive purposes at any points on or near the coast of the region east of the meridian 121° 40′ east of Greenwich, and to acquire on equitable compensation within that territory such sites as may be necessary for water supply, communications, and hospitals. Within that zone Chinese administration will not be interfered with, but no troops other than Chinese or British shall be allowed therein.

Jurisdiction within the Walled City.

It is also agreed that within the walled city of Weihaiwei Chinese officials shall continue to exercise jurisdiction, except so far as may be inconsistent with naval and military requirements for the defence of the territory leased.

Rights of Chinese Ships of War.

It is further agreed that Chinese vessels of war, whether neutral or otherwise, shall retain the right to use the waters herein leased to Great Britain.

No Expropriation or Expulsion of Natives.

It is further understood that there will be no expropriation or expulsion of the inhabitants of the territory herein specified, and that if land is required for fortifications, public offices, or any official or public purpose, it shall be bought at a fair price.

Ratifications.

This Convention shall come into force on signature. It shall be ratified by the Sovereigns of the two countries, and the ratifications shall be exchanged in London as soon as possible.

In witness whereof the Undersigned, duly authorized thereto by their respective Governments, have signed the present Agreement.

Done at Peking in quadruplicate (four copies in English and four in

Chinese), the 1st day of July, in the year of our Lord 1898, being the 13th day of the 5th moon of the 24th year of Kuang Hsü.

(L.S.)   CLAUDE M. MacDONALD.

(L.S.)   [Seal of Chinese Plenipotentiary.]

150

EXCHANGE OF LETTERS MODIFYING THE FRANCO-RUSSIAN CONVENTION OF 1893.

Count Mouravieff, Russian Minister of Foreign Affairs, to M. Delcassé, French Minister of Foreign Affairs.

St. Petersburg, July 28/August 9, 1899.

The last few days that Your Excellency has just spent among us will, I hope, have permitted you to note once more the solidity of the bonds of lively and unchanging friendship which unite Russia to France.

In order to give fresh expression to these sentiments and to respond to the desire that you have expressed to His Majesty, the Emperor has deigned to authorize me, Mr. Minister, to propose to you an exchange of letters between us which shall establish that:

The Imperial Government of Russia and the Government of the French Republic, ever solicitous for the maintenance of the general peace and of the European balance of power,

Confirm the diplomatic arrangement formulated in the letter of August 9/21, 1891, of M. de Giers, that of August 15/27, 1891, of Baron Mohrenheim, and the letter in reply of M. Ribot, likewise bearing the date of August 15/27, 1891.

They decide that the draft of a military convention which was the complement thereof and which is mentioned in the letter of M. de Giers of December 15/27, 1893, and that of Count de Montebello of December 23, 1893/January 4, 1894, shall remain in force as long as the diplomatic agreement concluded for the safeguarding of the common and permanent interests of the two countries.

The most absolute secrecy as to the tenor and even as to the existence of the said arrangements must be scrupulously observed on either side.

In addressing this communication to you, Mr. Minister, I avail myself of the opportunity it offers me to renew to you the assurance of my high consideration.

COUNT MOURAVIEFF.

M. Delcassé, Minister of Foreign Affairs of the French Republic,
to Count Mouravieff, Minister of Foreign Affairs of Russia.

St. Petersburg, July 28-August 9, 1899.

Mr. Minister,

Last Sunday, when, with his consent, I had expressed to His Majesty the Emperor my opinion upon the utility of confirming our diplomatic arrangement of August, 1891, and of assigning to the military Convention which followed it the same duration as to the arrangement itself, His Majesty was kind enough to tell me that his own sentiments were in complete accord with the views of the Government of the Republic.

By your letter of this morning, you have done me the honour to inform me that it has pleased His Majesty the Emperor to approve the following formula: which has, moreover, the entire adherence of the President of the Republic and of the French Government, and on which the understanding was previously established between Your Excellency and myself:

[*Here follow the third to the sixth paragraphs, inclusive, of the preceding note.*]

I congratulate myself, Minister, that these few days spent at St. Petersburg have permitted me to note once more the solidity of the bonds of lively and unchanging friendship which unite France and Russia; and I beg you to accept the fresh assurance of my high regard.

DELCASSÉ.

151

Exchange of notes respecting regulations to be applied in any future extension of the British or French concession at Hankow. 15th January, 1900.

(1). *Note Verbale communicated to M. Cambon.*

It is understood on the part of Her Majesty's Government that, in the event of any extension of the French Concession at Hankow being obtained subsequently to this date, the following conditions as regards British property therein will be strictly observed:—

1. All deeds applying to British property to be registered in the British Consulate.

2. All Municipal Regulations to be submitted to Her Majesty's Minister at Peking before they can be enforced on British subjects.

3. All titles to British property which are declared in order by the British Consul-General are to be so considered by the French authorities.

With respect to the British claims to land situated in the present French Concession, which are believed to be four in number, and all of which are represented by Mr. Greaves, of Hankow, as it is understood that the validity of the titles is questioned by the French authorities, Her Majesty's Government consent to the question being referred to the British and French Consuls-General at Shanghai, and failing an agreement being arrived at by them, to an Arbitrator, by whom the matter would be decided in accordance with precedent and local usage.

Foreign Office, London, December 22, 1899.

(2). *M. Cambon to the Marquess of Salisbury.*

Embassy of France, London, January 15, 1900.

M. LE MARQUIS,

I have the honour to acknowledge the receipt from Your Lordship of the memorandum that you were so good as to send me, on December 22 last, on the subject of the Regulations to be applied in the French Concession at Hankow, in the event of its being extended.

My Government, to which I have not failed to refer it, instructs me to make known to you that it gives its adherence to the four points embodied in that document. It is, on the other hand, clearly understood between the two Governments that, in case the British Concession should hereafter be extended, the conditions hereinafter set forth would be applied, insofar as concerns such lands belonging to Frenchmen as might be found situated in the area to be included in the British Concession:—

1. All documents relative to French properties must be registered at the French Consulate.

2. All Municipal Regulations must be submitted to the Minister of France at Peking, before they may be applied to French citizens.

3. All the title-deeds of properties belonging to Frenchmen which are recognized as valid by the French Consul are to be accepted as such by the British authorities.

Accept, etc.

PAUL CAMBON.

152

DECLARATIONS accepting the commercial policy of the 'Open Door' in China by the United States, France, Germany, Great Britain, Italy, Japan and Russia. 20th March, 1900.

(I.)—FRANCE.
MR. HAY TO MR. VIGNAUD.
DEPARTMENT OF STATE,
Washington, September 6, 1899.

SIR: I have to enclose, for your confidential information, copies of instructions I have sent under this date to the United States Ambassadors at London, Berlin, and St. Petersburg in reference to the desire of this Government that the Governments of Great Britain, Germany, and Russia make formal declaration of an "open-door" policy in the territories held by them in China.

I am, etc.,   JOHN HAY.

MR. HAY TO MR. PORTER.
[Telegram.]
DEPARTMENT OF STATE,
Washington, November 21, 1899.

PORTER, *Ambassador, Paris.*

Informally submit to French Government form of declaration outlined in enclosures with instruction No. 664 of September 6 and ask whether France will join.

HAY.

MR. DELCASSÉ TO MR. PORTER.
FOREIGN AFFAIRS.

(Received at United States Embassy at Paris, December 16, 1899.)

MY DEAR AMBASSADOR: I find your note awaiting me on my return. The declarations which I made in the Chamber on the 24th of November last, and which I have had occasion to recall to you since then, show clearly the sentiments of the Government of the Republic. It desires throughout the whole of China and, with the quite natural reservation that all the Powers interested give an assurance of their willingness to act likewise, is ready to apply in the territories which are leased to it, equal treatment to the citizens and subjects of all nations, especially in the matter of customs duties and navigation dues, as well as transportation tariffs on railways.

I beg you, my dear Ambassador, to accept, etc.

DELCASSÉ.

(II.)—GERMANY.
MR. HAY TO MR. WHITE.
No. 927.]   DEPARTMENT OF STATE,
Washington, September 6, 1899.

SIR: At the time when the Government of the United States was informed by that of Germany that it had leased from His Majesty the Emperor of China the port of Kiao-chao and the adjacent territory in the province of Shantung, assurances were given to the Ambassador of the United States at Berlin by the Imperial German Minister for Foreign Affairs that the rights and privileges insured by treaties with China to citizens of the United States would not thereby suffer or be in anywise impaired within the area over which Germany had thus obtained control.

More recently, however, the British Government recognized by a formal agreement with Germany the exclusive right of the latter country to enjoy in said leased area and the contiguous "sphere of influence or interest" certain privileges, more especially those relating to railroads and mining enterprises; but, as the exact nature and extent of the rights thus recognized have not been clearly defined, it is possible that serious conflicts of interests may at any time arise, not only between British and German subjects within said area, but that the interests of our citizens may also be jeopardized thereby.

Earnestly desirous to remove any cause of irritation and to insure at the same time to the commerce of all nations in China the undoubted benefits which should accrue from a formal recognition by the various Powers claiming " spheres of interest " that they shall enjoy perfect equality of treatment for their commerce and navigation within such " spheres," the Government of the United States would be pleased to see His German Majesty's Government give formal assurances, and lend its co-operation in securing like assurances from the other interested Powers, that each within its respective sphere of whatever influence—

First. Will in no way interfere with any treaty port or any vested interest within any so-called " sphere of interest " or leased territory it may have in China.

Second. That the Chinese treaty tariff of the time being shall apply to all merchandise landed or shipped to all ports as are within said " sphere of interest " (unless they be " free ports "), no matter to what nationality it may belong, and that duties so leviable shall be collected by the Chinese Government.

Third. That it will levy no higher harbour dues on vessels of another nationality frequenting any port in such " sphere " than shall be levied on vessels of its own nationality, and no higher railroad charges over lines built, controlled, or operated within its " sphere " on merchandise belonging to citizens or subjects of other nationalities transported through such " sphere " than shall be levied on similar merchandise belonging to its own nationals transported over equal distances.

The liberal policy pursued by His Imperial German Majesty in declaring Kiao-chao a free port and in aiding the Chinese Government in the establishment there of a custom-house are so clearly in line with the proposition which this Government is anxious to see recognized that it entertains the strongest hope that Germany will give its acceptance and hearty support.

The recent Ukase of His Majesty the Emperor of Russia declaring the port of Ta-lien-wan open during the whole of the lease under which it is held from China to the merchant ships of all nations, coupled with the categorical assurances made to this Government by His Imperial Majesty's representative at this capital at the time, and since repeated to me by the present Russian Ambassador, seem to insure the support of the Emperor to the proposed measure. Our Ambassador at the Court of St. Petersburg has in consequence been instructed to submit it to the Russian Government and to request their early consideration of it. A copy of my instruction on the subject to Mr. Tower is herewith enclosed for your confidential information.

The commercial interests of Great Britain and Japan will be so clearly served by the desired declaration of intentions, and the views of the Governments of these countries as to the desirability of the adoption of measures insuring the benefits of equality of treatment of all foreign trade throughout China are so similar to those entertained by the United States, that their acceptance of the propositions herein outlined and their co-operation in advocating their adoption by the other Powers can be confidently expected. I enclose herewith copy of the instruction which I have sent to Mr. Choate on the subject.

In view of the present favourable conditions, you are instructed to submit the above considerations to His Imperial German Majesty's Minister for Foreign Affairs, and to request his early consideration of the subject.

Copy of this instruction is sent to our Ambassadors at London and at St. Petersburg for their information.

I have, etc.,   JOHN HAY.

COUNT VON BÜLOW TO MR. WHITE.
FOREIGN OFFICE,
Berlin, February 19, 1900.

MR. AMBASSADOR: Your Excellency informed me, in a memorandum presented on the 24th of last month, that the Government of the United States of America had received satisfactory written replies from all the Powers to which an inquiry had been addressed similar to that contained in Your Excellency's note of September 26 last, in regard to the policy of the open door in China. While referring to this, Your Excellency thereupon expressed the wish that the Imperial Government would now also give its answer in writing.

Gladly complying with this wish, I have the honour to inform Your Excellency, repeating the statements already made verbally, as follows: As recognized by the Government of the United States of America, according to Your Excellency's note referred to above, the Imperial Government has, from the beginning, not only asserted, but also practically carried out to the fullest extent, in its Chinese possessions absolute equality of treatment of all nations with regard to trade, navigation, and commerce. The Imperial Government entertains no thought of departing in the future from this principle, which at once excludes any prejudicial or disadvantageous commercial treatment of the citizens of the United States of America, so long as it is not forced to do so, on account of considerations of reciprocity, by a divergence from it by other governments. If, therefore, the other Powers interested in the industrial development of the Chinese Empire are willing to recognize the same principles, this can only be desired by the Imperial Government, which in this case upon being requested will gladly be ready to participate with the United States of America and the other Powers in an agreement made upon these lines, by which the same rights are reciprocally secured.

I avail myself, etc. BÜLOW.

(III).—GREAT BRITAIN.
MR. CHOATE TO LORD SALISBURY.
EMBASSY OF THE UNITED STATES,
London, September 22, 1899.

MY LORD: I am instructed by the Secretary of State to present to Your Lordship a matter which the President regards as of great and equal importance to Great Britain and the United States—in the maintenance of trade and commerce in the East, in which the interest of the two nations differs, not in character, but in degree only—and to ask for action on the part of Her Majesty's Government which the President conceives to be in exact accord with its uniformly declared policy and traditions, and which will greatly promote the welfare of commerce.

He understands it to be the settled policy and purpose of Great Britain not to use any privileges which may be granted to it in China as a means of excluding any commercial rivals, and that freedom of trade for it in that Empire means freedom of trade for all the world alike. Her Majesty's Government, while conceding by formal agreements with Germany and Russia the possession of " spheres of influence or interest " in China, in which they are to enjoy especial rights and privileges, particularly in respect to railroads and mining enterprises, has at the same time sought to maintain what is commonly called the " open-door " policy, to secure to the commerce and navigation of all nations equality of treatment within such " spheres." The maintenance of this policy is alike urgently demanded by the commercial communities of our two nations, as it is justly held by them to be the only one which will improve existing conditions, enable them to maintain their positions in the markets of China, and extend their future operations.

While the Government of the United States will in no way commit itself to any recognition of the exclusive rights of any power within or control over any portion of the Chinese Empire, under such agreements as have been recently made, it can not conceal its apprehensions that there is danger of complications arising between the treaty powers which may imperil the rights insured to the United States by its treaties with China.

It is the sincere desire of my Government that the interests of its citizens may not be prejudiced through exclusive treatment by any of the controlling powers within their respective " spheres of interests " in China, and it hopes to retain there an open market for all the world's commerce, remove dangerous sources of international irritation, and thereby hasten united action of the powers at Pekin to promote administrative reforms so greatly needed for strengthening the Imperial Government and maintaining the integrity of China, in which it believes the whole western world is alike concerned. It believes that such a result may be greatly aided and advanced by declarations by the various Powers claiming " spheres of interest " in China as to their intentions in regard to the treatment of foreign trade and commerce therein, and that the present is a very favourable moment for informing Her Majesty's Government of the desire of the United States it make on its own part and to lend its powerful support in an effort to obtain from each of the various Powers claiming " spheres of interest " in China a declaration substantially to the following effect:

(1) That it will in no wise interfere with any treaty port or any vested interest within any so-called " sphere of interest " or leased territory it may have in China.

(2) That the Chinese treaty tariff of the time being shall apply to all merchandise landed or shipped to all such ports as are within such " spheres of interest " (unless they be " free ports "), no matter to what nationality it may belong, and that duties so leviable shall be collected by the Chinese Government.

(3) That it will levy no higher harbour dues on vessels of another nationality frequenting its own " sphere " than shall be levied on vessels of its own nationality, and no higher railroad charges over

lines built, controlled, or operated within its "sphere" on merchandise belonging to citizens or subjects of other nationalities transported through such "sphere" than shall be levied on similar
merchandise belonging to its own nationals transported over equal
distances.

The President has strong reason to believe that the Governments of
both Russia and Germany will co-operate in such an understanding as
is here proposed. The recent Ukase of His Majesty the Emperor of
Russia declaring the port of Ta-lien-wan open to the merchant ships of
all nations during the whole term of the lease under which it is to be
held by Russia removes all uncertainty as to the liberal and conciliatory
policy of that Power, and justifies the expectation that His Majesty
would accede to the similar request of the United States now being
presented to him and make the desired declaration.

The recent action of Germany in declaring the port of Kiao-chao a
"free port" and the aid which its Government has given China in
establishing there a Chinese custom-house, coupled with oral assurances
given the United States by Germany that the interests of the United
States and its citizens within its "sphere" would in no wise be affected
by its occupation of this portion of the province of Shantung, encourage
the belief that little opposition is to be anticipated to the President's
request for a similar declaration from that Power.

It is needless also to add that Japan, the Power next most largely
interested in the trade of China, must be in entire sympathy with the
views here expressed, and that its interests will be largely served by the
proposed arrangement; and the declarations of its statesmen within the
last year are so entirely in line with it that the co-operation of that
Power is confidently relied upon.

It is therefore with the greatest pleasure that I present this matter to
Your Lordship's attention and urge its prompt consideration by Her
Majesty's Government, believing that the action is in entire harmony
with its consistent theory and purpose, and that it will greatly redound
to the benefit and advantage of all commercial nations alike. The
prompt and sympathetic co-operation of Her Majesty's Government
with the United States in this important matter will be very potent in
promoting its adoption by all the Powers concerned.

I have, etc.,

JOSEPH H. CHOATE.

LORD SALISBURY TO MR. CHOATE.
FOREIGN OFFICE,
London, September 29, 1899.

YOUR EXCELLENCY: I have read with great interest the communication which you handed to me on the 23d instant, in which you inform me of the desire of the United States Government to obtain from the various Powers claiming spheres of interest in China declarations as to their intentions in regard to the treatment of foreign trade and commerce therein.

I have the honour to inform Your Excellency that I will lose no time in consulting my colleagues in regard to a declaration by Her Majesty's Government and on the proposal that they should co-operate with the Government of the United States in obtaining similar declarations by the other Powers concerned.

In the meantime, I may assure Your Excellency that the policy consistently advocated by this country is one of securing equal opportunity for the subjects and citizens of all nations in regard to commercial enterprise in China, and from this policy Her Majesty's Government have no intention or desire to depart.

I have, etc.,

SALISBURY.

LORD SALISBURY TO MR. CHOATE.

FOREIGN OFFICE,
London, November 30, 1899.

YOUR EXCELLENCY: With reference to my note of September 29 last, I have the honour to state that I have carefully considered, in communication with my colleagues, the proposal contained in Your Excellency's note of September 22 that a declaration should be made by foreign Powers claiming " spheres of interest " in China as to their intentions in regard to the treatment of foreign trade and interest therein.

I have much pleasure in informing Your Excellency that Her Majesty's Government will be prepared to make a declaration in the sense desired by your Government in regard to the leased territory of Wei-hai Wei and all territory in China which may hereafter be acquired by Great Britain by lease or otherwise, and all spheres of interest now held or that may hereafter be held by her in China, provided that a similar declaration is made by other Powers concerned.

I have, etc.,

SALISBURY.

MR. CHOATE TO LORD SALISBURY.

EMBASSY OF THE UNITED STATES,
London, December 6, 1899.

MY LORD: I have the honour to acknowledge the receipt of Your Lordship's note of November 30, in which you inform me that, after having carefully considered, in connection with your colleagues, the proposals contained in my note of September 22 last, Her Majesty's Government is prepared to make a declaration in the sense desired by my Government in regard to the leased territory of Wei-hai Wei and all territory in China which may hereafter be acquired by Great Britain by lease or otherwise, and all " spheres of interest " now held, or which may hereafter be held, by her in China, provided that a similar declaration is made by other Powers.

In acknowledging Your Lordship's note, I have also, under instructions from the Secretary of State, to express to Your Lordship the gratification he feels at the cordial acceptance by Her Britannic Majesty's Government of the proposals of the United States.

I have, etc.,   JOSEPH H. CHOATE.

(IV.)—ITALY.
MR. HAY TO MR. DRAPER.

No. 434.]   DEPARTMENT OF STATE,
Washington, November 17, 1899.

SIR: This Government, animated with a sincere desire to insure to the commerce and industry of the United States and of all other nations perfect equality of treatment within the limits of the Chinese Empire for their trade and navigation, especially within the so-called " spheres of influence or interest " claimed by certain European Powers in China, has deemed the present an opportune moment to make representations in this direction to Germany, Great Britain, Japan, and Russia.

To attain the object it has in view and to remove possible causes of international irritation and reestablish confidence so essential to commerce, it has seemed to this Government highly desirable that the various Powers claiming " spheres of interest or influence " in China should give formal assurances that—

First. They will in no way interfere with any treaty port or any vested interest within any so-called " sphere of interest " or leased territory they may have in China.

Second. The Chinese treaty tariff of the time being shall apply to all merchandise landed or shipped to all such ports as are within said " sphere of interest " (unless they be " free ports "), no matter to what nationality it may belong, and that duties so leviable shall be collected by the Chinese Government.

Third. They will levy no higher harbour dues on vessels of another nationality frequenting any port in such " sphere " than shall be levied on vessels of their own nationality, and no higher railroad charges over lines built, controlled, or operated within its " sphere " on merchandise belonging to citizens or subjects of other nationalities transported through such " sphere " than shall be levied on similar merchandise belonging to their own nationals transported over equal distances.

The policy pursued by His Imperial German Majesty in declaring Tsing-tao (Kiao-chao) a free port and in aiding the Chinese Government in establishing there a custom-house and the Ukase of His Imperial Russian Majesty of August 11 last erecting a free port at Dalny (Ta-lien-wan) are thought to be proof that these Powers are not disposed to view unfavourably the proposition to recognize that they contemplate nothing which will interfere in any way with the enjoyment by the commerce of all nations of the rights and privileges guaranteed to them by existing treaties with China.

Repeated assurances from the British Government of its fixed policy to maintain throughout China freedom of trade for the whole world insure, it is believed, the ready assent of that Power to our proposals. The commercial interests of Japan will also be greatly served by the above-mentioned declaration, which harmonizes with the assurances conveyed to this Government at various times by His Imperial Japanese Majesty's diplomatic representative at this capital.

In view of the important and growing commercial interests of Italy in eastern Asia, it would seem desirable that His Majesty's Government should also be informed of the steps taken by the United States to insure freedom of trade in China, in which it would find equal advantages to those which the other nations of Europe expect.

You are therefore instructed to submit to His Majesty's Minister for Foreign Affairs the above considerations and to invite his early attention to them, expressing, in the name of your Government, the hope that they will prove acceptable, and that His Majesty's Government will lend its aid and valuable assistance in securing their acceptance by the other interested Powers.

I enclose, for your personal and confidential information, copies of the instructions sent to our Ambassadors at Berlin, London, St. Petersburg, and to our Minister at Tokyo.

I am, etc., JOHN HAY.

THE MARQUIS VISCONTI VENOSTA TO MR. DRAPER.
[Translation.]

ROME, *January* 7, 1900.

MR. AMBASSADOR: Supplementary to what you had already done me the honour of communicating to me in your note of December 9, 1899, Your Excellency informed me yesterday of the telegraphic note received from your Government that all the Powers consulted by the Cabinet of Washington concerning the suitability of adopting a line of policy which would insure to the trade of the whole world equality of treatment in China have given a favourable reply.

Referring to your communications and to the statements in my note of December 23 last, I take pleasure in saying that the Government of the King adheres willingly to the proposals set forth in said note of December 9.

I beg Your Excellency to kindly convey the notice of our adhesion to the Cabinet of Washington, and I avail myself of the occasion to renew to you, etc.   VISCONTI VENOSTA.

(V.)—JAPAN.
MR HAY TO MR. BUCK.

No. 263.]   DEPARTMENT OF STATE,
                                    Washington, November 13, 1899.

SIR: This Government, animated with a sincere desire to insure to the commerce and industry of the United States and of all other nations perfect equality of treatment within the limits of the Chinese Empire for their trade and navigation, especially within the so-called " spheres of influence or interest " claimed by certain European Powers in China, has deemed the present an opportune moment to make representations in this direction to Germany, Great Britain, and Russia.

To obtain the object it has in view and to remove possible causes of international irritation and reestablish confidence so essential to commerce, it has seemed to this Government highly desirable that the various Powers claiming " spheres of interest or influence " in China should give formal assurances that—

First. They will in no way interfere with any treaty port or any vested interest within any so-called " sphere of interest " or leased territory they may have in China.

Second. The Chinese treaty tariff of the time being shall apply to all merchandise landed or shipped to all such ports as are within said " sphere of interest " (unless they be " free ports "), no matter to what nationality it may belong, and that duties so leviable shall be collected by the Chinese Government.

Third. They will levy no higher harbour dues on vessels of another nationality frequenting any port in such " sphere " than shall be levied on vessels of their own nationality, and no higher railroad charges over lines built, controlled, or operated within such " sphere " on merchandise belonging to citizens or subjects of other nationalities transported through such " sphere " than shall be levied on similar merchandise belonging to their own nationals transported over equal distances.

The policy pursued by His Imperial German Majesty in declaring

Tsing-tao (Kiao-chao) a free port and in aiding the Chinese Government in establishing there a custom-house, and the Ukase of His Imperial Russian Majesty of August 11 last erecting a free port at Dalny ('Ta-lien-wan) are thought to be proof that these Powers are not disposed to view unfavourably the proposition to recognize that they contemplate nothing which will interfere in any way with the enjoyment by the commerce of all nations of the rights and privileges guaranteed to them by existing treaties with China.

Repeated assurances from the British Government of its fixed policy to maintain throughout China freedom of trade for the whole world insure, it is believed, the ready assent of that Power to our proposals. It is no less confidently believed that the commercial interests of Japan would be greatly served by the above-mentioned declaration, which harmonizes with the assurances conveyed to this Government at various times by His Imperial Japanese Majesty's diplomatic representative at this capital.

You are therefore instructed to submit to His Imperial Japanese Majesty's Government the above considerations, and to invite their early attention to them, and express the earnest hope of your Government that they will accept them and aid in securing their acceptance by the other interested Powers.

I am, etc.,

JOHN HAY.

VISCOUNT AOKI TO MR. BUCK.
DEPARTMENT OF FOREIGN AFFAIRS,
Tokyo, the 26th day, the 12th month of the 32d year of Meiji.
(December 26, 1899.)

MR. MINISTER: I have the honour to acknowledge the receipt of the note No. 176 of the 20th instant, in which, pursuing the instructions of the United States Government, Your Excellency was so good as to communicate to the Imperial Government the representations of the United States as presented in notes to Russia, Germany, and Great Britain on the subject of commercial interests of the United States in China.

I have the happy duty of assuring Your Excellency that the Imperial Government will have no hesitation to give their assent to so just and fair a proposal of the United States, provided that all the other Powers concerned shall accept the same.

I avail myself, etc.,

VISCOUNT AOKI SIUZO,
Minister for Foreign Affairs.

(VI.)—RUSSIA.
MR. HAY TO MR. TOWER.

No. 82.]   DEPARTMENT OF STATE,

Washington, September 6, 1899.

SIR: In 1898, when his Imperial Majesty had, through his diplomatic representative at this capital, notified this Government that Russia had leased from His Imperial Chinese Majesty the ports of Port Arthur, Ta-lien-wan, and the adjacent territory in the Liao-tung Peninsula in northeastern China for a period of twenty-five years, your predecessor received categorical assurances from the Imperial Minister for Foreign Affairs that American interests in that part of the Chinese Empire would in no way be affected thereby, neither was it the desire of Russia to interfere with the trade of other nations, and that our citizens would continue to enjoy within said leased territory all the rights and privileges guaranteed them under existing treaties with China. Assurances of a similar purport were conveyed to me by the Emperor's Ambassador at this capital; while fresh proof of this is afforded by the Imperial Ukase of July 30/August 11 last, creating the free port of Dalny, near Ta-lien-wan, and establishing free trade for the adjacent territory.

However gratifying and reassuring such assurances may be in regard to the territory actually occupied and administered, it can not but be admitted that a further, clearer, and more formal definition of the conditions which are henceforth to hold within the so-called Russian " sphere of interest " in China as regards the commercial rights therein of our citizens is much desired by the business world of the United States, inasmuch as such a declaration would relieve it from the apprehensions which have exercised a disturbing influence during the last four years on its operations in China.

The present moment seems particularly opportune for ascertaining whether His Imperial Russian Majesty would not be disposed to give permanent form to the assurances heretofore given to this Government on this subject.

The Ukase of the Emperor of August 11 of this year, declaring the port of Ta-lien-wan open to the merchant ships of all nations during the remainder of the lease under which it is held by Russia, removes the slightest uncertainty as to the liberal and conciliatory commercial policy His Majesty proposes carrying out in northeastern China, and would seem to insure us the sympathetic and, it is hoped, favourable consideration of the propositions hereinafter specified.

The principles which this Government is particularly desirous of seeing formally declared by His Imperial Majesty and by all the great

Powers interested in China, and which will be eminently beneficial to the commercial interests of the whole world, are:

First. The recognition that no Power will in any way interfere with any treaty port or any vested interest within any leased territory or within any so-called " sphere of interest " it may have in China.

Second. That the Chinese treaty tariff of the time being shall apply to all merchandise landed or shipped to all such ports as are within said " sphere of interest " (unless they be " free ports "), no matter to what nationality it may belong, and that duties so leviable shall be collected by the Chinese Government.

Third. That it will levy no higher harbour dues on vessels of another nationality frequenting any port in such " sphere " than shall be levied on vessels of its own nationality, and no higher railroad charges over lines built, controlled, or operated within its " sphere " on merchandise belonging to citizens or subjects of other nationalities transported through such " sphere " than shall be levied on similar merchandise belonging to its own nationals transported over equal distances.

The declaration of such principles by His Imperial Majesty would not only be of great benefit to foreign commerce in China, but would powerfully tend to remove dangerous sources of irritation and possible conflict between the various Powers; it would reestablish confidence and security; and would give great additional weight to the concerted representations which the treaty Powers may hereafter make to His Imperial Chinese Majesty in the interest of reform in Chinese administration so essential to the consolidation and integrity of that Empire, and which, it is believed, is a fundamental principle of the policy of His Majesty in Asia.

Germany has declared the port of Kiao-chao, which she holds in Shantung under a lease from China, a free port and has aided in the establishment there of a branch of the Imperial Chinese Maritime Customs. The Imperial German Minister for Foreign Affairs has also given assurances that American trade would not in any way be discriminated against or interfered with, as there is no intention to close the leased territory to foreign commerce within the area which Germany claims. These facts lead this Government to believe that the Imperial German Government will lend its co-operation and give its acceptance to the proposition above outlined, and which our Ambassador at Berlin is now instructed to submit to it.

That such a declaration will be favourably considered by Great Britain and Japan, the two other Powers most interested in the subject, there can be no doubt; the formal and oft-repeated declarations of the British and Japanese Governments in favour of the maintenance throughout China of freedom of trade for the whole world insure us, it is believed, the ready assent of these Powers to the declaration desired.

The acceptance by His Imperial Majesty of these principles must therefore inevitably lead to their recognition by all the other Powers interested, and you are instructed to submit them to the Emperor's Minister for Foreign Affairs and urge their immediate consideration.

A copy of this instruction is sent to our Ambassadors at London and Berlin for their confidential information, and copies of the instructions sent to them on this subject are enclosed herewith.

I have, etc.,   JOHN HAY.

COUNT MOURAVIEFF TO MR. TOWER.
MINISTRY OF FOREIGN AFFAIRS,
December 18-30, 1899.

MR. AMBASSADOR: I had the honour to receive Your Excellency's note dated the 8th-20th of September last, relating to the principles which the Government of the United States would like to see adopted in commercial matters by the Powers which have interests in China.

In so far as the territory leased by China to Russia is concerned, the Imperial Government has already demonstrated its firm intention to follow the policy of " the open door " by creating Dalny (Ta-lien-wan) a free port; and if at some future time that port, although remaining free itself, should be separated by a customs limit from other portions of the territory in question, the customs duties would be levied, in the zone subject to the tariff, upon all foreign merchandise without distinction as to nationality.

As to the ports now opened or hereafter to be opened to foreign commerce by the Chinese Government, and which lie beyond the territory leased to Russia, the settlement of the question of customs duties belongs to China herself, and the Imperial Government has no intention whatever of claiming any privileges for its own subjects to the exclusion of other foreigners. It is to be understood, however, that this assurance of the Imperial Government is given upon condition that a similar declaration shall be made by other Powers having interests in China.

With the conviction that this reply is such as to satisfy the inquiry made in the aforementioned note, the Imperial Government is happy to have complied with the wishes of the American Government, especially as it attaches the highest value to anything that may strengthen and consolidate the traditional relations of friendship existing between the two countries.

I beg you to accept, etc.,

COUNT MOURAVIEFF.

INSTRUCTIONS SENT *MUTATIS MUTANDIS* TO THE UNITED STATES AMBASSADORS AT LONDON, PARIS, BERLIN, ST. PETERSBURG, AND ROME, AND TO THE UNITED STATES MINISTER AT TOKYO.

DEPARTMENT OF STATE,

Washington, March 20, 1900.

SIR: The ———— Government having accepted the declaration suggested by the United States concerning foreign trade in China, the terms of which I transmitted to you in my instruction No. — of ———,
and like action having been taken by all the various Powers having leased territory or so-called " spheres of interest " in the Chinese Empire, as shown by the notes which I herewith transmit to you, you will please inform the Government to which you are accredited that the condition originally attached to its acceptance—that all other Powers concerned should likewise accept the proposals of the United States—having been complied with, this Government will therefore consider the assent given to it by ———— as final and definitive.

You will also transmit to the Minister for Foreign Affairs copies of the present enclosures, and by the same occasion convey to him the expression of the sincere gratification which the President feels at the successful termination of these negotiations, in which he sees proof of the friendly spirit which animates the various Powers interested in the untrammelled development of commerce and industry in the Chinese Empire, and a source of vast benefit to the whole commercial world.

I am, etc., JOHN HAY.

153

AGREEMENT between Germany and Great Britain relative to China. 16th October, 1900.

Her Britannic Majesty's Government and the Imperial German Government, being desirous to maintain their interests in China and their rights under existing Treaties, have agreed to observe the following principles in regard to their mutual policy in China:—

1. It is a matter of joint and permanent international interest that the ports on the rivers and littoral of China should remain free and open to trade and to every other legitimate form of economic activity for the nationals of all countries without distinction; and the two Governments agree on their part to uphold the same for all Chinese territory as far as they can exercise influence.

2. Her Britannic Majesty's Government and the Imperial German

Government will not, on their part, make use of the present complication to obtain for themselves any territorial advantages in Chinese dominions, and will direct their policy towards maintaining undiminished the territorial condition of the Chinese Empire.

3. In case of another Power making use of the complications in China in order to obtain under any form whatever such territorial advantages, the two Contracting Parties reserve to themselves to come to a preliminary understanding as to the eventual steps to be taken for the protection of their own interests in China.

4. The two Governments will communicate this Agreement to the other Powers interested, and especially to Austria-Hungary, France, Italy, Japan, Russia, and the United States of America, and will invite them to accept the principles recorded in it.

154

AGREEMENT between Austria-Hungary and Italy in regard to Albania. 1900.

Despatch of the Italian Government to the Ambassador in Vienna containing the Agreement between Austria-Hungary and Italy in regard to Albania. Rome, December 20, 1900.

His Excellency Count Nigra, Ambassador of Italy, Vienna.
Copy.

Rome, December 20, 1900.

Mr. Ambassador,

I call the attention of Your Excellency to my reply to an interpellation recently addressed to me in the Chamber of Deputies on the subject of Albania. Here is the text of that reply:

" I am able to give the assurance that the Italian Government and the Austro-Hungarian Government have had occasion to consider their interests on the Ottoman coasts of the Adriatic and to recognize that these interests find their safeguard in respect for, and in the maintenance, of, the status quo."

I think it would be useful for you to bring my declarations to the knowledge of His Excellency Count Goluchowski. I have no doubt that the Imperial and Royal Minister of Foreign Affairs will find them in conformity with the understanding which was established between him and me on this subject on the occasion of the visit at Monza in 1897. In the exchange of views which took place during our conversations in respect to this question, we found ourselves agreed upon the following points:

1. To maintain the status quo as long as circumstances permitted;

2. In case the present state of affairs could not be preserved, or in case changes should be imperative, to use our efforts to the end that the modifications relative thereto should be made in the direction of autonomy;

3. In general, and as a mutual disposition on both sides, to seek in common, and as often as there is a reason for it, the most appropriate ways and means to reconcile and to safeguard our reciprocal interests.

I should appreciate being assured that Count Goluchowski, like myself, sees in the preceding the faithful summary of the substance of what was agreed between us upon this subject. In consequence, I authorize Your Excellency to communicate this despatch to him.

Accept, Mr. Ambassador, the assurance of my high consideration.

(signed)   VISCONTI VENOSTA.

Despatch in acknowledgment from the Austrian Government to the Ambassador in Rome. Vienna, February 9, 1901.

Submitted to His Majesty

Draft

of a strictly confidential despatch to Baron Pasetti at Rome.

On his return from Rome, Count Nigra directed my attention to the reply given by His Excellency the Minister of Foreign Affairs of the Kingdom of Italy to the interpellation recently addressed to him in the Chamber of Deputies on the subject of Albania; and at the same time expressed the hope that I might find the declarations which it contains in conformity with the principles upon which we came to an agreement in 1897 at the time of my interview with Marquis Visconti-Venosta at the Castle of Monza.

In the strictly confidential exchange of views which took place in our conversations in respect to that question, we recognized in effect the necessity

1. Of maintaining the status quo as long as circumstances permitted;

2. In case the present state of affairs could not be preserved, or in case changes should be imperative, of using our efforts to the end that the modifications relative thereto should be made in the direction of autonomy, just as we have decided; in general,

3. The disposition on both sides to seek in common, and as often as there is a reason for it, the most appropriate ways and means to reconcile and to safeguard our reciprocal interests.

Such being the case, I am pleased to state that the pronouncement of Marquis Visconti-Venosta has been received with lively satisfaction by the Imperial and Royal Cabinet; and requesting you, my dear Baron, to inform his Excellency the Minister of Foreign Affairs of this, I avail myself of this occasion, etc.

155

FINAL PROTOCOL for the settlement of the disturbances of 1900 in China. 7th September, 1901.

The plenipotentiaries of Germany, His Excellency M. A. Mumm von Schwarzenstein; of Austria-Hungary, His Excellency M. M. Czikann von Wahlborn; of Belgium, His Excellency M. Joostens; of Spain, M. B. J. de Cologan; of the United States, His Excellency M. W. W. Rockhill; of France, His Excellency M. Paul Beau; of Great Britain, His Excellency Sir Ernest Satow; of Italy, Marquis Salvago Raggi; of Japan, His Excellency M. Jutaro Komura; of the Netherlands, His Excellency M. F. M. Knobel; of Russia, His Excellency M. M. de Giers; and of China, His Highness Yi-K'uang Prince Ching of the first rank, President of the Ministry of Foreign Affairs, and His Excellency Li Hung-chang, Earl of Su-i of the first rank, Tutor of the Heir Apparent, Grand Secretary of the Wen-hua Throne Hall, Minister of commerce, Superintendent of the northern trade, Governor-General of Chihli, have met for the purpose of declaring that China has complied to the satisfaction of the Powers with the conditions laid down in the note of the 22nd of December, 1900 and which were accepted in their entirety by His Majesty the Emperor of China in a decree dated the 27th of December. (Annex No. 1.)

ART. I*a*. By an Imperial Edict of the 9th of June last (Annex No. 2), Tsai Feng, Prince of Ch'ün, was appointed Ambassador of His Majesty the Emperor of China, and directed in that capacity to convey to His Majesty the German Emperor the expression of the regrets of His Majesty the Emperor of China and of the Chinese Government for the assassination of His Excellency the late Baron von Ketteler, German minister.

Prince Ch'ün left Peking the 12th of July last to carry out the orders which had been given him.

ART. I*b*. The Chinese Government has stated that it will erect on the spot of the assassination of His Excellency the late Baron von Ketteler a commemorative monument, worthy of the rank of the deceased, and bearing an inscription in the Latin, German, and Chinese languages, which shall express the regrets of His Majesty the Emperor of China for the murder committed.

Their Excellencies the Chinese Plenipotentiaries have informed His

Excellency the German Plenipotentiary, in a letter dated the 22nd of July last (Annex No. 3) that an arch of the whole width of the street would be erected on the said spot, and that work on it was begun the 25th of June last.

ART. II*a*. Imperial Edicts of the 13th and 21st of February, 1901 (Annexes Nos. 4, 5, and 6), inflicted the following punishments on the principal authors of the outrages and crimes committed against the foreign Governments and their nationals:

Tsai-I Prince Tuan and Tsai Lan Duke Fu-kuo were sentenced to be brought before the autumnal court of assize for execution, and it was agreed that if the Emperor saw fit to grant them their lives, they should be exiled to Turkestan and there imprisoned for life, without the possibility of commutation of these punishments.

Tsai Hsün Prince Chuang, Ying Nien, President of the Court of censors, and Chao Shu-Chiao, President of the Board of punishments, were condemned to commit suicide.

Yü Hsien, Governor of Shanhsi, Chi Hsiu, President of the Board of rites, and Hsü Cheng-yu, formerly senior vice-President of the Board of punishments, were condemned to death.

Posthumous degradation was inflicted on Kang Yi, assistant Grand Secretary, President of the Board of Works, Hsü Tung, Grand Secretary, and Li Ping-heng, formerly Governor-General of Szu-ch'uan.

An Imperial Edict of February 13th, 1901 (Annex No. 7), rehabilitated the memories of Hsü Yung-yi, President of the Board of war, Li Shan, President of the Board of works, Hsü Ching-cheng, senior vice-President of the Board of works, Lien Yuan, vice-Chancellor of the Grand Council, and Yuan Chang, vice-President of the Court of sacrifices, who had been put to death for having protested against the outrageous breaches of international law of last year.

Prince Chuang committed suicide the 21st of February, 1901, Ying Nien and Chao Shü-chiao the 24th, Yü Hsien was executed the 22nd, Chi Hsiu and Hsü Cheng-yu on the 26th. Tung Fu-hsiang, General in Kan-su, has been deprived of his office by Imperial Edict of the 13th of February, 1901, pending the determination of the final punishment to be inflicted on him.

Imperial Edicts dated the 29th of April and 19th of August, 1901, have inflicted various punishments on the provincial officials convicted of the crimes and outrages of last summer.

ART. II*b*. An Imperial Edict promulgated the 19th of August, 1901 (Annex No. 8), ordered the suspension of official examinations for five years in all cities where foreigners were massacred or submitted to cruel treatment.

ART. III. So as to make honourable reparation for the assassination of Mr. Sugiyama, chancellor of the Japanese legation, His Majesty the Emperor of China by an Imperial Edict of the 18th of June, 1901 (Annex No. 9), appointed Na Tung, vice-President of the Board of revenue, to be his Envoy Extraordinary, and specially directed him to convey to His Majesty the Emperor of Japan the expression of the regrets of His Majesty the Emperor of China and of his Government at the assassination of the late Mr. Sugiyama.

ART. IV. The Chinese Government has agreed to erect an expiatory monument in each of the foreign or international cemeteries which were desecrated and in which the tombs were destroyed.

It has been agreed with the Representatives of the Powers that the legations interested shall settle the details for the erection of these monuments, China bearing all the expenses thereof, estimated at ten thousand taels for the cemeteries at Peking and within its neighbour-hood, and at five thousand taels for the cemeteries in the provinces. The amounts have been paid and the list of these cemeteries is enclosed herewith. (Annex No. 10.)

ART. V. China has agreed to prohibit the importation into its territory of arms and ammunition, as well as of materials exclusively used for the manufacture of arms and ammunition.

An Imperial Edict has been issued on the 25th of August, 1901 (Annex No. 11), forbidding said importation for a term of two years. New Edicts may be issued subsequently extending this by other successive terms of two years in case of necessity recognized by the Powers.

ART. VI. By an Imperial Edict dated the 29th of May, 1901 (Annex No. 12), His Majesty the Emperor of China agreed to pay the Powers an indemnity of four hundred and fifty millions of Haikwan Taels. This sum represents the total amount of the indemnities for States, companies or societies, private individuals, and Chinese referred to in Article VI of the note of December 22nd, 1900.

(a) These four hundred and fifty millions constitute a gold debt calculated at the rate of the Haikwan tael to the gold currency of each country, as indicated below.

Haikwan tael=marks 3.055
           =Austro-Hungary crown 3.595
           =gold dollar 0.742
           =francs 3.750
           =pound sterling . . . .   3s. 0d.
           =yen 1.407
           =Netherlands florin 1.796
           =gold rouble (17.424 dolias fine) 1.412

This sum in gold shall bear interest at 4 per cent per annum, and the capital shall be reimbursed by China in thirty-nine years in the manner indicated in the annexed plan of amortization. (Annex No. 13.)

Capital and interest shall be payable in gold or at the rates of exchange corresponding to the dates at which the different payments fall due.

The amortization shall commence the 1st of January, 1902, and shall finish at the end of the year 1940. The amortizations are payable annually, the first payment being fixed on the 1st of January, 1903.

Interest shall run from the 1st of July, 1901, but the Chinese Government shall have the right to pay off within a term of three years, beginning January, 1902, the arrears of the first six months, ending the 31st of December, 1901, on condition, however, that it pays compound interest at the rate of 4 per cent per annum on the sums the payments of which shall have thus been deferred. Interest shall be payable semiannually, the first payment being fixed on the 1st of July, 1902.

(*b*) The service of the debt shall take place in Shanghai, in the following manner:

Each Power shall be represented by a delegate on a commission of bankers authorized to receive the amount of interest and amortization which shall be paid to it by the Chinese authorities designated for that purpose, to divide it among the interested parties, and to give a receipt for the same.

(*c*) The Chinese Government shall deliver to the Doyen of the Diplomatic Corps at Peking a bond for the lump sum, which shall subsequently be converted into fractional bonds bearing the signatures of the delegates of the Chinese Government designated for that purpose. This operation and all those relating to issuing of the bonds shall be performed by the above-mentioned Commission, in accordance with the instructions which the Powers shall send their delegates.

(*d*) The proceeds of the revenues assigned to the payment of the bonds shall be paid monthly to the Commission.

(*e*) The revenues assigned as security for the bonds are the following:

1. The balance of the revenues of the Imperial maritime Customs after payment of the interest and amortization of preceding loans secured on these revenues, plus the proceeds of the raising to five per cent effective of the present tariff on maritime imports, including articles until now on the free list, but exempting foreign rice, cereals, and flour, gold and silver bullion and coin.

2. The revenues of the native customs, administered in the open ports by the Imperial maritime Customs.

3. The total revenues of the salt gabelle, exclusive of the fraction previously set aside for other foreign loans.

The raising of the present tariff on imports to five per cent effective is agreed to on the conditions mentioned below.

It shall be put in force two months after the signing of the present protocol, and no exceptions shall be made except for merchandise shipped not more than ten days after the said signing.

1°. All duties levied on imports " ad valorem " shall be converted as far as possible and as soon as may be into specific duties. This conversion shall be made in the following manner: The average value of merchandise at the time of their landing during the three years 1897, 1898, and 1899, that is to say, the market price less the amount of import duties and incidental expenses, shall be taken as the basis for the valuation of merchandise. Pending the result of the work of conversion, duties shall be levied " ad valorem."

2°. The beds of the rivers Peiho and Whangpu shall be improved with the financial participation of China.

ART. VII. The Chinese Government has agreed that the quarter occupied by the legations shall be considered as one specially reserved for their use and placed under their exclusive control, in which Chinese shall not have the right to reside and which may be made defensible.

The limits of this quarter have been fixed as follows on the annexed plan (Annex No. 14):

On the west, the line, 1, 2, 3, 4, 5.

On the north, the line 5, 6, 7, 8, 9, 10.

On the east, Ketteler street (10, 11, 12).

Drawn along the exterior base of the Tartar wall and following the line of the bastions, on the south of the line 12, 1.

In the protocol annexed to the letter of the 16th of January, 1901, China recognized the right of each Power to maintain a permanent guard in the said quarter for the defense of its legation.

ART. VIII. The Chinese Government has consented to raze the forts of Taku and those which might impede free communication between Peking and the sea; steps have been taken for carrying this out.

ART. IX. The Chinese Government has conceded the right to the Powers in the protocol annexed to the letter of the 16th of January, 1901, to occupy certain points, to be determined by an agreement between them, for the maintenance of open communication between the capital and the sea. The points occupied by the powers are:

Huang-tsun, Lang-fang, Yang-tsun, Tientsin, Chun-liang Ch'eng, Tang-ku, Lu-tai, Tang-shan, Lan-chou, Chang-li, Ch'in-wang tao, Shan-hai kuan.

ART. X. The Chinese Government has agreed to post and to have published during two years in all district cities the following Imperial edicts:

(*a*) Edict of the 1st of February (Annex No. 15), prohibiting forever, under pain of death, membership in any antiforeign society.

(*b*) Edicts of the 13th and 21st February, 29th April, and 19th August, enumerating the punishments inflicted on the guilty.

(*c*) Edict of the 19th August, 1901, prohibiting examinations in all cities where foreigners were massacred or subjected to cruel treatment.

(*d*) Edict of the 1st of February, 1901 (Annex No. 16), declaring all governors-general, governors, and provincial or local officials responsible for order in their respective districts, and that in case of new antiforeign troubles or other infractions of the treaties which shall not be immediately repressed and the authors of which shall not have been punished, these officials shall be immediately dismissed, without possibility of being given new functions or new honours.

The posting of these edicts is being carried on throughout the Empire.

ART. XI. The Chinese Government has agreed to negotiate the amendments deemed necessary by the foreign Governments to the treaties of commerce and navigation and the other subjects concerning commercial relations, with the object of facilitating them.

At present, and as a result of the stipulation contained in Article VI concerning the indemnity, the Chinese Government agrees to assist in the improvement of the courses of the rivers Peiho and Whangpu, as stated below.

(*a*) The works for the improvement of the navigability of the Peiho, begun in 1898 with the co-operation of the Chinese Government, have been resumed under the direction of an international Commission. As soon as the administration of Tientsin shall have been handed back to the Chinese Government, it will be in a position to be represented on this commission, and will pay each year a sum of sixty thousand Haikwan taels for maintaining the works.

(*b*) A conservancy Board, charged with the management and control of the works for straightening the Whangpu and the improvement of the course of that river, is hereby created.

This Board shall consist of members representing the interests of the Chinese Government and those of foreigners in the shipping trade of Shanghai. The expenses incurred for the works and the general management of the undertaking are estimated at the annual sum of four hundred and sixty thousand Haikwan taels for the first twenty years. This sum shall be supplied in equal portions by the Chinese Government and the foreign interests concerned. Detailed stipulations concerning the composition, duties, and revenues of the conservancy board are embodied in annex No. 17.

ART. XII. An Imperial Edict of the 24th of July, 1901 (Annex No. 18), reformed the Office of foreign affairs (Tsungli Yamen), on the lines indicated by the Powers, that is to say, transformed it into a Ministry of foreign affairs (Wai-wu Pu), which takes precedence over the six other Ministries of State. The same edict appointed the principal members of this Ministry.

An agreement has also been reached concerning the modification of Court ceremonial as regards the reception of foreign Representatives and has been the subject of several notes from the Chinese Pleni-potentiaries, the substance of which is embodied in a memorandum herewith annexed (Annex No. 19).

Finally, it is expressly understood that as regards the declarations specified above and the annexed documents originating with the foreign Plenipotentiaries, the French text only is authoritative.

The Chinese Government having thus complied to the satisfaction of the Powers with the conditions laid down in the above-mentioned note of December 22nd, 1900, the Powers have agreed to accede to the wish of China to terminate the situation created by the disorders of the summer of 1900. In consequence thereof the foreign Plenipotentiaries are authorized to declare in the names of their Governments that, with the exception of the legation guards mentioned in Article VII, the international troops will completely evacuate the city of Peking on the 17th September, 1901, and, with the exception of the localities men-tioned in Article IX, will withdraw from the province of Chihli on the 22nd of September.

The present final Protocol has been drawn up in twelve identic copies and signed by all the Plenipotentiaries of the Contracting Countries. One copy shall be given to each of the foreign Plenipotentiaries, and one copy shall be given to the Chinese Plenipotentiaries.

Peking, 7th September, 1901.

A. v. MUMM.
M. CZIKANN.
JOOSTENS.
B. J. DE COLOGAN.
W. W. ROCKHILL.
BEAU.
ERNEST SATOW.
SALVAGO RAGGI.
JUTARO KOMURA.
F. M. KNOBEL.
M. DE GIERS.

} Signatures and seals of Chinese plenipotentiaries.

ANNEX No. 1.

IMPERIAL EDICT of the 27th December, 1900.
[Seal of the Emperor.]

The 6th day of the 11th moon of the 26th year of Kuang-hsü (27 December, 1900), the following Edict was rendered:

" We have taken cognizance of the whole telegram of Yi-K'uang and Li Hung-chang. It is proper that We accept in their entirety the twelve articles which they have submitted to us."

Respect this!

Correct copy.

A. D'ANTHOUARD.
B. KROUPENSKY.
REGINALD TOWER.
G. BOHLEN-HALBACH.

ANNEX No. 2.

IMPERIAL EDICT of the 9th of June, 1901.

" We confer on Tsai Feng, Prince Ch'ün of the first rank, the title of Ambassador extraordinary, and We direct him to proceed to Germany to respectfully discharge the mission which We confide to him.

" Chang Yi, reader of the Grand Chancellery, and Yin Ch'ang, military Lieutenant-Governor, shall accompany him as secretaries.

" Respect this!"

Correct copy.

A. D'ANTHOUARD.
B. KROUPENSKY.
REGINALD TOWER.
G. BOHLEN-HALBACH.

ANNEXES TO THE FINAL PROTOCOL.

3. Letter of the Chinese plenipotentiaries of 22 July, 1901.
4. Imperial Edict of 13 February, 1901.
5. Imperial Edict of 13 February, 1901.
6. Imperial Edict of 21 February, 1901.
7. Imperial Edict of 13 February, 1901.
8. Imperial Edict of 19 August, 1901.
9. Imperial Edict of 18 June, 1901.
10. List of desecrated cemeteries.
11. Imperial Edict of 25 August, 1901.
12. Imperial Edict of 29 May, 1901.
13. Table of amortization.
14. Plan of the diplomatic quarter and notice.
15. Imperial Edict of 1st February, 1901.
16. Imperial Edict of 1st February, 1901.
17. Regulations for the improvement of the Whangpu.
18. Imperial Edict of 24 July, 1901.
19. Memorandum concerning court ceremonial.

156

TREATY BETWEEN GREAT BRITAIN AND THE USA to Facilitate the Construction of a Ship Canal connecting the Atlantic and the Pacific Oceans. Concluded 18th November, 1901. Ratifications exchanged 21st February, 1902

THE United States of America and His Majesty Edward the Seventh, of the United Kingdom of Great Britain and Ireland, and of the British Dominions beyond the Seas, King, and Emperor of India, being desirous to facilitate the construction of a ship canal to connect the Atlantic and Pacific Oceans, by whatever route may be considered expedient, and to that end to remove any objection which may arise out of the Convention of the 19th April, 1850, commonly called the Clayton-Bulwer Treaty, to the construction of such canal under the auspices of the Government of the United States, without impairing the "general principle" of neutralization established in Article VIII of that Convention, have for that purpose appointed as the Plenipotentiaries:

The President of the United States, John Hay, Secretary of State of the United States of America;

And His Majesty Edward the Seventh, of the United Kingdom of Great Britain and Ireland, and of the British Dominions beyond the Seas, King, and Emperor of India, the Right Honourable Lord Pauncefote, G. C. B., G. C. M. G., His Majesty's Ambassador Extraordinary and Plenipotentiary to the United States;

Who, having communicated to each other their full powers which were found to be in due and proper form, have agreed upon the following Articles:—

ART. I. The High Contracting Parties agree that the present Treaty shall supersede the afore-mentioned Convention of the 19th April, 1850.

ART. II. It is agreed that the canal may be constructed under the auspices of the Government of the United States, either directly at its own cost, or by gift or loan of money to individuals or Corporations, or through subscription to or purchase of stock or shares, and that, subject to the provisions of the present Treaty, the said Government shall have and enjoy all the rights incident to such construction, as well as the exclusive right of providing for the regulation and management of the canal.

ART. III. The United States adopts, as the basis of the neutralization of such ship canal, the following Rules, substantially as embodied in the Convention of Constantinople, signed the 28th October, 1888, for the free navigation of the Suez Canal, that is to say:

1. The canal shall be free and open to the vessels of commerce and of war of all nations observing these Rules, on terms of entire equality. so that there shall be no discrimination against any such nation, or its citizens or subjects, in respect of the conditions or charges of traffic, or otherwise. Such conditions and charges of traffic shall be just and equitable.

2. The canal shall never be blockaded, nor shall any right of war be exercised nor any act of hostility be committed within it. The United States, however, shall be at liberty to maintain such military police along the canal as may be necessary to protect it against lawlessness and disorder.

3. Vessels of war of a belligerent shall not revictual nor take any stores in the canal except so far as may be strictly necessary; and the transit of such vessels through the canal shall be effected with the least possible delay in accordance with the Regulations in force, and with only such intermission as may result from the necessities of the service.

Prizes shall be in all respects subject to the same Rules as vessels of war of the belligerents.

4. No belligerent shall embark or disembark troops, munitions of war, or warlike materials in the canal, except in case of accidental hindrance of the transit, and in such case the transit shall be resumed with all possible dispatch.

5. The provisions of this Article shall apply to waters adjacent to the canal, within 3 marine miles of either end. Vessels of war of a belligerent shall not remain in such waters longer than twenty-four hours at any one time, except in case of distress, and in such case, shall depart as soon as possible; but a vessel of war of one belligerent shall not depart within twenty-four hours from the departure of a vessel of war of the other belligerent.

6. The plant, establishments, buildings, and all work necessary to the construction, maintenance, and operation of the canal shall be deemed to be part thereof, for the purposes of this Treaty, and in time of war, as in time of peace, shall enjoy complete immunity from attack or injury by belligerents, and from acts calculated to impair their usefulness as part of the canal.

ART. IV. It is agreed that no change of territorial sovereignty or of the international relations of the country or countries traversed by the before-mentioned canal shall affect the general principle of neutralization or the obligation of the High Contracting Parties under the present Treaty.

ART. V. The present Treaty shall be ratified by the President of the United States, by and with the advice and consent of the Senate thereof, and by His Britannic Majesty; and the ratifications shall be exchanged at Washington or at London at the earliest possible time within six months from the date hereof.

In faith whereof the respective Plenipotentiaries have signed this Treaty and thereunto affixed their seals.

Done in duplicate at Washington, the 18th day of November, in the year of Our Lord one thousand nine hundred and one.

JOHN HAY.

PAUNCEFOTE.

157

AGREEMENT relative to China and Korea, between Great Britain and Japan, 30th January, 1902. Published 11th February, 1902.

THE governments of Great Britain and Japan, actuated solely by a desire to maintain the *status quo* and general peace in the Extreme East, being moreover specially interested in maintaining the independence and territorial integrity of the Empire of China and the Empire of Korea, and in securing equal opportunities in those countries for the commerce and industry of all nations, hereby agree as follows:

ART. I. The High Contracting Parties, having mutually recognised the independence of China and Korea, declare themselves to be entirely uninfluenced by any aggressive tendencies in either country. Having in view, however, their special interests of which those of Great Britain relate principally to China, while Japan, in addition to the interests which she possesses in China, is interested in a peculiar degree politically as well as commercially and industrially in Korea, the High Contracting Parties recognise that it will be admissible for either of them to take such measures as may be indispensable in order to safeguard those interests if threatened either by the aggressive action of any other Power, or by disturbances arising in China or Korea, and necessitating the intervention of either of the High Contracting Parties for the protection of the lives and property of its subjects.

ART. II. If either Great Britain or Japan, in the defence of their respective interests as above described, should become involved in war with another Power, the other High Contracting Party will maintain a strict neutrality, and use its efforts to prevent other Powers from joining in hostilities against its ally.

ART. III. If, in the above event, any other Power or Powers should join in hostilities against that ally, the other High Contracting Party will come to its assistance, and will conduct the war in common, and make peace in mutual agreement with it.

ART. IV. The High Contracting Parties agree that neither of them will, without consulting the other, enter into separate arrangements with another Power to the prejudice of the interests above described.

ART. V. Whenever, in opinion of either Great Britain or Japan, the above-mentioned interests are in jeopardy, the two Governments will communicate with one another fully and frankly.

ART. VI. The present Agreement shall come into effect immediately after the date of its signature, and remain in force for five years from that date.

In case neither of the High Contracting Parties should have notified twelve months before the expiration of the said five years the intention of terminating it, it shall remain binding until the expiration of one year from the day on which either of the High Contracting Parties shall have denounced it. But if, when the date fixed for its expiration arrives, either ally is actually engaged in war, the alliance, shall, *ipso facto*, continue until peace is concluded.

In faith whereof the Undersigned, duly authorised by their respective Governments, have signed this Agreement, and have affixed thereto their seals.

Done in duplicate at London, the 30th of January, 1902.

> (L.S.) LANSDOWNE, His Britannic Majesty's Principal Secretary of State for Foreign Affairs.
>
> (L.S.) HAYASHI, Envoy Extraordinary and Minister Plenipotentiary of His Majesty the Emperor of Japan at the Court of St. James.

158

THIRD TREATY between Austria-Hungary and Roumania renewing the Alliances of 1892 and 1896. Bucharest, 4th/17th April, 1902. Ratifications exchanged 13th/26th April, 1902.

HIS Majesty the Emperor of Austria, King of Bohemia, etc., and Apostolic King of Hungary, and His Majesty the King of Roumania, animated by an equal desire to maintain the general peace, in conformity with the purpose pursued by the Austro-Hungarian and

German Alliance, to assure the political order, and to guarantee against all eventualities the perfect friendship which binds Them together, having taken into consideration the stipulations of the Treaty signed to this end on July 25, 1892, between Austria-Hungary and Roumania, a Treaty which by its essentially conservative and defensive nature pursues only the aim of forestalling the dangers which might menace the peace of their States, and desiring to record once more the understanding established between Their Majesties in prospect of certain eventualities mentioned in the Treaty of July 25, 1892, the duration of which has been prolonged until July 25, 1903, by the Protocol signed at Sinaia on September 30, 1896, have resolved to renew and to confirm by a new agreement the engagements contained in the aforesaid Treaty.

For this purpose Their said Majesties have named as Their Plenipotentiaries, to wit:

His Majesty the Emperor of Austria, King of Bohemia, etc., and Apostolic King of Hungary:

the Sieur John Marquis Pallavicini, His Chamberlain, Envoy Extraordinary and Minister Plenipotentiary to His Majesty the King of Roumania, Commander of the Imperial Austrian Order of Francis Joseph with medal, Chevalier of the Imperial Austrian Order of Leopold,

His Majesty the King of Roumania:

the Sieur Demetrius A. Sturdza, President of the Council of Ministers, His Minister of Finance and ad interim for War, Grand Cross of the Orders of the Star of Roumania, of the Crown of Roumania, and of the Imperial Austrian Order of Leopold in brilliants, Chevalier of the First Class of the Imperial Austrian Order of the Iron Crown, who, after having communicated to each other their full powers, found in good and due form, have agreed upon the following Articles:

ART. I. Renewed and confirmed by common agreement are the stipulations contained in Articles 1, 2, 3, 4 and 6 of the Treaty signed on July 25, 1892, between Austria-Hungary and Roumania, and the text of which follows below:

ART. 1. The High Contracting Parties promise one another peace and friendship, and will enter into no alliance or engagement directed against any one of their States. They engage to follow a friendly policy, and to lend one another mutual support within the limits of their interests.

ART. 2. If Roumania, without any provocation on her part, should be attacked, Austria-Hungary is bound to bring her in ample time help and assistance against the aggressor. If Austria-Hungary be attacked under the same circumstances in a portion of her states bordering on Roumania, the *casus foederis* will immediately arise for the latter.

ART. 3. If one of the High Contracting Parties should find itself threatened by an aggression under the abovementioned conditions, the respective Governments shall put themselves in agreement as to the measures to be taken with a view to a co-operation of their armies. These military questions, especially that of the unity of operations and of passage through the respective territories, shall be regulated by a military convention.

ART. 4. If, contrary to their desire and hope, the High Contracting Parties be forced into a common war under the circumstances foreseen by the preceding Articles, they engage neither to negotiate nor to conclude peace separately.

ART. 6. The High Contracting Parties mutually promise secrecy as to the contents of the present Treaty.

ART. II. The Articles reproduced above shall remain in force for a new period of five years dating from July 25, 1903, that is to say, until July 25, 1908. If the present Treaty is not denounced one year before its expiration, or if its revision is not demanded by either of the High Contracting Parties, it shall be regarded as prolonged for a period of three years more; and so on from three years to three years in default of denunciation.

ART. III. The present Treaty shall be ratified and the ratifications shall be exchanged within a period of three weeks, or sooner if may be.

In witness whereof the respective Plenipotentiaries have signed it and have affixed thereto the seal of their arms.

Done at Bucharest, the seventeenth/fourth day of the month of April in the year of grace one thousand nine hundred and two.

PALLAVICINI.   D. STURDZA.
  (L.S.)   (L.S.)

Treaty between Austria-Hungary, the German Empire, and Roumania providing for the accession of Germany to the Alliance.
Sinaia, July 12/25, 1902. Ratifications exchanged, July 13/26, 1902.
HIS Majesty the Emperor of Austria, King of Bohemia, etc., and Apostolic King of Hungary, and His Majesty the King of Roumania having concluded at Bucharest on April 17 of the current year the following Treaty of friendship and alliance:

[*Articles I-III of the Treaty of April* 17, 1902, *follow.*]
have invited His Majesty the Emperor of Germany, King of Prussia, to accede to the provisions of the aforesaid Treaty.

Consequently His Majesty the Emperor of Germany, King of Prussia, has furnished with His full powers for this purpose His Representative at Bucharest, the undersigned Sieur Alfred von Kiderlen-Waechter,

His Privy Counsellor of Legation, Envoy Extraordinary and Minister Plenipotentiary, to adhere formally to the provisions contained in the abovementioned Treaty. In virtue of this Act of Accession His Majesty the Emperor of Germany, King of Prussia, takes in the name of the German Empire towards Their Majesties the Emperor of Austria, King of Bohemia, etc., and Apostolic King of Hungary, and the King of Roumania, and at the same time Their Majesties the Emperor of Austria, King of Bohemia, etc., and Apostolic King of Hungary, and the King of Roumania, by the undersigned, the Sieur John Marquis Pallavicini, His Chamberlain, Envoy Extraordinary and Minister Plenipotentiary to His Majesty the King of Roumania, and the Sieur Demetrius A. Sturdza, President of the Council of Ministers, His Minister of Finance and ad interim for War, duly authorized for this purpose, take towards His Majesty the Emperor of Germany, King of Prussia, the same engagements by which the High Contracting Parties have mutually bound themselves according to the stipulations of the said Treaty inserted above.

The present Act of Accession shall be ratified and the ratifications shall be exchanged within a period of three weeks, or sooner if may be.

In witness whereof the respective Plenipotentiaries have signed it and have affixed thereto the seal of their arms.

Done at Sinaia, the twenty-fifth/twelfth day of the month of July of the year of grace one thousand nine hundred and two.

(L.S.)   PALLAVICINI.
(L.S.)   KIDERLEN.
(L.S.)   D. STURDZA.

Treaty between Austria-Hungary and Italy providing for the accession of Italy to the Alliance. December 12, 1902.
Ratifications exchanged, January 14, 1902.

His Majesty the Emperor of Austria, King of Bohemia, etc., and Apostolic King of Hungary, and His Majesty the King of Roumania having concluded on April 17/4, 1902, a Treaty of friendship and alliance, the tenor of which follows:

[The text of the Treaty as above follows.]

This Treaty having received on July 25/12, 1902, the accession of His Majesty the Emperor of Germany, King of Prussia, and having been then communicated by the High Contracting Parties abovementioned to His Majesty the King of Italy, with an invitation to accede thereto, His Majesty the King of Italy, approving the purpose for which this Treaty has been concluded, and which is the preservation of the general peace and of the existing order, has authorized the undersigned Sieur

Emmanuel Marquis Beccaria-Incisa, His Envoy Extraordinary and Minister Plenipotentiary to His Majesty the King of Roumania, to declare in His name that He accedes to the said Treaty within the limits indicated below, so far as concerns the stipulations of Articles 2 and 3 of the Treaty signed on July 25, 1892, between Austria-Hungary and Roumania, Articles which are reproduced in Article I of the Treaty inserted above, to wit:

If eventualities that could give rise to the *casus foederis* as it is foreseen in the said Articles 2 and 3 should chance to occur, Their Majesties the Emperor of Austria, King of Bohemia, etc., and Apostolic King of Hungary, the King of Italy, and the King of Roumania assume a mutual engagement to take counsel together in ample time as to common action, the detailed procedure of which shall be regulated by a special convention.

The present Accession shall be in force, dating from July 25/12, 1903, for the whole duration of the principal Treaty of April 17/4, 1902, unless it be denounced by one of the High Contracting Parties at the proper time in conformity with the provisions of Article II of the said principal Treaty.

This Act of Accession shall be kept secret, and cannot be revealed without the consent of each of the High Contracting Parties.

His Majesty the Emperor of Austria, King of Bohemia, etc., and Apostolic King of Hungary has for his part authorized the undersigned Sieur John Marquis Pallavicini, His Chamberlain, Envoy Extraordinary and Minister Plenipotentiary to His Majesty the King of Roumania, to declare in His name that He accepts in the terms above stated, and with the same mutual obligations, the Accession of His Majesty the King of Italy to the Treaty of April 17/4, 1902.

The present Act of Accession and of acceptance shall be ratified by His Majesty the Emperor of Austria, King of Bohemia, etc., and Apostolic King of Hungary, and by His Majesty the King of Italy, and the ratifications shall be exchanged as soon as possible.

In witness whereof the respective Plenipotentiaries have signed the present Act of Accession and have affixed thereto the seal of their arms.

Done at Bucharest, the twelfth day of the month of December of the year of grace one thousand nine hundred and two.

PALLAVICINI.   E. DI BECCARIA-INCISA.

    (L.S.)   (L.S.)

159

PROTOCOL between Austria-Hungary and the German Empire concerning the continuation of the Treaty of 1879 and the Protocol of 1883. Berlin, 1st June, 1902.

The undersigned, Ladislas Szögyény-Marich of Magyar-Szögyén and Szolgaegyhaza, Ambassador Extraordinary and Plenipotentiary of His Majesty the Emperor of Austria, King of Bohemia, etc., and Apostolic King of Hungary, and Count Bernhard von Bülow, Chancellor of the German Empire, have, by reason of the Most Exalted authorization of their Sovereigns, met together on this day in Berlin for deliberation concerning the further maintenance of the secret Treaty signed at Vienna on October 7, 1879, ratified on the twenty-first of the same month, and already once expressly prolonged through the Protocol executed at Vienna on March 22, 1883, ratified on April 1 of the same year, between His Majesty the Emperor of Austria, King of Bohemia, etc., and Apostolic King of Hungary, and His Majesty the German Emperor, King of Prussia, and they have, with full power from Their Majesties, made the following declaration:

The provisions of Article III of the secret Treaty signed on October 7, 1879, and ratified on the twenty-first of the same month, between Their Majesties the Emperor of Austria, Apostolic King of Hungary, and the German Emperor, King of Prussia, as well as the provisions of Sections 1 and 2 of the Protocol of March 22, 1883, renewing the Treaty, are, according to the intentions which prevailed in this respect at the conclusion of the Treaty, to be so understood that the duration of the Treaty shall automatically be prolonged from three to three years for so long as the two Contracting Parties do not, within the interval agreed upon in Section 2 of the Protocol of March 22, 1883, before the expiration of one of these three-year periods, enter into negotiations over the question whether the conditions serving as the basis for the Treaty still prevail.

The present Protocol will be submitted and recommended for ratification to the two Exalted Sovereigns, and the exchange of documents of ratification shall take place within three weeks in Berlin.

In witness whereof this Protocol has been executed, signed, and sealed in duplicate.

Done at Berlin, on the first of June, one thousand nine hundred and two.

SZÖGYÉNY.   BÜLOW.
  (L. S.)   (L. S.)

160
Exchange of Letters between France and Italy concerning Morocco and Tripolitania.

M. Barrère, Ambassador of the French Republic at Rome, to His Excellency the Marquis Visconti-Venosta, Minister of Foreign Affairs of Italy.

Rome, December 14, 1900

Following the conclusion of the convention of March 21, 1899, between France and Great Britain, my Government, replying to your honourable predecessor, had the opportunity to give him through me explanations of a nature to dissipate all ambiguity as to the scope of that instrument.

Since then, Your Excellency has expressed the opinion that these assurances, reiterated in a more explicit manner, would contribute to strengthen the good relations between our two countries.

Consequently, I have been authorized by the Minister of Foreign Affairs to inform Your Excellency, in view of the friendly relations which have been established between France and Italy, and in that belief that this explanation will conduce further to improve them, that the Convention of March 21, 1899, while leaving the vilayet of Tripoli outside of the partition of influence which it sanctions, marks for the French sphere of influence, in relation to Tripolitania-Cyrenaica, a limit which the Government of the Republic has not the intention of exceeding; and that it does not enter into its plans to interrupt communications by caravan from Tripoli with the regions contemplated by the aforesaid convention.

These explanations, which we are agreed to keep secret, will contribute, I have no doubt, to strengthen, on this as upon other points, the friendly relations between our two countries.

BARRÈRE

Marquis Visconti-Venosta, Minister of Foreign Affairs of Italy, to M. Barrèré, Ambassador of the French Republic at Rome.

Rome, December 16, 1900

The present situation in the Mediterranean and the eventualities which might occur there have been the subject of a friendly interchange of ideas between us, our two Governments being equally animated by the desire to eliminate, in this respect also, everything that would be susceptible of compromising, in the present and in the future, their mutual good understanding.

So far as concerns Morocco more particularly, it appeared from our conversations that the action of France has as its purpose the exercise and the safeguarding of the rights which are the result for her of the proximity of her territory with that Empire.

So defined, I recognized that such action is not in our view of a nature to prejudice the interests of Italy as a Mediterranean power.

It was likewise understood that, if a modification of the political or territorial status of Morocco should result therefrom, Italy would reserve to herself, as a measure of reciprocity, the right eventually to develop her influence with regard to Tripolitania-Cyrenaica.

These explanations, which we are agreed to keep secret, will contribute, I have no doubt, to strengthen the friendly relations between our two countries.

VISCONTI-VENOSTA

Autograph Note of M. Delcassé

June 4, 1902

Count Tornielli has just read me the following telegram, containing the declaration stated, and has left a copy with me at my request.

June 4, 1902. 4 P.M.

DELCASSÉ

Copy left by Count Tornielli

I have been authorized by His Excellency, M. Prinetti, to communicate to Your Excellency a telegram in which the Minister of Foreign Affairs of Italy assures me that, in the renewal of the Triple Alliance, there is nothing directly or indirectly aggressive toward France, no engagement binding us in any eventuality to take part in an aggression against her, finally no stipulation which menaces the security and tranquility of France.

M. Prinetti likewise desires that I should know that the protocols or additional conventions to the Triple Alliance, of which there has been much talk of late, and which would alter its completely defensive character, and which would even have an aggressive character against France, do not exist.

The Minister of Foreign Affairs of Italy expresses at the same time his firm confidence that this communication will have the effect of strengthening more and more the good relations existing between the two countries and of assuring the fruitful development thereof.

This communication is meant to remain secret.

Exchange of Letters Declaring that no Divergence Subsists between the Two Countries as to their Respective Interests in the Mediterranean.

M. Prinetti, Minister of Foreign Affairs of Italy, to M. Barrère, Ambassador of the French Republic at Rome.

Rome, November 1, 1902

In continuation of the conversations which we have had concerning the reciprocal situation of Italy and of France in the Mediterranean basin, and concerning more especially the respective interests of the two countries in Tripolitania-Cyrenaica and in Morocco, it seemed to us opportune to define the engagements which result from the letters exchanged on this subject, between Your Excellency and Marquis Visconti-Venosta, on December 14 and 16, 1900, in this sense, that each of the two Powers can freely develop its sphere of influence in the above mentioned regions at the moment it deems it opportune, and without the action of one of them being necessarily subordinated to that of the other. It was explained on that occasion that the limit of French expansion in Northern Africa contemplated in the above-mentioned letter of Your Excellency of December 14, 1900, was fully understood to be the frontier of Tripolitania indicated by the map attached to the Declaration of March 21, 1899, additional to the Franco-English Convention of June 14, 1898.

We noted that this interpretation left no divergence still existing between our Governments as to their respective interests in the Mediterranean.

Profiting by the occasion of these conferences, and in order to eliminate in a definitive manner any possible misunderstanding between our two countries, I do not hesitate, in order to define their general relations, to make of my own accord to Your Excellency, in the name of the Government of His Majesty the King, the following declarations:

In case France should be the object of a direct or indirect aggression on the part of one or more Powers, Italy will maintain a strict neutrality.

The same shall hold good in case France, as the result of a direct provocation, should find herself compelled, in defence of her honour or of her security, to take the initiative of a declaration of war. In that eventuality, the Government of the Republic shall previously communicate its intention to the Royal Government, which will thus be enabled to determine whether there is really a case of direct provocation.

In order to remain faithful to the spirit of friendship which has inspired the present declarations, I am authorized further to confirm to you that on the part of Italy no protocol or military provision in the nature of an international contract which would be in disagreement with the present declarations exists or will be concluded by her.

I may add that—save as concerns the interpretation of the Mediterranean interests of the two Powers, which has a final character—in conformity with the spirit of the correspondence exchanged between Your Excellency and Marquis Visconti-Venosta, on December 14 and 16, 1900, as the preceding declarations are in harmony with the present international engagements of Italy, the Royal Government understands that they shall retain their full validity so long as it has not notified the Government of the Republic that these engagements have been modified.

I should be obliged if Your Excellency would be kind enough to acknowledge receipt of the present communication, which must remain secret, and to take note thereof in the name of the Government of the Republic.

Prinetti

M. Barrère, Ambassador of the French Republic at Rome, to M. Prinetti, Minister of Foreign Affairs of Italy.

Rome, November 1, 1902

By your letter of today's date, Your Excellency has been kind enough to recall to me that in the continuation of our conversations relative to the reciprocal situation of France and of Italy in the Mediterranean basin, and more especially to the respective interests of the two countries in Tripolitania-Cyrenaica and in Morocco, it seemed to us opportune to define the engagements which result from the letters exchanged on this subject between Marquis Visconti-Venosta and myself on December 14 and 16, 1900, in this sense, that each of the two Powers can freely develop its sphere of influence in the abovementioned regions at the moment it deems it opportune, and without the action of one of them being necessarily subordinated to that of the other.

It was explained on that occasion that the limit of French expansion in Northern Africa contemplated in my abovementioned letter of December 14, 1900, was fully understood to be the frontier of Tripolitania indicated by the map attached to the Declaration of March 21, 1899, additional to the English Convention of June 14, 1898.

This interpretation leaving, as we have noted, no divergence as to their respective interests in the Mediterranean still existing between our Governments, and with the purpose of eliminating in a definitive manner any possible misunderstanding between our two countries, you have been authorized by the Government of His Majesty to formulate of your own accord certain declarations intended to define the general relations of Italy towards France.

I have the honour to acknowledge receipt thereof to Your Excellency and to give you note of these declarations in the name of my Government.

I am authorized, in return, to formulate in the following manner the conditions under which France on her side intends, in the same friendly spirit, to order her general relations towards Italy.

In case Italy should be the object of a direct or indirect aggression on the part of one or more Powers, France will maintain a strict neutrality.

The same shall hold good in case Italy, as the result of a direct provocation, should find herself compelled, in defence of her honour or of her security, to take the initiative of a declaration of war. In that eventuality, the Royal Government shall previously communicate its intention to the Government of the Republic, which will thus be enabled to determine whether there is really a case of direct provocation.

I am authorized equally to declare to you that on the part of France no protocol or military provision in the nature of an international contract which would be in disagreement with the present declarations exists or will be concluded by her.

It is fully understood finally that—save as concerns the interpretation of the Mediterranean interests of the two Powers, which has a final character—in conformity with the spirit of the correspondence exchanged between Marquis Visconti-Venosta and myself, on December 14 and 16, 1900, as the declarations which precede, and which must remain secret, are in harmony with the present international engagements of Italy, they shall retain their full validity so long as the Royal Government has not notified the Government of the Republic that these engagements have been modified.

BARRÈRE

Definition of the word " direct " as used above.
M. Barrère, Ambassador of the French Republic at Rome, to M. Prinetti,
Minister of Foreign Affairs of Italy.

Rome, November 2, 1902.

On the subject of the declarations which we have exchanged by our letters of yesterday's date respecting the general relations of France and Italy, it would seem to me necessary, in order to avoid every possibility of misunderstanding, to define the sense and the scope which ought to be attributed to the word " direct " in the expression " direct provocation " employed in the said declarations.

I should be obliged to you if you would confirm to me the interpretation which, in your opinion, belongs to the term in question.

BARRÈRE

M. Prinetti, Minister of Foreign Affairs of Italy,
to M. Barrère, Ambassador of the French
Republic at Rome.

Rome, November 2, 1902.

You have been kind enough to express to me, by your letter of today, the desire to see defined by me, in order to avoid every possibility of misunderstanding, the sense and the scope which ought to be attributed to the word *direct* in the expression *direct provocation*, employed in the declarations which I made to you by my letter of yesterday.

I hasten to confirm to you on this subject what I had occasion to say to you by word of mouth. The word *direct* has this sense and this meaning, to wit, that the facts capable of being eventually invoked as constituting the provocation must concern the direct relations between the Power provoking and the Power provoked.

GIULIO PRINETTI

161

FOURTH TREATY of Triple Alliance between Austria-Hungary, the German Empire, and Italy. Berlin, 28th June, 1902. Ratifications exchanged, 8th July, 1902.

Their Majesties the Emperor of Austria, King of Bohemia, etc., and Apostolic King of Hungary, the Emperor of Germany, King of Prussia, and the King of Italy, firmly resolved to assure to Their States the continuation of the benefits which the maintenance of the Triple Alliance guarantees to them, from the political point of view as well as from the monarchical and social point of view, and wishing with this object to prolong the duration of this Alliance, concluded on May 20, 1882, renewed a first time by the Treaties of February 20, 1887, and a second time by the Treaty of May 6, 1891, have for this purpose appointed as Their Plenipotentiaries, to wit:

His Majesty the Emperor of Austria, King of Bohemia, etc., and Apostolic King of Hungary: the Sieur Ladislas Szögyény-Marich of Magyar-Szögyén and Szolgaegyháza, His Ambassador Extraordinary and Plenipotentiary to His Majesty the Emperor of Germany, King of Prussia;

His Majesty the Emperor of Germany, King of Prussia: Count Bernhard von Bülow, Chancellor of the Empire, His President of the Council of Ministers of Prussia; and

His Majesty the King of Italy: Count Carlo Lanza di Busca, Lieutenant-General, Senator, His Ambassador Extraordinary and Plenipotentiary to His Majesty the Emperor of Germany, King of Prussia, who, after exchange of their full powers, found in good and due form, have agreed upon the following Articles:

Art. I. The High Contracting Parties mutually promise peace and friendship, and will enter into no alliance or engagement directed against any one of their States.

They engage to proceed to an exchange of ideas on political and economic questions of a general nature which may arise, and they further promise one another mutual support within the limits of their own interests.

Art. II. In case Italy, without direct provocation on her part, should be attacked by France for any reason whatsoever, the two other Contracting Parties shall be bound to lend help and assistance with all their forces to the Party attacked.

This same obligation shall devolve upon Italy in case of an aggression without direct provocation by France against Germany.

Art. III. If one, or two, of the High Contracting Parties, without direct provocation on their part, should chance to be attacked and to be engaged in a war with two or more Great Powers nonsignatory to the present Treaty, the *casus foederis* will arise simultaneously for all the High Contracting Parties.

Art. IV. In case a Great Power nonsignatory to the present Treaty should threaten the security of the states of one of the High Contracting Parties, and the threatened Party should find itself forced on that account to make war against it, the two others bind themselves to observe towards their Ally a benevolent neutrality. Each of them reserves to itself, in this case, the right to take part in the war, if it should see fit, to make common cause with its Ally.

Art. V. If the peace of one of the High Contracting Parties should chance to be threatened under the circumstances foreseen by the preceding Articles, the High Contracting Parties shall take counsel together in ample time as to the military measures to be taken with a view to eventual co-operation.

They engage, henceforth, in all cases of common participation in a war, to conclude neither armistice, nor peace, nor treaty, except by common agreement among themselves.

Art. VI. Germany and Italy, having in mind only the maintenance, so far as possible, of the territorial status quo in the Orient, engage to use their influence to forestall on the Ottoman coasts and islands in the Adriatic and the Aegean Seas any territorial modification which might be injurious to one or the other of the Powers signatory to the present

Treaty. To this end, they will communicate to one another all information of a nature to enlighten each other mutually concerning their own dispositions, as well as those of other Powers.

ART. VII. Austria-Hungary and Italy, having in mind only the maintenance, so far as possible, of the territorial status quo in the Orient, engage to use their influence to forestall any territorial modification which might be injurious to one or the other of the Powers signatory to the present Treaty. To this end, they shall communicate to one another all information of a nature to enlighten each other mutually concerning their own dispositions, as well as those of other Powers. However, if, in the course of events, the maintenance of the status quo in the regions of the Balkans or of the Ottoman coasts and islands in the Adriatic and in the Aegean Sea should become impossible, and if, whether in consequence of the action of a third Power or otherwise, Austria-Hungary or Italy should find themselves under the necessity of modifying it by a temporary or permanent occupation on their part, this occupation shall take place only after a previous agreement between the two Powers, based upon the principle of a reciprocal compensation for every advantage, territorial or other, which each of them might obtain beyond the present status quo, and giving satisfaction to the interests and well founded claims of the two Parties.

ART. VIII. The stipulations of Articles VI and VII apply in no way to the Egyptian question, with regard to which the High Contracting Parties preserve respectively their freedom of action, regard being always paid to the principles upon which the present Treaty rests.

ART. IX. Germany and Italy engage to exert themselves for the maintenance of the territorial status quo in the North African regions on the Mediterranean, to wit, Cyrenaica, Tripolitania, and Tunisia. The Representatives of the two Powers in these regions shall be instructed to put themselves into the closest intimacy of mutual communication and assistance.

If unfortunately, as a result of a mature examination of the situation, Germany and Italy should both recognize that the maintenance of the status quo has become impossible, Germany engages, after a formal and previous agreement, to support Italy in any action in the form of occupation or other taking of guaranty which the latter should undertake in these same regions with a view to an interest of equilibrium and of legitimate compensation.

It is understood that in such an eventuality the two Powers would seek to place themselves likewise in agreement with England.

ART. X. If it were to happen that France should make a move to extend her occupation, or even her protectorate or her sovereignty, under any form whatsoever, in the North African territories, and that in consequence thereof Italy, in order to safeguard her position in the Mediterranean, should feel that she must herself undertake action in the said North African territories, or even have recourse to extreme measures in French territory in Europe, the state of war which would thereby ensue between Italy and France would constitute *ipso facto*, on the demand of Italy, and at the common charge of Germany and Italy, the *casus foederis* foreseen by Articles II and V of the present Treaty, as if such an eventuality were expressly contemplated therein.

ART. XI. If the fortunes of any war undertaken in common against France by the two Powers should lead Italy to seek for territorial guaranties with respect to France, for the security of the frontiers of the Kingdom and of her maritime position, as well as with a view to stability and to peace, Germany will present no obstacle thereto, and, if need be, and in a measure compatible with circumstances, will apply herself to facilitating the means of attaining such a purpose.

ART. XII. The High Contracting Parties mutually promise secrecy as to the contents of the present Treaty.

ART. XIII. The Signatory Powers reserve the right of subsequently introducing, in the form of a Protocol and of a common agreement; the modifications of which the utility should be demonstrated by circumstances.

ART. XIV. The present Treaty shall remain in force for the space of six years, dating from the exchange of ratifications; but if it has not been denounced one year in advance by one or another of the High Contracting Parties, it shall remain in force for the same duration of six more years.

ART. XV. The ratifications of the present Treaty shall be exchanged at Berlin within a period of a fortnight, or sooner if may be.

In witness whereof the respective Plenipotentiaries have signed the present Treaty, and have affixed thereto the seal of their arms.

Done at Berlin, in triplicate, the twenty-eighth day of the month of June, one thousand nine hundred and two.

(L. S.)   SZÖGYÉNY.
(L. S.)   BÜLOW.
(L. S.)   C. LANZA.

Final Protocol to the Treaty.   Berlin, June 28, 1902.
PROTOCOL.

At the moment of proceeding to the signing of the Treaty of this day between Austria-Hungary, Germany, and Italy, the undersigned Plenipotentiaries of these three Powers, thereto duly authorized, mutually declare themselves as follows:

1. Under reserve of parliamentary approval for the executory stipu-

lations proceeding from the present declaration of principle, the High Contracting Parties promise each other, from this moment, in economic matters (finances, customs, railroads), in addition to most-favoured-nation treatment, all of the facilities and special advantages which would be compatible with the requirements of each of the three States and with their respective engagements with third Powers.

2. The accession of England being already acquired, in principle, to the stipulations of the Treaty of this day which concern the Orient, properly so-called, to wit, the territories of the Ottoman Empire, the High Contracting Parties shall exert themselves at the opportune moment, and to the extent that circumstances may permit it, to bring about an analogous accession with regard to the North African territories of the central and western part of the Mediterranean, including Morocco. This accession might be realized by an acceptance, on the part of England, of the programme established by Articles IX and X of the Treaty of this day.

In witness whereof the three Plenipotentiaries have signed the present Protocol in triplicate.

Done at Berlin, the twenty-eighth day of the month of June, one thousand nine hundred and two.

SZÖGYÉNY.
BÜLOW.
C. LANZA.

Austrian Declaration to Italy concerning Tripoli. Rome, June 30, 1902.

Secret.

DECLARATION.

I the undersigned, Ambassador of His Imperial and Royal Apostolic Majesty, have been authorized to declare to the Government of His Majesty the King of Italy, that, while desiring the maintenance of the territorial status quo in the Orient, the Austro-Hungarian Government, having no special interest to safeguard in Tripolitania and Cyrenaica, has decided to undertake nothing which might interfere with the action of Italy, in case, as a result of fortuitous circumstances, the state of things now prevailing in those regions should undergo any change whatsoever and should oblige the Royal Government to have recourse to measures which would be dictated to it by its own interests.

It is understood that the present Declaration shall remain secret; and that it may be produced only in virtue of a previous agreement between the two Governments.

Rome, June 30, 1902.
Baron Pasetti, m.p.

Note of the Italian Government acknowledging the Austrian
Declaration concerning Tripoli. Rome, June 30, 1902.
Ministry of Foreign Affairs.
Secret.
To His Excellency.

Baron Pasetti,
Imperial and Royal Ambassador of Austria-Hungary,
Rome.

Rome, June 30, 1902.
Mr. Ambassador,
In conformity with the desire which Your Excellency has been kind enough to express to me in your secret Note dated today, No. 27, I have the honour to acknowledge the receipt of the Declaration concerning Tripolitania-Cyrenaica which Your Excellency has transmitted to me with your abovementioned Note in accordance with the instruction of your Government.

Pray accept, Mr. Ambassador, the assurance of my very high consideration.

PRINETTI
Rome. June 30, 1902

162

CONVENTION BETWEEN GREAT BRITAIN AND THE USA as to the Alaskan boundary. Concluded 24th January 1903. Ratifications Exchanged, 3rd March 1903.

The United States of America and His Majesty Edward the Seventh, of the United Kingdom of Great Britain and Ireland, and of the British Dominions beyond the Seas, King, and Emperor of India, equally desirous for the friendly and final adjustment of the differences which exist between them in respect to the true meaning and application of certain clauses of the convention between Great Britain and Russia, signed under date of February 28/16, A.D. 1825, which clauses relate to the delimitation of the boundary line between the territory of Alaska, now a possession of the United States, and the British possessions in North America, have resolved to provide for the submission of the questions as hereinafter stated to a tribunal, and to that end have appointed their respective plenipotentiaries as follows:

The President of the United States of America, John Hay, Secretary of State of the United States; and

His Britannic Majesty, The Right Honourable Sir Michael H. Herbert, K.C.M.G., C.B., His Britannic Majesty's Ambassador Extraordinary and Plenipotentiary;

Who, after an exchange of their full powers which were found to be in good and due form, have agreed upon the following articles:

ART. I. A tribunal shall be immediately appointed to consider and decide the questions set forth in Article IV of this convention. The tribunal shall consist of six impartial jurists of repute who shall consider judicially the questions submitted to them, each of whom shall first subscribe an oath that he will impartially consider the arguments and evidence presented to the tribunal and will decide thereupon according to his true judgment. Three members of the tribunal shall be appointed by the President of the United States, and three by His Britannic Majesty. All questions considered by the tribunal, including the final award, shall be decided by a majority of all the members thereof.

In case of the refusal to act, or of the death, incapacity or abstention from service of any of the persons so appointed, another impartial jurist of refute shall be forthwith appointed in his place by the same authority which appointed his predecessor.

The tribunal may appoint a secretary and a bailiff to perform such duties as they may prescribe, and may employ scientific experts if found to be necessary, and may fix a reasonable compensation for such offers. The tribunal shall keep an accurate record of all its proceedings.

Each of the High Contracting Parties shall make compensation for the services of the members of the tribunal of its own appointment and of any agent, counsel, or other person employed in its behalf, and shall pay all costs incurred in the preparation of its case. All expenses reasonably incurred by the tribunal in the performance of its duties shall be paid by the respective governments in equal moieties. The tribunal may, subject to the provisions of this convention, establish all proper rules for the regulation of its proceedings.

ART. II. Each of the High Contracting Parties shall also name one person to attend the tribunal as its agent.

The written or printed case of each of the two parties, accompanied by the documents, the official correspondence and all other evidence in writing or print on which each party relies, shall be delivered in duplicate to each member of the tribunal and to the agent of the other party as soon as may be after the organization of the tribunal, but within a period not exceeding two months from the date of the exchange of ratifications of this convention.

Within two months after the delivery on both sides of the written or printed case, either party may, in like manner, deliver in duplicate to each member of the tribunal, and to the agent of the other party, a counter-case and additional documents, correspondence and evidence in reply to the case, documents, correspondence and evidence so presented by the other party. The tribunal may, however, extend this last mentioned period when in their judgement it becomes necessary by reason of special difficulties which may arise in the procuring of such additional papers and evidence.

If in the case submitted to the tribunal either party shall have specified or referred to any report or document in its own exclusive possession without annexing a copy, such party shall be bound, if the other party shall demand it, within thirty days after the delivery of the case, to furnish to the party applying for it a duly certified copy thereof; and either party may call upon the other, through the tribunal, to produce the original or certified copies of any papers adduced as evidence, giving in each instance such reasonable notice as the tribunal may require; and the original or copy so requested shall be delivered as soon as may be and within a period not exceeding forty days after receipt of notice.

Each party may present to the tribunal all pertinent evidence, documentary, historical, geographical, or topographical, including maps and charts, in its possession or control and applicable to the rightful decision of the questions submitted; and if it appears to the tribunal that there is evidence pertinent to the case in the possession of either party, and which has not been produced, the tribunal may in its discretion order the production of the same by the party having control thereof.

It shall be the duty of each party through its agent or counsel, within two months from the expiration of the time limited for the delivery of the counter-case on both sides, to deliver in duplicate to each member of the said tribunal and to the agent of the other party a written or printed argument showing the points and referring to the evidence upon which his Government relies, and either party may also support the same before the tribunal by oral argument of counsel. The tribunal may, if they shall deem further elucidation with regard to any point necessary, require from either party a written, printed, or oral statement or argument upon the point; but in such case the other party shall have the right to reply thereto.

ART. III. It is agreed by the High Contracting Parties that the tribunal shall consider in the settlement of the questions submitted to its decision the Treaties respectively concluded between His Britannic Majesty and the Emperor of All the Russias under date of 28/16 February, A.D. 1825, and between the United States of America and the Emperor of All the Russias concluded under date of March 30/18, A.D. 1867; and particularly the Articles III, IV, V, of the first mentioned treaty, which in the original text are word for word as follows:

" La ligne de démarcation entre les Possessions des Hautes Parties

Contractantes sur la Côte du Continent et les Iles de l'Amérique Nord-Ouest, sera tracée ainsi qu'il suit:

" A partir du Point le plus méridional de l'Ile dite *Prince of Wales*, lequel Point se trouve sous la parallèle du 54me degré 40 minutes de latitude Nord, et entre le 131me et 133 me degré de longitude Ouest (Méridien de Greenwich), la dite ligne remontera au Nord de long de la passe dite *Portland Channel*, jusqu'au Point de la terra ferme où elle atteint le 56me degré latitude Nord; de ce dernier point la ligne de démarcation suivra la crête des montagnes situées parallèlement a la Côte, jusqu'au point d'intersection du 141me degré de longitude Ouest (même Méridien); et finalement, du dit point d'intersection, la meme ligne méridienne du 141me degré formera, dans son prolongement jusqu'a la Mer Glaciale, la limite entre les Possessions Russes et Britanniques sur les Continent de l'Amérique Nord-Ouest."

IV. " Il est entendu, par rapport à la ligne de démarcation déterminée dans l'Article précédent;

" 1. Que l'Isle dite *Prince of Wales* appartiendra toute entière à la Russie.

" 2. Que partoute où la crête des montagnes qui s'étendent dans une direction parallèle à la Côte depuis le 56me degré de latitude Nord au point d'intersection du 141me degré de longitude Ouest, se trouveroit à la distance de plus de dix lieues marines de l'Océan, la limite entre les Possessions Britanniques et la lisière de Côte mentionnée ci-dessus comme devant appartenir à la Russie, sera formée par une ligne parallèle aux sinuosités de la Côte, et qui ne pourra jamais en être éloignée que de dix lieues marines."

V. " Il est convenue en outre, que nul Etablissement ne sera formé par l'une des deux Parties dans les limites que les deux Articles précédens assignent aux Possessions de l'Autre. En conséquence, les Sujets Britanniques ne formeront aucun Etablissement soit sur la Côte, soit sur la lisière de terre ferme comprise dans les limites des Possessions Russes, telles qu'elles sont désignées dans les deux Articles précédens; et, de même, nul Etablissement ne sera formé par des Sujets Russes au delà des dîtes limites."

The tribunal shall also take into consideration any action of the several governments or of their respective representatives preliminary or subsequent to the conclusion of said treaties so far as the same tends to show the original and effective understanding of the parties in respect to the limits of their several territorial jurisdictions under and by virtue of the provisions of said treaties.

ART. IV. Referring to Articles III, IV, and V of the said treaty of 1825 the said tribunal shall answer and decide the following questions:—

1. What is intended as the point of commencement of the line?

2. What channel is the Portland Channel?

3. What course should the line take from the point of commencement to the entrance to Portland Channel?

4. To what point on the 56th parallel is the line to be drawn from the head of the Portland Channel, and what course should it follow between these points?

5. In extending the line of demarcation northward from said point on the parallel of the 56th degree of North latitude, following the crest of the mountains situated parallel to the coast until its intersection with the 141st degree of longitude west of Greenwich, subject to the condition that if such line should anywhere exceed the distance of ten marine leagues from the ocean then the boundary between the British and the Russian territory should be formed by a line parallel to the sinuosities of the coast and distant therefrom not more than ten marine leagues, was it the intention and meaning of said convention of 1825 that there should remain in the exclusive possession of Russia a continuous fringe or strip of coast on the mainland, not exceeding ten marine leagues in width, separating the British Possessions from the bays, ports, inlets, havens, and waters of the ocean, and extending from the said point on the 56th degree of latitude north to a point where such line of demarcation should intersect the 141st degree of longitude west of the Meridian of Greenwich?

6. If the foregoing question should be answered in the negative, and in the event of the summit of such mountains proving to be in places more than ten marine leagues from the coast, should the width of the lisière which was to belong to Russia be measured (1) from the mainland coast of the ocean, strictly so-called, along a line perpendicular thereto, or (2) was it the intention and meaning of the said convention that where the mainland coast is indented by deep inlets, forming part of the territorial waters of Russia, the width of the lisière was to be measured (a) from the line of the general direction of the mainland coast, or (b) from the line separating the waters of the ocean from the territorial waters of Russia, or (c) from the heads of the aforesaid inlets?

7. What, if any exist, are the mountains referred to as situated parallel to the coast, which mountains, when within ten marine leagues from the coast, are declared to form the eastern boundary?

ART. V. The tribunal shall assemble for their first meeting at London as soon as practicable after receiving their commissions; and shall themselves fix the times and places of all subsequent meetings.

The decision of the tribunal shall be made so soon as possible after the conclusion of the arguments in the case, and within three months thereafter, unless the President of the United States and His Britannic Majesty shall by common accord extend the time therefor. The decision shall be made in writing, and dated, and shall be signed by the members of the tribunal assenting to the same. It shall be signed in duplicate, one copy whereof shall be given to the agent of the United States of America for his government, and the other to the agent of His Britannic Majesty for his government.

ART. VI. When the High Contracting Parties shall have received the decision of the tribunal upon the questions submitted as provided in the foregoing articles, which decision shall be final and binding upon all parties, they will at once appoint, each on its own behalf, one or more scientific experts who shall with all convenient speed proceed together to lay down the boundary line, in conformity with such decision.

Should there be, unfortunately, a failure by a majority of the tribunal to agree upon any of the points submitted for their decision, it shall be their duty to so report in writing to the respective governments through their respective agents. Should there be an agreement by a majority upon a part of the questions submitted, it shall be their duty to sign and report their decision upon the points of such agreement in the manner hereinbefore prescribed.

ART. VII. The present Convention shall be ratified by the President of the United States, by and with the advice and consent of the Senate, and by His Britannic Majesty, and the ratifications shall be exchanged in Washington or in London so soon as the same may be effected.

In faith whereof we, the respective plenipotentiaries, have signed this Convention and have hereunto affixed our seals.

Done at Washington, in duplicate, this 24th day of January, A.D. 1903.

JOHN HAY
MICHAEL H. HERBERT

DECISION OF THE ALASKAN BOUNDARY TRIBUNAL UNDER THE TREATY OF JANUARY 24, 1903, BETWEEN THE UNITED STATES AND GREAT BRITAIN.

Whereas by a Convention signed at Washington on the 24th day of January 1903, by Plenipotentiaries of and on behalf of His Majesty the King of the United Kingdom of Great Britain and Ireland and of the British Dominions beyond the Seas, Emperor of India, and of and on behalf of the United States of America, it was agreed that a Tribunal should be appointed to consider and decide the questions hereinafter set forth, such Tribunal to consist of six impartial Jurists of repute, who should consider judicially the questions submitted to them each of whom should first subscribe an oath that he would impartially consider the arguments and evidence presented to the said

Tribunal, and would decide thereupon according to his true judgement, and that three members of the said Tribunal should be appointed by His Britannic Majesty and three by the President of the United States:

And whereas it was further agreed by the said Convention that the said Tribunal should consider in the settlement of the said questions submitted to its decision the Treaties respectively concluded between His Britannic Majesty and the Emperor of All the Russias under date of the 28th (16th) February A.D. 1825 and between the United States of America and the Emperor of all the Russias, concluded under date of the 18th (30th) March A.D. 1867, and particularly the Articles III, IV and V of the first mentioned Treaty, and should also take into consideration any action of the several Governments or of their respective Representatives, preliminary or subsequent to the conclusion of the said Treaties so far as the same tended to show the original and effective understanding of the parties in respect to the limits of their several territorial jurisdictions under and by virtue of the provisions of the said Treaties.

And whereas it was further agreed by the said Convention, referring to Articles III, IV and V of the said Treaty of 1825, that the said Tribunal should answer and decide the following questions:—

1. What is intended as the point of commencement of the line?

2. What channel is the Portland Channel?

3. What course should the line take from the point of commencement to the entrance to Portland Channel?

4. To what point on the 56th parallel is the line to be drawn from the head of the Portland Channel, and what course should it follow between these points?

5. In extending the line of demarcation northward from said point on the parallel of the 56th degree of north latitude, following the crest of the mountains situated parallel to the coast until its intersection with the 141st degree of longitude west of Greenwich, subject to the conditions that if such line should anywhere exceed the distance of 10 marine leagues from the ocean, then the boundary between the British and the Russian territory should be formed by a line parallel to the sinuosities of the coast and distant therefrom not more than 10 marine leagues, was it the intention and meaning of the said Convention of 1825 that there should remain in the exclusive possession of Russia a continuous fringe, or strip, of coast on the mainland not exceeding 10 marine leagues in width, separating the British possessions from the bays, ports, inlets, havens, and waters of the ocean, and extending from the said point on the 56th degree of latitude north

to a point where such line of demarcation should intersect the 141st degree of longitude west of the meridian of Greenwich?

6. If the foregoing question should be answered in the negative and in the event of the summit of such mountains proving to be in places more than 10 marine leagues from the coast should the width of the *lisière*, which was to belong to Russia be measured (1) from the mainland coast of the ocean, strictly so-called along a line perpendicular thereto, or (2) was it the intention and meaning of the said Convention that where the mainland coast is indented by deep inlets forming part of the territorial waters of Russia, the width of the *lisière* was to be measured (*a*) from the line of the general direction of the mainland coast, or (*b*) from the line separating the waters of the ocean from the territorial waters of Russia, or (*c*) from the heads of the aforesaid inlets?

7. What, if any exist, are the mountains referred to as situated parallel to the coast, which mountains, when within 10 marine leagues from the coast, are declared to form the eastern boundary?

And whereas His Britannic Majesty duly appointed Richard Everard, Baron Alverstone, G.C.M.G. Lord Chief Justice of England, Sir Louis Amable Jetté K.C.M.G. Lieutenant-Governor of the Province of Quebec, and Allen Bristol Aylesworth one of His Majesty's Counsel, and the President of the United States of America duly appointed the Honourable Elihu Root Secretary of War of the United States, the Honourable Henry Cabot Lodge, Senator of the United States from the State of Massachusetts and the Honourable George Turner of the State of Washington, to be members of the said Tribunal.

Now therefore we the Undersigned having each of us first subscribed an oath as provided by the said Convention and having taken into consideration the matters directed by the said Convention to be considered by us, and having judicially considered the said questions submitted to us, do hereby make Answer and Award as follows:—

In answer to the *first* question

The Tribunal unanimously agrees that the point of commencement of the line is Cape Muzon.

In answer to the *second* question

The Tribunal unaminously agrees that the Portland Channel is the Channel which runs from about 55° 56' NL and passes to the north of Pearse and Wales Islands.

A majority of the Tribunal that is to say Lord Alverstone Mr Root Mr Lodge and Mr Turner decides that the Portland Channel after passing to the north of Wales Island is the channel between Wales Island and Sitklan Island called Tongass Channel. The Portland Channel above mentioned is marked throughout its length by a dotted red line from the point B to the point marked C on the map signed in duplicate by the members of the Tribunal at the time of signing their decision.

In answer to the *third* question.

A majority of the Tribunal that is to say Lord Alverstone Mr Root Mr Lodge and Mr Turner decides that the course of the line from the point of commencement to the entrance to Portland Channel is the line marked A B in red on the aforesaid map.

In answer to the *fourth* question

A majority of the Tribunal that is to say Lord Alverstone Mr Root Mr Lodge and Mr Turner decides that the point to which the line is to be drawn from the head of the Portland Channel is the point on the 56th parallel of latitude marked D on the aforesaid map and the course which the line should follow is drawn from C to D on the aforesaid map.

In answer to the *fifth* question

A majority of the Tribunal, that is to say Lord Alverstone Mr Root Mr Lodge and Mr Turner decides that the answer to the above question is in the affirmative

Question five having been answered in the affirmative question *six* requires no answer.

In answer to the *seventh* question

A majority of the Tribunal that is to say Lord Alverstone, Mr Root, Mr Lodge and Mr Turner decides that the mountains marked S on the aforesaid map are the mountains referred to as situated parallel to the coast on that part of the coast where such mountains marked S are situated and that between the points marked P (mountain marked S 8,000) on the north and the point marked T (mountain marked S 7,950) in the absence of further survey the evidence is not sufficient to enable the Tribunal to say which are the mountains parallel to the coast within the meaning of the Treaty.

In witness whereof we have signed the above written decision upon the questions submitted to us.

Signed in duplicate this twentieth day of October 1903.

ALVERSTONE
ELIHU ROOT
HENRY CABOT LODGE
GEORGE TURNER

Witness
REGINALD TOWER:
Secretary.

163

TREATY of Alliance Between the Principality of Bulgaria and the Kingdom of Serbia, 30th March, 1904. Ratifications exchanged in Sofia, 9th April, 1904.

THE government of H.R.H. Prince Ferdinand I of Bulgaria and the government of H.M. King Peter I of Serbia, guided by the principle of "The Balkans for the Balkan nations," and inspired by a desire to safeguard the peace and security of their peoples, to preserve the territorial *status quo* on the Balkan peninsula, and to improve the condition of their fellow-countrymen in the Ottoman Empire, agree on the following:

I. Convinced of the utility of the programme of reforms adopted at Mürzsteg for the vilayets of Salonica, Bitolya and Kossovo (Macedonia and Old Serbia), the two allied states hereby promise to promote jointly and by all peaceful means at their disposal the execution of these reforms in the said three vilayets, at the same time encouraging their introduction into the vilayet of Adrianople, thus safeguarding the lives, property and free development of their fellow-countrymen in these vilayets, on the basis of political and national equality in all respects.

II. Firmly resolved to apply all of their loyal efforts and goodwill for the preservation of peace on the Balkan peninsula, the two allied states hereby promise jointly to defend themselves with all the power and resources at their command, against any encroachment from whatever source, be it on the present territorial unity and independence of their respective states, or on the security and inviolability of the reigning dynasties.

III. Likewise the two allied states promise to oppose, with all the power and resources at their command, any hostile act or isolated occupation of the above-mentioned four vilayets, whatever nation may be responsible.

IV. In the circumstances foreseen in Articles II and III, the two allied states will conclude a special military convention, in which all possible eventualities and all their consequences will be provided for.

V. In the desire to prepare the ground for the full co-operation between the Slavs on the Balkan peninsula and to create favourable circumstances for an immediate agreement between the Kingdom of Serbia and the Principality of Montenegro, the two allied states hereby promise—whenever the question of Albania should arise—to support such a solution as would favour the interests of Montenegro.

VI. The two allied states hereby promise to discuss and decide jointly all questions which, by their nature and spirit, are within the sphere of this treaty.

VII. The two allied states hereby promise to submit to the final decision of His Imperial Majesty the Tsar of All Russians, all of those controversies which they are not able to decide among themselves. In case the Russian emperor declines to award a decision on such a controversial question, it will be placed in the hands of the Permanent Court of Arbitration at The Hague.

VIII. The present allied treaty remains secret. It may be communicated to a third party—in whole or in part—only after a preliminary agreement between the two allied governments.

After five years this treaty may be brought up for revision if the two allied states consider it desirable.

It becomes valid on the day of its ratification.

Concluded in Belgrade the thirtieth day of the month of March [O.S.] the one thousand nine hundred and fourth year after the birth of Christ, the third day of Easter.

In the name of the Principality of Bulgaria:

(s) D. RIZOV.

(s) Colonel of the General Staff HESAPCHIEV.

In the name of the Kingdom of Serbia:

(s) GENERAL SAVA GRUIĆ.

(s) NIKOLA PAŠIĆ.

TREATY of Friendship between the Principality of Bulgaria and the Kingdom of Serbia, 31st March, 1904. Ratifications exchanged in Sofia, 9th April, 1904.

THE government of His Royal Highness Prince Ferdinand I of Bulgaria and the government of His Majesty King Peter I of Serbia, deeply conscious of the common destinies of their neighbouring and related states, and sincerely inspired by the desire of safeguarding the advantages of the regulated and peaceful political and cultural development of their nations through a friendly and brotherly union between them, agree on the following:

I. To permit the free importation of their respective products (of domestic origin), at the same time attempting to conduct similar customs policies with respect to other states, aiming at an eventual customs union (Zollverein).

II. To facilitate the mutual exchange and transit of their products by reducing the corresponding freight and passenger rates.

III. To equalise their telegraph and postal rates with their internal rates and to introduce the Cyrillic alphabet into their telegraphic communication.

IV. To abolish their frontier passports, and to remove all other hindrances to free communication between their peoples.

V. To conclude a judicial convention for the mutual execution of decisions under civil law as well as for the extradition of criminals according to common law (du droit commun), and of deserters.

VI. To conclude a monetary convention for the establishment of the free circulation of Serbian and Bulgarian money in their states, and thus to facilitate commercial relations.

VII. This treaty may be made public only after a preliminary agreement between the two states. It shall enter into force from the day of its ratification.

Concluded in Belgrade on the thirtieth of March [O.S.], 1904 (one thousand nine hundred fourth year) after the birth of Christ, the third day of the Resurrection.

In the name of the Kingdom of Serbia:

(s) GENERAL SAVA GRUIĆ
(s) NIKOLA PAŠIĆ.

In the name of the Principality of Bulgaria:

(s) D. RIZOV.
(s) Colonel of the General Staff HESAPCHIEV.

Approved: Chargé d'Affaires of the Agency, for the General Staff, Colonel HESAPCHIEV.

(By mutual consent the two allied states agree that this treaty be made public.)

Concluding Protocol.

Today, March 31, 1904, we the undersigned: D. Rizov, Bulgarian diplomatic agent in Cetinje, and Hristofor Hesapchiev, Colonel of the General Staff, chargé d'affaires of the Bulgarian diplomatic agency in Belgrade, appointed by His Royal Highness Prince Ferdinand I of Bulgaria with plenipotentiary letters, issued in Plovdiv on March 22 [O.S.], as plenipotentiaries of the Principality of Bulgaria, and General Sava Gruić, president of the ministerial council, and N. P. Pašić, minister of foreign affairs of the Kingdom of Serbia, appointed by H.M. King Peter I of Serbia with a plenipotentiary letter, issued in Belgrade on March 28 [O.S.], as plenipotentiaries of the Kingdom of Serbia, with the aim of conducting negotiations for the drawing up and conclusion of a convention to guarantee the political and economic development of the said two states through joint action for protecting their national rights and interests, having exchanged our plenipotentiary letters which were found in good and due form, we proceeded to the execution of the mission entrusted to us.

After a long and varied exchange of opinions as to the foundations which should form the basis of such a convention, we decided:

I. That the convention should consist of two parts: the one, which may be made public after the condition foreseen in its text has been fulfilled, to be entitled: " A Treaty of Friendship between the Principality of Bulgaria and the Kingdom of Serbia " and to contain agreements of a cultural and economic character; the other, which is secret, to be entitled: " A Treaty of Alliance between the Principality of Bulgaria and the Kingdom of Serbia," and to contain agreements of a political and military character.

II. That, in order to avoid misinterpretations in the application of the said treaties, the following explanations are included in this protocol:

1. Concerning the Treaty of Friendship: (a) in Article I the phrase: " to conduct similar customs policies " is to be understood: as far as the existing commercial treaties of the two states permit this; and (b) as a supplement to Article III: the two states will agree upon making a joint proposal to the imperial Russian government for the immediate establishment of telegraphic communication between Russia and Bulgaria—if possible in the Cyrillic alphabet.

2. Concerning the Treaty of Alliance: (a) in Article I, the vilayet of Kossovo is understood to include the Sanjak of Novibazar. (b) in Article I, above the Serbian text of the Bulgarian-Serbian copy the last word *pogledu*, as synonymous with the word *otnoshtayu*, is not to be considered erroneous; (c) supplementary to Article I, the two allied states will promote mutual tolerance between their fellow-countrymen in the Ottoman Empire, and (d) in Article V " Albania " is to be understood within the boundaries of the vilayets of Scutari and Janina.

III. That the two treaties be written parallel and with two copies of each one, in the Serbian and Bulgarian languages; also that the copies for the Kingdom of Serbia should be in Bulgarian and Serbian, and the copies for the Principality of Bulgaria should be in Serbia and Bulgarian.

IV. That the original copies of the two treaties, duly ratified by the two sovereigns and their respective ministers, after the plenipotentiary letters and the present protocol have been attached, be kept in the private archives of H.M. King Peter I of Serbia and H.R.H. Prince Ferdinand I of Bulgaria. Only a copy of the Treaty of Friendship may be deposited in the archives of the Ministries of Foreign Affairs of the two states.

Concluded in Belgrade on March 31 [O.S.], the one thousand nine hundred and fourth year after the birth of Christ, the third day of Easter.

In the name of the Principality of Bulgaria:

(s) D. RIZOV.

(s) Colonel of the General Staff H. HESAPCHIEV.

In the name of the Kingdom of Serbia:

(s) GENERAL S. GRUIĆ.

(s) NIKOLA P. PAŠIĆ.

164

CONVENTION between the United Kingdom and France respecting Newfoundland, and West and Central Africa. Signed at London, April 8, 1904. Ratifications exchanged at London, December 8, 1904. (see Appendix 2 for Supplementary matter.)

His Majesty the King of the United Kingdom of Great Britain and Ireland and of the British Dominions beyond the Seas, Emperor of India, and the President of the French Republic, having resolved to put an end, by a friendly Arrangement, to the difficulties which have arisen in Newfoundland, have decided to conclude a Convention to that effect, and have named as their respective Plenipotentiaries:

His Majesty the King of the United Kingdom of Great Britain and Ireland and of the British Dominions beyond the Seas, Emperor of India, the Most Honourable Henry Charles Keith Petty-Fitzmaurice, Marquess of Lansdowne, His Majesty's Principal Secretary of State for Foreign Affairs; and

The President of the French Republic, His Excellency Monsieur Paul Cambon, Ambassador of the French Republic at the Court of His Majesty the King of the United Kingdom of Great Britain and Ireland and of the British Dominions beyond the Seas, Emperor of India;

Who, after having communicated to each other their full powers, found in good and due form, have agreed as follows, subject to the approval of their respective Parliaments:—

ART. I. France renounces the privileges established to her advantage by Article XIII of the Treaty of Utrecht, and confirmed or modified by subsequent provisions.

ART. II. France retains for her citizens, on a footing of equality with British subjects, the right of fishing in the territorial waters on that portion of the coast of Newfoundland comprised between Cape St. John and Cape Ray, passing by the north; this right shall be exercised during the usual fishing season closing for all persons on the 20th October of each year.

The French may therefore fish there for every kind of fish, including bait and also shell fish. They may enter any port or harbour on the said coast and may there obtain supplies or bait and shelter on the same conditions as the inhabitants of Newfoundland, but they will remain subject to the local Regulations in force; they may also fish at the mouths of the rivers, but without going beyond a straight line drawn between the two extremities of the banks, where the river enters the sea.

They shall not make use of stake-nets or fixed engines without permission of the local authorities.

On the above-mentioned portion of the coast, British subjects and French citizens shall be subject alike to the laws and Regulations now in force, or which may hereafter be passed for the establishment of a close time in regard to any particular kind of fish, or for the improvement of the fisheries. Notice of any fresh laws or Regulations shall be given to the Government of the French Republic three months before they come into operation.

The policing of the fishing on the above-mentioned portion of the coast, and for prevention of illicit liquor traffic and smuggling of spirits, shall form the subject of Regulations drawn up in agreement by the two Governments.

ART. III. A pecuniary indemnity shall be awarded by His Britannic Majesty's Government to the French citizens engaged in fishing or the preparation of fish on the " Treaty Shore," who are obliged, either to abandon the establishments they possess there, or to give up their occupation, in consequence of the modification introduced by the present Convention into the existing state of affairs.

This indemnity cannot be claimed by the parties interested unless they have been engaged in their business prior to the closing of the fishing season of 1903.

Claims for indemnity shall be submitted to an Arbitral Tribunal, composed of an officer of each nation, and, in the event of disagreement, of an Umpire appointed in accordance with the procedure laid down by Article XXXII of The Hague Convention. The details regulating the constitution of the Tribunal and the conditions of the enquiries to be instituted for the purpose of substantiating the claims, shall form the subject of a special Agreement between the two Governments.

ART IV. His Britannic Majesty's Government, recognising that, in addition to the indemnity referred to in the preceding Article, some territorial compensation is due to France in return for the surrender of her privilege in that part of the Island of Newfoundland referred to in

Article II, agree with the Government of the French Republic to the provisions embodied in the following Articles:—

ART V. The present frontier between Senegambia and the English Colony of the Gambia shall be modified so as to give to France Yarbutenda and the lands and landing-places belonging to that locality.

In the event of the river not being open to maritime navigation up to that point, access shall be assured to the French Government at a point lower down on the River Gambia, which shall be recognised by mutual agreement as being accessible to merchant ships engaged in maritime navigation.

The conditions which shall govern transit on the River Gambia and its tributaries, as well as the method of access to the point that may be reserved to France in accordance with the preceding paragraph, shall form the subject of future agreement between the two Governments.

In any case, it is understood that these conditions shall be at least as favourable as those of the system instituted by application of the General Act of the African Conference of the 26th February, 1885, and of the Anglo-French Convention of the 14th June, 1898, to the English portion of the basin of the Niger.

ART. VI. The group known as the Iles de Los, and situated opposite Konakry, is ceded by His Britannic Majesty to France.

ART. VII. Persons born in the territories ceded to France by Articles V and VI of the present Convention may retain British nationality by means of an individual declaration to that effect, to be made before the proper authorities by themselves, or, in the case of children under age, by their parents or guardians.

The period within which the declaration of option referred to in the preceding paragraph must be made shall be one year, dating from the day on which French authority shall be established over the territory in which the persons in question have been born.

Native laws and customs now existing will, as far as possible, remain undisturbed.

In the Iles de Los, for a period of thirty years from the date of exchange of the ratifications of the present Convention, British fishermen shall enjoy the same rights as French fishermen with regard to anchorage in all weathers, to taking in provisions and water, to making repairs, to transhipment of goods, to the sale of fish, and to the landing and drying of nets, provided always that they observe the conditions laid down in the French Laws and Regulations which may be in force there.

ART. VIII. To the east of the Niger the following line shall be substituted for the boundary fixed between the French and British possessions by the Convention of the 14th June, 1898, subject to the modifications which may result from the stipulations introduced in the sixth and seventh paragraphs of the present Article.

Starting from the point on the left bank of the Niger laid down in Article III of the Convention of the 14th June, 1898, that is to say, the median line of the Dallul Mauri, the frontier shall be drawn along this median line until it meets the circumference of a circle drawn from the town of Sokoto as a centre, with a radius of 160,932 mètres (100 miles). Thence it shall follow the northern arc of this circle to a point situated 5 kilomètres south of the point of intersection of the above-mentioned arc of the circle with the route from Dosso to Matankari via Maourédé.

Thence it shall be drawn in a direct line to a point 20 kilomètres north of Konni (Birni-N'Kouni), and then in a direct line to a 15 kilomètres south of Maradi, and thence shall be continued in a direct line to the point of intersection of the parallel 13° 20′ north latitude with a meridian passing 70 miles to the east of the second intersection of the 14th degree of north latitude and the northern arc of the above-mentioned circle.

Thence the frontier shall follow in an easterly direction the parallel of 13° 20′ north latitude until it strikes the left bank of the River Komadugu Waubé (Komadougou Ouobé), the thalweg of which it will then follow to Lake Chad. But, if before meeting this river the frontier attains a distance of 5 kilomètres from the caravan route from Zinder to Yo, through Sua Kolulua (Soua Kololoua), Adeber, and Kabi, the boundary shall then be traced at a distance of 5 kilomètres to the south of this route until it strikes the left bank of the River Komadugu Waubé (Komadougou Ouobé), it being nevertheless understood that, if the boundary thus drawn should happen to pass through a village, this village, with its lands, shall be assigned to the Government to which would fall the larger portion of the village and its lands. The boundary will then, as before, follow the thalweg of the said river to Lake Chad.

Thence it will follow the degree of latitude passing through the thalweg of the mouth of the said river up to its intersection with the meridian running 35′ east of the centre of the town of Kouka, and will then follow this meridian southwards until it intersects the southern shore of Lake Chad.

It is agreed, however, that, when the Commissioners of the two Governments at present engaged in delimiting the line laid down in Article IV of the Convention of the 14th June, 1898, return home and can be consulted, the two Governments will be prepared to consider any modifications of the above frontier line which may seem desirable for the purpose of determining the line of demarcation with greater accuracy. In order to avoid the inconvenience to either party which might result from the adoption of a line deviating from recognised and well-established frontiers, it is agreed that in those portions of the projected line where the frontier is not determined by the trade routes, regard shall be had to the present political divisions of the territories so that the tribes belonging to the territories of Tessaoua-Maradi and Zinder shall, as far as possible, be left to France, and those belonging to the territories of the British zone shall, as far as possible, be left to Great Britain.

It is further agreed that, on Lake Chad, the frontier line shall, if necessary, be modified so as to assure to France a communication through open water at all seasons between her possessions on the north-west and those on the south-east of the Lake, and a portion of the surface of the open waters of the Lake at least proportionate to that assigned to her by the map forming Annex 2 of the Convention of the 14th June, 1898.

In that portion of the River Komadugu which is common to both parties, the populations on the banks shall have equal rights of fishing.

ART. IX. The present Convention shall be ratified, and the ratifications shall be exchanged, at London, within eight months, or earlier if possible.

In witness whereof his Excellency the Ambassador of the French Republic at the Court of His Majesty the King of the United Kingdom of Great Britain and Ireland and of the British Dominions beyond the Seas, Emperor of India, and His Majesty's Principal Secretary of State for Foreign Affairs duly authorised for that purpose, have signed the present Convention and have affixed thereto their seals.

Done at London, in duplicate, the 8th day of April, 1904.

(L. S.)   LANSDOWNE.
(L. S.)   PAUL CAMBON.

165

DECLARATION between the United Kingdom and France respecting Egypt and Morocco. Signed at London, April 8, 1904. (See Appendix 3 for Supplementary matter.)

ART. I. His Britannic Majesty's Government declare that they have no intention of altering the political status of Egypt.

The Government of the French Republic, for their part, declare that they will not obstruct the action of Great Britain in that country by asking that a limit of time be fixed for the British occupation or in any other manner, and that they give their assent to the draft Khedivial Decree annexed to the present Arrangement, containing the guarantees considered necessary for the protection of the interests of the Egyptian bondholders, on the condition that, after its promulgation, it cannot be modified in any way without the consent of the Powers Signatory of the Convention of London of 1885.

It is agreed that the post of Director-General of Antiquities in Egypt shall continue, as in the past, to be entrusted to a French *savant*.

The French schools in Egypt shall continue to enjoy the same liberty as in the past.

ART. II. The Government of the French Republic declare that they have no intention of altering the political status of Morocco.

His Britannic Majesty's Government, for their part, recognise that it appertains to France, more particularly as a Power whose dominions are conterminous for a great distance with those of Morocco, to preserve order in that country, and to provide assistance for the purpose of all administrative, economic, financial, and military reforms which it may require.

They declare that they will not obstruct the action taken by France for this purpose, provided that such action shall leave intact the rights which Great Britain, in virtue of Treaties, Conventions, and usage, enjoys in Morocco, including the right of coasting trade between the ports of Morocco, enjoyed by British vessels since 1901.

ART. III. His Britannic Majesty's Government, for their part, will respect the rights which France, in virtue of Treaties, Conventions, and usage, enjoys in Egypt, including the right of coasting trade between Egyptian ports accorded to French vessels.

ART. IV. The two Governments, being equally attached to the principle of commercial liberty both in Egypt and Morocco, declare that they will not, in those countries, countenance any inequality either in the imposition of customs duties or other taxes, or of railway transport charges.

The trade of both nations with Morocco and with Egypt shall enjoy the same treatment in transit through the French and British possessions in Africa. An Agreement between the two Governments shall settle the conditions of such transit and shall determine the points of entry.

This mutual engagement shall be binding for a period of thirty years. Unless this stipulation is expressly denounced at least one year in advance, the period shall be extended for five years at a time.

Nevertheless, the Government of the French Republic reserve to themselves in Morocco, and His Britannic Majesty's Government reserve to themselves in Egypt, the right to see that the concessions for roads, railways, ports, &c., are only granted on such conditions as will maintain intact the authority of the State over these great undertakings of public interest.

ART. V. His Britannic Majesty's Government declare that they will use their influence in order that the French officials now in the Egyptian service may not be placed under conditions less advantageous than those applying to the British officials in the same service.

The Government of the French Republic, for their part, would make no objection to the application of analogous conditions to British officials now in the Moorish service.

ART. VI. In order to insure the free passage of the Suez Canal, His Britannic Majesty's Government declare that they adhere to the stipulations of the Treaty of the 29th October, 1888, and that they agree to their being put in force. The free passage of the Canal being thus guaranteed, the execution of the last sentence of paragraph 1 as well as of paragraph 2 of Article VIII of that Treaty will remain in abeyance.

ART. VII. In order to secure the free passage of the Straits of Gibraltar, the two Governments agree not to permit the erection of any fortifications or strategic works on that portion of the coast of Morocco comprised between, but not including, Melilla and the heights which command the right bank of the River Sebou.

This condition does not, however, apply to the places at present in the occupation of Spain on the Moorish coast of the Mediterranean.

ART. VIII. The two Governments, inspired by their feeling of sincere friendship for Spain, take into special consideration the interests which that country derives from her geographical position and from her territorial possessions on the Moorish coast of the Mediterranean. In regard to these interests the French Government will come to an understanding with the Spanish Government.

The agreement which may be come to on the subject between France and Spain shall be communicated to His Britannic Majesty's Government.

ART. IX. The two Governments agree to afford to one another their diplomatic support, in order to obtain the execution of the clauses of the present Declaration regarding Egypt and Morocco.

In witness whereof his Excellency the Ambassador of the French Republic at the Court of His Majesty the King of the United Kingdom of Great Britain and Ireland and of the British Dominions beyond the Seas, Emperor of India, and His Majesty's Principal Secretary of State for Foreign Affairs, duly authorized for that purpose, have signed the present Declaration and have affixed thereto their seals.

Done at London, in duplicate, the 8th day of April, 1904.

(L.S.) LANSDOWNE. (L.S.) PAUL CAMBON.

Secret Article I.

In the event of either Government finding themselves constrained, by the force of circumstances, to modify their policy in respect to Egypt and Morocco, the engagements which they have undertaken towards each other by Articles IV, VI and VII of the Declaration of today's date would remain intact.

Secret Article II.

His Britannic Majesty's Government have no present intention of proposing to the Powers any changes in the system of the Capitulations, or in the judicial organisation of Egypt.

In the event of their considering it desirable to introduce in Egypt reforms tending to assimilate the Egyptian legislative system to that in force in other civilised countries, the Government of the French Republic will not refuse to entertain any such proposals, on the understanding that His Britannic Majesty's Government will agree to entertain the suggestions that the Government of the French Republic may have to make to them with a view of introducing similar reforms in Morocco.

Secret Article III.

The two Governments agree that a certain extent of Moorish territory adjacent to Melilla, Ceuta and other *Présides* should, whenever the Sultan ceases to exercise authority over it, come within the sphere of influence of Spain, and that the administration of the coast from Melilla as far as, but not including, the heights on the right bank of the Sebou shall be intrusted to Spain.

Nevertheless, Spain would previously have to give her formal assent to the provisions of Articles IV and VII of the Declaration of today's date, and undertake to carry them out.

She would also have to undertake not to alienate the whole or a part of the territories placed under her authority or in her sphere of influence.

Secret Article IV.

If Spain, when invited to assent to the provisions of the preceding article, should think proper to decline, the Arrangement between France and Great Britain, as embodied in the Declaration of today's date, would be none the less applicable.

Secret Article V.

Should the consent of the other Powers to the draft Decree mentioned in Article I of the Declaration of today's date not be obtained, the

Government of the French Republic will not oppose the repayment at par of the Guaranteed, Privileged and Unified Debts after the 15th July, 1910.

Done at London, in duplicate, the 8th day of April, 1904.

(L.S.) LANSDOWNE. (L.S.) PAUL CAMBON.

166

DECLARATION between the United Kingdom and France concerning Siam, Madagascar, and the New Hebrides. Signed at London, April 8, 1904.

I.—SIAM.

THE Government of His Britannic Majesty and the Government of the French Republic confirm Articles 1 and 2 of the Declaration signed in London on the 15th January, 1896, by the Marquess of Salisbury, then Her Britannic Majesty's Principal Secretary of State for Foreign Affairs, and Baron de Courcel, then Ambassador of the French Republic at the Court of Her Britannic Majesty.

In order, however, to complete these arrangements, they declare by mutual agreement that the influence of Great Britain shall be recognized by France in the territories situated to the west of the basin of the River Menam, and that the influence of France shall be recognized by Great Britain in the territories situated to the east of the same region, all the Siamese possessions on the east and south-east of the zone above described and the adjacent islands coming thus henceforth under French influence, and, on the other hand, all Siamese possessions on the west of this zone and of the Gulf of Siam, including the Malay Peninsula and the adjacent islands, coming under English influence.

The two Contracting Parties, disclaiming all idea of annexing any Siamese territory, and determined to abstain from any act which might contravene the provisions of existing Treaties, agree that, with this reservation, and so far as either of them is concerned, the two Governments shall each have respectively liberty of action in their spheres of influence as above defined.

II.—MADAGASCAR.

In view of the agreement now in negotiation on the questions of Jurisdiction and the postal service in Zanzibar, and on the adjacent coast, His Britannic Majesty's Government withdraw the protest which they had raised against the introduction of the Customs tariff established at

Madagascar after the annexation of that island to France. The Government of the French Republic take note of this Declaration.

III.—NEW HEBRIDES.

The two Governments agree to draw up in concert an Arrangement which, without involving any modification of the political *status quo*, shall put an end to the difficulties arising from the absence of jurisdiction over the natives of the New Hebrides.

They agree to appoint a Commission to settle the disputes of their respective nationals in the said islands with regard to landed property. The competency of this Commission and its rules of procedure shall form the subject of a preliminary Agreement between the two Governments.

In witness whereof His Britannic Majesty's Principal Secretary of State for Foreign Affairs and His Excellency the Ambassador of the French Republic at the Court of His Majesty the King of the United Kingdom of Great Britain and Ireland and of the British Dominions beyond the Seas, Emperor of India, duly authorised for that purpose, have signed the present Declaration and have affixed thereto their seals.

Done at London in duplicate, the 8th day of April, 1904.

(L.S.)   LANSDOWNE.
(L.S.)   PAUL CAMBON.

167

JOINT DECLARATION of Austria-Hungary and Russia in regard to the maintenance of neutrality by either if the other is at war. St. Petersburg, October 2/15, 1904.[1]

The undersigned, duly authorized by their August Sovereigns, have met together today at the Imperial Ministry of Foreign Affairs to sign the following Declaration:

Austria-Hungary and Russia, united by identical views as to the conservative policy to be followed in the Balkan countries, and much satisfied with the result obtained so far by their close collaboration, are firmly decided to persevere in this course. Happy to record once more this understanding, the Cabinets of Vienna and of St. Petersburg attach great importance to offering each other in due form a mark of friendship and reciprocal confidence.

It is with this purpose that the two Powers have come to an agreement

---

[1] The ratification is lacking, since the Treaty was rendered valid by this declaration with the authority of both Chiefs of State.

to observe a loyal and absolute neutrality in case one of the two Parties signatory to this Declaration should find itself, alone and without provocation on its part, in a state of war with a third Power which sought to endanger its security or the status quo; the maintenance of which constitutes the basis of their understanding, as pacific as it is conservative.

The engagement between Austria-Hungary and Russia stipulated in the above naturally does not apply to the Balkan countries, whose destinies are obviously closely attached to the agreement established between the two neighbouring Empires. The said engagement is understood to remain valid so long as these two great Powers shall pursue their policy of an understanding in the affairs of Turkey; it shall be kept secret, and cannot be communicated to any other Government, except after a previous understanding between the Cabinets of Vienna and of St. Petersburg.

Done in duplicate at St. Petersburg, October 2/15, 1904.

(L.S.) L. AEHRENTHAL.   (L.S.) COUNT LAMSDORFF.

168

FRANCO-SPANISH DECLARATION AND CONVENTION Respecting Morocco. Signed at Paris, 3rd October, 1904.

DECLARATION.

The Government of the French Republic and the Government of His Majesty the King of Spain, having reached accord over fixing the extent of the rights and the guarantee of interests which arise for France from her Algerian possessions; and for Spain from her possessions on the coast of Morocco, and, the Government of His Majesty the King of Spain having in consequence its adherence to the Franco-British Declaration Relating to Morocco and Egypt, communication of which had been made to it by the French Government, DECLARE that they remain firmly attached to the integrity of the Moroccan Empire under the sovereignty of the Sultan.

In testimony whereof, the undersigned, His Excellence the Minister of Foreign Affairs and His Excellency the Ambassador Extraordinary and Plenipotentiary of His Majesty the King of Spain to the President of the French Republic, duly authorised to this effect, have drawn up the present Declaration to which they have apposed their seals.

Done in duplicate at Paris, 3rd October, 1904.

Signed

DELCASSÉ

F. de LÉON y CASTILLO.

CONVENTION.

The President of the French Republic and His Majesty the King of Spain, wishing to fix the extent of the rights and the guarantee of interests which arise for France from her Algerian possessions and for Spain from her possessions on the coast of Morocco, have decided to conclude a Convention and have nominated for this purpose as their Plenipotentiaries the following: The President of the French Republic, His Excellence M. Th. Delcassé, Deputy, Minister of Foreign Affairs of the French Republic, etc; His Majesty the King of Spain, His Excellence M. de Léon y Castillo, Marquis del Muni, his Ambassador Extraordinary and Plenipotentiary to the President of the French Republic etc.;

Who, after having had their plenary powers communicated to them, drawn up in due and proper form, have agreed upon the following articles:—

ART. I. Spain adheres under the terms of the present Convention to the Franco-British Declaration of 8th April, 1904 Relating to Morocco and Egypt.

ART. II. The region situated to the West and North of the line hereinafter determined constitutes the sphere of influence which arises for Spain from her possessions on the coast of Morocco.

In this zone the same right of action is reserved for Spain as is accorded to France by the second paragraph of Article II of the Declaration of 8th April, 1904 Relating to Morocco and Egypt.

However, taking into account of the existing difficulties and of the mutual interest there is in settling them, Spain declares that she will not exercise this right of action except after previous accord with France during the first period of application of the present Convention—a period which shall not exceed fifteen years from the signature of the Convention.

On its part, during the same period, France, desirous that the rights and interests accorded to Spain by the present should always be respected, will make known beforehand to the King's Government its action at the Court of the Sultan of Morocco in matters concerning the Spanish sphere of influence.

After this first period has expired and so long as the status quo endures, French action in relation to the Moroccan Government over matters concerning the sphere of influence reserved to Spain will not be taken except after previous accord with the Spanish Government.

During the first period the Government of the French Republic will do its best to secure that in two of the Customs ports of the region determined below the delegate of the Representative General of the

Bondholders of the Moroccan loan of the 12th July, 1904 should be of Spanish nationality.

Starting from the point where the Moulouia enters the Mediterranean Sea, the abovementioned dividing line will run upstream along the Thalweg of this river as far as the line of the ridge of heights nearest to the left bank of the Wadi Defla. From this point, without under any circumstances being allowed to intersect the course of the Moulouia, the demarcation line shall proceed as directly as possible to the watershed separating the basins of the Moulouia and the Wadi Inaouen from that of the Wadi Kert. Then it will run on westwards along the watershed separating the basins of the Wadi Inaouen and the Wadi Sebou from those of the Wadi Kert and the Wadi Ouergha to reach the Jebel Moulai Bou Chta by the most northern ridge. Then it will head north remaining at a distance of at least twenty-five kilometres to the east of the road from Fez to Kear-el-Kebir by way of Ouezzan as far as the meeting place with the Wadi Loukkos or Wadi el Kous, the Thalweg of which it will descend for five kilometres downstream from the meeting of this river with the abovementioned road from Fear-el-Kebir by way of Ouezzan. From this point it will reach shore of the Atlantic Ocean as directly as possible above the lagoon of Ez Zerga.

This delimitation is in conformity with the delimitation marked out on the map attached to the present Convention designated No. 1.

ART. III. In the case where the political state of Morocco and the Sherifean Government would be able to remain in existence no longer, or if, through the weakness of this government and through its persistent inability to guarantee safety and public order, or for any other reason to establish mutual agreement, the maintenance of the status quo should become impossible, Spain would be able to act freely in the region delimited in the previous Article, which from now on constitutes her sphere of influence.

ART. IV. The Moroccan Government having, by Article VII of the treaty of 26th April, 1860, conceded to Spain a colony at Santa Cruz de mar Pequeña (Ifni), it is agreed that the territory of this colony shall not go beyond the course of the Wadi Tazeroualt from its source up to its confluence with the Wadi Mesa and the course of the Wadi Mesa from this confluence as far as the sea, in accordance with the map attached to the present Convention.

ART. V. To complete the delimitation laid down by Article I of the Convention of 27th June, 1900, it is agreed that the demarcation between the French and Spanish spheres of influence will begin from the intersection of the meridian 14° 20' West of Paris and the line of 26° of latitude North, which it will follow eastwards as far as the meeting point with meridian 11° West of Paris. It will go up this meridian as far as the place where it reaches the Wadi Draa, then along the Thalweg of the Wadi Draa until it meets meridian 10° West of Paris, finally keeping to meridian 10° West of Paris as far as the watershed between the basins of the Wadi Draa and the Wadi Sous, and will follow the watershed between the basins of the Wadi Draa and the Wadi Sous in a westerly direction, afterwards going between coastal basins of the Wadi Messa and the Wadi Noun as far as the point nearest to the source of the Wadi Tazeroualt.

This delimitation is in conformity with the delimitation marked out on Map No 2 already cited and attached to the present Convention.

ART. VI. Articles IV and V will be applicable at the same time as Article II of the present Convention.

However, the Government of the French Republic allows that Spain can establish herself at any time within the area defined by Article IV, on the condition of being in agreement beforehand with the Sultan.

In the same way, the Government of the French Republic accords from now on to the Spanish Government full liberty of action in the region contained between 26° and 27° 40′ North and meridian 11° West of Paris which are outside Moroccan territory.

ART. VII. Spain undertakes not to alienate or cede in any way whatsoever, even by way of temporary title, all or part of the territories designated in Articles II, IV and V of the present Convention.

Art. VIII. If, in the application of Articles II, IV, and V of the present Convention one of the two contracting parties has a military operation forced upon it, it shall notify the other of it at once. In no case will it call upon a foreign power for assistance.

ART. IX. The town of Tangiers shall retain the special character given it by the presence of the diplomatic corps and its municipal and sanitary institutions.

ART. X. As long as the existing political condition shall endure, public works enterprizes, railways, roads, canals leaving from a point in Morocco and leading into the region specified in Article II and vice versa, will be carried out by the companies which the French and Spanish shall be able to set up.

In the same way, it shall be permissible for the French and the Spanish in Morocco to join together for the exploitation of mines, quarries and economic enterprizes generally.

ART. XI. The Spanish schools and institutions acting existing in Morocco shall be respected. The circulation of Spanish money will be neither prevented nor hindered. Spaniards will continue to enjoy in Morocco the rights secured them by the Treaties, Conventions and usages in force, including the right of navigation and fishing in Moroccan waters and ports.

ART. XII. The French shall enjoy, in the regions designated in Articles II, IV, and V of the present Convention, the same rights recognised for the Spaniards in the remainder of Morocco by the preceding Article.

ART. XIII. In the case where the Moroccan Government should forbid the sale of arms and ammunition in its territory, the two contracting Powers undertake to introduce in their African possessions the measures necessary to prevent them being brought into Morocco as contraband.

ART. XIV. It is agreed that the zone defined in paragraph I of Article VII of the Franco-English Convention of 8th April, 1904 relating to Morocco and Egypt begins on the coast thirty kilometres south-east of Melilla.

ART. XV. In the case where the denunciation provided for under paragraph III of Article IV of the Franco-English relating to Morocco and Egypt were to have taken place, the French and Spanish Governments will act in concert for the establishment of an economic administration especially in keeping with their reciprocal interests.

ART. XVI. The present Convention will be published when the two governments shall judge, by mutual agreement, that it can be done without disadvantages.

In any case, it will be able to be published by one of the two governments at the expiration of its first period of application—a period defined by paragraph III of Article II.

In testimony whereof the respective Plenipotentaries have signed the present Convention and have apposed to it their seals.

Done in duplicate at Paris, 3rd October, 1904.

(L.S.)   (Signé) DELCASSÉ.

(L.S.)   (Signé) F. de LÉON y CASTILLO.

169

AGREEMENT between **GREAT BRITAIN AND JAPAN** respecting the integrity of China, the general peace of eastern Asia and India, and the territorial rights and special interests of the parties in those regions, August 12, 1905.

Preamble.

THE Governments of Great Britain and Japan, being desirous of replacing the Agreement concluded between them on the 30th of January, 1902, by fresh stipulations, have agreed upon the following Articles, which have for their object:

(a) The consolidation and maintenance of the general peace in the regions of Eastern Asia and of India.

(b) The preservation of the common interests of all Powers in China by insuring the independence and integrity of the Chinese Empire and the principle of equal opportunities for the commerce and industry of all nations in China.

(c) The maintenance of the territorial rights of the High contracting parties in the regions of Eastern Asia and of India, and the defence of their special interests in the said regions.

ART. I. It is agreed that whenever, in the opinion of either Great Britain or Japan, any of the rights and interests referred to in the preamble of this Agreement are in jeopardy, the two Governments will communicate with one another fully and frankly, and will consider in common the measures which should be taken to safeguard those menaced rights or interests.

ART. II. If by reason of unprovoked attack or aggressive action, whenever arising, on the part of any other Power or Powers, either contracting party should be involved in war in defence of its territorial rights or special interests mentioned in the preamble of this Agreement, the other contracting party will at once come to the assistance of its ally, and will conduct the war in common, and make peace in mutual agreement with it.

ART. III. Japan possessing paramount political, military, and economic interests in Korea, Great Britain recognises the right of Japan to such measures of guidance, control, and protection in Korea as she may deem proper and necessary to safeguard and advance those interests, provided always such measures are not contrary to the principle of equal opportunities for the commerce and industry of all nations.

ART. IV. Great Britain having a special interest in all that concerns the security of the Indian frontier, Japan recognises her rights to take such measures in the proximity of that frontier as she may find necessary for safeguarding her Indian possessions.

ART. V. The high contracting parties agree that neither of them will, without consulting the other, enter into separate arrangements with another Power to the prejudice of the objects described in the preamble of this Agreement.

ART. VI. As regards the present war between Japan and Russia, Great Britain will continue to maintain strict neutrality unless some other Power or Powers should join in hostilities against Japan, in which case Great Britain will come to the assistance of Japan, and will conduct the war in common, and make peace in mutual agreement with Japan.

ART. VII. The conditions under which armed assistance shall be afforded by either Power to the other in the circumstances mentioned in the present Agreement, and the means by which such assistance is to be made available, will be arranged by naval and military authorities of the contracting parties, who will from time to time consult one another fully and freely upon all questions of mutual interest.

ART. VIII. The present Agreement shall, subject to the provisions of Article VI, come into effect immediately after the date of its signature, and remain in force for ten years from that date.

In case neither of the high contracting parties should have notified twelve months before the expiration of the said ten years the intention of terminating it, it shall remain binding until the expiration of one year from the day on which either of the high contracting parties shall have denounced it. But if, when the date fixed for its expiration arrives, either ally is actually engaged in war, the alliance shall, *ipso facto*, continue until peace is concluded.

In faith whereof, the undersigned, duly authorised by their respective Governments, have signed this Agreement, and have affixed thereto their seals.

Done in duplicate at London, the 12th day of August, 1905.

> (L.S.) LANSDOWNE, His Britannic Majesty's Principal Secretary of State for Foreign Affairs.

> (L.S.) TADASU HAYASHI, Envoy Extraordinary and Minister Plenipotentiary of His Majesty the Emperor of Japan at the Court of St. James.

170

The GENERAL ACT of the Algeciras Conference relating to the Affairs of Morocco (Great Britain, Austria-Hungary, Belgium, France, Germany, Italy, Morocco, Netherlands, Portugal, Russia, Spain, Sweden, United States). Signed at Algeciras, 7th April, 1906. Ratifications deposited at Madrid, 31st December, 1906.

In the name of Almighty God!

His Majesty the Emperor of Germany, King of Prussia, in the name of the German Empire; His Majesty the Emperor of Austria, King of Bohemia, etc., and Apostolic King of Hungary; His Majesty the King of the Belgians; His Majesty the King of Spain; the President of the United States of America; the President of the French Republic; His Majesty the King of the United Kingdom of Great Britain and Ireland

TEL. 34657
(COMMON ROOM)

BRISTOL GRAMMAR SCHOOL
UNIVERSITY ROAD
BRISTOL
BS8 1SR

and the British Territories Beyond the Seas, Emperor of India; His Majesty the King of Italy; His Majesty the Sultan of Morocco; Her Majesty the Queen of the Netherlands; His Majesty the King of Portugal and the Algarves etc.; His Majesty the Emperor of All the Russias; His Majesty the King of Sweden, being convinced of the advantage flowing from the reign of order, peace and prosperity in Morocco, and having recognised that this precious end cannot be attained except through the introduction of reforms based upon the triple principle of the sovereignty and independence of His Majesty the Sultan, of the integrity of his domains, and of economic freedom without any inequality, have resolved, upon the invitation which had been addressed to them by His Sherifean Majesty, to convene a Conference at Algeciras to arrive at an agreement upon the said reforms, as also to examine the means for obtaining the resources necessary for their implementation, and have designated as their Delegates Plenipotentiary, the following:

His Majesty the Emperor of Germany, King of Prussia, in the name of the German Empire: Joseph von Radowitz, his Ambassador Extraordinary and Plenipotentiary at the court of His Catholic Majesty; and Christian, Count von Tattenbach, his Envoy-Extraordinary and Minister Plenipotentiary to His Most Faithful Majesty;

His Majesty the Emperor of Austria, King of Bohemia etc., and Apostolic King of Hungary: Leopold Count Bolesta-Koziebrodzki, his Envoy Extraordinary and Minister Plenipotentiary to Morocco;

His Majesty the King of the Belgians: Marice, Baron Joostens, his Envoy Extraordinary and Minister Plenipotentiary at the court of His Catholic Majesty; and Conrad, Count de Buisseret-Steenbecque de Blarenghein, his Envoy Extraordinary and Minister Plenipotentiary to Morocco;

His Majesty the King of Spain: Don Juan Manuel Sanchez y Gutiérrez de Castro, Duke de Almodovar del Rio, his Minister of State; and Don Juan Pérez-Caballero y Ferrer, his Envoy Extraordinary and Minister Plenipotentiary at the court of His Majesty the King of the Belgians;

The President of the United States: Henry White, Ambassador Extraordinary and Plenipotentiary of the United States at the court of the King of Italy; and Samuel R. Gummeré, Envoy Extraordinary and Minister Plenipotentiary of the United States to Morocco;

The President of the French Republic: Paul Révoil, Ambassador Extraordinary and Plenipotentiary of the French Republic to the Swiss Confederation; and Eugène Regnault, Minister Plenipotentiary;

His Majesty the King of the United Kingdom of Great Britain and Ireland, and the Territories Beyond the Seas, Emperor of India: Sir

Arthur Nicolson, his Ambassador Extraordinary at the court of His Majesty the Emperor of All the Russias;

His Majesty the King of Italy: Emile, Marquis Visconti Venosta, Chevalier of the Order of the Most Holy Annunciation; and Giulio Malmusi, his Envoy Extraordinary and Minister Plenipotentiary to Morocco;

His Majesty the Sultan of Morocco: El-Hadj Mohamed Ben-el-Arbi Ettorres, his Delegate at Tangiers and his Ambassador Extraordinary; El-Hadj Mohamed-ben-Abdesselam-el-Mokri, his Minister of Expenditure; El-hadj Mohamed-es-Seffar; and Sid Abderrhaman Bennis;

Her Majesty the Queen of the Netherlands: Jonkheer Hannibal Testa, her Envoy Extraordinary and Minister Plenipotentiary at the court of His Catholic Majesty;

His Majesty the King of Portugal and the Algarves: Antoine, Count de Tovar, his Envoy Extraordinary and Minister Plenipotentiary at the court of His Catholic Majesty; and Francois-Robert, Count de Martens Ferrao, Peer of the Kingdom, his Envoy Extraordinary and Minister Plenipotentiary to Morocco;

His Majesty the Emperor of All the Russia: Arthur, Count Cassini, his Ambassador Extraordinary and Plenipotentiary to the court of His Catholic Majesty; and Basil Bacheracht, his Minister to Morocco;

His Majesty the King of Sweden; Robert Sager, his Envoy Extraordinary and Plenipotentiary to the court of His Catholic Majesty and to that of his Most Faithful Majesty;

The which, furnished with full powers, which have been found to be in good and proper order, have, in conformity with the programme on which His Sherifean Majesty and the Powers have agreed upon, successively discussed and adopted:—

1. A Declaration relating to the organisation of the police.
2. A Settlement concerning the surveillance and repression of armaments contraband.
3. An Instrument of Concession for a Moroccan State Bank.
4. A declaration concerning a better yield of taxes and the creation of new revenues.
5. A Settlement concerning the Customs of the Empire and the repression of fraud and of contraband.
6. A Declaration relating to the Public Services and to Public Works;

and, having decided that these different documents could usefully be coordinated into a single instrument, they have been put together into a General Act consisting of the following Articles:—

CHAPTER I

Declaration relating to the Organisation of the Police

ARTICLE 1. The Conference, called upon by His Majesty the Sultan of Morocco to pronounce upon the measures necessary for organising the police, declares that the measures to take are as follows:—

ARTICLE 2. The police shall be placed under the sovereign authority of His Majesty the Sultan. It will be recruited by the Makhzen from among the Moroccan Moslems, commanded by the Moroccan Caids and distributed in the eight ports open to commerce.

ARTICLE 3. For assisting the Sultan in the organisation of this police, Spanish officers and non-commissioned officer instructors and French officers and non-commissioned officer instructors will be put at his disposal by their respective governments, which will submit their designation to the approval of His Sherifean Majesty. A contract entered into between the Makhzen and the instructors, in conformity with the Settlement provided for in Article 4, shall determine the conditions of their engagement and shall fix their pay, which shall not be less than double the corresponding pay of each rank of officer or non-commissioned officer. There shall be awarded to them in addition a residence grant variable according to the localities. Suitable accommodation shall be put at their disposal by the Makhzen, which will also provide the necessary mounts and fodder.

The Governments under whom the instructors serve reserve to themselves the right to recall them and replace them by others, agreed upon and taken on in accordance with the same conditions.

ARTICLE 4. These officers and non-commissioned officers shall give assistance in the organisation of the Sherifean police for a period of five years from the ratification of the Act of the Conference. They shall enforce instruction and discipline in conformity with the Settlement which shall be laid down on the point; they shall likewise see to it that the men enrolled possess the aptitude for military service. They must generally oversee the administration of the troops and inspect the payment of wages which will be carried out by the Amin, assisted by accountant instructor officer. They shall afford the Moroccan authorities entrusted with the command of these corps their technical aid for carrying out this responsibility.

The prescribed arrangements suitable for ensuring the recruitment, discipline, instruction and administration of the police corps will be laid down by a mutual agreement between the Moroccan Minister of War, or his delegate, the Inspector as provided for in Article 7, the French Instructor and the Spanish Instructor—both of the highest rank.

The Settlement must be submitted to the Corps Diplomatique at

Tangiers, which will formulate its verdict within a month. The Settlement shall take effect if the delay exceeds this time limit.

ARTICLE 5. The effective total of police troops shall not exceed 2,500 men nor be less than 2,000. It shall be distributed according to the importance of the ports in groups varying from 150 to 600 men. The number of Spanish and French shall be between 16 and 20; that of Spanish and French non-commissioned officers between 30 and 40.

ARTICLE 6. The funds necessary for the maintenance and payment of the troops and officers and non-commissioned officers shall be advanced to the Sherifean Treasury by the State Bank within the limits of the annual budget earmarked for the police, which should not exceed 2,500,000 pesetas for an effective force of 2,500 men.

ARTICLE 7. The functioning of the police will be, during the same period of five years, the object of a general inspection, which will be entrusted by His Sherifean Majesty to a high officer of the Swiss Army, whose selection will be submitted for his approval by the Swiss Federal Government.

This officer will take the title of Inspector-General and will have his residence at Tangiers.

At least once a year he will inspect the different corps of police and, following these inspections, he will draw up a report which he will send to the Makhzen.

Besides the regular reports he shall be able, if he deems it necessary, to draw up special reports on all questions concerning the functioning of the police.

Without intervening directly in the command or instruction, the Inspector-General shall ascertain the results obtained by the Sherifian police from the point of view of the maintenance of order and of security in the localities where that police shall be installed.

ARTICLE 8. The reports and communications made to the Makhzen by the Inspector-General on the subject of his mission shall at the same time be remitted in the form of copies to the doyen of the Corps Diplomatique at Tangiers, so that the Corps Diplomatique be in a position to state that the Sherifean police is functioning in accordance with the decisions taken by the Conference, and to watch whether it guarantees in a manner efficacious and in conformity with the treaties, the security of persons and property of foreign nationals as well as that of commercial transactions.

ARTICLE 9. In the case of complaints of which the Corps Diplomatique has been appraised by the interested Legation the Corps Diplomatique shall be able, while informing the representative of the Sultan, to require the Inspector-General to make an enquiry and to draw up a report on these complaints, for all useful purposes.

ARTICLE 10. The Inspector-General shall receive an annual salary of 25,000 francs. He will besides be allowed an indemnity of 6,000 francs for travelling expenses. The Makhzen will put at his disposition a suitable house and will provide the upkeep of his horses.

ARTICLE 11. The material conditions of his appointment and of his installation, laid down in Article 10, will form the subject matter of a contract made between him and the Makhzen. This contract will be communicated in the form of copies to the Corps Diplomatique.

ARTICLE 12. The cadre of the instructors of the Sherifean police (Officers and non-commissioned officers) shall be Spanish at Tetuan, mixed at Tangiers, Spanish at Larache, French at Rabat, mixed at Casablanca, and French in the three other ports.

CHAPTER II

Settlement concerning the surveillance and repression of armaments contraband.

ARTICLE 13. Except in the cases specified in Articles 14 and 15, the importation and trade in armaments, spare parts for armaments, charged and uncharged munitions of all kinds, gunpowders, saltpetre, gun-cotton, nitro-glycerine, and all compositions intended exclusively to the manufacture of munitions are prohibited throughout the Sherifean Empire.

ARTICLE 14. Explosives necessary to industry and to public works can nevertheless be brought in. A regulation, drawn up in accordance with the forms indicated in Article 18, shall determine conditions under which their importation shall be effected.

ARTICLE 15. The armaments, spare parts for armaments and munitions intended for the troops of His Sherifean Majesty shall be admitted after the satisfaction of the following conditions:—

A declaration, signed by the Moroccan Minister of War, listing the number and type of supplies ordered from foreign industry must be presented at the Legation of the country of origin, which will appose its visa to it. The clearing through the customs of the cases and packages containing the arms and munitions delivered in accordance with the order of the Moroccan Government shall be effected upon the production of:—

1. The declaration specified above.

2. The Bill of Lading indicating the number, the weight of the parcels, the number and type of arms and munitions which they contain. This document must be countersigned by the Legation of the country of origin, which will indicate on the reverse side the successive quantities already cleared through customs. The visa will not be granted from the moment when the order has been fully met.

ARTICLE 16. The importation of sporting and pleasure weapons, spare parts, cartridges, charge and uncharged, is likewise forbidden. It can, nevertheless, be authorised:—

1. For the strictly personal needs of the importer.

2. For the supplying of authorised arms magazines in conformity with Article 18.

ARTICLE 17. Sporting arms and munitions or those for pleasure will be admitted for the strictly personal use of the importer on the production of a permit granted by the Representative of the Makhzen at Tangier. If the importer is a foreigner the permit will not be issued except at the request of the Legation to which he is answerable. In regard to sporting munitions, each permit will cover a maximum of 1,000 cartridges, or the supplies necessary for the manufacture of 1,000. The permit will not be given except to persons who have not been subject to any criminal conviction.

ARTICLE 18. Trade in sporting and luxury arms of the non-rifled variety of foreign manufacture, as well as that in the munitions which go with them, will be regulated, in so far as circumstances allow, by the decision of the Sherifean Government, taken in conformity with the opinion of the majority of the Diplomatic Corps at Tangier. In the same way the decisions governing the suspension or the restraint of the exercise of this trade will rest with the same body.

Only persons who have obtained special and temporary licences from the Government of Morocco will be allowed to open and operate retail shops for sporting arms and munitions. This licence will not be accorded except upon the written request of the interested party, supported by a favourable reference from the Legation to which he is answerable.

The regulations drawn up in the form indicated in the first paragraph of this Article will determine the number of retail shops which can be opened in Tangier and, eventually, in the ports which ultimately shall be designated. They will lay down the formalities imposed on the importation of explosives for the use of industry and public works, arms and munitions intended for the supply of the retail shops and also the maximum quantities which can be stored in the depots. In case of breaches of the regulations, the licence can be rescinded temporarily or definitively, without prejudice to other penalties incurred by the delinquents.

ARTICLE 19. All introduction, or attempted introduction of prohibited goods will give rise to their confiscation and, in addition, to the penalties and fines laid down below, which will be decided upon by the competent authority.

ARTICLE 20. The introduction, or attempted introduction, through a port open to commerce or through a customs post will be punished:—

1. By a fine of between 500 and 2,000 pesetas and by a supplementary fine equal to three times the value of the imported goods.

2. By imprisonment ranging from five days to one year, or, by one only of the two penalties.

ARTICLE 21. The introduction or, attempted introduction outside a port open to commerce or of a customs post will be punished:—

1. By a fine of between 1,000 and 5,000 pesetas and by a supplementary fine equal to three times the value of the imported goods.

2. By imprisonment ranging from three months to two years, or by one only of the two penalties.

ARTICLE 22. The fraudulent sale, receiving and peddling of goods prohibited by the present regulations will be punished by the penalties laid down in Article 20.

ARTICLE 23. The accomplices to the offences set out in Articles 20, 21 and 22 will be liable to the same punishments as the principal perpetrators. The factors comprising complicity will be determined according to the laws of the relevant tribunal.

ARTICLE 24. When there is evidence arousing serious suspicion that a ship moored in a port open to trade is carrying arms, munitions or other prohibited goods with a view to their importation into Morocco, the Sherifean customs officials must pass on this evidence to the competent consular authority, so that it can proceed, with the assistance of a representative of the Sherifean customs, to such enquiries, examinations or visits as it deems necessary.

ARTICLE 25. In the case of importation, or of attempted importation, of prohibited goods by sea outside a port open to trade, the Sherifean customs authority can conduct the ship to the nearest port to be delivered to the Consular authority, which can seize it and maintain the seizure until payment of the decreed fines. Nevertheless, the seizure of the ship must be lifted at any stage of the hearing, in so far as doing so does not contravene the orders of the court, upon the deposit of a sum amounting to the ceiling of the fine in the hands of the Consular authority, or under a fully covered guarantee to pay it accepted by the Customs authority.

ARTICLE 26. The Makhzen shall keep the confiscated goods, either for its own use if they can be employed for such a purpose, provided the subjects of the Empire cannot obtain them, or for sale abroad. Forms of land transport can be confiscated and sold for the benefit of the Sherifean Treasury.

ARTICLE 27. The sale of arms abandoned by the Moroccan Government shall be prohibited throughout the Sherifean Empire.

ARTICLE 28. The rewards to be deducted from the total sum of fines inflicted shall be assigned to the informers who have led to the discovery of the prohibited goods and to the agents who carry out their seizure. These rewards will be assigned after deduction, should there be occasion, of the expenses of the trial, thus—one third for the Customs authority to distribute among the informers; one third to the agents who seized the goods; and one third to the Moroccan Treasury.

If the seizure has been carried out without the aid of an informer, half of the fines will be assigned to the seizing agents and half to the Sherifean Treasury.

ARTICLE 29. The Moroccan Customs authorities must make known directly to the Diplomatic or Consular Agents the infractions of the present regulations committed by their nationals, so that they can be brought before the competent jurisdiction. The same infractions, when committed by Moroccan subjects, will be referred by the Customs authority directly to the Sherifean authority.

A representative of the Customs authority will be entrusted with following the procedure of cases pending before the various jurisdictions.

ARTICLE 30. In the frontier region of Algeria, the application of the regulations on arms contraband will remain the exclusive concern of France and Morocco. Similarly, the application of the regulations on arms contraband in the Riff and generally in the frontier regions of Spanish possessions will remain the exclusive concern of Spain and Morocco.

CHAPTER III.

Acting Granting a State Bank.

ARTICLE 31. A bank will be set up in Morocco under the name of " State Bank of Morocco " to exercise the rights specified below, the concession of which has been accorded it by His Majesty, the Sultan of Morocco for a period of forty years beginning from the ratification of this present Act.

ARTICLE 32. The Bank, which will be able to carry out all the operations generally regarded as within the competence of a bank, will have the exclusive privilege of issuing notes to the bearer, reimbursable on presentation, which will be legal tender in all public money houses of the Moroccan Empire.

The Bank will maintain, for a term of two years beginning from the date of its commencing its functions, a cash reserve amounting to not less than half the value of its notes in circulation and one of not less than a third of it after this period of two years is completed. At least one third of this reserve will consist of bullion or gold coins.

ARTICLE 33. The Bank will fulfil the functions of the Treasury-Paymaster of the Empire to the exclusion of every other bank or credit establishment. To this end the Moroccan Government will take the measures necessary to have the proceeds of the customs revenues lodged in the coffers of the Bank, except for that portion affected by the interest on the loan of 1904 and other revenues it shall designate.

As for the proceeds of the special tax created with a view to carrying out certain public works, the Moroccan Government must have it deposited in the Bank; so too with the revenues which it could ultimately earmark for the guarantee of its loans, the Bank being especially charged to assure the interest upon them, with the exception, nevertheless, of the loans of 1904, which are covered by a special arrangement.

ARTICLE 34. The Bank will be the special financial agent of the Government, both inside and outside the Empire, without prejudice to the right of the Government to turn to other banking houses or credit establishments for its public loans. Nevertheless, in relation to the said loans, the Bank will enjoy a right of preference, given equal conditions, over all banking houses or credit establishments.

But, for Government Bonds and other Treasury Stock of a short term variety which the Moroccan Government should wish to negotiate, without recourse to a public issue, the Bank will be entrusted, to the exclusion of all other establishments, with carrying out the negotiation, whether in Morocco or abroad, for the account of the Moroccan Government.

ARTICLE 35. The Bank will grant advances to the Government of Morocco on current account a sum not exceeding one million francs on account of the Treasury receipts.

The Bank will open, besides, for a period of ten years from the outset of its establishment, a credit for the Government which shall not exceed two-thirds of its initial capital.

This credit will be spread out over several years and used in the first place to cover the cost of creating and maintaining the police corps organised in conformity with the decisions taken by the Conference, and secondarily for the cost of works of general interest which could not be charged to the special funds provided for in the following Article. The rate of these two advances will be at a maximum of seven per cent, bank commission included, and the Bank will be able to demand that the Government remit to it as a guarantee of their whole amount an equivalent sum in Treasury Bonds.

If, before the expiry of these ten years, the Moroccan Government wishes to contract a loan, the Bank will have the power to obtain an immediate reimbursement of the advances made in accordance with the second paragraph of the present Article.

ARTICLE 36. The receipts from the special tax (Articles 33 and 66) shall form a special fund of which the Bank will keep a separate account. This fund will be used in conformity with the regulations laid down by the Conference.

In case of a deficit and on account of prospective receipts the Bank can open credit for this fund, the extent of which shall not exceed the total sum received during the previous year.

The conditions governing interest and commission rates shall be the same as those fixed in the previous Article for the advance to the Treasury on current account.

ARTICLE 37. The Bank shall take the measures which it deems necessary for setting the monetary situation in Morocco to rights. Spanish currency will continue to be admitted into circulation as full legal tender. Consequently, the Bank will have exclusive charge of the purchase of precious metals, of the minting and of the recoining of money, as well as of all other monetary operations which it shall take for the account and for the benefit of the Moroccan Government.

ARTICLE 38. The Bank, the head office of which will be at Tangiers, shall establish branches and agencies in the principal towns of Morocco and in all other places where it judges it useful so to do.

ARTICLE 39. The sites necessary for the setting up of the Bank as well for the branches and agencies in Morocco shall be put at its disposition at no cost by the Government and, at the expiry of the concession, the Government will retake possession of them and reimburse the Bank for the expenses incurred for the construction of these establishments. The Bank will be authorised, in addition, to acquire all buildings and land of which it has need for the same object.

ARTICLE 40. The Sherifean Government takes full responsibility for the security and protection of the Bank, its branches and agencies. To this end, it will place a sufficient force in each town at the disposal of each of these establishments.

ARTICLE 41. The Bank, its branches and agencies will be exempt from all tax or royalties ordinary or extraordinary, in existence or to be created in the future. The same holds good in respect of the premises used for its functions, the securities and dividend warrants of its shares and its notes. The import and export of metals and coins intended for operations of the Bank shall be authorised and exempt from all dues.

ARTICLE 42. The Sherifean Government shall exercise overall surveillance over the Bank through a Moroccan High Commissioner, nominated by it after previous agreement with the Administrative Council of the Bank.

This High Commissioner will have the right to enquire into the administration of the Bank; he will control the issue of banknotes and ensure the strict observation of the conditions of the concession.

The High Commissioner must sign each note or attach his seal to it; he is charged with overseeing the relations between the Bank and the Moroccan Treasury.

He shall not involve himself in the administration and the management of the Bank, but he shall always have the right to attend the meetings of the auditors.

The Sherifean Government will nominate one or two assistant Commissioners who will be specially charged with supervising the financial operations of the Treasury with the Bank.

ARTICLE 43. A regulation, specifying the relations between the Bank and the Moroccan Government, shall be established by the special committee envisaged in Article 57 and approved by the auditors.

ARTICLE 44. The Bank, set up with the approval of the Government of His Sherifean Majesty in the form of a limited liability company, is subject to French law governing that sphere.

ARTICLE 45. Actions brought by the Bank in Morocco will be brought before the Consular Tribunal of the defendant or before the Moroccan jurisdiction, in conformity with the rules of competence established by the treaties and Firmans of Morocco.

Actions brought in Morocco against the Bank will be brought before a special tribunal, composed of two Consular magistrates and two assessors. The Corps Diplomatique will lay down each year the list of magistrates, assessors and their substitutes.

This Tribunal will apply to these cases the rules of law, procedure and competence laid down for commercial matters by the law of France. Appeal from judgements pronounced by this Tribunal will be brought before Federal Court at Lausanne from which there will be no appeal.

ARTICLE 46. In the case of dispute about the clauses of the concession or disputes possibly arising between the Moroccan Government and the Bank, the disagreement shall be submitted to the Federal Court at Lausanne without right of appeal or further remedy.

Likewise, all disputes which may possibly arise between the shareholders and the Bank over the application of the statutes or because of trouble stemming from matters relating to employees shall be referred to this Court without right of appeal or further remedy.

ARTICLE 47. The Bank statutes shall be set up along the following lines by a special Committee provided for in Article 57. They shall be approved of by the auditors and ratified by the general meeting of the shareholders.

ARTICLE 48. The constituent general meeting of the company shall fix the place where the meetings of the shareholders and the gathering of the Administrative Council shall take place; nevertheless, the latter shall have the right to meet in any other town if it deems it useful so to do.

The management of the Bank will be based on Tangiers.

ARTICLE 49. The Bank will be administered by an Administrative Council composed as far as possible of members who shall have been allotted shares in the initial capital.

The administrators will have the widest powers for the administration and management of the company; notably it is they who shall nominate the Directors, Under-Directors and members of the Commission indicated in Article 54, as well as the managers of the branches and agencies. All the employees of the company will be recruited as far as possible from among the nationals of the different powers who have contributed to the raising of capital.

ARTICLE 50. The administrators, nomination of whom will be made by the general meeting of the shareholders, will be designated for its approval by the groups subscribing the capital.

The first Council will remain in office for five years. On the expiry of this period it should proceed to its renewal to the extent of three members per year. The order of retirement of the administrators shall be determined by lot; they shall be re-eligible for election. At the foundation of the company each subscribing group will have the right of designating administrators in proportion to its subscription of paid up partnership shares, without the groups being obliged to choose a candidate of their own nationality.

The groups of subscribers will not retain their right of designating administrators, either at the time of their replacement or at that of the renewal of their mandate, except in so far as they are able to prove themselves still in possession of not less than half of each partnership share by dint of which they are exercising this right. In the case where, by reason of these regulations, a subscribing group no longer finds itself in a position to nominate an administrator, the general meeting of the shareholders should proceed directly to such designation.

ARTICLE 51. Each of the institutions named below: The Bank of the German Empire, The Bank of England, The Bank of Spain and The Bank of France—shall nominate, with the agreement of its Government, an auditor to be attached to the State Bank of Morocco.

These auditors shall exercise their duties for four years. Retiring auditors can be renominated.

In case of death or resignation, the vacancy can be filled by the institution which designated the previous holder, but only for the time which the latter had to run.

ARTICLE 52. The auditors who shall exercise their mandate by virtue of the present Act of the Signatory Powers must, in their interest, see to the proper running of the Bank and ensure strict observance of the provisions of the Concession and the statutes. They shall oversee the precise implementation of the regulations concerning the issuing of notes and must supervise the operations aiming at the reorganisation of the monetary situation. But they shall never, under any pretext whatsoever, become involved in the management side nor in the internal administration of the Bank.

Each auditor shall be able to scrutinise the accounts of the Bank at all times, to ask, either from the Administrative Council, or from the Board of Directors, for information about the running of the Bank, and to be present at the meetings of the Administrative Council, but in a consultative capacity only.

The four auditors shall meet at Tangiers for the fulfilment of their duties not less than once every two years on a date mutually agreed upon among themselves. Other meetings, at Tangiers or elsewhere, must be called if three auditors so require.

The four auditors shall prepare, by common agreement, an annual report, which shall be affixed to that of the Administrative Council. The Administrative Council shall transmit without delay a copy of this report to each of the Governments signatory to the Act of the Conference.

ARTICLE 53. The salaries and travel indemnities earmarked for the auditors shall be fixed by the Committee for Preparing the Statutes. They shall be paid directly to these agents by the banks charged with their designation and reimbursed to these establishments by the State Bank of Morocco.

ARTICLE 54. A Commission shall be set up at Tangiers attached to the Board of Directors, the members of which shall be chosen by the Administrative Council without distinction as to nationality and by those of standing, being owners of partnership shares in the Bank, who are resident at Tangiers.

This Commission will be presided over by one of the Directors or Under-Directors and give its opinion on discounts and the opening up of credits.

It shall prepare a monthly report on these diverse questions for the Administrative Council.

ARTICLE 55. The capital, the extent of which shall be fixed by the special Committee designated in Article 57, except that it cannot be less than 15,000,000 francs nor more than 20,000,000 francs, shall consist of gold coin and the share certificates, of which the smallest denomination shall represent a value equivalent to 500 francs and made payable in diverse gold coinages at a fixed determined by the statutes.

This capital shall ultimately be increased, one or more times, by the general meeting of the shareholders.

The subscription of these increases of capital shall be reserved to all shareholders, irrespective of group, in proportion to the stocks and shares held by each one of them.

ARTICLE 56. The initial capital of the Bank shall be divided into as many equal foundation shares as there shall be stockholding parties among the Powers represented at the Conference.

To this effect, each Power shall designate a bank, which shall exercise, either for itself, or for a group of banks, the right of subscribing specified above as well as the right of designating the administrators laid down in Article 50. Every bank chosen as the head of a group can, with the authorisation of its Government, be replaced by another bank of the same country.

The states which wish to avail themselves of their right of subscription shall communicate this intention to the Royal Government of Spain within a period of four weeks from the signing of the present Act by the representatives of the Powers.

Nevertheless, two foundation shares equal to those reserved to each of the subscribing groups shall be assigned to a Consortium of banks, being signatories of the Contract of 12 June 1904, in compensation for the surrender which was made by the Consortium to the State Bank of Morocco relating to:

1. The rights specified in Article 33 of the Contract.

2. The right written into Article 32 (no. 2) of the Contract concerning the disposable balance of customs receipts under express reserve of the general privilege conferred as a top priority by Article 11 of the same Contract to holders of claims on the total earnings of the customs.

ARTICLE 57. Within a period of three weeks from the point when the subscription time closed (after notification to the interested Powers by the Royal Spanish Government), a special committee, composed of delegates nominated by the subscribing groups according to the conditions laid down in Article 50 for the nomination of administrators, shall meet to formulate the Statutes of the Bank.

The constituent general meeting of the company shall take place within a period of two months from the ratification of the present Act. The role of the special committee shall cease immediately after the formation of the company.

The special committee shall itself fix the place for its meetings.

ARTICLE 58. No modification of the Statutes can be brought forward unless proposed by the Administrative Council and with the joint approval of the auditors and the Imperial High Commissioner.

Such modifications must be approved of in the general meeting of the shareholders by a majority of three quarters of the members present or represented there.

CHAPTER IV.

Declaration Concerning a Better Yield of Taxes and the Creation of New Revenues.

ARTICLE 59. From the time that the "Tertib" shall be levied regularly from Moroccan subjects the representatives of the Powers at Tangiers shall render their nationals within the Empire liable to it. But it is understood that the said tax shall not apply to foreigners:—

(a) Except under the conditions laid down by the Ruling of the Corps Diplomatique at Tangier on 23rd November, 1903.

(b) Except in the localities where it is levied on Moroccan subjects.

The Consular authorities shall retain a given percentage of the sums collected from their nationals to cover the expenses incurred through drawing up the lists and recovering the tax.

The rate of this deduction shall be fixed by joint agreement between the Makhzen and the Corps Diplomatique at Tangier.

ARTICLE 60. In conformity with the right accorded to them by Article XI of the Madrid Convention, foreign nationals shall be able to acquire properties throughout the extent of the Sherifean Empire, and His Majesty the Sultan shall give the administrative and judicial authorities the necessary instructions, although the authorisation for allowing the procedures cannot be refused without a legitimate reason. As for subsequent transferences, by due process between living parties or after decease, they shall continue to be made without let or hindrance.

In the ports open to commerce and within a radius of ten kilometres around them His Majesty the Sultan makes a general grant of the assent required under Article XI of the Madrid Convention, so that it will not be necessary to obtain special permission for each purchase of property by foreign nationals.

At Ksar-el-Kebir, Arzila, Azemmour and eventually in the other localities of the littoral or of the interior the above-mentioned general authorisation is likewise granted to foreign nationals, but only for acquisitions within a radius of 2 kilometres around these towns. Everywhere in places where foreign nationals have acquired properties they shall be entitled to raise constructions conforming to the regulations and usages.

Before authorising the drawing up of transfer deeds the Cadi must satisfy himself, in conformity with Moslem law, as to the regularity of the titles. The Makhzen shall designate in each of the towns and the areas around them indicated in the present Article the Cadi who shall be entrusted with making these verifications.

ARTICLE 61. With the purpose of creating new resources for the Makhzen, the Conference recognised in principle that a tax should be established for urban construction.

A part of the receipts so raised shall be set aside for the needs of the refuse dumps and municipal hygiene and for the cost of improving and maintaining the towns.

The tax shall be payable by the proprietor, whether he be Moroccan or a foreign national, without distinction; but the tenant or holder of the key will be responsible for it to the Moroccan Treasury.

A regulation laid down by joint agreement by the Sherifean Government and the Corps Diplomatique at Tangiers shall fix the tax rate, its method of collection and its application and shall determine the proportion of the resources so created which must be set aside towards the expenses for the improvement and maintenance of the towns.

At Tangier this quota shall be turned over to the International Sanitary Committee, which will regulate its use until the creation of a municipal organisation.

ARTICLE 62. His Sherifean Majesty, having decided in 1901 that the Moroccan functionaries entrusted with the collection of agricultural taxes should no longer receive either sokhri or mouna from the populations, the Conference considers that this rule should be given general application to the greatest extent possible.

ARTICLE 63. The Sherifean Delegates have explained that some " habous " assets or certain national properties, in particular some landed estates of the Makhzen, taken over as security for payment of the 6 per cent dues have been retained by foreign nationals without regular titles or by virtue of contracts subject to revision. The Conference, being desirous of remedying this state of things, charges the Corps Diplomatique at Tangier with finding an equitable solution to these two questions in accord with the Special Commissioner whom His Sherifean Majesty wishes to appoint for this purpose.

ARTICLE 64. The Conference takes note of the proposals formulated by the Sherifean Delegates on the subject of the creation of taxes on certain trades, industries and professions.

If, following the application of these taxes to Moroccan subjects, the Corps Diplomatique at Tangier considered it necessary to extend them to foreign nationals, it is specified from now on that the said taxes shall be exclusively municipal.

ARTICLE 65. The Conference supports the proposals formulated by the Moroccan delegation for establishing, with the assistance of the Corps Diplomatique:—

(a) A stamp duty on the contracts and legal instruments passed before the " adoul ";

(*b*) A transfer duty, with a two per cent maximum, on the sales of property;

(*c*) A duty on inward and outward trade to cover the cost of trade statistics and one for weight, with a maximum one per cent ad valorem value, on goods carried by coastal traffic;

(*d*) A passport duty to levy on Moroccan subjects;

(*e*) Should occasion arise, the harbour and lighthouse duties, the yield of which must be devoted to the improvement of the ports.

ARTICLE 66. On a temporary basis, goods of foreign origin shall be subject upon entry into Morocco to a special ad valorem tax rising to a maximum of two and a half per cent. The entire yield of this tax shall form a special fund, which shall be devoted to the expenses and the carrying out of public works designed for the development of navigation and commerce generally in the Sherifean Empire.

The programme of works and their order of priority shall be decided by joint agreement by the Sherifean Government and the Corps Diplomatique at Tangier.

The surveys, estimates, plans and specifications having reference to it shall be carried out by a qualified engineer nominated by the Sherifean Government in accord with the Corps Diplomatique. This engineer, can, should need arise, be assisted by one or several deputy engineers. Their salaries shall be charged on the funds of the special account.

The funds of the special account shall be deposited in the State Bank of Morocco, which will keep the books.

Awards of public contracts shall be dealt with in the forms and in accordance with the general conditions prescribed by a regulation which the Corps Diplomatique has been desired to set up with the representative of His Sherifean Majesty.

The adjudication Board shall consist of a representative of the Sherifean Government, five delegates of the Corps Diplomatique and the engineer. The award shall be given in favour of the party tendering who, while conforming with the conditions of the specifications, presents the offer containing the best general conditions.

So far as concerns the sums yielded by the special tax, which will be collected in the customs offices in the areas dealt with by Article 103 of the Customs Regulations, their use shall be regulated by the Makhzen in agreement with the limitrophe power in conformity with the conditions of the present Article.

ARTICLE 67. The Conference, without prejudice to opinions presented on this subject, expresses the wish that the export duties on the below-mentioned goods should be reduced in the following manner:—

	Per cent.
Chick peas	20
Maize	20
Barley	50
Wheat	34

ARTICLE 68. His Sherifean Majesty shall agree to raise to 10,000 the figure of 6,000 head of cattle which each Power shall have the right to export from Morocco. The export can take place at all customs offices. If, on account of unfortunate circumstances, a dearth of livestock has been declared in a defined region, His Sherifean Majesty can temporarily forbid the departure of cattle from the port or ports which serve this region. This measure must not exceed a period of more than two years. It cannot be applied simultaneously to all the ports of the Empire.

It is, moreover, understood, that the above conditions do not modify the other regulations governing the export of livestock laid down by earlier Firmans.

The Conference is in addition of the opinion that a veterinary inspection service should be organised at top speed in the ports of the coast.

ARTICLE 69. In conformity with the earlier decisions of His Sherifian Majesty and especially with that of 28th September 1901, transport by coastal trade between the ports of the Empire of cereals, grains, vegetables, eggs, fruits, poultry and, in general, goods and animals of all kinds has been authorised, with the exception of horses, mules, donkeys and camels, for which a special permit from the Makhzen will be necessary. The coastal trade can be carried on by the ships of all nationalities, without the said articles being subject to export duty, but complying with special charges and with the regulations on the matter.

ARTICLE 70. The rate of stopping and anchorage charges imposed on ships in Moroccan ports are laid down by the treaties concluded with certain Powers—these Powers being prepared to agree to the revision of the said charges. The Corps Diplomatique at Tangier has been entrusted with the establishment, by agreement with the Makhzen, of conditions for the revision, which cannot take place until after the improvement of the ports.

ARTICLE 71. The dues for customs warehousing shall be collected in all Moroccan ports where adequate repositories exist, conforming to the regulations made or to be made by the Government of His Sherifean Majesty in agreement with the Corps Diplomatique at Tangier.

ARTICLE 72. Opium and kif shall continue to be a monopoly for the benefit of the Sherifean Government. Nevertheless, the import of opium especially intended for pharmaceutical purposes shall be authorised by special permit, provided by the Makhzen, upon the request of the Legation to which the importing pharmacist or doctor is answerable. The Sherifean Government and the Corps Diplomatique shall regulate by common agreement the maximum quantity to be brought in.

ARTICLE 73. The Representatives of the Powers take cognizance ot the intention of the Sherifean Government to extend to tobacco, shops of all kinds the present monopoly relating to snuff. They reserve the right of their nationals to be duly indemnified for losses which the said monopoly could occasion those of them who had created enterprises under the current rule concerning tobacco. Failing a friendly agreement, the indemnity shall be fixed by the Makhzen and by the Corps Diplomatique in conformity with the regulations governing cases of expropriation for reasons of public utility.

ARTICLE 74. The principle of adjudication shall be applied to the farms concerning the opium and kif monopoly. It would be applied in the same way to the tobacco monopoly if it was established.

ARTICLE 75. In the case where there would be grounds for modifying any one of the arrangements made by the present Declaration, an agreement must be come to on the subject between the Makhzen and the Corps Diplomatique at Tangiers.

ARTICLE 76. In all the cases provided for in the present Declaration where the Corps Diplomatique will be called upon to intervene, the decisions shall be made by majority vote, except in what concerns Articles 64, 70 and 75.

CHAPTER V.

Regulation for the Imperial Customs and the Suppression of Fraud and Contraband.

ARTICLE 77. Every Captain of a trading vessel, coming from abroad or from Morocco, must, within twenty-four hours of his admission to pratique in one of the ports of the Empire, deposit an exact copy of his ship's manifest, signed by him and certified true by the consignee of the ship, at the customs office. He must, in addition, if so required, make available the original of this manifest to the customs officials.

The customs shall have the right to one or several guardians to prevent all illegal traffic.

ARTICLE 78. The following are exempt from deposit of the manifest:

(1) Warships or those chartered on behalf of a Power.

(2) Dinghies belonging to the individuals who employ them for their use, while abstaining from all carrying of merchandise.

(3) The boats or small craft used for offshore fishing.

(4) Yachts employed solely for pleasure sailing and registered as such at its home port.

(5) Ships especially entrusted with the laying and repair of telegraphic cables.

(6) Boats assigned solely to life-saving.

(7) Hospital ships.

(8) Training ships of the merchant marine not engaged in commercial operations.

ARTICLE 79. The manifest deposited with the customs must declare the nature and origin of the cargo along with the registered trade marks and numbers of the cases, bales, packages and casks, etc.

ARTICLE 80. When there are serious pointers arousing suspicion as to the inexactitude of the manifest, or when the captain of the ship refuses to cooperate over the inspection and examinations made by the customs officials, the matter shall be drawn to the attention of the competent Consular authority in order that it proceed, along with a delegate of the Sherifean customs, with the enquiries, inspections and examinations which it shall deem necessary.

ARTICLE 81. If, on the expiry of the period of twenty-four hours indicated in Article 77 the captain has not deposited his manifest, he shall be liable, provided the delay has not resulted from a case of main force, to a fine of 150 pesetas for each day of default, without, nevertheless, the said fine exceeding a total of 600 pesetas. If the captain has fraudulently presented an inexact or incomplete manifest, he shall personally be fined a sum equal to the value of the goods for which he has failed to produce the manifest, and a further fine of between 500 and 1,000 pesetas, and in addition the ship and the merchandise can be seized by the competent Consular authority as security for the fine.

ARTICLE 82. Everyone, at the moment of clearing goods imported or intended for export through the customs, must present the customs with a detailed declaration, setting out the category, quality, weight, number, size and value of the goods, as well as the type, registered trade marks and numbers of the cases containing them.

ARTICLE 83. In the case where, at the time of the visit fewer packages or goods are found than had been declared, the declarer, unless he can prove his good faith, must pay double duty for the missing goods and the presented goods shall be held by the customs as security for this double duty; if, on the other hand the visit reveals an excess as to the number of packages, and as to the quantity or weight of the goods, this excess shall be seized and confiscated for the benefit of the Makhzen, unless the declarer can prove his good faith.

ARTICLE 84. If the declaration had been recognised as inexact as to the category or as to quality and if the declarer cannot prove his good faith, the goods inaccurately declared shall be seized and confiscated for the benefit of the Makhzen by the competent authority.

ARTICLE 85. In the case where the declaration is seen to be inexact as to declared value and if the declarer cannot establish his good faith, the customs can either deduct the duty in kind then and there, or, in the case of the goods being indivisible, acquire the said goods by paying to the declarer immediately the declared value plus five per cent.

ARTICLE 86. If the declaration has been seen to be false as to the nature of the goods, those goods shall be considered as not having been declared and the offence shall come under the application of Articles 88 and 90 below and shall be punished in the ways laid down in the said Articles.

ARTICLE 87. All attempted or all flagrant offences as to importation and all attempted or flagrant offences as to export by way of smuggling of goods subject to duties, whether by sea or by land, shall render the goods subject to confiscation, without prejudice to the penalties and fines listed below, which shall be inflicted by a competent jurisdiction. Over and above that the means of transport by land shall be seized and confiscated where the contraband constitutes the main part of the cargo.

ARTICLE 88. All attempted or all flagrant offences as to importation and all attempted or flagrant offences as to export by way contraband through an open commercial port or through a customs office shall be punished by a fine not exceeding three times the value of the goods constituting the subject of the fraud and by imprisonment of between five days and six months, or by one of the two penalties alone.

ARTICLE 89. All attempted or all flagrant offences as to importation and all attempted or all flagrant offences as to export outside an open commercial port or customs office shall be punished by a fine of between 300 and 500 pesetas and by a supplementary fine equal to three times the value of the goods, or by imprisonment of between one month and one year.

ARTICLE 90. The accessories to the offences laid down in Articles 88 and 89 shall be liable to the same penalties as the principals. The factors constituting complicity shall be determined in accordance with the law of the relevant tribunal.

ARTICLE 91. In the case of attempted or flagrant offences as to importation and in that of attempted or flagrant export of goods by a ship outside an open commercial port, the Moroccan customs shall be able to conduct the ship to the nearest port to be handed over to the Consular authority, which shall be able to seize it and maintain the seizure until it has fully paid up the total of fines imposed.

The seizure of the ship must be lifted, whatever the stage of the hearing, in so far as this does not interfere with the judicial process, upon the deposit of the maximum sum of the fine in the hands of the

Consular authority, or upon the acceptance by the customs of security for payment.

ARTICLE 92. The provisions of the preceding Articles will be applicable to coastal trade navigation.

ARTICLE 93. Goods not subject to export duties taken on board in a Moroccan port for the purpose of being transported by sea to another port of the Empire must be accompanied by an exit certificate provided by the customs, under pain of being subject to the payment of import duty and even to confiscation if they were not included in the manifest.

ARTICLE 94. The transport by coastal trade of products subject to export duties cannot be carried on except by depositing at the customs office of departure in exchange for a receipt the total amount of export duties relating to these goods.

This deposit shall be repaid to the depositor by the office where it was lodged upon production of a declaration furnished by the customs containing proof of arrival and of the receipt verifying the deposit of the duties. The documents establishing the arrival of the goods must be produced within three months of their despatch. Beyond this period, unless the delay arises from a case of main force, the sum deposited must be forfeited to the Makhzen.

ARTICLE 95. Entry and exit duties shall be payable in cash at the customs office where the settlement of the account will be made. The ad valorem duties shall be settled according to the approximate cash value of the goods submitted to the customs office and shall not include customs and warehouse duties. In the case of damage, the depreciation in value of the goods will be taken into account in the valuation. The goods cannot be removed without payment of customs and warehouse duties.

Everything taken over or levied must be the subject of a regular receipt provided by the agent entrusted with the operation.

ARTICLE 96. The value of the principal items of goods taxed by the Moroccan customs shall be fixed each year, in accordance with the conditions specified in the preceding Article, by a Commission of Customs Values called together at Tangiers and composed of:—

1. Three members designated by the Moroccan Government.

2. Three members designated by the Corps Diplomatique at Tangiers.

3. A Delegate of the State Bank.

4. An official of the delegates of the Moroccan 5 per cent Loan of 1904. The Commission shall nominate between twelve and twenty honorary members domiciled in Morocco, whom it shall consult when there are values to be fixed and at all such times as they judge appropriate. These honorary members shall be chosen from lists of persons of standing drawn up by each Legation for foreign nationals and by the Representa-

tive of the Sultan for Moroccans. They shall be nominated as far as possible in proportion to the importance of the trade of each nation. The list of values it shall fix shall be used as a basis for the valuations which shall be made in each office by the Moroccan Customs Administration. It shall be displayed in the customs offices and in the chancelleries of the Legations or Consulates at Tangiers.

The list will be subject to revision at the end of six months if considerable changes in the value of certain goods have occurred.

ARTICLE 97. A Permanent Committee, called " The Customs Committee " has been set up at Tangiers and appointed for three years. It shall consist of a Special Commissioner of His Sherifean Majesty, of a member of the Corps Diplomatique or Consular Service nominated by the Corps Diplomatique at Tangiers, and a Delegate of the State Bank. It can co-opt one or several representatives of the Customs.

This Committee shall devote the closest attention to the operation of the customs and can propose to His Sherifean Majesty measures suitable for improving the service and for ensuring the regularity and supervision of operations and collection of duties (discharges of cargo, loadings of cargo, transport to land, handling, entries and exits of goods, warehouse dues, valuation, clearing of accounts and collection of taxes). The creation of " The Customs Committee " shall in no way call in question the rights laid down in favour of bondholders by Articles 15 and 16 of the Contract of Loan of 12th June 1904.

Instructions formulated by " The Customs Committee " and the interested services shall determine the detailed application of Article 96 and of the present Article. They shall be submitted for the opinion of the Corps Diplomatique.

ARTICLE 98. In the customs posts where sufficient warehouses exist the customs service shall take charge of goods discharged for despatch from the moment when they have been handed over, in return for a receipt, by the captain of the ship to the agents employed for lighterage, until the moment when they have been regularly cleared through the customs. It is responsible for any damages caused by loss or injury of goods which are due to the mistakes or the negligence of its agents. It is not responsible for injuries resulting either from the natural deterioration of the goods or from an unduly long period in storage, or in cases of main force.

In the customs posts where there are not sufficient warehouses the agents of the Makhzen alone are empowered to use the methods of preservation which the customs office has at its disposal.

A revision of the rulings as to warehouse dues actually in force shall be effected by the good offices of the Corps Diplomatique in accord with the Sherifean Government.

ARTICLE 99. Goods and means of transportation to land which are confiscated shall be sold through the good offices of the customs within a period of eight days from the time a definitive judgement is delivered by the competent tribunal.

ARTICLE 100. The net yield of the sale of goods and confiscated objects goes definitively to the state; that of monetary fines, just as the proceeds of transactions, shall, after deduction of all expenses, be divided between the Sherifean Treasury and those who have brought about the repression of the fraud or of the contraband.

One third shall be divided by the customs among the informers.
One third shall go to the agents who seized the merchandise.
One third to the Moroccan Treasury.

If the seizure has been effected without the assistance of an informer, half the fines shall be distributed to the seizing agents and the other half to the Moroccan Treasury.

ARTICLE 101. The Moroccan customs authorities must notify the Corps Diplomatique or Consular Agents directly of violations of the present ruling committed by their nationals, so that the same can be brought before the competent jurisdiction.

The same offences, when committed by Moroccan subjects shall be referred directly by the customs to the Sherifean authority.

A Delegate of the customs shall be charged with following the course of cases pending before the various jurisdictions.

ARTICLE 102. All confiscations, fines or penalties shall be inflicted upon foreign nationals by the Consular jurisdiction and for Moroccan subjects by the Sherifean jurisdiction.

ARTICLE 103. In the frontier region of Algeria the application of the present ruling shall rest exclusively in the hands of France and Morocco.

In the same way, the application of this ruling in the Riff and generally in the frontier areas of Spanish possessions shall rest exclusively in the hands of Spain and Morocco.

ARTICLE 104. The provisions of the present ruling, other than those relating to penalties, can be revised by the Corps Diplomatique at Tangiers, provided it is unanimous, and by agreement with the Makhzen at the end of a period of two years running from the time of its coming into force.

CHAPTER VI.

Declaration Relating to Public Services and to Public Works.

ARTICLE 105. With a view to ensuring the application of the principle of economic liberty without any differentiation, the Signatory Powers declare that the Public Services of the Sherifean Empire cannot be alienated for the profit of individual interests.

ARTICLE 106. In the case where the Sherifean Government believes it should call in foreign capital or foreign industry for the exploitation of public services or for the carrying out of public works, construction of roads, railways, ports, telegraphs and so on, the Signatory Powers reserve themselves the right to see that the authority of the state over these great enterprises of general interest remains complete.

ARTICLE 107. The validity of concessions made in accordance with the terms of Article 106, just as for those for state supplies, shall be subject to the principle of adjudication throughout the Sherifean Empire, without differentiation as to nationality, for all matters which, in conformity with the rules followed in foreign legislation, require its application.

ARTICLE 108. The Sherifean Government, as soon as it has decided to proceed by way of adjudication to the carrying out of public works, must inform the Corps Diplomatique; subsequently, it shall convey to them the specifications, plans and all the documents appertaining to the adjudication project in such a way that the nationals of all the Signatory Powers may be fully aware of the projected works and be in a position to compete. A suitable period for this purpose shall be fixed by notice from the court.

ARTICLE 109. The specifications must not include, directly or indirectly, any condition or provision which can interfere with free competition and put the competitors of one nationality in a position of inferiority vis-a-vis those of another.

ARTICLE 110. The adjudications shall be drawn up according to the forms and following the general conditions laid down by a ruling which the Sherifean Government shall decide upon with the help of the Corps Diplomatique.

The adjudication shall be given by the Sherifean Government in favour of the tenderer, who, while conforming with the provisions of the specifications, shall make the offer containing the most advantageous general conditions.

ARTICLE 111. The provisions of Articles 106 to 110 shall be applied to concessions for the exploitation of cork-oak forests in conformity with the arrangements used in foreign law.

ARTICLE 112. A Sherifean Firman shall determine the conditions governing the concession and exploitation of mines, open cast workings and quarries. In the formulation of this Firman the Sherifean Government shall take their pattern from existing foreign legislation on the subject.

ARTICLE 113. If, in the cases mentioned in Articles 106 to 112 it was necessary to take over certain properties, their expropriation can be proceeded with fairly by pre-payment of a just indemnity and in conformity with the following rules.

ARTICLE 114. The expropriation cannot take place except for public purposes and only in so far as the necessity has been established by an administrative enquiry, of which a Sherifean ruling, drawn up with the assistance of the Corps Diplomatique, shall fix the formalities.

ARTICLE 115. If the owners of the properties are Moroccan subjects, His Sherifean Majesty shall take the measures necessary so that no obstacle shall be put in the way of carrying out the works which it has declared are for public purposes.

ARTICLE 116. If the matter concerns foreign owners, the expropriation shall be proceeded with in the following way:—

In case of disagreement between the competent administration and the owner of the property to be expropriated, the indemnity shall be fixed by a special jury, or, if there is cause, by arbitration.

ARTICLE 117. This jury shall be composed of six valuation experts, three chosen by the owner and three by the administration which seeks appropriation. The opinion of the absolute majority shall prevail.

If it proves impossible to assemble a majority, the owner and the administration shall each nominate an arbitrator and these two arbitrators shall designate a third.

In default of agreement over the designation of a third arbitrator, he shall be nominated by the Corps Diplomatique at Tangiers.

ARTICLE 118. The arbitrators must be chosen from a list drawn up at the beginning of the year by the Corps Diplomatique and, as far as is possible, from among experts not resident in the locality where the work is to be carried out.

ARTICLE 119. The owner can make an appeal from the decision given by the arbitrators before the competent jurisdiction and in conformity with the rules laid down on the matter of arbitration by the legislation to which it had recourse.

CHAPTER VII.

General Provisions.

ARTICLE 120. So as to put its legislation, if there is need, into harmony with the obligations undertaken by the present General Act, each of the Signatory Powers binds itself to secure the adoption of the legislative measures necessary in regard to matters concerning it.

ARTICLE 121. The present General Act shall be ratified according to the particular constitutional laws of each state; the ratifications shall be deposited at Madrid as soon as possible and at latest on the 31st December 1906. A Procès-Verbal shall be drawn up upon deposit, a certified true copy of which shall be sent to the Signatory Powers by the ordinary channels of diplomacy.

ARTICLE 122. The present General Act shall come into effect on the day by which all the deposits shall have been made and at the latest on 31st December 1906.

In the case where the special legislative measures, which in certain countries are necessary to ensure the application to their nationals resident in Morocco of several of the stipulations of the present General Act, shall not have been adopted before the date fixed for ratification, these stipulations shall not become applicable to what concerns them until after the legislative measures laid down above shall have been promulgated.

ARTICLE 123. All the Treaties, Conventions and Agreements of the Signatory Powers with Morocco remain in force. Nevertheless, it is understood that in case of conflict between their provisions and those of the present General Act, the stipulations of the latter shall prevail.

In witness whereof the Plenipotentiaries have signed the present General Act and attached their seal to it.

Done at Algeciras the 7th April 1906 in one copy, which shall remain deposited in the archives of the Government of His Catholic Majesty, and of which copies certified as true shall be forwarded to the Signatory Powers by the ordinary channels of diplomacy.

For Germany:

(L.S.)   RADOWITZ.

(L.S.)   TATTENBACH.

For Austria-Hungary:

(L.S.)   WELSERSHEIMB.

(L.S.)   BOLESTA-KOZIEBRODZKI.

For Belgium:

(L.S.)   JOOSTENS.

(L.S.)   COMTE CONRAD DE BUISSERE.

For Spain:

(L.S.)   EL DUQUE DE ALMODOVAR DEL RIO.

(L.S.)   J. PÉREZ-CABALLERO.

For the United States of America (subject to the Declaration made in plenary session of the Conference on 7th April 1906).

(L.S.)   HENRY WHITE.

(L.S.)   SAMUEL R. GUMMERÉ.

Declaration by the United States Delegate.

The Government of the United States of America, not having any political interests in Morocco, and not having been, in taking part in this Conference, actuated by desires and intentions other than to contribute towards assuring to all nations the fullest equality in Morocco in the spheres of trade, treatment and prerogatives, and to facilitate there the introduction of reforms of which the result will·be a general well-being, based upon a complete cordiality of foreign relations and an internal administrative stability, declares: that in associating itself with the settlements and declarations of the Conference by signing the General Act, without prejudice to ratification in conformity with the constitutional laws, and the Additional Protocol, and in accepting their application to American citizens and interests in Morocco, it is not taking upon itself any obligation or responsibility with respect to the measures which may be necessary for carrying the said settlements and declarations into effect.)

For France:
  (L.S.)   RÉVOIL.
  (L.S.)   REGNAULT.

For Great Britain:
  (L.S.)   A. NICOLSON.

For Italy:
  (L.S.)   VISCONTI VENOSTA.
           G. MALMUSI.

For Morocco:
(Imperial Decree Ratifying the General Act of the International Conference at Algeciras, June 18th, 1906.

Glory to the One God: His absolute rule is eternal.

(Seal of SULTAN ABDULAZIS-BEN-HASSAN).

By the present Edict we make it known that we have read that which has been formulated by our Sherifean Delegates and the Delegates of the Great and High friendly Powers in the sessions of the Conference assembled in the town of Algeciras in the year 1324 of the Hegira, corresponding to the year 1906 of the Christian era, to examine the reforms to be introduced into this Maghrebin Empire, based in the first place upon three principles, namely: the maintenance of our sovereignty, the independence of our abovementioned Empire and economic liberty in carrying out public works. Then, the reforms based on the above principles have been brought under seven headings, which are:—

  1. Declaration relating to the organisation of the police in the ports of the Empire open to trade.

  2. Settlement concerning the surveillance and repression of arms contraband in the territory of this Empire.

  3. Act of concession of a bank in the name of the Moroccan Government.

4. Declaration concerning a better payment of existing taxes and the creation of new revenues.

5. Ruling on the imperial customs and the repression of fraud and contraband.

6. Ruling concerning the means of carrying out public works.

7. General arrangements for the ratification and execution of the General Act.

Each of these sections consists of a number of Articles—123 in all. After having examined the Act which consolidates the above-mentioned Articles and carries the date of 12 Safar of the current year, corresponding to the 7th April 1906, and after having probed into this same Act from one end to the other, we have made the Sherifean decision to approve, ratify, accept and execute it in its entirety.

Thus given by our order; an order strong and powerful through the will of God, the 26th day of Rabi', 1324, corresponding to the 18th June 1906 of the Christian era.

For a certified true translation copy:

A. M. LAREDO, Vice-Consul, Interpreter of the Italian Legation.

For the Netherlands:

(L.S.)   H. TESTA.

For Portugal:

(L.S.)   CONDE DE TOVAR.

(L.S.)   CONDE DE MARTENS FERRAO.

For Russia:

(L.S.)   CASSINI.

(L.S.)   BASILE BACHERACHT.

For Sweden:

(L.S.)   ROBERT SAGER.

(The Swedish Delegate stated that he signed with the same reservation as that made by the United States' Delegate.)

For a certified true copy:

Under-Secretary of State,

(L.S.)   E. DE OJÉDA.

Additional Protocol.

At the moment of proceeding to the signature of the General Act of the Conference of Algeciras, the Delegates of Germany, Austria-Hungary, Belgium, Spain, the United States of America, France, Great Britain, Italy, the Netherlands, Portugal, Russia, and Sweden, taking into account that the Moroccan Delegates have declared that for the moment they are not in a position to add their signatures, postponement not allowing them to obtain at short notice the response of His Sherifean Majesty concerning the points on the subject of which they believed they should refer to him, undertake reciprocally, in virtue of their similar plenary powers, to unite their efforts with a view to the complete ratification of the said General Act by His Sherifean Majesty and with a view to the simultaneous putting into effect of the reforms contained in it, and which are bound up with each other.

They agree, therefore, to entrust His Excellency M. Malmusi, Italian Minister in Morocco and doyen of the Corps Diplomatique at Tangiers, with taking the steps necessary to this end, in calling the attention of His Majesty the Sultan to the great advantages which will result for his Empire from the provisions unanimously adopted at the Conference by the Signatory Powers.

The adherence given by His Sherifean Majesty to the General Act of the Conference at Algeciras must be communicated by the intermediary of the Government of His Catholic Majesty to the Governments of the other Signatory Powers. This adherence shall have the same force as if the Moroccan Delegates had apposed their signatures to the General Act and shall take the place of ratification by His Sherifean Majesty. In witness whereof the Delegates of Germany, Austria-Hungary, Belgium, Spain, the United States of America, France, Great Britain, Italy, the Netherlands, Portugal, Russia and Sweden have signed the present Additional Protocol and apposed their seals to it.

Done at Algeciras the 7th day of April 1906 in a single copy, which shall remain deposited in the archives of the Government of His Catholic Majesty and of which copies certified as true shall be sent by the usual diplomatic channels to the Signatory Powers.

For Germany:
(L.S.)   RADOWITZ.
(L.S.)   TATTENBACH.

For Austria-Hungary:
(L.S.)   WELSERHEIMB.
(L.S.)   BOLESTA-KOZIEBRODZKI.

For Belgium:
(L.S.)   JOOSTENS.
(L.S.)   COMTE CONRAD DE BUISSERET.

For Spain:
(L.S.)   EL DUQUE DE ALMADOVAR DEL RIO.
(L.S.)   J. PÉREZ-CABALLERO.

For the United States of America:
(Subject to the declaration made in plenary session of the Conference on 7th April 1906).
(L.S.)   HENRY WHITE.
(L.S.)   SAMUEL R. GUMMERÉ.

For France:
(L.S.)   REVOIL.
(L.S.)   REGNAULT.
For Great Britain:
(L.S.)   A. NICOLSON.
For Italy:
(L.S.)   VISCONTI-VENOSTA.
(L.S.)   G. MALMUSI.
For the Netherlands:
(L.S.)   H. TESTA.
For Portugal:
(L.S.)   CONDE DE TOVAR.
(L.S.)   CONDE DE MARTENS FERRAO.
For Russia:
(L.S.)   CASSINI.
(L.S.)   BASILE BACHERACHT.
For Sweden:
(L.S.)   ROBERT SAGER.
For a certified true copy:
The Under-Secretary of State (L.S.)   E. DE OJÉDA.

Procès-Verbal of the Deposit of Ratifications of the General Act of the International Conference at Algeciras. Madrid, December 31st 1906.

In execution of Article 121 of the General Act of the International Conference of Algeciras, the undersigned Representatives of Great Britain, Germany, Austria-Hungary, Belgium, Spain, the United States of America, France, Italy, the Netherlands, Portugal, Russia and Sweden have come together at the Ministry of State at Madrid in order to make deposit into the hands of the Government of His Catholic Majesty the ratifications of the High Contracting Parties.

The Instruments of Ratification:—

1. From His Majesty the King of the United Kingdom of Great Britain and Ireland and the British Territories Beyond the Seas, Emperor of India;

2. From His Majesty the Emperor of Germany, King of Prussia, in the name of the German Empire;

3. From His Majesty the Emperor of Austria, King of Bohemia and King Apostolic of Hungary;

4. From the King of the Belgians;

5. From His Majesty the King of Spain;

6. From the President of the United States of America;

7. From the President of the French Republic;

8. From His Majesty the King of Italy;

9. From Her Majesty the Queen of the Netherlands;

10. From His Majesty the King of Portugal and the Algarves etc., etc.;

11. From His Majesty the Emperor of All the Russias;

12. And from His Majesty the King of Sweden;

have been brought forward and having, after examination, been found in proper and due form, have been handed over to the Government of His Catholic Majesty for deposit in the archives of the Department of State. The Chargé d'Affaires of the United States declares that the ratification of the President of the United States of America has been given subject to the declaration made by the principal Delegate of his country at the closing session of the Conference on 7th April 1906 and to the resolution adopted by the American Senate on 12th December 1906; a declaration and a resolution which have been inserted in the instrument of ratification and of which copies have been provided.

The adherence of His Sherifean Majesty to the General Act of the international Conference of Algeciras having been communicated by the intermediary of the Government of His Catholic Majesty to the Governments of the other Powers, this adherence, conforming with the Additional Protocol of the said Act, takes the place of ratification in what concerns Morocco.

In witness whereof the present Procès-Verbal has been prepared, a certified true copy of which shall be provided by the Government of His Catholic Majesty to the Signatory Powers of the General Act.

Done at Madrid on the 31st day of December 1906.

For Great Britain:
(L.S.)   MAURICE DE BUNSEN.
For Germany:
(L.S.)   RADOWITZ.
For Austria-Hungary:
(L.S.)   WELSERHEIMB.
For Belgium:
(L.S.)   JOOSTENS.
For Spain:
(L.S.)   J. PÉREZ-CABALLERO.
For the United States of America:
(L.S.)   WINTROP.
For France:
(L.S.)   CAMBON.
For Italy:
(L.S.)   SILVESTRELLI.
For the Netherlands:
(L.S.)   H. TESTA.

For Portugal:
(L.S.)   CONDE DE TOVAR.
For Russia:
(L.S.)   CASSINI.
For Sweden:
(L.S.)   SAGER.

171

CONVENTION between GREAT BRITAIN AND RUSSIA relating to Persia, Afghanistan, and Thibet. August 31, 1907.

His Majesty the King of the United Kingdom of Great Britain and Ireland and of the British Dominions beyond the Seas, Emperor of India, and His Majesty the Emperor of All the Russias, animated by the sincere desire to settle by mutual agreement different questions concerning the interests of their States on the Continent of Asia, have determined to conclude Agreements destined to prevent all cause of misunderstanding between Great Britain and Russia in regard to the questions referred to, and have nominated for this purpose their respective Plenipotentiaries, to wit;

His Majesty the King of the United Kingdom of Great Britain and Ireland and of the British Dominions beyond the Seas, Emperor of India, the Right Honourable Sir Arthur Nicolson, His Majesty's Ambassador Extraordinary and Plenipotentiary to His Majesty the Emperor of All the Russias;

His Majesty the Emperor of All the Russias, the Master of his Court Alexander Iswolsky, Minister for Foreign Affairs;

Who, having communicated to each other their full powers, found in good and due form, have agreed on the following:—

AGREEMENT CONCERNING PERSIA.

The Governments of Great Britain and Russia having mutually engaged to respect the integrity and independence of Persia, and sincerely desiring the preservation of order throughout that country and its peaceful development, as well as the permanent establishment of equal advantages for the trade and industry of all other nations;

Considering that each of them has, for geographical and economic reasons, a special interest in the maintenance of peace and order in certain provinces of Persia adjoining, or in the neighbourhood of, the Russian frontier on the one hand, and the frontiers of Afghanistan and

Baluchistan on the other hand; and being desirous of avoiding all cause of conflict between their respective interests in the above-mentioned provinces of Persia;

Have agreed on the following terms:—

I.—Great Britain engages not to seek for herself, and not to support in favour of British subjects, or in favour of the subjects of third Powers, any Concessions of a political or commercial nature—such as Concessions for railways, banks, telegraphs, roads, transport, insurance, &c.— beyond a line starting from Kasr-i-Shirin, passing through Isfahan, Yezd, Kakhk, and ending at a point on the Persian frontier at the inter-section of the Russian and Afghan frontiers, and not to oppose, directly or indirectly, demands for similar Concessions in this region which are supported by the Russian Government. It is understood that the above-mentioned places are included in the region in which Great Britain engages not to seek the Concessions referred to.

II.—Russia, on her part, engages not to seek for herself and not to support, in favour of Russian subjects, or in favour of the subjects of third Powers, any Concessions of a political or commercial nature—such as Concessions for railways, banks, telegraphs, roads, transport, insur-ance, &c.—beyond a line going from the Afghan frontier by way of Gazik, Birjand, Kerman, and ending at Bunder Abbas, and not to oppose, directly or indirectly, demands for similar Concessions in this region which are supported by the British Government. It is understood that the above-mentioned places are included in the region in which Russia engages not to seek the Concessions referred to.

III.—Russia, on her part, engages not to oppose, without previous arrangement with Great Britain, the grant of any Concessions whatever to British subjects in the regions of Persia situated between the lines mentioned in Articles I and II.

Great Britain undertakes a similar engagement as regards the grant of Concessions to Russian subjects in the same regions of Persia.

All Concessions existing at present in the regions indicated in Articles I and II are maintained.

IV.—It is understood that the revenues of all the Persian customs, with the exception of those of Farsistan and of the Persian Gulf, revenues guaranteeing the amortization and the interest of the loans concluded by the Government of the Shah with the "Banque d'Escompte et des Prêts de Perse" up to the date of the signature of the present Agreement, shall be devoted to the same purpose as in the past.

It is equally understood that the revenues of the Persian customs of Farsistan and of the Persian Gulf, as well as those of the fisheries on the Persian shore of the Caspian Sea and those of the Posts and Telegraphs, shall be devoted, as in the past, to the service of the loans concluded by the Government of the Shah with the Imperial Bank of Persia up to the date of the signature of the present Agreement.

V.—In the event of irregularities occurring in the amortization or the payment of the interest of the Persian loans concluded with the "Banque d'Escompte et des Prets de Perse" and with the Imperial Bank of Persia up to the date of the signature of the present Agreement, and in the event of the necessity arising for Russia to establish control over the sources of revenue guaranteeing the regular service of the loans concluded with the first-named bank, and situated in the region mentioned in Article II of the present Agreement, or for Great Britain to establish control over the sources of revenue guaranteeing the regular service of the loans concluded with the second-named bank, and situated in the region mentioned in Article I of the present Agreement, the British and Russian Governments undertake to enter beforehand into a friendly exchange of ideas with a view to determine, in agreement with each other, the measures of control in question and to avoid all interference which would not be in conformity with the principles governing the present Agreement.

CONVENTION CONCERNING AFGHANISTAN.

The High Contracting Parties, in order to ensure perfect security on their respective frontiers in Central Asia and to maintain in these regions a solid and lasting peace, have concluded the following Convention:—

ARTICLE I.—His Britannic Majesty's Government declare that they have no intention of changing the political status of Afghanistan.

His Britannic Majesty's Government further engage to exercise their influence in Afghanistan only in a pacific sense, and they will not themselves take, nor encourage Afghanistan to take, any measures threatening Russia.

The Russian Government, on their part, declare that they recognize Afghanistan as outside the sphere of Russian influence, and they engage that all their political relations with Afghanistan shall be conducted through the intermediary of His Britannic Majesty's Government; they further engage not to send any Agents into Afghanistan.

ARTICLE II.—The Government of His Britannic Majesty having declared in the Treaty signed at Kabul on the 21st March, 1905, that they recognize the Agreement and the engagements concluded with the late Ameer Abdur Rahman, and that they have no intention of interfering in the internal government of Afghan territory, Great Britain engages neither to annex nor to occupy in contravention of that Treaty any portion of Afghanistan or to interfere in the internal administration of the country, provided that the Ameer fulfils the engagements already contracted by him towards His Britannic Majesty's Government under the above-mentioned Treaty.

ARTICLE III.—The Russian and Afghan authorities, specially designated for the purpose on the frontier or in the frontier provinces, may establish direct relations with each other for the settlement of local questions of a non-political character.

ARTICLE IV.—His Britannic Majesty's Government and the Russian Government affirm their adherence to the principle of equality of commercial opportunity in Afghanistan, and they agree that any facilities which may have been, or shall be hereafter, obtained for British and British-Indian trade and traders, shall be equally enjoyed by Russian trade and traders. Should the progress of trade establish the necessity for Commercial Agents, the two Governments will agree as to what measures shall be taken, due regard, of course, being had to the Ameer's sovereign rights.

ARTICLE V.—The present arrangements will only come into force when His Britannic Majesty's Government shall have notified to the Russian Government the consent of the Ameer to the terms stipulated above.

AGREEMENT CONCERNING THIBET.

The Governments of Great Britain and Russia recognizing the suzerain rights of China in Thibet, and considering the fact that Great Britain, by reason of her geographical position, has a special interest in the maintenance of the *status quo* in the external relations of Thibet, have made the following Agreement:—

ARTICLE I.—The two High Contracting Parties engage to respect the territorial integrity of Thibet and to abstain from all interference in its internal administration.

ARTICLE II.—In conformity with the admitted principle of the suzerainty of China over Thibet, Great Britain and Russia engage not to enter into negotiations with Thibet except through the intermediary of the Chinese Government. This engagement does not exclude the direct relations between British Commercial Agents and the Thibetan authorities provided for in Article V of the Convention between Great Britain and Thibet of the 7th September, 1904, and confirmed by the Convention of 27th April, 1906, between Great Britain and China; nor does it modify the engagements assumed by Great Britain and China by virtue of Article I of the said Convention of 1906.

It is agreed that the Buddhists, whether British or Russian subjects, can enter into direct relations with the Dalai-Lama and the other representatives of Buddhism in Thibet on strictly religious grounds, the Governments of Great Britain and Russia undertake, in so far as it is within their power, not to allow these relations to bring into question the conditions of the present arrangement.

ARTICLE III.—The British and Russian Governments each undertake not to send representatives to Lhasa.

ARTICLE IV.—The Two High Contracting parties undertake not to seek out or obtain, either on their own account or for the sake of their subjects, any railway, road, telegraph and mining concessions, or any other rights in Thibet.

ARTICLE V.—The two Governments are agreed that no part of the revenues of Thibet, be it in kind or in specie, can be promised or assigned either to Great Britain or to Russia or their subjects.

Annexe to the Agreement between Great Britain and Russia Concerning Thibet.

Great Britain reaffirms the Declaration signed by His Excellency the Viceroy and Governor-General of India and annexed to the ratification of the Convention of 7th September, 1904, stipulating that the occupation of the valley of Chumbi by British forces would end after payment of three annual payments of the indemnity of 2,500,000 rupees, on condition that the marts mentioned in Article II of the said Convention had been effectively opened for three years and that the Thibetan authorities should during this period have conformed strictly according to all the reports to the terms of the said Convention of 1904. It is agreed that, if the occupation of the valley of the Chumbi by British forces has not, for any reason whatsoever, come to an end by the time laid down by the above Declaration, the British and Russian Governments will enter into a friendly exchange of views on this topic.

The present Convention will be ratified and the ratifications will be exchanged at St. Petersbourg as soon as possible.

In testimony whereof the Plenipotentiaries have signed the present Convention and to which they have apposed their seals.

Done in duplicate at St. Petersbourg, 18th/31st August, 1907.

A. NICOLSON.   ISWOLSKY.
   (L.S.)   (L.S.)

172

AGREEMENT Between Japan and the United States (The Root—Takahira Agreement), November 30, 1908.

The Note addressed to Secretary of State Root from Ambassador Takahira ran as follows:

"The exchange of views between us, which has taken place at the several interviews which I have recently had the honour of holding with you, has shown that Japan and the United States holding important outlying insular possessions in the region of the Pacific Ocean, the Governments of the two countries are animated by a common aim, policy, and intention in that region.

"Believing that a frank avowal of that aim, policy, and intention would not only tend to strengthen the relations of friendship and good neighbourhood, which have immemorially existed between Japan and the United States, but would materially contribute to the preservation of the general peace, the Imperial Government have authorized me to present to you an outline of their understanding of that common aim, policy, and intention:

1. It is the wish of the two Governments to encourage the free and peaceful development of their commerce on the Pacific Ocean;

2. The policy of both Governments, uninfluenced by any aggressive tendencies, is directed to the maintenance of the existing status quo in the region above-mentioned and to the defence of the principle of equal opportunity for commerce and industry in China;

3. They are accordingly firmly resolved reciprocally to respect the territorial possessions belonging to each other in the said region;

4. They are also determined to preserve the common interests of all Powers in China, by supporting, by all pacific means at their disposal, the independence and integrity of China and the principle of equal opportunity for commerce and industry of all nations in that Empire;

5. Should any event occur threatening the status quo as above described or the principle of equal opportunity as above defined, it remains for the two Governments to communicate with each other, in order to arrive at an understanding as to what measures they may consider it useful to take."

In reply to the Note of Ambassador Takahira, the Note of the same date from Secretary of State Root to Ambassador Takahira affirmed the American-Japanese declaration of policy and stated as follows:

"It is a pleasure to inform you that this expression of mutual understanding is welcome to the Government of the United States as appropriate to the happy relations of the two countries and as the occasion for a concise mutual affirmation of that accordant policy respecting the Far East, which the two Governments have so frequently declared in the past."

It is not too much to say that the unofficial advice of Great Britain had played an important part in inducing the Japanese Government to make the proposal to conclude the American-Japanese Agreement. Ambassador Takahira asked the advice of James Bryce, the British

Ambassador in the United States, in a rather guarded way as to whether it would be desirable that Japan should conclude such an agreement, to which Ambassador Bryce replied that the conclusion of such an agreement would have a good effect on the relations between Japan and the United States.

On the other hand, the United States confidentially communicated the text of the proposed agreement before its consummation to Sir Edward Grey, the British Foreign Minister, who stated that the Government of Great Britain had learned with sincere satisfaction of the impending conclusion of such an agreement, and that they were confident that the agreement could not fail to have beneficial results not only to the respective interests of the United States and of Japan but to the general peace in the Pacific and Far East. The Japanese Chargé d'Affaires in London also informed Foreign Minister Grey that Japan had made an agreement with the United States, to which Grey stated that "it was very good news. I welcomed it sincerely and all my colleagues would do so too. As the ally of Japan we were very pleased with it, because we ourselves were especially desirous of remaining on good terms with the United States."

173

DECLARATION of France and Germany Respecting Morocco. Signed at Berlin, 9th February 1909.

[The Treaty of Algeciras did not make a final adjustment between France and Germany on the question of Morocco; incidents occurred which gave occasion for a reaffirmation of the principles upon which it was based. This 1909 convention, although favourably proclaimed from many sides at the time it was announced, proved to be of doubtful value because it, too, was hard to put into effect. The immediate causes for the friction which resulted in the Crisis of 1911, lay in the attempts at application of the following accord, which provided for the working out of schemes of Franco-German economic co-operation.]

The Government of the French Republic and the Imperial German Government, animated by an equal desire to facilitate the execution of the Act of Algeciras, have agreed to define the meaning that they attach to its clauses, in order to avoid all cause of misunderstanding between them in the future.

In consequence,

the Government of the French Republic, entirely attached to the maintenance of the integrity and independence of the Sherifean Empire, has resolved to safeguard the economic equality and consequently not to hinder the German commercial and industrial interests,

and the Imperial German Government, pursuing only economic interests in Morocco, recognising on the other hand that the particular political interests of France there are closely bound up with the consolidation of order and internal peace, has decided not to impede these interests,

declare that they will not pursue nor encourage any measure of a nature to create in their favour or in the favour of any other Power an economic privilege, and that they will endeavour to associate their citizens in the affairs for which they may obtain concessions.

174

AGREEMENT between Austria-Hungary and Italy explaining and supplementing Article VII of the Treaty of the Triple Alliance of 1887. Vienna, November 30; Rome, December 15, 1909.

Secret.

In the conferences which I [you] have lately had with Duke Avarna [Count Aehrenthal] with a view to defining and perfecting Article VII of the Treaty of the Triple Alliance, we [you] have agreed, to begin with, that, Austria-Hungary having renounced the rights which the Treaty of Berlin had conferred upon her in respect to the Sanjak of Novibazar, the provisions of the aforesaid Article of the Triple Alliance apply to the Sanjak as well as to the other parts of the Ottoman Empire. If, then, in consequence of the impossibility of maintaining the status quo in the Balkans, Austria-Hungary should be compelled by the force of circumstances to proceed to a temporary or permanent occupation of the Sanjak of Novibazar, that occupation shall be effected only after a previous agreement with Italy, based on the principle of compensation.

Faithful to the spirit which has inspired the Treaty of the Triple Alliance, and with a view to defining exactly and by mutual agreement the procedure which the two Allied Cabinets intend to adopt in certain eventualities, we, Duke Avarna and I, [you, with Count Aehrenthal,] have also agreed upon the following:

Each of the two Cabinets binds itself not to conclude with a third Power any agreement whatsoever concerning Balkan questions without the participation of the other Cabinet on a footing of absolute equality; likewise, the two Cabinets bind themselves to communicate to each other every proposition which may be made to the one or to the other by a third Power, running contrary to the principle of non-intervention and tending to a modification of the status quo in the regions of the Balkans or of the Ottoman coasts and islands in the Adriatic and of the Aegean Sea.

It goes without saying that Article VII of the Treaty of the Triple Alliance, which the above provisions only render more specific and complete, remains in force in its entirety.

As to the duration of the engagement which the two Cabinets assume in virtue of the above, it is understood that it shall coincide with that of the Treaty of the Triple Alliance, so that the engagement itself will be implicitly renewed with the renewal of the Triple Alliance.

In conformity with analogous provisions of that Treaty, the two Cabinets mutually promise secrecy as to the engagement they have just entered into; only the Cabinet of Berlin, in its capacity as an Ally, shall be informed thereof by the two Governments without delay.

In order to fix exactly what has been agreed upon in the conferences I have conducted through Duke Avarna [through you] with the Royal [Imperial and Royal] Cabinet, I request you, Mr. Ambassador, to communicate this despatch to the Minister of Foreign Affairs and to leave with him a copy thereof.

Accept, etc. [Accept, Mr. Ambassador, the assurance of my high consideration. Signed: Guicciardini.]

175

AGREEMENT between GREAT BRITAIN AND JAPAN RESPECTING THE INTEGRITY OF CHINA, THE GENERAL PEACE OF EASTERN ASIA AND INDIA, AND THE TERRITORIAL RIGHTS AND SPECIAL INTERESTS OF THE PARTIES IN THOSE REGIONS, 13th, JULY 1911.

Preamble

The Government of Japan and the Government of Great Britain having in view the important changes which have taken place in the situation since the conclusion of the Anglo-Japanese Agreement of August 12, 1905, and believing that the revision of that Agreement responding to such changes would contribute to general stability and repose, have agreed upon the following stipulations to replace the Agreement above mentioned, such stipulations having the same object as the said Agreement, namely:

A.—The consolidation and maintenance of the general peace in the regions of Eastern Asia and India.

B.—The preservation of the common interests of all the Powers in China by insuring the independence and integrity of the Chinese Empire and the principle of equal opportunities for the commerce and industry of all nations in China.

C.—The maintenance of the territorial rights of the High Contracting Parties in the regions of Eastern Asia and of India and the defence of their special interests in those regions:

ART. I. It is agreed that whenever, in the opinion of either Japan or Great Britain, any of the rights and interests referred to in the preamble of this Agreement are in jeopardy, the two Governments will communicate with one another fully and frankly, and will consider in common the measures which should be taken to safeguard those menaced rights and interests.

ART. II. If by reason of an unprovoked attack or aggressive action, wherever arising, on the part of any other Power or Powers, either of the High Contracting Parties should be involved in war in defence of its territorial rights or special interests mentioned in the preamble of this Agreement, the other High Contracting Party will at once come to the assistance of its Ally and will conduct the war in common and make peace in mutual agreement with it.

ART. III. The High Contracting Parties agree that neither of them will, without consulting the other, enter into a separate agreement with another Power to the prejudice of the objects described in the preamble of this Agreement.

ART. IV. Should either of the High Contracting Parties conclude a treaty of general arbitration with a third Power, it is agreed that nothing in this Agreement shall impose on such contracting party an obligation to go to war with the Power with whom such an arbitration treaty is in force.

ART. V. The conditions under which armed assistance shall be afforded by either Power to the other in circumstances entered into the present Agreement, and the means by which such assistance is to be made available, will be arranged by the military and naval authorities of the High Contracting Parties, who will from time to time consult one another fully and frankly upon all questions of mutual interests.

ART. VI. The present Agreement shall come into effect immediately after the date of its signature, and remain in force for ten years from that date. In case neither of the High Contracting Parties should have notified twelve months before the expiration the intention of terminating it, it shall remain binding until the expiration of one year from the day on which either of the High Contracting Parties shall have denounced it.

But if, when the date fixed for its expiration arrives, either ally is actually engaged in war, the Alliance shall, *ipso facto*, continue until peace is concluded.

In faith whereof the undersigned, duly authorised by their respective Governments, have signed this Agreement and have affixed their seals thereto. Done at London July 13, 1911.

> (L.S.)   T. KATO, the Ambassador of His Majesty the Emperor of Japan at the Court of St. James.
>
> (L.S.)   EDWARD GREY. H. B. M.'s Secretary of State for Foreign Affairs.

176

FRANCO-GERMAN CONVENTION Respecting Morocco. Signed at Berlin, 4th November, 1911.

The Government of the French Republic and the Government of His Majesty the Emperor of Germany, following the troubles which have arisen in Morocco and which have demonstrated the necessity of pursuing there, in the general interest, the work of pacification and progress provided for by the Act of Algeciras, having judged it necessary to specify and complete the Franco-German Agreement of 9th February, 1909, have resolved to conclude a Convention to this effect. In consequence, M. Jules Cambon, Ambassador Extraordinary of the French Republic accredited to His Majesty the Emperor of Germany and Herr von Kiderlen-Waechter, Secretary of State for Foreign Affairs of the German Empire, having had their plenary powers communicated to them, drawn up in due and proper form, have agreed upon the following arrangements:

ARTICLE I. The Imperial German Government declares that as it is only pursuing economic interests in Morocco it will not hinder the action of France with a view to lending its assistance to the Moroccan Government for introducing all the administrative, judicial, economic, financial and military reforms of which there is need to secure the good government of the Empire, so too for all the new regulations and the modifications to existing regulations which these reforms require. Consequently, it accedes to the measures of reorganisation, of inspection and of financial guarantee which, after agreement with the Moroccan Government, the French Government shall consider it ought to take to this end, with the reservation that French action shall safeguard in Morocco equality of economic opportunity between the nations.

In the case where France were to take steps to specify and to extend her control and protection, the German Imperial Government, recognising full liberty of action for France and with that the reservation relating to commercial liberty laid down by earlier treaties shall be maintained, will not raise any obstacle.

It is understood that it will not impede the rights and functions of the State Bank of Morocco, such as were defined by the Act of Algeciras.

ARTICLE II. In accordance with this scheme of things, it is agreed that the Imperial Government will place no obstacle in the way of France when, after agreement with the Moroccan Government, she proceeds to military occupations of Moroccan territory deemed necessary for the maintenance of order and for the security of commercial transactions. Likewise in regard to what she does by way of police action on land and in Moroccan waters.

ARTICLE III. Henceforth, if His Majesty the Sultan of Morocco should decide to confer upon the diplomatic and consular agents of France the representation and protection of the subjects and interests of Morocco abroad, the Imperial Government declares that it will raise no objection.

If, elsewhere, His Majesty the Sultan of Morocco should confer upon the French representative accredited to the Moroccan Government the duty of being his intermediary with foreign representatives, the German Government would not raise any objection.

ARTICLE IV. The French Government declares that being firmly attached to the principle of commercial freedom in Morocco, it will not countenance any inequality in the imposition of customs duties and in other taxes any more than in the setting up of transport tariffs for railways, river travel or any other means of transportation—especially in all questions of transit.

The French Government will likewise strive in its relations with the Moroccan Government to prevent all differential treatment between the nationals of the different powers; it will especially oppose to the utmost for example in the promulgation of administrative ordinances on weights and measures, gauging and hallmarking and so on anything which could put the merchandise of any power at a disadvantage.

The French Government undertakes to use its influence with the State Bank so that it will confer in turn upon the members of its management at Tangiers the posts of delegate of which it disposes on the Commission for fixing customs and on the permanent Committee for customs.

ARTICLE V. The French Government will take care that no export duty shall be levied upon iron ore exported from Moroccan ports. The working operations for iron ore shall not be subjected to any special tax either on their production or means of work. They will only be subject, over and above general taxes, to a fixed rent, calculated by hectare and by year, and a royalty proportional to the amount of raw material extracted. These royalties, which will be fixed in accordance with Article 35 and 49 of the proposal for mining regulation annexed to the Protocol of the Conference of Paris of 7th July, 1910 will be equally upheld by all the mining enterprises.

The French Government will see to it that the mining taxes will be regularly levied without the possibility of any individual remissions from the total or from a part of these taxes being agreed to on any pretext whatsoever.

ARTICLE VI. The French Government undertakes to see that the works and supplying of goods and materials necessitated by the eventual construction of roads, railways, ports, telegraphs etc. should be allocated by the Moroccan Government in accordance with the rules of the award.

It undertakes also to see to it that the conditions of awarding contracts, particularly in what concerns the supplying of materials and the time allowed for submitting tenders, do not place the nationals of any power in a position of inferiority.

The execution of the large enterprises mentioned above will be reserved to the Moroccan Government or freely conceded by it to third parties who will be able to be made responsible for furnishing the funds necessary to this end. The French Government will ensure that, in the working of the railways and other means of transport as in the regulations designed to ensure it, no difference of treatment should be made between the nationals of the different powers who make use of these means of transport.

The Government of the Republic will use its influence with the State Bank so that it confers in turn to the members of its management at Tangiers the post of delegate to the General Commission for awards of contracts and markets which lies in its gift.

In the same way, the French Government will exert influence on the Moroccan Government in order that during the period when Article 66 of the Act of Algeciras shall remain in force it confers upon a national of one of the powers represented in Morocco one of the three posts of Sherifean delegate to the special Committee of public works.

ARTICLE VII. The French Government will exert itself with the Moroccan Government in order that the proprietors of mines and other industrial or agricultural undertakings, without distinction of nationality and in conformity with the regulations which will be laid down in accordance with French legislation on the matter, may be authorised to build industrial railways intended to link their production centres with lines for general use or to the ports.

ARTICLE VIII. It will have presented every year a report on the working of railways in Morocco, which will be drawn up in accordance with the same methods of procedure and conditions as the reports presented to the meetings of shareholders of French railways.

The Government of the Republic will entrust one of the administrators of the State Bank with the drafting of this report which, together with the data upon which it will be based, will be communicated to the auditors, then made public with, if necessary, the observations they shall judge it necessary to add after their own reports.

ARTICLE IX. In order to avoid diplomatic protests as much as possible, the French Government will so work with the Moroccan Government as to persuade it to submit to an arbitrator, designated ad hoc for each matter by common accord between the French Consul and the one of the interested power, or failing them, by the two governments of these Consuls, the complaints brought by foreign nationals against the Moroccan authorities, or the agents acting for the Moroccan authorities, and which could not be settled through the instrumentality of the French Consul and of the consul of the interested government.

This procedure will remain in force until the time when a judicial system based upon the juridical rules of legislation of the interested powers and intended to replace, following mutual agreement, the Consular Tribunals, shall have been introduced.

ARTICLE X. The French Government will take care that foreign nationals continue to enjoy the right to fish in Moroccan ports and waters.

ARTICLE XI. The French Government will exert itself with the Moroccan government to see that the latter opens once more to foreign trade as required by this trade.

ARTICLE XII. In response to a request of the Moroccan Government, the two governments undertake to bring about the revision, in agreement with the other powers and on the basis of the Convention of Madrid, the lists and the position of foreign protected persons and the agricultural stockholders in Morocco referred to in Articles 8 and 16 of this Convention.

They agree also to pursue with the signatory powers all the modifications of the Convention of Madrid which circumstances now demand— the change in the system for protected persons and agricultural stockholders.

ARTICLE XIII. All clauses of any agreement, convention, treaty or settlement contrary to the forgoing stipulations are and remain abrogated.

ARTICLE XIV. The present agreement will be communicated to the other signatory powers of the Act of Algeciras in relation to whom the two governments undertake to lend each other mutual support to obtain their accession.

ARTICLE XV. The present Convention will be ratified and the ratifications exchanged at Paris as soon as possible.

Done at Berlin, 4th November 1911 in duplicate.

Signed	(L.S.)	JULES CAMBON.
Signed	(L.S.)	KIDERLEN.

177

TREATY of Friendship and Alliance between Bulgaria and Serbia. Signed in Sofia, 29th February, 1912.

His Majesty Ferdinand I, Tsar of the Bulgarians, and His Majesty Peter I, King of Serbia, being firmly convinced of the unity of interests and the identity of fate of their States and of the two kindred nations, the Bulgarian and the Serbian, and determined to defend those interests with united force and to work for their general advancement, have agreed upon the following:

Article 1.—The kingdom of Bulgaria and the kingdom of Serbia guarantee to each other their national independence and the integrity of their national territories, binding themselves absolutely and without reservation to succour each other with their entire forces, in the event of one of them being attacked by one or more States.

Article 2.—The two contracting parties also undertake to come to each other's assistance with all their forces in the event of any Great Power attempting to annex, occupy, or even temporarily to invade with its armies any part of the Balkan territories which are today under Turkish rule, if one of the parties should consider this as contrary to its vital interests and a *casus belli*.

Article 3.—The two contracting parties bind themselves not to conclude peace except jointly and after a preliminary understanding.

Article 4.—For the complete and most appropriate application of this treaty, a military convention will be concluded which will provide minutely for everything that may have to be undertaken by either side in the event of a war, or that appertains to the military organisation, disposition, or mobilisation of the armies and the relations between the higher commands which must be settled in time of peace, as a preparation for the war and its successful prosecution. The military convention will form an integral part of the present treaty. Its formulation must being at the latest fifteen days after the signature of the present treaty, and the convention must be ready within a maximum period of two months.

Article 5.—This treaty and the military convention will remain in force from the day of their signature to December 31, 1920 (old style), inclusive. They can be prolonged after that date through an additional understanding, explicitly ratified by the two parties. If, on the day when the treaty and convention expire, the contracting parties should be engaged in war, or should not yet have wound up the situation arising from a war, the treaty and convention will retain their force until the conclusion of peace, or until the situation resulting from a war has been definitely settled.

Article 6.—The treaty will be signed in two identical copies, both of them in Bulgarian and Serbian. They will be signed by the two Rulers and their Ministers of Foreign Affairs. The military convention, also in two copies, both of them in Bulgarian and Serbian, will be signed by the Rulers, the respective Ministers of Foreign Affairs, and by special military plenipotentiaries.

Article 7.—The treaty and the convention may be published, or communicated to other States, only after a preliminary agreement between the two contracting parties, and even then only jointly and simultaneously by the two sides.

In the same way, a third party may be admitted to join the alliance after a preliminary understanding between the two parties.

Made in Sofia, on February 29, 1912 (old style).

Iv. Ev. Gueshoff

I. Milovanovitch

Secret Annex to Treaty of Friendship and Alliance between the Kingdom of Bulgaria and the Kingdom of Serbia

Article 1.—In the event of internal troubles arising in Turkey which might endanger the State or the national interests of the contracting parties, or of either of them; or in the event of internal or external difficulties of Turkey raising the question of the maintenance of the status quo in the Balkan Peninsula, that contracting party which first arrives at the conclusion that in consequence of all this military action has become indispensable must make a reasoned proposal to the other party, which is bound immediately to enter into an exchange of views and, in the event of disagreement, must give to the proposing party a reasoned reply.

Should an agreement favourable to action be reached, it will be communicated to Russia, and if the latter Power is not opposed to it, military operations will begin as previously arranged, the parties being guided in everything by the sentiment of solidarity and community of their interests. In the opposite case, when no agreement has been reached, the parties will appeal to the opinion of Russia, which opinion, if and in so far as Russia pronounces herself, will be binding on both parties.

If, Russia declining to state an opinion and the parties still failing to agree, the party in favour of action should on its own responsibility open war on Turkey, the other contracting party is bound to observe towards its ally a friendly neutrality, ordering at once a mobilisation in the limits fixed by the military convention, and coming to its assistance in the event of any third party taking the side of Turkey.

Article 2.—All territorial gains acquired by combined action within the scope of articles 1 and 2 of the treaty, and of article 1 of this secret annex, shall constitute common property (condominium) of the two allies, and their repartition will take place immediately or, at the latest, within a period of three months after the restoration of peace, the following principles being observed:

Serbia recognises the right of Bulgaria to the territory east of the Rhodope Mountains and the River Strouma; while Bulgaria recognises a similar right of Serbia to the territory north and west of Shar Mountain.

As regards the territory lying between Shar Mountain and the Rhodope Mountains, the Archipelago and the Lake of Ochrida, if the two parties should become convinced that the organisation of this territory into an autonomous province is impossible, in view of the common interests of the Bulgarians and Serbian nationalities, or owing to other internal and external causes, in such a case the said territory will be disposed of in accordance with the following declarations: Serbia undertakes to ask for nothing beyond a line, drawn on the accompanying map. . . . Bulgaria undertakes to accept this line, if His Majesty the Russian Emperor, who will be requested to act as supreme arbitrator, pronounces in its favour. It is understood that the two parties bind themselves to accept as a definite frontier the line between the indicated frontiers which His Majesty the Russian Emperor will esteem to correspond best to the rights and the interests of the two parties.

Article 3.—A copy of the treaty and of the secret annex, as also of the military convention, will be jointly communicated to the Russian Government, which will be asked to take note of them, to show itself benevolent towards their aims, and to request His Majesty the Russian Emperor to accept and sanction the parts reserved by the treaty for His Majesty and the Imperial Government.

Article 4.—All disputes concerning the interpretation and the execution of any part of this treaty, of its secret annex, and of the military convention will be submitted to the final decision of Russia, as soon as one of the contracting parties declares that, in its opinion, an agreement by direct negotiations is impossible.

Article 5.—No disposition of the present secret annex shall be made

public, or communicated to another State, without the previous consent
of the two parties and the permission of Russia.

Made in Sofia, on February 29, 1912 (old style).

Iv. Ev. GUESHOFF

M. MILOVANOVITCH

178

MILITARY CONVENTION between the Kingdom of
Bulgaria and the Kingdom of Serbia. Signed at Varna,
29th April, 1912.

IN conformity with the spirit and in virtue of article 3 of the treaty of
friendship and alliance between the King of the Bulgarians and the
King of Serbia, as also in order to ensure the successful prosecution
of the war and the attainment of the objects of the alliance, the two
contracting parties have agreed upon the following conditions which
will have the same force and value as the dispositions of the treaty itself.

ARTICLE 1. The King of the Bulgarians and the King of Serbia undertake, in the eventualities specified by articles 1 and 2 of the treaty of
alliance, and by article 1 of its secret annex, to render each other mutual
help: Bulgaria, with an army not less than 200,000 strong; and Serbia,
with an army not less than 150,000 strong, fit to fight on their frontiers
and to take part in military operations outside their countries.

These figures do not comprise soldiers of a supernumerary character,
the third class of the Serbian reserve troops, or the second class of
Bulgarian reserve troops.

This army must be sent to the frontiers, or beyond the frontiers of
the two countries, in the direction where military operations are expected to take place, in accordance with the causes and objects of the
war, not later than twenty-one days after the declaration of the war,
or after one of the allied Governments shall have announced that a
casus fœderis has arisen. In all events and before the specified period
has elapsed, the two parties will consider it their duty as allies—in so
far as this shall be compatible with the nature of the military operations,
or might have a favourable influence on the issue of the war—to send
their armies to the theatres of war in sections, while the mobilisation
and the concentration are still proceeding, immediately after the seventh
day following the declaration of the war, or the announcement of the
casus fœderis.

ARTICLE 2. If Roumania attacks Bulgaria, Serbia must at once declare
war on her, and send a force at least 100,000 strong to the middle
Danube, or to the Dobrudja theatre of war.

If Bulgaria is attacked by Turkey, Serbia undertakes to invade the Turkish territory, and to send to the Vardar theatre of war a force of at least 100,000 men.

Should Serbia be then at war with another country, separately or jointly with Bulgaria, she will use all her free forces against Roumania or Turkey.

ARTICLE 3. If Austria-Hungary attacks Serbia, Bulgaria must immediately declare war on Austria-Hungary and undertakes to send to Serbia an army at least 200,000 strong which, united to the Serbian army, will act offensively or defensively against Austria-Hungary.

Bulgaria owes Serbia the same assistance if Austria-Hungary sends, on whatever pretext, her troops to the Sandjak of Novi Bazar, with or without the consent of Turkey, Serbia being thereby forced to declare war on her or to order her army into the Sandjak in defence of her interests, thus provoking an armed contest with Austria-Hungary.

If Turkey attacks Serbia, Bulgaria must immediately cross the Turkish frontiers and set aside at least 100,000 men of her army, mobilised in accordance with article 1 of the present convention, sending them to the Vardar theatre of war.

In the event of Roumania attacking Serbia, Bulgaria undertakes to attack the Roumanian forces as soon as they cross the Danube and invade the Serbian territory.

If, in any of the eventualities specified in this article, Bulgaria should find herself, separately or together with Serbia, in a state of war with another country, she binds herself to send all her free forces to the assistance of Serbia.

ARTICLE 4. Should Bulgaria and Serbia declare war on Turkey in accordance with a previous agreement, both parties undertake, in the absence of any special disposition to the contrary, to detach from their armies, mobilised in accordance with article 1 of the present convention at least 100,000 men each and to send them to the Vardar theatre of war.

ARTICLE 5. If one of the contracting parties declares war on a third party without a preliminary understanding with the other party, or without the latter's consent, the non-consenting party is relieved of the liabilities specified in article 1 of the present convention, but must observe throughout the war a friendly neutrality towards its ally, mobilising immediately at least 50,000 men and concentrating them in such a way as to ensure freedom of movement to its ally.

ARTICLE 6. In the event of a joint war, neither party has the right to conclude with the enemy an armistice for more than twenty-four hours in the absence of a preliminary understanding with its ally, or without the latter's consent.

No peace negotiations may be opened, nor a treaty of peace concluded, without the previous consent of both parties, given in writing.

ARTICLE 7. During the war, the armies of each contracting party will be commanded by its own officers, and their operations will be conducted through the same medium.

When army corps belonging to both parties are engaged against one and the same enemy force, the general command will devolve, both armies being equal, on the officer of senior rank, effective command being taken into account.

When one or more armies of one contracting party are placed under the orders of the other party, they will be commanded by their own officers, who, as regards the strategic operations, will follow the orders of the officer commanding the army to which they are attached.

In the event of a joint war against Turkey, the chief command in the Vardar theatre of war will belong to Serbia, if the principal Serbian army is operating in that theatre and is numerically superior to the Bulgarian army, sent to function in that quarter in virtue of article 4 of the present convention. But if the main Serbian army does not operate in that theatre or is numerically weaker than the Bulgarian forces, the chief command will devolve on Bulgaria.

ARTICLE 8. If the armies of the two contracting parties are placed under one command, all the orders and directions regarding the strategic leadership of the general tactical operations will be issued in two languages—Bulgarian and Serbian.

ARTICLE 9. As regards the clothing and the commissariat, housing, medical assistance, transport of sick and wounded, burial of dead, transport of war materials and of other similar articles, the armies of each contracting party will enjoy equal rights and facilities on the territories of the other party, utilising the same methods as the allied armies and conforming themselves to the local laws and regulations. All local authorities are bound to give the allied armies every assistance to that effect.

The payment of supplies will be effected by each side separately on the basis of local prices, preferably in money, and only in exceptional cases by bonds.

The transport of troops and all military materials, provisions and other articles by railway, and the cost of the transport, will be at the charge of the party through whose territories the transport is effected.

ARTICLE 10. The trophies belong to the army which has captured them.

If these trophies have been captured as a result of fighting in which the two armies have participated, the two armies will divide them in proportion with the strength of the operating forces.

ARTICLE 11. In time of war, each contracting party will be represented on the staff of the Headquarters, or of the commanders of armies, by special delegates who will maintain relations between the two armies.

ARTICLE 12. All strategic operations and unforeseen cases, as well as the disputes which may arise, will be settled by mutual agreement between the two Headquarters.

ARTICLE 13. The chiefs of the General Staffs of the allied armies will, immediately after the conclusion of the present convention, agree as to the repartition of the mobilised armies, in accordance with article 1 of the convention, and as to their dispatch to the zones of concentration in the cases hereafter described. They will also determine what roads must be mended or freshly built for the rapid concentration of the armies on the frontiers and for all further operations.

ARTICLE 14. The present convention becomes operative from the day of its signature, and will retain its force as long as the treaty of friendship and alliance, of which it forms an integral part.

> Iv. Ev. GUESHOFF.
> M. MILOVANOVITCH.
> Lieut.-Gen. N. NIKIPHOROFF.

Varna, April 29, 1912.   General R. PUTNIK.

179

TREATY of Defensive Alliance between Bulgaria and Greece. Signed at Sofia, 16/29th, May 1912. Ratifications exchanged, 16/29th, June 1912.

Taking into consideration that the two kingdoms strongly desire the maintenance of peace in the Balkan Peninsula and can, by means of a solid defensive treaty, better secure that end;

Bearing in mind that the peaceable existence of the various nationalities in Turkey, based on a real and genuine political equality and on the respect of all the rights of the Christian nationalities in the Empire, whether they derive from treaties or have been conceded to them in a different way, constitutes an indispensable condition for the consolidation of peace in the East;

Lastly, taking into account that the joint efforts of the two kingdoms in that direction would facilitate and strengthen the good understanding between Greeks and Bulgarians in Turkey, thereby helping their good relations with the Ottoman Empire;

The Government of His Majesty the Tsar of the Bulgarians and that of His Majesty the King of the Hellenes, promising not to impart to their purely defensive agreement any aggressive tendency and determined on concluding with each other a peaceable and mutually protective treaty, on the lines indicated hereafter, have appointed as their plenipotentiaries H. E. Mr. I. E. Gueshoff and H. E. Mr. D. Panas.

Who, after verifying their credentials, agreed upon the following:

ART. 1. If, notwithstanding the sincere wish of the two high contracting parties and efforts of their Governments to avoid all aggression or provocation against Turkey, one of the parties should be attacked by Turkey, either on its territory or through systematic disregard of its rights, based on treaties or on the fundamental principles of international law, the two contracting parties undertake to assist each other with all their armed forces, and not to conclude peace except by joint agreement.

ART. 2. The two high contracting parties promise each other to use their moral influence over their co-nationalists in Turkey so as sincerely to assist the peaceable existence of the nationalities forming the population of the Empire; they also promise to support each other and to act together, both as regards the Turkish Government and towards the Great Powers, in all actions having for object to secure the respect of the privileges deriving from treaties or otherwise conceded to the Greek and Bulgarian nationalities, and to obtain political equality and constitutional guarantees.

ART. 3. The present treaty will remain in force for a period of three years from the date of its signature, and will be tacitly prolonged for another year, unless previously denounced. The denunciation must take place at least six months before the end of the third year from the day of its signature.

ART. 4. The present treaty will be kept secret and may not be communicated to any third State, totally or in part, nor be published, totally or in part, except with the consent of the two contracting parties.

The present treaty will be ratified as soon as possible. The exchange of the ratifications will take place in Sofia (or in Athens).

In proof whereof, the respective plenipotentiaries have signed the present treaty and affixed their seals.

Made in Sofia, in two copies, on May 16, 1912 (old style).

IV. EV. GUESHOFF

D. PANAS.

DECLARATION

The first article does not apply to the case of a war breaking out between Greece and Turkey in consequence of the admission in the Greek Parliament of the Cretan deputies, against the wishes of Turkey.

In that event, Bulgaria is only bound to observe towards Greece a benevolent neutrality. As the settlement of the Eastern crisis, due to the events of 1909, and of the Cretan question harmonises with the general interest, and is even likely to consolidate the international situation favourably to peace, without upsetting the equilibrium in the Balkan Peninsula, Bulgaria (independently of any engagements assumed by the present treaty) promises in no way to embarrass any eventual action of Greece tending to solve this problem.

IV. EV. GUESHOFF
D. PANAS

180

NAVAL CONVENTION BETWEEN FRANCE AND RUSSIA OF 16th JULY, 1912.

Draft of Naval Convention.

ARTICLE 1. The naval forces of France and Russia shall co-operate in every eventuality where the alliance contemplates and stipulates combined action of the land armies.

ARTICLE 2. The co-operation of the naval forces shall be prepared while there is still peace.

To this end the Chiefs of General Staff of the two Navies are authorized from now on to correspond directly, to exchange any information, to study all hypotheses of war, to counsel together on all strategic problems.

ARTICLE 3. The Chiefs of General Staff of the two Navies shall confer in person at least once a year; they will draw up minutes of their conferences.

ARTICLE 4. As to duration, effectiveness, and secrecy, the present Convention is to run parallel to the Military Convention of August 17, 1892, and to the subsequent Agreements.

Paris, July 16, 1912.

Chief of the General Staff of the French Navy, Signed: AUBERT.	Chief of the General Staff of the Imperial Russian Navy, Signed: PRINCE LIEVEN.
Minister of Marine, Signed: M. DELCASSÉ.	Minister of Marine, Signed: J. GRIGOROVITCH.

Convention for the Exchange of Information between the Russian Navy and the French Navy.

Following an exchange of views that occurred during the month of

July, 1912, between Vice Admiral Prince Lieven, Chief of the General Staff of the Imperial Russian Navy, and Vice Admiral Aubert, Chief of the General Staff of the French Navy, the following decisions of principle have been reached between the two conferees:

1. Dating from September 1/14, 1912, the Chief of the General Staff of the Imperial Russian Navy and the Chief of the General Staff of the French Navy shall exchange all information as to their respective navies, and regularly every month, in writing, any information which these two countries may obtain; telegraphic cipher may be used in certain urgent cases;

2. In order to avoid any indiscretion or any disclosure relative to this information, it is indispensable to adopt the following procedure in transmission:

Any request for information about the French Navy of interest to the Russian Navy shall be addressed by the Russian Naval Attaché at Paris to the Chief of the General Staff of the French Navy; and, reciprocally, any request for information about the Russian Navy of interest to the French Navy shall be addressed by the French Naval Attaché at St. Petersburg to the Chief of the General Staff of the Russian Navy.

This procedure will be exclusive of all other. In principle, therefore, a direct request is not to be made to the Naval Attachés for information respecting their own Navies.

Paris, July 16, 1912.

Chief of the General Staff	Chief of the General Staff of the
of the French Navy,	Imperial Russian Navy,
Signed: AUBERT.	Signed: PRINCE LIEVEN.

181

ALLIANCE Between Serbia and Montenegro. Signed at Lucerne, 12th September/6th October, 1912.

POLITICAL CONVENTION

The King of Serbia and the King of Montenegro, deeply convinced that the interests and the destiny of their respective states and of the Serbian people are identical, and determined to defend these interests most decisively with their united forces, have agreed to the following:

ART. I. The Kingdom of Serbia and the Kingdom of Montenegro bind themselves without any reservation to aid each other with their entire strength, should either of them be attacked by one or more states.

ART. II. The Kingdom of Serbia and the Kingdom of Montenegro pledge to aid each other with their entire strength should Austria-Hungary attempt to annex, occupy or even temporarily hold with its army a part of European Turkey, and should one of the contracting parties regard this as contrary to its vital interests.

ART. III. Should one of the contracting parties regard the situation in Turkey and general conditions in Europe as favourable, to initiate action for the liberation of Serbs under the Turkish yoke, and should it turn to the other party with a proposal in this regard, the other party must immediately enter into negotiations thereon.

ART. IV. Inasmuch as the governments of the Kingdom of Serbia and the Kingdom of Montenegro regard the present situation in Turkey and general conditions in Europe as very favourable for action aimed at the liberation of Serbs under the Turkish yoke, they have agreed that war should be declared upon Turkey at the latest by October 1 of the current year. If, however, for special reasons, one party were to find this impossible within the stated time limit, it is bound to give ample notice to the other party as to the date to which it proposes to defer action. There can be only one postponement.

ART. V. The Allies must not negotiate with the enemy for any special advantage, nor conclude an armistice or peace without mutual agreement.

ART. VI. The boundaries between the allied Serbian Kingdoms must be regulated by a joint commission.

If the commission cannot reach agreement, it will be left to the King of Bulgaria and the King of Greece to resolve the issue of our common frontiers.

Luzern, September 1912.

For Serbia
General Staff Infantry Colonel:
PETAR PEŠIĆ

For Montenegro
Minister, JOVAN PLAMENAC
Brigadier, JOVO BEĆIR

MILITARY CONVENTION

ART. I. In case of war with Austria-Hungary the manner of warfare on the part of Montenegro and Serbia will be that of strategic defensive, not excluding tactical offensive in certain directions and at appropriate moments.

ART. II. In a war with Turkey the character of warfare pursued by the armies of both Kingdoms will be that of strategic offensive.

ART. III. In this latter case the Montenegrin army will operate with its main force in the operational direction of Skadar, Northern Albania, Debar, Kičevo, Bitolj. Secondary Montenegrin forces will operate in the Sanjak of Novipazar.

ART. IV. In this event the Serbian army will move with its main force

in the operational direction of the Vardar Valley, with Skoplje and the
Veles-Štip line as its principal and primary objective. The next
operational objective will be determined by the situation on the battlefield. Secondary Serbian forces will operate in the operational zone
Sanjak of Novipazar-Poreč-Vardar.

ART. V. In its main movements the Montenegrin army will seek to out-
manœuvre the Turkish army through action in its rear in order to cut its
communications with Salonika and the sea, and so that the Montenegrin
army will constitute the right wing of the Serbian army.

ART. VI. At the beginning of operations, the supreme commands
of both armies will be independent in their performance. Following
the first successful operations and the attainment of joint objectives,
both supreme commands must come to agreement on the subsequent
course of operations, in the interests of unity of action and solidarity of
operations.

ART. VII. Both armies must undertake all necessary measures in
peace to insure the most effective organization of military forces, and
must facilitate, as speedily as possible, mobilization and concentration.

ART. VIII. The operational forces of both Kingdoms must be fully
prepared to operate abroad, and not only in defense of the state.

ART. IX. The relationship of the main army force to secondary forces
will be determined by the war plan of the respective armies, but no less
than three-fourths of all the operational forces must be directed into the
main battle-zone.

ART. X. This Convention becomes effective on the day when it is
signed by the Royal governments, will last three years and can be
extended by agreement. It can be denounced half a year in advance.

ART. XI. This agreement is to remain secret in its particulars, and
can be communicated only to allies.

Luzern, September 1912.

For Serbia   For Montenegro
General Staff Infantry Colonel: Minister, JOVAN PLAMENAC
PETAR PEŠIĆ   Brigadier, JOVO BEĆIR

182

MILITARY CONVENTION BETWEEN BULGARIA AND GREECE.

His Majesty the Tzar of the Bulgarians and His Majesty the King of
the Hellenes, desirous to complete by a military convention the treaty of
defensive alliance, concluded in Sofia on May 16, 1912, between the

kingdom of Bulgaria and the kingdom of Greece, have appointed as their plenipotentiaries for that purpose:

H.M. the Tzar of the Bulgarians—H.E. Monsieur Iv. Ev. Gueshoff, etc., etc.;

H.M. the King of the Hellenes—H.E. Monsieur D. Panas, etc., etc.;

Who, after having examined each other's credentials and found them to be in good and regular form, agreed upon the following:

ARTICLE 1. If, in conformity with the engagements assumed by the treaty of defensive alliance, concluded in Sofia on May 16, 1912, between Bulgaria and Greece, this latter country should intervene by arms against Turkey in the event of a Turco-Bulgarian war, or should Bulgaria intervene against Turkey in the event of a Greco-Turkish war, the two parties, Bulgaria and Greece, undertake to cooperate with each other, viz.: Greece, with an army at least 120,000 strong; and Bulgaria, with an army at least 300,000 strong. These forces must be ready to start towards the frontiers and to participate in any military operations outside the boundaries of their respective territory.

The said forces must complete their concentration on the frontiers and be ready to cross them at the latest on the twelfth day after the mobilisation order, or after one of the contracting parties shall have announced that a *casus fœderis* has arisen.

ARTICLE 2. In the event of Greece being attacked by Turkey, Bulgaria undertakes to declare war on the latter State, and to attack it with all her forces, consisting of at least 300,000 men, conforming her movements with the plan previously elaborated by the Bulgarian General Staff.

If Bulgaria is attacked by Turkey, Greece binds herself to declare war on the latter State, and to attack it with all her forces, consisting of at least 120,000 men, conforming her operations to the plan previously elaborated by the Greek General Staff. The chief aim of the Greek fleet will be to secure naval supremacy over the Ægean sea, thus interrupting all communications by that route between Asia Minor and European Turkey.

In the eventualities specified by the previous two articles, Bulgaria undertakes to assume with an important part of her army offensive operations against the Turkish forces concentrated in the vilayets of Kossovo, Monastir, and Salonica. If Serbia should take part in the war, in accordance with her agreement with Bulgaria, the latter will be allowed to use her forces in Thrace; but in that case she guarantees to Greece by this convention that a Serbian army of at least 120,000 men will act on the offensive against the Turkish forces concentrated in the said vilayets.

ARTICLE 3. If Bulgaria and Greece should declare war on Turkey, in accordance with a special agreement, they undertake to place in the field the number of men mentioned in article 1 of the present convention, unless it be otherwise stipulated.

The dispositions of the last two paragraphs of article 2 are in such a case obligatory.

ARTICLE 4. If one of the contracting parties declares war on a State other than Turkey without a previous understanding with the other party and without its consent, the non-consenting party is relieved of the obligations entailed by article 1, but must observe all through the war a friendly neutrality towards its ally.

ARTICLE 5. In the event of a joint war, neither party will have the right of concluding an armistice for more than twenty-four hours without the consent and preliminary agreement of the allied State.

Similarly, the consent of the two parties, specially given in writing, is indispensable for either party to open peace negotiations or to conclude a treaty of peace.

ARTICLE 6. If, after Bulgaria and Greece have mobilised or commenced a joint war, the latter country should find itself obliged to settle the Cretan question in accordance with the wishes of the inhabitants of Crete and, in consequence of that action, is attacked by Turkey, Bulgaria undertakes to assist Greece in accordance with article 1 of the present convention.

ARTICLE 7. The Chiefs of the Bulgarian and Greek Staffs undertake, in the event of a war, to communicate to each other their plans of operations, as opportunity may offer. They also undertake every year to inform each other of the alterations in those plans, rendered necessary by new circumstances.

ARTICLE 8. The present convention will become binding on the two parties immediately after its signature, and will retain its force as long as the treaty of defensive alliance, signed on May 16, 1912, of which it forms an integral part.

Made in Sofia, in two copies, on September 22, 1912 (old style).

IV. EV. GUESHOFF.
GENERAL FITCHEFF.
D. PANAS.
CAPTAIN G. G. METAXAS.

183

EXCHANGE OF NOTES BETWEEN FRANCE AND ITALY RESPECTING LIBYA AND MOROCCO. PARIS, 28th OCTOBER, 1912.

The Government of the French Republic [Royal Government of Italy] and the Royal Government of Italy [Government of the French Republic], desirous of executing in the most friendly spirit their agreements of 1902, confirm their mutual intention of reciprocally not putting any obstacle in the way of the realization of all measures they shall deem it opportune to enact, France in Morocco and Italy in Libya [Italy in Libya and France in Morocco].

They agree likewise that the most-favoured-nation treatment shall be reciprocally assured to France in Libya and Italy in Morocco [Italy in Morocco and to France in Libya]: said treatment to be applied in the largest sense to the nationals, the products, the establishments, and the enterprises of both states, without exception.

(Signed) POINCARÉ
TITTONI.

Paris, October 28, 1912.

184

FIFTH TREATY of Triple Alliance between Austria-Hungary, the German Empire, and Italy. Vienna, 5th December 1912. Ratifications exchanged, 19th December, 1912.

Their Majesties the Emperor of Austria, King of Bohemia, etc., and Apostolic King of Hungary, the Emperor of Germany, King of Prussia, and the King of Italy, firmly resolved to assure to Their States the continuation of the benefits which the maintenance of the Triple Alliance guarantees to them, from the political point of view as well as from the monarchical and social point of view, and wishing with this object to prolong the duration of this Alliance, concluded on May 20, 1882, renewed a first time by the Treaties of February 20, 1887, a second time by the Treaty of May 6, 1891, and a third time by the Treaty of June 28, 1902, have, for this purpose, appointed as Their Plenipotentiaries, to wit:

His Majesty the Emperor of Austria, King of Bohemia, etc., and Apostolic King of Hungary: Count Leopold Berchtold von und zu Ungarschitz, His Minister of the Imperial and Royal Household and of Foreign Affairs, President of the Common Council of Ministers; His Majesty the Emperor of Germany, King of Prussia: the Sieur Heinrich von Tschirschky und Bögendorff, His Ambassador Extraordinary and Plenipotentiary to His Majesty the Emperor of Austria, King of Bohemia, etc., and Apostolic King of Hungary; and His Majesty the King of Italy: Duke Giuseppe d'Avarna, His Ambassador Extraordinary and Plenipotentiary to His Majesty the Emperor of Austria, King of Bohemia, etc., and Apostolic King of Hungary, who, after exchange of their full powers, found in good and due form, have agreed upon the following Articles:

ARTICLE I. The High Contracting Parties mutually promise peace and friendship, and will enter into no alliance or engagement directed against any one of their States.

They engage to proceed to an exchange of ideas on political and economic questions of a general nature which may arise, and they further promise one another mutual support within the limits of their own interests.

ARTICLE II. In case Italy, without direct provocation on her part, should be attacked by France for any reason whatsoever, the two other Contracting Parties shall be bound to lend help and assistance with all their forces to the Party attacked.

This same obligation shall devolve upon Italy in case of any aggression without direct provocation by France against Germany.

ARTICLE III. If one, or two, of the High Contracting Parties, without direct provocation on their part, should chance to be attacked and to be engaged in a war with two or more Great Powers nonsignatory to the present Treaty, the *casus foederis* will arise simultaneously for all the High Contracting Parties.

ARTICLE IV. In case a Great Power nonsignatory to the present Treaty should threaten the security of the states of one of the High Contracting Parties, and the threatened Party should find itself forced on that account to make war against it, the two others bind themselves to observe towards their Ally a benevolent neutrality. Each of them reserves to itself, in this case, the right to take part in the war, if it should see fit, to make common cause with its Ally.

ARTICLE V. If the peace of one of the High Contracting Parties should chance to be threatened under the circumstances foreseen by the preceding Articles, the High Contracting Parties shall take counsel together in ample time as to the military measures to be taken with a view to eventual coöperation.

They engage, henceforth, in all cases of common participation in a war, to conclude neither armistice, nor peace, nor treaty, except by common agreement among themselves.

ARTICLE VI. Germany and Italy, having in mind only the maintenance, so far as possible, of the territorial status quo in the Orient, engage to use their influence to forestall on the Ottoman coasts and islands in the Adriatic and the Aegean Seas any territorial modification which might be injurious to one or the other of the Powers signatory to the present Treaty. To this end, they will communicate to one another all information of a nature to enlighten each other mutually concerning their own dispositions, as well as those of other Powers.

ARTICLE VII. Austria-Hungary and Italy, having in mind only the maintenance, so far as possible, of the territorial status quo in the Orient, engage to use their influence to forestall any territorial modification which might be injurious to one or the other of the Powers signatory to the present Treaty. To this end, they shall communicate to one another all information of a nature to enlighten each other mutually concerning their own dispositions, as well as those of other Powers. However, if, in the course of events, the maintenance of the status quo in the regions of the Balkans or of the Ottoman coasts and islands in the Adriatic and in the Aegean Sea should become impossible, and if, whether in consequence of the action of a third Power or otherwise, Austria-Hungary or Italy should find themselves under the necessity of modifying it by a temporary or permanent occupation on their part, this occupation shall take place only after a previous agreement between the two Powers, based upon the principle of a reciprocal compensation for every advantage, territorial or other, which each of them might obtain beyond the present status quo, and giving satisfaction to the interests and well founded claims of the two Parties.

ARTICLE VIII. The stipulations of Articles VI and VII shall apply in no way to the Egyptian question, with regard to which the High Contracting Parties preserve respectively their freedom of action, regard being always paid to the principles upon which the present Treaty rests.

ARTICLE IX. Germany and Italy engage to exert themselves for the maintenance of the territorial status quo in the North African regions on the Mediterranean, to wit, Cyrenaica, Tripolitania, and Tunisia. The Representatives of the two Powers in these regions shall be instructed to put themselves into the closest intimacy of mutual communication and assistance.

If unfortunately, as a result of a mature examination of the situation, Germany and Italy should both recognize that the maintenance of the status quo has become impossible, Germany engages, after a formal and previous agreement, to support Italy in any action in the form of occupation or other taking of guaranty which the latter should undertake in these same regions with a view to an interest of equilibrium and of legitimate compensation.

It is understood that in such an eventuality the two Powers would seek to place themselves likewise in agreement with England.

ARTICLE X. If it were to happen that France should make a move to extend her occupation, or even her protectorate on her sovereignty, under any form whatsoever, in the North African territories, and that in consequence thereof Italy, in order to safeguard her position in the Mediterranean, should feel that she must herself undertake action in the said North African territories, or even have recourse to extreme measures in French territory in Europe, the state of war which would thereby ensue between Italy and France would constitute *ipso facto*, on the demand of Italy, and at the common charge of Germany and Italy, the *casus foederis* foreseen by Articles II and V of the present Treaty, as if such an eventuality were expressly contemplated therein.

ARTICLE XI. If the fortunes of any war undertaken in common against France by the two Powers should lead Italy to seek for territorial guaranties with respect to France for the security of the frontiers of the Kingdom and of her maritime position, as well as with a view to stability and to peace, Germany will present no obstacle thereto, and, if need be, and in a measure compatible with circumstances, will apply herself to facilitating the means of attaining such a purpose.

ARTICLE XII. The High Contracting Parties mutually promise secrecy as to the contents of the present Treaty.

ARTICLE XIII. The Signatory Powers reserve the right of subsequently introducing, in the form of a Protocol and of a common agreement, the modifications of which the utility should be demonstrated by circumstances.

ARTICLE XIV. The present Treaty shall remain in force for the space of six years, dating from the expiration of the Treaty now in force; but if it has not been denounced one year in advance by one or another of the High Contracting Parties, it shall remain in force for the same duration of six more years.

ARTICLE XV. The ratifications of the present Treaty shall be exchanged at Vienna within a period of a fortnight, or sooner if may be.

In witness whereof the respective Plenipotentiaries have signed the present Treaty and have affixed thereto the seal of their arms.

Done at Vienna, in triplicate, the fifth day of the month of December, one thousand nine hundred and twelve.

(L.S.)	BERCHTOLD.
(L.S.)	VON TSCHIRSCHKY.
(L.S.)	AVARNA.

First Final Protocol concerning the mutual granting of commercial advantages, and concerning means of bringing about the accession of Great Britain to the Articles of the Treaty relating to Mediterranean questions. Vienna, December 5, 1912.

PROTOCOL.

At the moment of proceeding to the signing of the Treaty of this day between Austria-Hungary, Germany and Italy, the undersigned Plenipotentiaries of these three Powers, thereto duly authorized, mutually declare themselves as follows:

1. Under reserve of parliamentary approval for the executory stipulations proceeding from the present declaration of principle, the High Contracting Parties promise each other, from this moment, in economic matters (finances, customs, railroads), in addition to most-favoured-nation treatment, all of the facilities and special advantages which would be compatible with the requirements of each of the three States and with their respective engagements with third Powers.

2. The accession of England being already acquired, in principle, to the stipulations of the Treaty of this day which concern the Orient, properly so-called, to wit, the territories of the Ottoman Empire, the High Contracting Parties shall exert themselves at the opportune moment, and to the extent that circumstances may permit it, to bring about an analogous accession with regard to the North African territories of the central and western part of the Mediterranean, including Morocco. This accession might be realized by an acceptance, on the part of England, of the programme established by Articles IX and X of the Treaty of this day.

In witness whereof the three Plenipotentiaries have signed the present Protocol in triplicate.

Done at Vienna, the fifth day of the month of December, one thousand nine hundred and twelve.

BERCHTOLD.

VON TSCHIRSCHKY.

AVARNA.

Second Final Protocol concerning North Africa, Albania, and Novi-Bazar. Vienna, December 5, 1912.

PROTOCOL.

At the moment of proceeding to the signing of the Treaty of this day between Austria-Hungary, Germany, and Italy, the undersigned Plenipotentiaries of these three Powers, thereto duly authorized, mutually declare themselves as follows:

1. It is understood that the territorial status quo in the North African regions on the Mediterranean mentioned in Article IX of the Treaty of June 28, 1902, implies the sovereignty of Italy over Tripolitania and Cyrenaica.

2. It is likewise understood that Article X of the same Treaty has for its basis the existing territorial status quo in the North African regions at the moment of the signing of the Treaty.

3. It is understood that the special arrangements concerning Albania and the Sanjak of Novi-Bazar agreed upon between Austria-Hungary and Italy on December 20, 1900/February 9, 1901, and on November

20/December 15, 1909, are not modified by the renewal of the Treaty of Alliance between Austria-Hungary, Germany, and Italy.

In witness whereof the three Plenipotentiaries have signed the present Protocol in triplicate.

Done at Vienna, the fifth day of the month of December, one thousand nine hundred and twelve.

(L.S.)	BERCHTOLD.
(L.S.)	VON TSCHIRSCHKY.
(L.S.)	AVARNA.

185

TREATY between Austria-Hungary and Roumania renewing the Alliances of 1892, 1896, and 1903. Bucharest, 5th February, 1913. Ratifications exchanged, 30th January/ 12 February, 1913.

His Majesty the Emperor of Austria, King of Bohemia, etc., and Apostolic King of Hungary, and His Majesty the King of Roumania, animated by an equal desire to maintain the general peace, in conformity with the purpose pursued by the Austro-Hungarian-German Alliance, to assure the political order, and to guarantee against all eventualities the perfect friendship which binds Them together, having taken into consideration the stipulations of the Treaty signed to this end on July 25, 1892, between Austria-Hungary and Roumania, a Treaty which by its essentially conservative and defensive nature pursues only the aim of forestalling the dangers which might menace the peace of Their States, and desiring to record once more the understanding established between Their Majesties in prospect of certain eventualities mentioned in the Treaty of July 25, 1892, the duration of which was prolonged until July 25, 1903, by the Protocol signed at Sinaia on September 30, 1896, and which was renewed by the Treaty signed at Bucharest on April 17, 1902, have resolved to renew and to confirm by a new agreement the engagements contained in the aforesaid Treaty.

For this purpose Their said Majesties have named as Their Plenipotentiaries, to wit:

His Majesty the Emperor of Austria, King of Bohemia, etc., and Apostolic King of Hungary: the Sieur Charles Emil Prince von Fürstenberg, His Chamberlain, Envoy Extraordinary and Minister Plenipotentiary to His Majesty the King of Roumania, Chevalier of the Imperial Austrian Orders of Leopold and of the Iron Crown,

Third Class; His Majesty the King of Roumania: the Sieur Titus Majoresco, President of the Council of Ministers, His Minister of Foreign Affairs, Grand Cross of the Order of the Star of Roumania and of the Imperial Austrian Order of Leopold, who, after having communicated to each other their full powers, found in good and due form, have agreed upon the following Articles:

ART. I. Renewed and confirmed by common agreement are the stipulations contained in Articles 1, 2, 3, 4, and 6 of the Treaty signed on July 25, 1892, between Austria-Hungary and Roumania, and the text of which follows below:

ART. 1. The High Contracting Parties promise one another peace and friendship, and will enter into no alliance or engagement directed against any one of their States.

They engage to follow a friendly policy, and to lend one another mutual support within the limits of their interests.

ART. 2. If Roumania, without any provocation on her part, should be attacked, Austria-Hungary is bound to bring her in ample time help and assistance against the aggressor. If Austria-Hungary be attacked under the same circumstances in a portion of her states bordering on Roumania, the *casus foederis* will immediately arise for the latter.

ART. 3. If one of the High Contracting Parties should find itself threatened by an aggression under the abovementioned conditions, the respective Governments shall put themselves in agreement as to the measures to be taken with a view to co-operation of their armies. These military questions, especially those of the unity of operations and of passage through the respective territories, shall be regulated by a military convention.

ART. 4. If, contrary to their desire and hope, the High Contracting Parties are forced into a common war under the circumstances foreseen by the preceding Articles, they engage neither to negotiate nor to conclude peace separately.

ART. 6. The High Contracting Parties mutually promise secrecy as to the contents of the present Treaty.

ART. II. The Articles reproduced above shall remain in force until July 8, 1920. If the present Treaty is not denounced one year before its expiration, or if its revision is not demanded by either of the High Contracting Parties, it shall be regarded as prolonged for a period of six years, and so on from six years to six years in default of denunciation.

ART. III. The present Treaty shall be ratified and the ratifications shall be exchanged within a period of three weeks, or sooner if may be.

In witness whereof the respective Plenipotentiaries have signed it and have affixed thereto the seal of their arms.

Done at Bucharest, the fifth day of the month of February in the year of grace one thousand nine hundred and thirteen.

(L.S.)   PRINCE CHARLES EMILE DE FÜRSTENBERG.
(L.S.)   T. MAÏORESCO.

Treaty between Austria-Hungary, the German Empire, and Roumania providing for the accession of Germany to the Alliance.   Bucharest, February 13/26, 1913.
Ratifications exchanged February 23/March 8, 1913.

His Majesty the Emperor of Austria, King of Bohemia, etc., and Apostolic King of Hungary, and His Majesty the King of Roumania having concluded at Bucharest on February 5 of the current year the following Treaty of friendship and alliance:

[*Articles I-III of the Treaty of February 5, 1913, follow.*]
have invited His Majesty the Emperor of Germany, King of Prussia, to accede to the provisions of the aforesaid Treaty.

Consequently His Majesty the Emperor of Germany, King of Prussia, has furnished with His full powers for this purpose His Representative at Bucharest, the undersigned Sieur Julius von Waldthausen, His Envoy Extraordinary and Minister Plenipotentiary to His Majesty the King of Roumania, to adhere formally to the provisions contained in the abovementioned Treaty. In virtue of this Act of Accession His Majesty the Emperor of Germany, King of Prussia, takes in the name of the German Empire towards Their Majesties the Emperor of Austria, King of Bohemia, etc., and Apostolic King of Hungary, and the King of Roumania, and at the same time Their Majesties the Emperor of Austria, King of Bohemia, etc., and Apostolic King of Hungary, and the King of Roumania by the undersigned, the Sieur Charles Emil Prince von Fürstenberg, His Chamberlain, Envoy Extraordinary and Minister Plenipotentiary to His Majesty the King of Roumania, and the Sieur Titus Majoresco, President of the Council of Ministers, His Minister of Foreign Affairs, duly authorized for this purpose, take towards His Majesty the Emperor of Germany, King of Prussia, the same engagements by which the High Contracting Parties have mutually bound themselves according to the stipulations of the said Treaty inserted above.

The present Act of Accession shall be ratified and the ratifications shall be exchanged within a period of three weeks, or sooner if may be.

In witness whereof the respective Plenipotentiaries have signed it and have affixed thereto the seal of their arms.

Done at Bucharest, the twenty-sixth/thirteenth day of the month of

February of the year of grace one thousand nine hundred and thirteen.

(L.S.)   PRINCE CHARLES EMILE DE FÜRSTENBERG.
(L.S.)   WALDTHAUSEN.
(L.S.)   T. MAÏORESCO.

Treaty between Austria-Hungary and Italy providing for the accession of Italy. Bucharest, March 5, 1913.
Ratifications exchanged March 13/26, 1913.

His Majesty the Emperor of Austria, King of Bohemia, etc., and Apostolic King of Hungary, and His Majesty the King of Roumania, having concluded on February 5 of the current year the following Treaty of friendship and alliance:

[The text of the Treaty as above follows.]

This Treaty having received [on February 13/26, 1913] the accession of His Majesty the Emperor of Germany, King of Prussia, and having been then communicated by the High Contracting Parties above-mentioned to His Majesty the King of Italy with an invitation to accede thereto, His Majesty the King of Italy, approving the purpose for which this Treaty has been concluded, and which is the preservation of the general peace and of the existing order, has authorized the under-signed Sieur Ch. Baron Fasciotti, His Envoy Extraordinary and Minister Plenipotentiary to His Majesty the King of Roumania, to declare in His name that He accedes to the said Treaty within the limits indicated below, so far as concerns the stipulations of Articles 2 and 3 of the Treaty of July 25, 1892, between Austria-Hungary and Roumania, Articles which are reproduced in Article I of the Treaty inserted above, to wit:

If eventualities that could give rise to the *casus foederis* as it is fore-seen in the said Articles 2 and 3 should chance to occur, Their Majesties the Emperor of Austria, King of Bohemia, etc., and Apostolic King of Hungary, the King of Italy, and the King of Roumania assume a mutual engagement to take counsel together in ample time as to common action, the detailed procedure of which shall be regulated by a special convention.

The present Accession shall be in force, dating from July 8, 1914, for the whole duration of the principal Treaty of February 5, 1913, unless it be denounced by one of the High Contracting Parties in the proper time in conformity with the provisions of Article II of the said principal Treaty.

This Act of Accession shall be kept secret, and cannot be revealed without the consent of each of the High Contracting Parties.

His Majesty the Emperor of Austria, King of Bohemia, etc., and Apostolic King of Hungary has for his part authorized the undersigned

Sieur Charles Emil Prince von Fürstenberg, His Chamberlain, Envoy Extraordinary and Minister Plenipotentiary to His Majesty the King of Roumania, to declare in His name that He accepts in the terms above stated, and with the same mutual obligations, the Accession of His Majesty the King of Italy to the Treaty of February 5, 1913.

The present Act of Accession and of acceptance shall be ratified by His Majesty the Emperor of Austria, King of Bohemia, etc., and Apostolic King of Hungary, and by His Majesty the King of Italy, and the ratifications shall be exchanged as soon as possible.

In witness whereof the respective Plenipotentiaries have signed the present Act and have affixed thereto the seal of their arms.

Done at Bucharest, the fifth day of the month of March of the year of grace one thousand nine hundred and thirteen.

(L.S.)   PRINCE CHARLES EMILE DE FÜRSTENBURG.
(L.S.)   FASCIOTTI.

186

PROTOCOL concerning the conclusion of a Treaty of Alliance between Greece and Serbia. Signed, 22nd April/ 5th May, 1913.

His Excellency Mr. Lambros A. Coromilas, Minister for Foreign Affairs of Greece, and His Excellency Mr. Mathias Boschkovitch, Minister of Serbia in Athens, acting on behalf of their governments and in accordance with their instructions, held a conference today and agreed as follows:

1. The Governments of Greece and Serbia bind themselves to conclude and sign a treaty of amity and of defensive alliance within the period of twenty days from the signature of the present instrument.

2. It will be covenanted in that treaty that the two governments will give mutual aid to each other in order that Greece and Serbia may have contiguous boundaries to the west of the Axios (Vardar) river and that the fixing of the new boundaries shall be done in principle on the basis of effective occupation.

The general direction of this boundary shall be as follows:

Starting from the mountain range of Kamena Planina (Kamna) which delimits the upper Schkoumbi to the southwest side of the Ochrida lake, the boundary line will pass round this lake to the south; it will reach the western shore of the Prespa lake at the village Kousko, and passing through the lake it will reach Dolni Dupliani on the eastern shore; from there it will pass eastward near Rahmanli, will follow the line of the water-shed between the Erigon (Tserna) river and the

Moglenica and will reach the Axios (Vardar) river at about three kilometres to the south of Ghevgheli.

The Greco-Bulgarian as well as the Serbo-Bulgarian boundary lines shall be fixed on the basis of the principle of effective possession and the equilibrium between the three states.

The Serbian boundary line to the north of Ghevgheli will follow the Axios (Vardar) river as far as the confluence of the Bregalnitza river, which it will ascend to a point of the old Turkish-Bulgarian boundary.

The Greco-Bulgarian boundary line will run to the south of Kilkitch, to the north of Nigrita, through Orliako, and from there, by the Achinos (Tachinos) lake and the Angitis (Anghista) river, will descend to the sea a little to the east of the harbour of Eleutherai.

All these boundary lines will be fixed in a more detailed manner and will be inserted in the text of the aforesaid treaty of alliance.

3. The Governments of Greece and Serbia bind themselves to act in unison, to afford to each other constant assistance in the negotiations which will be opened in regard to the division of the territories ceded by Turkey, and to mutually support the boundary lines indicated above, between Greece and Serbia, Greece and Bulgaria, Serbia and Bulgaria.

4. Should a dissension arise with Bulgaria in regard to the boundaries above indicated and a friendly settlement become impossible, the Governments of Greece and Serbia reserve to themselves the right to propose jointly to Bulgaria that the dispute be submitted to mediation or arbitration. In case Bulgaria should refuse to accept this mode of peaceful settlement and assume a menacing attitude or attempt to impose her claims by force, the two governments, in order to secure the integrity of their possessions, bind themselves to afford to each other military assistance and not to conclude peace except jointly and together.

5. A military convention shall be concluded with the least possible delay for the purpose of preparing and insuring the necessary defensive measures in case one of the two states, without provocation on its part, should be attacked by a third Power.

6. . . . .

7. The Greek Government binds itself to afford all the facilities and to guarantee for fifty years the entire freedom of the Serbian export and import trade through the port of Salonika and the railway lines from Salonika to Uskup and Monastir.

8. The present instrument shall be kept strictly secret.

Done in duplicate, Athens, this twenty-second day of April in the year one thousand, nine hundred and thirteen.

The Minister of Foreign Affairs	The Minister of
of Greece.	Serbia.
L. A. COROMILAS.	M. BOSCHKOVITCH.

1 8 7

MILITARY CONVENTION between the Kingdom of Greece and the Kingdom of Serbia. Signed, 1st/14th, May 1913.

His Majesty the King of the Hellenes and His Majesty the King of Serbia, desiring to complete the treaty of alliance concluded between the Kingdom of Greece and the Kingdom of Serbia, by a military convention, have appointed for that purpose as their plenipotentiaries:

His Majesty the King of the Hellenes, Captain John Metaxas, of the Corps of Engineers and of the General Staff of the Army; His Majesty the King of Serbia, Colonel Petar Pechitch of the General Staff, and Colonel Douchan Toufegdjitch, of the Infantry, who, after having communicated to each other their full powers found in good and due form, have agreed as follows:

ARTICLE 1. In case of war between Greece and Bulgaria or between Serbia and Bulgaria, or in case of a sudden attack by the Bulgarian army against the Greek or the Serbian army, the two states, namely Greece and Serbia, promise to each other mutual military assistance, Greece with all her land and sea forces, and Serbia with all her land forces.

ARTICLE 2. In the beginning of the hostilities, at whatever moment they begin, Greece is bound to have an army of ninety thousand fighting men concentrated in the region between the Pangaion Mountain, Salonika and Goumenitsa, and Serbia an army of one hundred and fifty thousand fighting men concentrated in the region of Ghevgheli, Veles (Kioprulu), Koumanovo, Pirot. Besides, Greece is at the same time bound to have her fleet in the Ægean Sea ready for action.

ARTICLE 3. The two states are bound to transport to the zone of operations the remainder of their military forces, as soon as these shall become available.

ARTICLE 4. A decrease of the forces mentioned in Article 2, either by demobilization or the transportation of troops elsewhere, is not permitted, unless there is a written agreement to that effect between the General Staffs of the armies of the two allied states.

ARTICLE 5. The military operations against Bulgaria shall be based upon a common plan of operations. This plan of operations shall be drawn up by the respective General Staffs of the two states, or by their delegates. It may subsequently be modified in consequence of a change of the military situation by a common agreement in writing of the two General Staffs.

ARTICLE 6. After the opening of hostilities, whatever the course of the military operations may be and whatever the localities through which, during the military operations, the troops of the one or the other allied states may pass, and whatever the cities, villages or positions which may be occupied by these troops for military necessities, the occupation of the country lying beyond the boundary line between Greece and Serbia on the one hand and Bulgaria on the other, as provided for by the Greco-Serbian Treaty of Alliance, of which the present convention is a complement, is regulated as follows:

The Greek army has the right to occupy the country situated to the south and southeast of the line of Gradec,—the crest line of the Beles mountain,—summit 1800 to the northwest of Karakioi,—altitude 2194 Perelik; the Serbian army, the country lying to the north and northwest of the said line.

If during the military operations one of the two armies shall occupy part of the country, cities, or villages situated in the zone which should be occupied by the other army, it shall evacuate them as soon as the army which, according to the previous paragraph, has the right to their occupation, demands it.

ARTICLE 7. The ultimate object of the military operations of the allied Greek and Serbian armies being the destruction of the military forces of Bulgaria, if one of the two armies can not attain that object in its own theatre of operations, it is bound to accept the assistance of the other army in the same theatre of operations. Still, the army which has attained this object in its own theatre of operations is bound to go to the assistance of the other, independently of whether this assistance was asked for or not, in order that by a joint action of the two allied armies, Bulgaria may be forced to submit to the conditions which shall be laid down by the two allied states and conclude peace.

ARTICLE 8. Neither of the two allied armies can conclude an armistice of a duration of more than twenty-four hours nor can it tacitly suspend hostilities.

An armistice of a duration of more than twenty-four hours can not be concluded except upon a joint agreement in writing of the two allied states; this agreement shall at the same time determine the conditions of the armistice.

ARTICLE 9. The present convention shall be valid as long as the treaty of alliance between Greece and Serbia, of which it forms a complement, remains in force.

Article 2 of the present convention may be modified by a joint agreement in writing of the General Staffs of the two respective states, after the passing of the present crisis and the ordering of demobilization.

ARTICLE 10. The present convention shall come into force from the day of its ratification by their Majesties the King of the Hellenes and the King of Serbia, or by the respective governments of the allied states.

In faith whereof, the plenipotentiaries have signed the present convention.

Done in duplicate, in Salonika, the first day of May in the year 1913.
For Greece:
CAPTAIN J. P. METAXAS.
For Serbia:
COLONEL PETAR PECHITCH.
COLONEL DOUCHAN TOUFEGDJITCH.

188

TREATY of Alliance between the Kingdom of Greece and the Kingdom of Serbia. Signed, 19th May/1st June, 1913; ratifications exchanged at Athens, 8th/21st June, 1913.

HIS Majesty the King of the Hellenes and His Majesty the King of Serbia, considering that it is their duty to look after the security of their people and the tranquillity of their kingdoms; considering furthermore, in their firm desire to preserve a durable peace in the Balkan Peninsula, that the most effective means to attain it is to unite themselves in a close defensive alliance;

Have resolved to conclude an alliance of peace, of friendship, and of mutual protection, promising to each other never to give to their purely defensive agreement an offensive character, and for that purpose they have appointed as their plenipotentiaries:

His Majesty the King of the Hellenes; Mr. John Alexandropoulos, his Minister at Belgrade, Commander of the Royal Order of the Saviour, Grand Commander of the Royal Order of Takovo; His Majesty the King of Serbia; Mr. Mathias Boschkovitch, his Minister at Athens, Grand Commander of the Royal Order of Saint Sava, Commander of the Royal Order of the Saviour, who, after having exchanged their full powers found in good and due form, have today agreed as follows:

ART. 1. The two high contracting parties covenant expressly the mutual guarantee of their possessions and bind themselves, in case, contrary to their hopes, one of the two kingdoms should be attacked without any provocation on its part, to afford to each other assistance with all their armed forces and not to conclude peace subsequently except jointly and together.

ART. 2. At the division of the territories of European Turkey, which will be ceded to the Balkan States after the termination of the present war by the treaty of peace with the Ottoman Empire, the two high contracting parties bind themselves not to come to any separate understanding with Bulgaria, to afford each other constant assistance, and to proceed always together, upholding mutually their territorial claims and the boundary lines hereafter to be indicated.

ART. 3. The two high contracting parties, considering that it is to the vital interest of their kingdoms that no other state should interpose between their respective possessions to the west of the Axios (Vardar) river, declare that they will mutually assist one another in order that Greece and Serbia may have a common boundary line. This boundary line, based on the principle of effective occupation, shall start from the highest summit of the mountain range of Kamna, delimiting the basin of the Upper Schkoumbi, it shall pass round the lake Achris (Ochrida), shall reach the western shore of the Prespa lake at the village Kousko and the eastern shore at Lower Dupliani (Dolni Dupliani), shall run near Rahmanli, shall follow the water-shed between the Erigon (Tserna) river and the Moglenica and shall reach the Axios (Vardar) river at a distance of nearly three kilometers to the south of Ghevgheli, according to the line drawn in detail in Annex I of the present treaty.

ART. 4. The two high contracting parties agree that the Greco-Bulgarian and Serbo-Bulgarian boundary lines shall be established on the principle of actual possession and the equilibrium between the three states, as follows:

The eastern frontier of Serbia from Ghevgheli shall follow the course of the Axios (Vardar) river up to the confluence of Bojimia-Dere, shall ascend that river, and, passing by the altitudes 120, 350, 754, 895, 571, and the rivers Kriva, Lakavitza, Bregalnica and Zletovska shall proceed towards a point of the old Turkish-Bulgarian frontier on the Osogovska Planina, altitude 2225, according to the line drawn in detail in Annex II of the present treaty.

The Greek frontier on the side of Bulgaria shall leave to Greece on the left shore of the Axios (Vardar) the territories occupied by the Greek and Serbian troops opposite Ghevgheli and Davidovo as far as the mountain Beles and the Doïran lake; then, passing to the south of Kilkitch it shall cross the Strymon river north of the Orliako bridge and shall proceed through the Achinos (Tachinos) lake and the Angitis (Anghista) river to the sea, a little to the east of the Gulf of Eleutherai according to the line drawn in detail in Annex III of the present treaty.

ART. 5. Should a dissension arise with Bulgaria in regard to the frontiers as indicated above, and every friendly settlement become impossible, the two high contracting parties reserve to themselves the right to propose, by common agreement, to Bulgaria, that the dispute be submitted to the mediation or arbitration of the sovereigns of the Entente Powers or the chiefs of other states. In case Bulgaria shall refuse to accept this mode of peaceful settlement and assume a menacing attitude against either of the two kingdoms, or attempt to impose her claims by force, the two high contracting parties bind themselves solemnly to afford assistance to each other with all their armed forces and not to conclude peace subsequently except jointly and together.

ART. 6. In order to prepare and to secure the means of military defence, a military convention shall be concluded with the least possible delay upon the signature of the present treaty.

ART. 7. His Majesty the King of the Hellenes covenants that his government shall grant all the necessary facilities and guarantee for a period of fifty years the complete freedom of the export and import trade of Serbia through the port of Salonika and the railway lines from Salonika to Uskup and Monastir. This freedom shall be as broad as possible, provided only it is compatible with the full and entire exercise of the Hellenic sovereignty.

A special convention shall be concluded between the two high contracting parties within one year from this day in order to regulate in detail the carrying out of this article.

ART. 8. The two high contracting parties agree that upon the final settlement of all the questions resulting from the present war, the General Staffs of the two armies shall come to an understanding with the view of regulating in a parallel manner the increase of the military forces of each state.

ART. 9. The two high contracting parties agree furthermore that, upon the final settlement of all the questions resulting from the present war, they will proceed by common agreement to the study of a plan for a customs convention, in order to draw closer the commercial and economic relations of the two countries.

ART. 10. The present treaty shall be put in force after its signature. It can not be denounced before the expiration of ten years. The intention for the cessation of its force shall be notified by one of the two high contracting parties to the other six months in advance, in the absence of which the agreement shall continue to be binding upon the two states until the expiration of one year from the date of the denunication.

ART. 11. The present treaty shall be kept strictly secret. It can not be communicated to another Power either totally or partially, except with the consent of the two high contracting parties.

It shall be ratified as soon as possible. The ratifications shall be exchanged in Athens.

In faith whereof the respective plenipotentiaries have signed this treaty and affixed their seals.

Executed in Salonika, in duplicate, the nineteenth day of May in the year one thousand nine hundred and thirteen.

JOHN ALEXANDROPOULOS.   M. BOSCHKOVITCH.

189

MILITARY CONVENTION between the Kingdom of Greece and the Kingdom of Serbia. Signed, 19th May/1st June, 1913; ratifications exchanged at Athens, 8th/21st June, 1913.

His Majesty the King of the Hellenes and His Majesty the King of Serbia, desiring to complete the treaty of alliance concluded between the Kingdom of Greece and the Kingdom of Serbia, by a military convention, have appointed for that purpose as their plenipotentiaries:

His Majesty the King of the Hellenes, Captain Xenophon Stratigos, of the Corps of Engineers, and of the General Staff of the Army; His Majesty the King of Serbia, Colonel Petar Pechitch, of the General Staff, and Colonel Douchan Toufegdjitch, of the Infantry, who, after having communicated to each other their full powers, found in good and due form, have agreed as follows:

ARTICLE 1. In case of war between one of the allied states and a third Power, arising in the circumstances provided for by the treaty of alliance between Greece and Serbia, or in case of a sudden attack by important masses—at least two divisions—of the Bulgarian army against the Greek or Serbian army, the two states, namely Greece and Serbia, promise to each other mutual military support, Greece with all her land and sea forces, and Serbia with all her land forces.

ARTICLE 2. In the beginning of the hostilities, at whatever moment they begin, Greece is bound to have an army of ninety thousand fighting men concentrated in the region between the Pangaion Mountain, Salonika, and Goumenitsa, and Serbia an army of one hundred and fifty thousand fighting men concentrated in the region of Ghevgheli, Veles (Kioprulu), Koumanovo, Pirot. Besides, Greece is bound to have at the same time her fleet in the Ægean Sea ready for action.

ARTICLE 3. The two states are bound to bring to the zone of operations their remaining military forces, as soon as these shall become available.

ARTICLE 4. A decrease of the forces mentioned in Article 2, either by demobilization or by the transportation of troops elsewhere, is not permitted, except on a written agreement between the General Staffs of the armies of the two allies states.

But if Greece, in the case provided for in Article 1, should, at the same time, be found under the necessity of defending herself against an attack of a Power other than Bulgaria, she shall be bound to go to the assistance of Serbia, attacked by Bulgaria, by a number of troops fixed by a joint agreement at the proper time between the two General Staffs, according to the military situation and having due regard to the security of the territory of the Kingdom of Greece.

Conversely, if Serbia should be in need of defending herself against an attack by a Power other than Bulgaria, she shall be bound to go to the assistance of Greece, attacked by Bulgaria, by a number of troops fixed by common agreement at the proper time between the two General Staffs, according to the military situation, and having due regard to the security of the territory of the Kingdom of Serbia.

ARTICLE 5. In case one of the contracting parties shall declare war against Bulgaria or against another Power, without a previous agreement and the consent of the other contracting party, the latter shall be released from the obligations imposed by Articles 1 and 2 of the present convention. It shall nevertheless maintain a benevolent neutrality towards its ally during the continuation of the war and shall be bound to mobilize immediately in its territory, Greece, at least forty thousand fighting men and Serbia at least fifty thousand fighting men, in such a manner as to protect its neutrality and consequently the liberty of movement of the allied army.

ARTICLE 6. The military operations against Bulgaria shall be based on a common plan of operations. This plan of operations shall be drawn up by the respective General Staffs of the two states or by their delegates. It may be subsequently modified in consequence of a change of the military situation, by a joint agreement in writing of the two General Staffs.

ARTICLE 7. After the opening of the hostilities, whatever the course of the military operations may be and whatever the localities through which, during the military operations, the troops of one or the other of the allied states may pass, and whatever may be the cities, villages or positions occupied by these troops for military necessities, the final occupation of the country lying beyond the boundary line between Greece and Serbia on the one hand and Bulgaria on the other, provided for by the treaty of alliance between Serbia and Greece, of which the present convention forms a complement, is regulated as follows:

Greece has the right to occupy definitely and to annex the country lying to the south and east of the line which, starting from a point on the Vardar immediately to the north of Sehovo, passes between the villages of Bogoroditsa and Mazucovo, afterwards by the crest line between the villages of Selimli and Dautli, it proceeds towards the altitudes 535, 227, runs through the lake proceeding towards the altitude 208, and afterwards towards the altitudes 397, 1494, the crest line of the Beles mountain, summit 1800 M to the northwest of Karakioi up to altitude 2194 (Perelik).

Serbia has the right to occupy definitely and to annex the country lying to the north and the northwest of the said line.

Greece concedes that Serbia shall occupy a zone of territory of a width of ten kilometers, lying on the left shore of the Nostos-Mosta (Karassou), to the north of Xanthi and to the east of Buru-Gölü. Serbia, on the other hand, is bound to allow Greece free passage through this zone and declares that she recognises the influence of Greece in all the territory lying to the east of this zone and recognizes that she has no claim whatever upon it.

If, during the military operations, one of the two armies occupies part of the country, cities or villages, situated in the zone which should be occupied by the other army, it is bound to evacuate them as soon as the army which, according to the previous paragraph, has the right to their occupation, demands it.

ARTICLE 8. The ultimate object of the military operations of the allied Greek and Serbian armies being the destruction of the military forces of Bulgaria, if one of the two armies can not attain that object in its own theatre of operations, it is bound to accept the assistance of the other in the same theatre of operations. Still, the army which has attained this object in its own theatre of operations is bound to go to the assistance of the other, independently of whether this assistance was asked for or not, in order that by a joint action of the two allied armies, Bulgaria may be forced to submit to the conditions which shall be laid down by the two allied states and conclude peace.

ARTICLE 9. Neither of the two allied armies can conclude an armistice of more than twenty-four hours' duration or tacitly suspend hostilities.

An armistice of more than twenty-four hours' duration can not be concluded except upon a joint agreement in writing of the two allied states. This agreement shall at the same time determine the conditions of the armistice.

ARTICLE 10. The allied armies shall mutually enjoy, each on the territory of the other high contracting party, all the rights and privileges granted to the (national) armies of the country by virtue of the laws and ordinances in force—except as to requisitions—in regard to general maintenance, revictualling, sanitary service, transportation of the wounded and sick, burial of the dead, and the transportation of all the material and provisions destined for the use of the troops. To these ends the military and civil authorities of the two contracting parties are bound to render every assistance and service requested by the allied troops.

The payment for the purchases made for the needs of the army of one of the two allied states stationed in the territory of the other, shall be made regularly in cash, at the market price. In exceptional cases payments may be made by vouchers placed at the disposal of the allied army at its request by the proper authorities of the other ally.

The current rate of the Greek and Serbian coin or paper money shall be fixed by a joint agreement of the two allied governments. It goes without saying that in the territories taken from the enemy and occupied by the allied armies, the two contracting parties shall enjoy in regard to the maintenance and the revictualling of their troops the rights conceded by the laws of war.

Each allied army shall enjoy these privileges only in the territory which belongs to its own zone of occupation, as this is indicated in Article 6 of the present convention. The expenses for the transportation of troops, all necessary material in general, war booty, etc., by railways or ships, shall be borne by the contracting state in whose territory such transportations shall be effected.

ARTICLE 11. The war booty shall belong to the allied army which captures it.

In case the booty is captured in a common battle of the allied armies, on the same battlefield, it shall be divided in proportion to the number of fighting men of the two armies who participate in it.

ARTICLE 12. The present convention shall be valid as long as the treaty of alliance between Greece and Serbia, of which it forms a complement, remains in force.

Article 2 of the present convention may be modified by a joint agreement in writing of the General Staffs of the two respective states, after the passing of the present crisis and the ordering of demobilization.

ARTICLE 13. The present convention shall come into force from the day of its ratification by their Majesties the King of the Hellenes and the King of Serbia, or by the respective governments of the allied states.

In faith whereof the plenipotentiaries have signed the present convention.

Done in duplicate, in Salonika, the nineteenth day of May in the year 1913.

For Greece: For Serbia:
X. STRATIGOS.   COLONEL PETAR PECHITCH.
                         COLONEL DOUCHAN TOUFEGDJITCH.

190

TREATY of Peace between Turkey and the Balkan Allies. Signed at London, 30th May, 1913. [Preamble omitted as of no importance.]

ARTICLE 1. Upon the exchange of ratifications of the present treaty there shall be peace and amity between His Imperial Majesty the Sultan of Turkey, on the one hand, and Their Majesties the Allied Sovereigns, on the other hand, as well as between their heirs and successors, their respective states and subjects forever.

ARTICLE 2. His Imperial Majesty the Sultan cedes to Their Majesties, the Allied Sovereigns, all the territories of his Empire on the continent of Europe west of a line drawn from Enos on the Aegean Sea to Midia on the Black Sea, with the exception of Albania.

The exact line of the frontier shall be determined by a commission appointed by the Powers.

ARTICLE 3. His Imperial Majesty the Sultan and Their Majesties the Allied Sovereigns declare that they submit to His Majesty the Emperor of Germany, His Majesty the Emperor of Austria and King of Hungary, the President of the French Republic, His Majesty the King of Great Britain and Ireland and Emperor of India, His Majesty the King of Italy, and His Majesty the Emperor of All the Russias the matter of arranging the delimitation of the frontiers of Albania and all other questions concerning Albania.

ARTICLE 4. His Imperial Majesty the Sultan declares that he cedes to Their Majesties the Allied Sovereigns the Island of Crete and renounces in their favour all rights of sovereignty and all other rights which he possessed over that island.

ARTICLE 5. His Imperial Majesty the Sultan and Their Majesties the Allied Sovereigns declare that they entrust to His Majesty the Emperor of Germany, His Majesty the Emperor of Austria and King of Hungary, the President of the French Republic, His Majesty the King of Great Britain and Ireland and Emperor of India, and His Majesty the Emperor of All the Russias the matter of passing upon the title to all the Ottoman Islands in the Ægean Sea (except the Island of Crete) and to the Peninsula of Mount Athos.

ARTICLE 6. His Imperial Majesty the Sultan and Their Majesties the Allied Sovereigns declare that they refer the matter of settling questions of a financial nature resulting from the war which is ending and from the above-mentioned cessions of territory to the international commission convened at Paris, to which they have sent their representatives.

ARTICLE 7. Questions concerning prisoners of war, questions of jurisdiction, of nationality and of commerce shall be settled by special conventions.

191

NAVAL AGREEMENT prepared between the Naval Section of the Austrian War Ministry, the Admiralty Staff of the German Navy, and the Admiralty Staff of the Italian Navy. Prepared in draft, 23rd June, 1913. Revised, 2nd August, 1913. Came into force, 1st November, 1913.

With the Most Exalted approbation of the Sovereigns of the Triple Alliance, the following Naval Agreement has been concluded between the Naval Section of the Imperial and Royal Austro-Hungarian Ministry of War, the Admiralty Staff of the Imperial German Navy and the Royal Italian Ministry of Marine (Admiralty Staff), in the contingency of a war involving the members of the Triple Alliance in common.

The Agreement concluded in Berlin on December 5, 1900, hereby ceases to be in force.

1. EMPLOYMENT OF THE NAVAL FORCES OF THE TRIPLE ALLIANCE IN WAR.

(a) In the Mediterranean.

The Naval forces of the Triple Alliance which may be in the Mediterranean shall unite for the purpose of gaining naval control of the Mediterranean by defeating the enemy fleets.

The basic outlines of the plan of operations for joint action in the Mediterranean shall be prepared in time of peace by the Admiralty Staffs, and correspondingly by the Naval Section of the Imperial and Royal Ministry of War, of the Triple Alliance Powers, in the form of a Supplementary Agreement, and must receive in principle the approbation of the three Sovereigns. According to the circumstances, details may be changed by the Admiralty Staffs and the Naval Section of the Imperial and Royal Ministry of War, acting in mutual understanding.

(b) Outside the Mediterranean.

Naval units which may be lying in the same foreign port or within reach of one another shall attempt to join forces, provided they have not received other orders, with a view to co-operating in the interests of the Triple Alliance.

In case it may be assumed from the general political situation that war will probably break out between the Triple Alliance and the Triple Entente, the commanders of such vessels of the Triple Alliance Powers as may find themselves in foreign waters in the same region shall be informed by their superior authorities, acting in accordance with a mutual understanding between the Admiralty Staffs and the Naval Section of the Imperial and Royal Ministry of War, of the existence of a Naval Agreement. In this case it shall be the duty of the respective commanders of vessels to come to a reciprocal understanding regarding the measures to be taken on the outbreak of hostilities, keeping before them the special instructions which they shall have received from their superior authorities.

2. THE SUPREME COMMAND

(*a*) The Supreme Command of the Naval Forces of the Triple Alliance in the Mediterranean may be intrusted to an Austro-Hungarian or to an Italian Flag-Officer, whose nomination shall have been decided on in time of peace by reciprocal agreement of the States of the Triple Alliance.

If, during the course of the joint operations, the Commander-in Chief shall become incapacitated for service or for other reasons shall have to be temporarily replaced, it shall be the duty of the officer next to him in rank, or, in the case of two officers of equal dignity, of the command of the larger force, to assume the Supreme Commander until the Commander-in-Chief resumes his duties, or until the appointment of a new joint Commander-in-Chief in accordance with the preceding paragraph.

(*b*) As regards the ships and commanders indicated under Section 1 (*b*), the Supreme Command of joint operations shall be determined by rank. In the case of two officers of equal dignity, the Supreme Command shall fall to the commander of the larger force.

3. COMMUNICATION BETWEEN THE ALLIES.

(*a*) *Preparation of Operations and Exchange of Intelligence.*

As often as it shall seem advantageous for the preparation of the operations of the United Fleet, the abovementioned authorities shall get in touch with one another, either directly or through specially assigned officers.

In the same way, when the occasion arises, there shall be an exchange of such news as has been obtained concerning the naval forces of the probable enemy, as well as information bearing on the development of their own fleets.

(*b*) *Reciprocal Assignment of Naval Officers to Supreme Headquarters.*

The swift and trustworthy collection of intelligence and transmission of information from Headquarters to Headquarters in matters concerning the Navy shall devolve upon the Naval Officers assigned by each Allied Power to the Supreme Headquarters of the other two Powers. As far as possible, secret communication with their own Supreme Headquarters shall be permitted and facilitated.

For this service the Naval Attachés are indicated, as they appear to be specially suited thereto through their personal relations with the Navies of their Allies.

The Naval Attachés shall be informed of the existence of a secret Naval Agreement, and, should the occasion arise, they may be acquainted with those provisions of the Agreement which, by reason of new circumstances, may undergo an alteration by reciprocal agreement between the Admiralty Staffs and the Naval Section of the Imperial and Royal Ministry of War.

(c) Assignment of Naval Officers to the Staff of the Commander-in-Chief in the Mediterranean.

In time of peace there shall be assigned to the Staff of the Commander-in-Chief in the Mediterranean: a Chief of Staff with the rank of Captain of a Ship of the Line by Austria-Hungary and Italy respectively, and an officer of the Admiralty Staff with the necessary staff by Austria-Hungary, Germany, and Italy respectively.

4. MEANS OF COMMUNICATION.

For the transmission of orders and the exchange of intelligence between the vessels (signal stations) of the Allied Navies, the joint Signal Book (Triple Code) shall be employed. This also contains provisions concerning secret signals of recognition and communication by cipher.

The joint Signal Book is to be regarded as highly confidential.

5. RECIPROCAL CONTRIBUTION OF MERCHANT VESSELS FOR PURPOSES OF WAR.

(a) Merchant vessels may, in case of war, be placed at the disposal of an Allied Power. The abovementioned authorities shall reach an agreement in time of peace concerning the rules for requisitioning merchant vessels of the Allied States. They shall also endeavour to facilitate as far as possible the availability of the vessels for special purposes.

(b) If in time of peace a Navy shall make preparations for war involving the use of particular merchant vessels of the Allied States, plans and descriptions of these vessels shall be placed at its disposal for temporary use through the agency of the above-mentioned authorities.

6. RECIPROCAL USE OF HARBOURS.

In the abovementioned event of war, the harbours of one of the Allied Powers may also be used by the naval forces and merchant vessels of the other Allied Powers in the same manner as by its own vessels.

Vienna, June 23, 1913.

Signed in draft:

KÖHLER M.P.   CICOLI M.P.   CONZ M.P.

For the true copy:

A. SUCHOMEL.

SUPPLEMENTARY AGREEMENT FOR THE MEDITERRANEAN.

(*Section 1 (a), Paragraph 2 of the Naval Agreement.*)

1. *Supreme Command.* In accordance with Section 2 (*a*) of the Naval Agreement, the Supreme Command of the Naval forces of the Triple Alliance in the Mediterranean shall be conferred on the Imperial and Royal Austro-Hungarian Admiral Anton Haus.

2. *Composition of the Staff of the Commander-in-Chief.* The Staff of the Commander-in-Chief shall be composed, in accordance with Section 3 (*c*) of the Naval Agreement, as follows:

1 Austro-Hungarian Chief of Staff with rank of Captain of a Ship of the Line, 1 Italian Chief of Staff with rank of Captain of a Ship of the Line, and 1 Officer each of the Admiralty Staffs of the Austro-Hungarian, the German, and the Italian Navies.

The two Chiefs of Staff and the German Officer of the Admiralty Staff are directly subordinate to the Commander-in-Chief.

Signal, wireless, and office personnel shall be assigned as assistants when requisite.

It is desirable that the Commander-in-Chief establish personal relations with the officers of his Staff in time of peace.

3. *War-Time Distribution of the Allied Forces.* The following shall be accepted as the principles for distribution in time of war:

(*a*) The various subordinate units shall be constituted from ships of the same nationality.

(*b*) A squadron shall, so far as possible, contain not more than eight battleships.

The war-time distribution is appended to the Supplementary Agreement as Annex I. The Commander-in-Chief shall be responsible for keeping it constantly up to date.

4. *Union of the Allied Naval Forces.* The Austro-Hungarian and the Italian fleets shall assemble as soon as possible in the neighbourhood of Messina and complete their supplies. The Italian fleet shall then proceed to its anchoring place between Milazzo and Messina, the Austro-Hungarian fleet to the harbour of Augusta. If need be, Italy shall retain a division for special duty in the north of the Tyrrhenian Sea and despatch a part of her torpedo flotillas mentioned in Annex I, heading A, together with mine layers, to Cagliari and Trapani. The Commander-in-Chief shall be notified of this in due season.

The German vessels shall endeavour to unit at Gaeta (or in the event of unfavourable conditions at sea, at Naples) in order to complete their supplies. Should special circumstances render it impossible to reach Gaeta (Naples), the German naval forces also shall join the Commander-in-Chief in the neighbourhood of Messina.

On the occasion of their first meeting all ships and torpedo boats must with particular care observe the provisions laid down in the Triple Code for secret signals of recognition.

Torpedo boats proceeding alone and groups of torpedo boats must as a fundamental principle avoid approaching vessels and anchoring places of the Allied Fleets after nightfall, as every torpedo boat not recognized with complete certainty as friendly will be fired upon.

5. *Scheme of Operations.* The chief objective of the Commander-in-Chief shall be the securing of naval control in the Mediterranean through the swiftest possible defeat of the enemy fleets.

Should a portion of the French fleet lie at Bizerta, the Commander-in-Chief shall attempt to deal separately with the scattered portions of this fleet. For the purpose of holding the portion of the enemy fleet at Bizerta, operations with mine layers and torpedo boats from Trapani and Cagliari are in contemplation; for action against a French fleet possibly proceeding eastward from Toulon, the light units of the local coast defence of the Western Ligurian coast are in contemplation.

The main action is to be carried out so swiftly that the decision shall be reached before the Russian forces in the Black Sea can interfere.

It shall remain with the Commander-in-Chief to decide whether, in addition to the main operations against the enemy fleets, simultaneous secondary actions shall be directed against possible French troop transports from North Africa or against sections of the enemy coasts.

6. *Provisioning of the Fleet and Bases.* Italy makes herself responsible for the preparations in time of peace specified herewith for the bases enumerated in this section, at her own expense. The Royal Italian Navy shall receive compensation for the supplies appropriated by the Austro-Hungarian and German vessels.

(*a*) *Bases for Assembling.* With reference to Section 4 of the Supplementary Agreement, the following places shall be prepared as bases for assembling:

(α) The harbour of Augusta for the Austro-Hungarian,

(β) Gaeta (Naples) for the German, and

(γ) Messina for the Italian Naval forces.

The stocks of supplies to be accumulated at Augusta and Gaeta (Naples) shall, while providing for a necessary reserve, be apportioned in such a manner that the vessels on the occasion of their first meeting may be certain of completing their stores.

After this last fitting out and after the final departure of the Austro-Hungarian Naval forces from Augusta, all stores remaining in the harbour there shall be removed or destroyed, in order to forestall any capture by the enemy.

Should the fitting out of the German vessels at Gaeta (Naples) be no longer possible, they shall complete their fitting out at Messina.

(*b*) *Bases for Further Operations.* With reference to Section 5 of the Supplementary Agreement, the following places shall be selected and prepared as the main bases for further operations:

(α) Maddalena for the Austro-Hungarian and German,

(β) Spezia for the Italian Naval forces,

(γ) Trapani, Cagliari, and the western coast of Liguria for lighter units.

Maddalena shall be supplied with rations for one month for the Austro-Hungarian fleet; a corresponding stock of fuel and machinery supplies shall be kept there permanently.

Annex II contains the list of the total amount of supplies requisite in accordance with Section 6.

7. *Defence of the Adriatic.* For the defence of the Adriatic there shall be employed the naval forces enumerated in Annex I, heading B, to the Supplementary Agreement, as well as the naval forces normally provided for the local defence of the coasts.

The naval forces enumerated in Annex I, heading B, shall assemble as rapidly as possible, as follows:

The Austro-Hungarian and German vessels in the Gulf of Cattaro,

The Italian vessels at Brindisi.

The operations in the Adriatic shall be conducted by the highest ranking officer of the Allied Naval forces, according to instructions from the Commander-in-Chief, who shall be empowered to re-enforce, or to withdraw vessels from, the Naval forces in that region, according to the war situation.

8. *Attacks on French Troop Transports from North Africa.* Since the first French troop transports from North Africa may be expected to proceed northward from the main embarkation centres of Bona-Philippeville, Algiers, Oran-Mostagenem, and Casablanca-Mogador within the first three days of the mobilization, Italy shall immediately establish a patrol off the North African coast with fast auxiliary cruisers. For the further obstruction of the sending forward of troops the operations of light warships from Cagliari (cf. Section 4, Paragraph 1 of the Supplementary Agreement), and secondarily from Maddalena, are in contemplation.

The joint carrying out of this undertaking shall be directed from Cagliari by a commander to be appointed by Italy, who shall be directly subordinate in this service to the Commander-in-Chief. The Commander-in-Chief also shall in case of necessity despatch fast cruisers for the interruption of the troop transports (cf. Section 5, last paragraph, of the Supplementary Agreement).

9. *Cutting off Enemy Commerce in the Mediterranean.* For cutting off enemy commerce in the Mediterranean Auxiliary Cruisers shall first be employed.

Apart from the measures which will probably be first taken in the second phase of the war for the obstruction of enemy commerce, it would appear advantageous to establish a patrol of the Suez Canal and the Dardanelles immediately on the outbreak of hostilities.

The necessary preparations for commerce destroying shall be made in time of peace by the Commander-in-Chief.

The vessels which shall primarily be available as auxiliary cruisers for commerce destroying are enumerated in Annex III to the Supplementary Agreement.

As bases for operations of this nature Taranto, the neighbourhood of Messina, and the Libyan coast (Tripoli, Tobruk) are in contemplation in the Eastern Mediterranean; for the Western Mediterranean, all the bases enumerated in Section 6 of the Supplementary Agreement.

10. *Utilization of Merchant Vessels of the Allied States for Special War Purposes.* The Merchant vessels available for purposes of war shall be divided into:

(*a*) Auxiliary cruisers (auxiliary warships),

(*b*) Vessels for transporting supplies and troops,

(*c*) Hospital ships

The abovementioned authorities shall exchange indications regarding the merchant vessels which may come in question, and shall reach more precise agreements by direct negotiation with regard to the right of utilizing and disposing of them. These indications and agreements shall be appended to the Supplementary Agreements Annex III. The Commander-in-Chief shall be responsible for keeping it constantly up to date.

Such auxiliary warships as are under military command shall be under the orders of the senior commander of warships of their nationality in the Mediterranean.

For the supply ships belonging to the Austro-Hungarian fleet, Messina and Maddalena shall be regarded as the proper bases.

Spezia, Naples, or Taranto, according to the location of the seat of war, shall serve as the main bases for the hospital ships of the Allied Nations.

The German shipowners shall be instructed to bring such of their vessels as may be in the Mediterranean at the outbreak of war to Italian ports: mail boats to Spezia whenever possible, the remaining merchant vessels to Taranto or other Italian harbours exclusive of Genoa.

Vienna, June 23, 1913.

Signed in draft:

KÖHLER M.P.   CICOLI. M.P.   CONZ M.P.

For the true copy:

A. SUCHOMEL.

Annex. I.

DISTRIBUTION IN TIME OF WAR OF THE NAVAL FORCES OF THE TRIPLE ALLIANCE FOR JOINT OPERATIONS.

(Valid for 1914.)

COMMANDER-IN-CHIEF OF THE ALLIED NAVAL FORCES:

The Imperial and Royal Austro-Hungarian Admiral Anton Haus.

A. IN THE MEDITERRANEAN.

I. Italy.

1st Squadron:

1st Division: Dante Alighieri, Giulio Cesare, Leonardo da Vinci.
     Scout Cruiser: Quarto.

2nd Division: Vittorio Emanuele, Regina Elena, Roma, Napoli.
     Scout Cruiser: Nino Bixio.

2nd Squadron:

1st Division: San Giorgio, San Marco, Pisa, Amalfi.
     Scout Cruiser: Marsala.

2nd Division: Garibaldi, Varese, Ferruccio.
     Scout Cruiser: Agordat.

Division for Special Purposes: Benedetto Brin, Regina Margherita, Emanuele Filiberto, Ammiraglio di St. Bon.

Scout Cruiser: Coatit.

Torpedo Flotillas:

16 Torpedo boat destroyers (6 of 1000 tons, 10 of 700 tons, Indomito-Ardente type);

10 Torpedo boat destroyers of 450 tons, Bersagliere type;

24 Topedo boats of 250 tons, Saffo-Cigno type;

30 Torpedo boats of 33 sea miles.

II. Austria-Hungary.

1st Squadron:

1st Division: Viribus Unitis, Tegetthoff, Prinz Eugen.

2nd Division: Erzherzog Franz Ferdinand, Radetzky, Zrinyi.

1st Cruiser Division: St. Georg, Kaiser Karl VI.

2nd Squadron:

3rd Division: Erzherzog Karl, Erzherzog Friedrich, Erzherzog Ferdinand Max.

4th Division: Habsburg, Árpád, Babenberg.

2nd Cruiser Division: Spaun, Helgoland, Saida, Novara.

Torpedo Flotillas:

6 Torpedo boat destroyers of 800 tons, Tátra type;

12 Torpedo boat destroyers of 400 tons, Huszár type;

12 Torpedo boats of 200 tons, Kaiman type.

III. Germany.

Cruiser Division (directly subordinate to the Commander-in-Chief): Goeben, Strassburg, Breslau, Dresden.

B. IN THE ADRIATIC.

I. Italy.

Vettor Pisani, Carlo Alberto, Marco Polo, Dandolo.

Scout Cruisers: Piemonte, Libia.

6 Torpedo boat destroyers and several Torpedo Divisions.

II. Austria-Hungary.

Monarch, Wien, Budapest.

Maria Theresia, Kaiser Franz Joseph I.

Zenta, Aspern, Szigetvár.

12 Torpedo boats of 200 tons, Kaiman type, and several Torpedo Divisions of older units.

III. Germany.

School ships and older cruisers which may be stationed in the Mediterranean.

KÖHLER M.P.   CICOLI M.P.   CONZ M.P.

For the true copy:
A. SUCHOMEL.

192

TREATY of Peace between Bulgaria and Roumania, Greece, Montenegro and Serbia. Signed at Bucharest 28th July-10th August, 1913; ratifications exchanged 30th August, 1913.

Their Majesties the King of Roumania, the King of the Hellenes; the King of Montenegro, and the King of Servia, on the one part, and His Majesty the King of the Bulgarians, on the other part, animated by the desire to bring to an end the state of war at present existing between their respective countries and wishing for the sake of order, to establish peace between their long-suffering peoples, have resolved to conclude a definitive treaty of peace. Their said Majesties have, therefore, appointed as their plenipotentiaries, to wit: (See conlusion of document.)

Who, in accordance with the proposal of the Royal Government of Roumania, have assembled in conference at Bucharest, with full powers, which were found to be in good and due form, and who having happily reached an accord, have agreed upon the following stipulations:

ARTICLE I. Dating from the day on which the ratifications of the present treaty are exchanged there shall be peace and amity between His Majesty the King of Roumania, His Majesty the King of the Bulgarians, His Majesty the King of the Hellenes, His Majesty the King of Montenegro, and His Majesty the King of Servia, as well as between their heirs and successors, their respective states and subjects.

ARTICLE II. The former frontier between the Kingdom of Bulgaria and the Kingdom of Roumania, from the Danube to the Black Sea, is, in conformity with the *procès-verbal* drawn up by the respective military delegates and annexed to Protocol No. 5 of July 22 (August 4), 1913, of the Conference of Bucharest, corrected in the following manner:

The new frontier shall begin at the Danube above Turtukaia and extend to the Black Sea south of Ekrene.

Between these two extreme points the frontier line shall follow the route indicated on the 1/100,000 and 1/200,000 maps of the Roumanian

General Staff, in accordance with the description annexed to the present article.

It is formally understood that within a period of not more than two years, Bulgaria shall dismantle existing fortifications and shall not construct new ones at Rustchuk, at Shumla, in the intervening country, and within a zone of twenty kilometers around Baltchik.

A mixed commission, composed of an equal number of representatives of each of the two high contracting parties, shall be charged, within fifteen days from the signing of the present treaty, with delimiting the new frontier in conformity with the preceding stipulations. This commission shall supervise the division of the lands and funds which up to the present time may have belonged in common to districts, communes or communities separated by the new frontier. In case of disagreement as to the line or as to the method of marking it, the two high contracting parties agree to request a friendly government to appoint an arbitrator, whose decision upon the points at issue shall be considered as final.

ARTICLE III. The frontier between the Kingdom of Bulgaria and the Kingdom of Servia shall follow, conformably to the *procès-verbal* drawn up by the respective military delegates, which is annexed to Protocol No. 9 of July 25 (August 7), 1913, of the Conference of Bucharest; the following line:

The frontier line shall begin at the old frontier, on the summit of Patarica, follow the old Turko-Bulgarian frontier and the dividing line of the waters between the Vardar and the Struma, with the exception of the upper valley of the Strumitza, which shall remain Servian territory; the line shall extend as far as the Belasica Mountain, where it will meet the Bulgaro-Greek frontier. A detailed description of this frontier and the 1/200,000 map of the Austrian General Staff, on which it is shown, are annexed to the present article.

A mixed commission, composed of an equal number of representatives of each of the two high contracting powers, shall be charged, within fifteen days from the signing of the present treaty, with delimiting the new frontier, in conformity with the preceding stipulations.

This commission shall supervise the division of the lands and funds, which up to the present time may have belonged in common to the district, communes or communities separated by the new frontier. In case of disagreement as to the line or as to method of marking it, the two high contracting parties agree to request a friendly government to appoint an arbitrator, whose decision upon the points at issue shall be considered as final.

ARTICLE IV. Matters relating to the old Serbo-Bulgarian frontier shall be settled in accordance with the understanding reached by the two high contracting parties, as set forth in the protocol annexed to the present article.

ARTICLE V. The frontier between the Kingdom of Greece and the Kingdom of Bulgaria shall follow, conformably to the *procès-verbal* drawn up by the respective military delegates and annexed to Protocol No. 9 of July 25 (August 7), 1913 of the Conference of Bucharest, the following line:

The frontier line shall begin at the new Bulgaro-Servian frontier on the crest of Belasica Planina and extend to the mouth of the Mesta on the Aegean Sea.

Between these two extreme points the frontier line shall follow the route indicated on the 1/200,000 map of the Austrian General Staff, in accordance with the description annexed to the present article.

A mixed commission, composed of an equal number of representatives of each of the two high contracting parties, shall be charged, within fifteen days from the signing of the present treaty, with delimiting the frontier in conformity with the preceding stipulations.

This commission shall supervise the division of the lands and funds, which up to the present time may have belonged in common to the districts, communes or communities separated by the new frontier. In case of disagreement as to the line or as to the method of marking it, the two high contracting parties engage to request a friendly government to appoint an arbitrator, whose decision upon the points at issue shall be considered as final.

It is formally understood that Bulgaria renounces from this time forth all claim to the Island of Crete.

ARTICLE VI. The headquarters of the respective armies shall be immediately informed of the signing of the present treaty. The Bulgarian Government engages to begin to reduce its army to a peace footing on the day after such notification. It shall order its troops to their garrisons, whence, with the least possible delay, the various reserves shall be returned to their homes.

If the garrison of any troops is situated in the zone occupied by the army of one of the high contracting parties, such troops shall be ordered to some other point in the old Bulgarian territory and may not return to their regular garrisons until after the evacuation of the above-mentioned occupied Zone.

ARTICLE VII. The evacuation of Bulgarian territory, both old and new, shall begin immediately after the demobilization of the Bulgarian army and shall be completed within a period of not more than fifteen days.

During this period, the zone of demarcation for the Roumanian army of operations shall be determined by a line running as follows:

Sistov - Lovcea - Turski - Isvor - Glozene - Zlatitza - Mirkovo - Araba - Konak - Orchania - Mezdra - Vratza - Berkovitza - Lom - Danube.

ARTICLE VIII. During the occupation of the Bulgarian territories, the various armies shall retain the right of requisition in consideration of cash payment.

Such armies shall have free use of the railroads for the transportation of troops and of provisions of all kinds, without compensation to the local authority.

The sick and wounded shall be under the protection of the said armies.

ARTICLE IX. As soon as possible after the exchange of ratifications of the present treaty, all prisoners of war shall be mutually surrendered.

The governments of the high contracting parties shall each appoint special commissioners to receive the prisoners.

All prisoners in the hands of any of the governments shall be delivered to the commissioner of the government to which they belong or to his duly authorized representative, at the place which shall be determined upon by the interested parties.

The governments of the high contracting parties shall present to each other, respectively, as soon as possible after all the prisoners have been returned, a statement of the direct expenses caused by the care and maintenance of the prisoners from the date of their capture or surrender to the date of their death or return. The sums due by Bulgaria to each one of the other high contracting parties shall be set off against the sums due by each of the other high contracting parties to Bulgaria, and the difference shall be paid to the creditor government in each case as soon as possible after the exchange of the above-mentioned statements of expense.

ARTICLE X. The present treaty shall be ratified and the ratifications thereof shall be exchanged at Bucharest within fifteen days, or sooner if it be possible.

In witness whereof, the respective plenipotentiaries have hereunto affixed their names and seals.

Done at Bucharest the twenty-eighth day of the month of July (tenth day of the month of August) in the year one thousand (nine hundred and thirteen.

(Signed)

For Roumania:	For Bulgaria:
(L.S.) T. MAOIRESCO	(L.S.) D. TONTCHEFF
AL. MARGHILOMAN	GENERAL FITCHEFF
TAKE IONESCO	DR. S. IVANTCHOFF

C. G. Dissesco

General Coanda, Aide-
de-Camp

Colonel C. Christesco

S. Radeff

Lt. Colonel Stancioff

For Greece:

(L.S.) E. K. Veniselos

D. Panas

N. Polits

Captain A. Exadactylos

Captain Pali

For Montenegro:

(L.S.) General Serdar I. Voukotitch

I. Matanovitch

For Servia:

(L.S.) Mik. P. Pachitch

M. G. Ristitch

M. Spalaikovitch

Colonel K. Smilianitch

Lt. Colonel D. Kalafatovitch

193

AGREEMENT between Great Britain and Germany regarding Turkish Petroleum, 19th March, 1914.

Agreements for Fusion of Interests in Turkish Petroleum Concessions of the d'Arcy Group and of the Turkish Petroleum Company

It is agreed that the interests shall be divided as follows:

Fifty per cent to the d'Arcy group,

Twenty-five per cent to the Deutsche Bank,

Twenty-five per cent to the Anglo-Saxon Petroleum Company,
[A Subsidiary of the Royal Dutch and Shell Companies, controlling 60% and 40% of the shares, respectively.]

and that, in order to carry out this division,

1. The shares in the Turkish Petroleum Company now held by the National Bank of Turkey shall be transferred in equal moieties to the Deutsche Bank and the Anglo-Saxon Petroleum Company.

2. The capital of the Turkish Petroleum Company shall be increased to £160,000 by the creation of 80,000 new shares of £1 each of the same class as those now existing.

3. These 80,000 new shares shall be allotted to the d'Arcy group on terms to be agreed upon between the parties

4. The Board of the Company shall consist of eight members, of whom four will be nominated by the d'Arcy group, two by the Deutsche Bank, and two by the Anglo-Saxon Company

5. The capital of the Turkish Petroleum Company shall be employed only in exploring, testing, and proving oil fields, a separate public company or companies being formed to work any field or fields the examination of which has proved satisfactory.

6. Such working company or companies shall issue to the Turkish Petroleum Company fully paid ordinary shares as consideration for the properties to be acquired; such ordinary shares shall carry full control of the working company or companies, which control shall in no circumstances be parted with by the Turkish Petroleum Company.

7. The working capital required by such working company or companies shall be raised by means of preference shares and (or) debentures which shall be offered to the public to such extent as the members of the Turkish Petroleum Company or any one of them shall elect not to subscribe for themselves.

8. The alterations in the memorandum and (or) articles of association of the Turkish Petroleum Company necessary to carry out the above conditions shall be made forthwith.

9. Mr. C. S. Gulbenkian shall be entitled to a beneficiary five per cent interest without voting rights in the Turkish Petroleum Company, this five per cent being contributed equally by the d'Arcy group and the Anglo-Saxon Company out of their respective holdings. The shares representing Mr. Gulbenkian's interest shall be registered in the names of nominees of the d'Arcy group and of the Anglo-Saxon Company, and shall be held by them, but undertakings shall be exchanged between these parties whereby

(1) Mr. Gulbenkian undertakes to pay the calls on the shares, and

(2) The d'Arcy group and the Anglo-Saxon Company undertake that Mr. Gulbenkian shall be [entitled to] all financial benefits of the shares.

(3) If Mr. Gulbenkian shall desire to dispose of this interest, and also in the event of his death, the d'Arcy group and the Anglo-Saxon Company shall have the option of purchasing the interests standing in their names as defined in Article 36 (b) of the articles of association of the Turkish Petroleum Company.

10. The three groups participating in the Turkish Petroleum Company shall give undertakings on their own behalf and on behalf of the companies associated with them not to be interested directly or indirectly in the production or manufacture of crude oil in the Ottoman Empire in Europe and Asia, except in that part which under the administration of the Egyptian Government or of the Sheikh of Koweit, or in the "trans-

ferred territories" on the Turco-Persian frontier, otherwise than through the Turkish Petroleum Company.

> For the Imperial German Government
>   R. VON KÜHLMANN
> For His Britannic Majesty's Government
>   EYRE A. CROWE
> For the National Bank of Turkey
>   H. BABINGTON-SMITH
> For the Anglo-Saxon Petroleum Company, Ltd.
>   H. DETERDING
>   WALTER H. SAMUEL
> For the Deutsche Bank
>   C. BERGMANN
> For the d'Arcy Group
>   C. GREENWAY
>   H. S. BARNES

The Foreign Office (London)
19 March, 1914

194

CONVENTION between Great Britain and Germany concerning the Bagdad Railway. Signed, 15th June, 1914.

Preamble: then the following Articles

Article 1. (a) In recognition of the general importance which the construction of the Bagdad Railway possesses for international trade, His Britannic Majesty's Government binds itself not to adopt or to support any measures which might render more difficult the construction or management of the Bagdad Railway by the Bagdad Railway Company or to prevent the participation of capital in this enterprise.

(b) The Imperial German Government declares that it will use its best endeavours to have elected to the Board of Directors of the Bagdad Railway Company, as representatives of the British shareholders, two English members acceptable to His Britannic Majesty's Government.

Article 2. (a) Whereas the Bagdad Railway Company has entered into an agreement with the Imperial Ottoman Government on the following basis, the Imperial German and His Britannic Majesty's Governments declare, in so far as they are concerned, (their intention) to uphold this agreement and to use their best efforts that the terms thereof may be regularly complied with:

(I) The terminus of the lines of the Bagdad Railway is to be Basra.

The Bagdad Railway Company has renounced the construction of the branch line from Basra (Zobeir) to the Persian Gulf, provided for in Article 1 of the Bagdad Railway Convention of March 5, 1903, and the construction of a port or a terminal on the Persian Gulf in accordance with Article 23 of the aforesaid Convention.

(II) On the lines of the Bagdad Railway Company, as hitherto, no direct or indirect discrimination in transit facilities or freight rates shall be made in the transportation of goods of the same kind between the same places, either on account of ownership or on account of origin or destination of the goods or because of any other consideration.

(III) The Bagdad Railway Company agrees that any changes in the conditions of transportation or in freight rates, as set forth in Article 21 of the Specification (of 1903) always shall be announced two months in advance. The announcement shall be published in the Official Journal of the Imperial Ottoman Government and in the Official Bulletin of the Ottoman Chamber of Commerce in Constantinople.

(IV) Should a branch line be constructed from Basra to the Persian Gulf, appropriate agreements shall be made to facilitate through traffic from and to the railhead of the Bagdad Railway, and full guarantees shall be provided against direct and indirect discriminatory treatment.

(V) The proposed port works in Basra and Bagdad, which were authorized by Article 23 of the Bagdad Railway Convention of March 5, 1903, are to be constructed and administered by a special Ottoman company.

The Port Company shall not collect tolls or duties of any kind or any description from ships or goods, except such as are imposed equally under the same circumstances and in similar cases on all ships and goods, regardless of the nationality of the ships or their owners, or of the owners of the goods, their country of origin or destination, and regardless of the place from which the ships or goods come or wither they are bound. . . .

The rights conferred upon the Port Company shall in no way hinder or interfere with the said Commission in the fulfilment of the tasks conferred upon it by the Anglo-Turkish agreement of July 29, 1913.

(b) The Imperial German Government declares that it will raise no objections to British interests acquiring 40 per cent of the capital of the separate Ottoman Company for the construction and operation of the ports of Basra and Bagdad as mentioned above under (V); or to their being represented on the Board of Directors (*Conseil d'Administration*) of the Port Company in proportion to their participation; or to their sharing in contracts for the construction or maintenance of the port.

Article 3. (a) The Imperial German and His Britannic Majesty's Governments declare that under no circumstances will they support the construction of a branch from Basra (Zobeir) or any other point on the main line of the Bagdad Railway to the Persian Gulf, unless a complete understanding be previously arrived at between the Imperial Ottoman, the Imperial German, and His Britannic Majesty's Governments.

(b) The Imperial German Government declares that it will under no circumstances undertake the construction of a harbour or a railway station on the Persian Gulf or support efforts of any persons or companies directed towards this end, unless a complete agreement be previously arrived at between the Imperial German and His Britannic Majesty's Governments.

(c) His Britannic Majesty's Government declares that under no circumstances will it undertake railway construction on Ottoman territory in direct competition with lines of the Bagdad Railway Company or in contravention of existing rights of this company or support the efforts of any persons or companies directed to this end, unless previously a complete agreement be arrived at between the Imperial German and His Britannic Majesty's Governments. For the provisions of this article the western terminus of the Bagdad Railway lines is considered to be Konia, the eastern terminus, Basra.

Article 4. (a) The Imperial German Government has taken official note of the declaration promulgated by the Imperial Ottoman Government on July 29, 1913, concerning the navigation of the Tigris and Euphrates and declares that it will neither raise objections to the execution of this declaration nor support any action directed against its execution as long as the navigation of these rivers is maintained in accordance with the principal provisions of the declaration.

(b) His Britannic Majesty's Government declares that it will raise no objections if the shareholders of the Bagdad Railway acquire 40 per cent of that part of the capital of the Ottoman River Navigation Company which is to be assigned to Ottoman interests at the first issue (*i.e.*, 27 per cent of the total capital). . . .

Article 5. [Both Powers pledged themselves unreservedly to observe the principle of the economic open door.]

Article 6. The Imperial German and His Britannic Majesty's Governments will together use their good offices with the Imperial Ottoman Government to the end that the Shatt-el-Arab shall be brought into a satisfactory navigable condition and permanently maintained in such condition so that ocean-going ships may always be assured of free and easy access to the port of Basra, and further, that the shipping on the Shatt-el-Arab shall always be open to ocean-going ships, under the same conditions to ships of all nations, regardless of the nationality of the ships or their cargo. . . .

Article 9. Any differences in opinion resulting from this Convention or the Explanatory Note attached thereto are subject to arbitration. If the two governments cannot agree on an arbitrator or a special court of arbitration, the case shall be submitted to the Permanent Court of Arbitration at the Hague.

Article 10. The present Convention and the attached Note shall be ratified and the deeds of ratification shall be exchanged within three months after the date of signature.

In witness whereof the plenipotentiaries on both sides have signed the present Convention and attached their seals.

Made in duplicate in London on the ——————————

Initialled in London, on the 15 day of June, 1914.

L. [ichnowsky]

E. [dward] G. [rey]

(His Britannic Majesty's Government in the Explanatory Note undertook to support a raising of the customs duties of the Ottoman Empire from an *ad valorem* tax of 11% to one of 15%) and to "raise no objection to the assignment to the Bagdad Railway Company of already existing Turkish State revenues, or of revenues from the intended increase in tariff duties, or of the proposed monopolies or taxes on the consumption of alcohol, petroleum, matches, tinder, cigarette-paper, playing cards, and sugar to the extent necessary for the completion of the Railway.")

APPENDIX 1

AGREEMENT between the British and German Governments, respecting Africa and Heligoland. Berlin, 1st July, 1890.

THE Undersigned,—

Sir Edward Baldwin Malet, Her Britannic Majesty's Ambassador Extraordinary and Plenipotentiary;

Sir Henry Percy Anderson, Chief of the African Department of Her Majesty's Foreign Office;

The Chancellor of the German Empire, General von Caprivi;

The Privy Councillor in the Foreign Office, Dr. Krauel,—

Have, after discussion of various questions affecting the Colonial interests of Germany and Great Britain, come to the following Agreement on behalf of their respective Governments:—

East Africa. German Sphere of Influence.

ART. I.—In East Africa the sphere in which the exercise of influence is reserved to Germany is bounded—

German Sphere. To the North. River Umba to Victoria Nyanza.

1. To the north by a line which, commencing on the coast at the north bank of the mouth of the River Umba [or Wanga], runs direct to Lake Jipé; passes thence along the eastern side and round the northern side of the lake, and crosses the River Lumé; after which it passes midway between the territories of Taveita and Chagga, skirts the northern base of the Kilimanjaro range, and thence is drawn direct to the point on the eastern side of Lake Victoria Nyanza which is intersected by the 1st parallel of south latitude; thence, crossing the lake on that parallel, it follows the parallel to the frontier of the Congo Free State, where it terminates.

Mount Mfumbiro.

It is, however, understood that, on the west side of the lake, the sphere does not comprise Mount Mfumbiro; if that mountain shall prove to lie to the south of the selected parallel, the line shall be deflected so as to exclude it, but shall, nevertheless, return so as to terminate at the above-named point.

German Sphere. To the South. Rovuma River to Lakes Nyassa and Tanganyika (Stevenson's Road).

2. To the south by a line which, starting on coast at the northern limit of the Province of Mozambique, follows the course of the River

Rovuma to the point of confluence of the Msinje; thence it runs westward along the parallel of that point till it reaches Lake Nyassa; thence striking northward, it follows the eastern, northern, and western shores of the lake to the northern bank of the mouth of the River Songwe; it ascends that river to the point of its intersection by the 33rd degree of east longitude; thence it follows the river to the point where it approaches most nearly the boundary of the geographical Congo Basin defined in the 1st Article of the Act of Berlin, as marked in the map attached to the 9th Protocol of the Conference.

From that point it strikes direct to the above-named boundary; and follows it to the point of its intersection by the 32nd degree of east longitude; from which point it strikes direct to the point of confluence of the northern and southern branches of the River Kilambo, and thence follows that river till it enters Lake Tanganyika.

Map.   Nyassa-Tanganyika Plateau.

The course of the above boundary is traced in general accordance with a map of the Nyassa-Tanganyika Plateau, officially prepared for the British Government in 1889.

German Sphere.   To the West.   River Kilambo to Congo Free State.

3. To the west by a line which, from the mouth of the River Kilambo to the 1st parallel of south latitude, is conterminous with the Congo Free State.

East Africa.   British Sphere of Influence.

The sphere in which the exercise of influence is reserved to Great Britain is bounded—

British Sphere.   To the South.   River Umba to Congo Free State.

1. To the south by the above-mentioned line running from the mouth of the River Umba (or Wanga) to the point where the 1st parallel of south latitude reaches the Congo Free State.

Mount Mfumbiro.

Mount Mfumbiro is included in the sphere.

British Sphere.   To the North.   River Juba to confines of Egypt
(Uganda, &c.).

2. To the north by a line commencing on the coast at the north bank of the mouth of the River Juba; thence it ascends that bank of the river and is conterminous with the territory reserved to the influence of Italy in Gallaland and Abyssinia, as far as the confines of Egypt.

British Sphere. To the West. Basin of Upper Nile to Congo Free State (Uganda, &c.).

3. To the west by the Congo Free State, and by the western watershed of the basin of the Upper Nile.

Withdrawal by Germany in favour of Great Britain of Protectorate over Witu.

ART. II. In order to render effective the delimitation recorded in the preceding Article, Germany withdraws in favour of Great Britain her Protectorate over Witu.

Recognition by Great Britain of Sultan of Witu's Sovereignty.

Great Britain engages to recognize the sovereignty of the Sultan of Witu over the territory extending from Kipini to the point opposite the Island of Kwyhoo, fixed as the boundary in 1887.

Withdrawal of German Protectorate over adjoining Coast up to Kismayu, to all other Territories North of Tana, and to Islands of Patta and Manda.

Germany also withdraws her Protectorate over the adjoining coast up to Kismayu, as well as her claims to all other territories on the mainland, to the north of the River Tana, and to the Islands of Patta and Manda.

South West Africa. German Sphere of Influence.

ART. III. In South-West Africa the sphere in which the exercise of influence is reserved to Germany is bounded.

Namaqualand. Damaraland, &c.

1. To the south by a line commencing at the mouth of the Orange River, and ascending the north bank of that river to the point of its intersection by the 20th degree of east longitude.

2. To the east by a line commencing at the above-named point, and following the 20th degree of east longitude to the point of its intersection by the 22nd parallel of south latitude, it runs eastward along that parallel to the point of its intersection by the 21st degree of east longitude; thence it follows that degree northward to the point of its intersection by the 18th parallel of south latitude; it runs eastward along that parallel till it reaches the River Chobe; and descends the centre of the main channel of that river to its junction with the Zambesi, where it terminates.

German Access to the Zambesi.

It is understood that under this arrangement Germany shall have free access from her Protectorate to the Zambesi by a strip of territory which shall at no point be less than 20 English miles in width.

South-West Africa.   British Sphere of Influence.   Bechuanaland,
Kalahari, &c.

The sphere in which the exercise of influence is reserved to Great
Britain is bounded to the west and north-west by the above-mentioned
line.

Lake Ngami.

It includes Lake Ngami.

Map.

The course of the above boundary is traced in general accordance
with a map officially prepared for the British Government in 1889.

Walfisch Bay.

The delimitation of the southern boundary of the British territory
of Walfisch Bay is reserved for arbitration, unless it shall be settled
by the consent of the two Powers within two years from the date of the
conclusion of this Agreement. The two Powers agree that, pending
such settlement, the passage of the subjects and transit of goods of
both Powers through the territory now in dispute shall be free; and the
treatment of their subjects in that territory shall be in all respects
equal. No dues shall be levied on goods in transit. Until a settlement
shall be effected the territory shall be considered neutral.

*Line of Boundary between the British Gold Coast Colony and the German
Protectorate of Togo.   Volta Districts.*

ART. IV. In West Africa—

1. The boundary between the German Protectorate of Togo and
the British Gold Coast Colony commences on the coast at the marks
set up after the negotiations between the Commissioners of the two
countries of the 14th and 28th of July, 1886; and proceeds direct
northwards to the 6° 10′ parallel of north latitude; thence it runs
along that parallel westward till it reaches the left bank of the River
Aka; ascends the mid-channel of that river to the 6° 20′ parallel of
north latitude; runs along that parallel westwards to the right bank
of the River Dchawe or Shavoe; follows that bank of the river till
it reaches the parallel corresponding with the point of confluence of
the River Deine with the Volta; it runs along that parallel westward
till it reaches the Volta; from that point it ascends the left bank of
the Volta till it arrives at the neutral zone established by the Agreement of 1888, which commences at the confluence of the River Dakka
with the Volta.

Each Power engages to withdraw immediately after the conclusion of this Agreement all its officials and employés from territory which is assigned to the other Power by the above delimitation.

Gulf of Guinea. Rio del Rey Creek.

2. It having been proved to the satisfaction of the two Powers that no river exists on the Gulf of Guinea corresponding with that marked on maps as the Rio del Rey, to which reference was made in the Agreement of 1885, a provisional line of demarcation is adopted between the German sphere in the Cameroons and the adjoining British sphere, which, starting from the head of the Rio del Rey Creek, goes direct to the point, about 9° 8′ of east longitude, marked "Rapids" in the British Admiralty chart.

Freedom of Goods from Transit Dues between River Benué and Lake Chad.

ART. V. It is agreed that no Treaty or Agreement, made by or on behalf of either Power to the north of the River Benué, shall interfere with the free passage of goods of the other Power, without payment of transit dues, to and from the shores of Lake Chad.

Treaties in Territories between the Benué and Lake Chad.

All Treaties made in territories intervening between the Benué and Lake Chad shall be notified by one Power to the other.

Lines of Demarcation subject to Modification.

ART. VI. All the lines of demarcation traced in Articles I to IV shall be subject to rectification by agreement between the two Powers, in accordance with local requirements.

Boundary Commissioners to be Appointed.

It is specially understood that, as regards the boundaries traced in Article IV, Commissioners shall meet with the least possible delay for the object of such rectification.

Non-interference of either Power in Sphere of Influence of the other.

ART. VII. The two Powers engage that neither will interfere with any sphere of influence assigned to the other by Articles I to IV. One Power will not in the sphere of the other make acquisitions, conclude Treaties, accept sovereign rights or Protectorates, nor hinder the extension of influence of the other.

No Companies or Individuals of either Power to exercise Sovereign Rights in Sphere of Influence of the other.

It is understood that no Companies nor individuals subject to one Power can exercise sovereign rights in a sphere assigned to the other, except with the assent of the latter.

Application of Berlin Act in Spheres of Influence within Limits of Free Trade Zone.

ART. VIII. The two Powers engage to apply in all the portions of their respective spheres, within the limits of the free zone defined by the Act of Berlin of 1885, to which the first five articles of that Act are applicable at the date of the present Agreement;

Freedom of Trade.

The provisions of those articles according to which trade enjoys complete freedom;

Navigation of Lakes, Rivers, &c.

The navigation of the lakes, rivers, and canals, and of the ports on those waters, is free to both flags;

Differential Duties.   Transport or Coasting Trade.

And no differential treatment is permitted as regards transport or coasting trade;

Duties on Goods.

Goods, of whatever origin, are subject to no dues except those, not differential in their incidence, which may be levied to meet expenditure in the interest of trade;

Transit Dues.

No transit dues are permitted;

Trade Monopolies.

And no monolopy or favour in matters of trade can be granted.

Settlements in Free Trade Zone.

The subjects of either Power will be at liberty to settle freely in their respective territories situated within the free trade zone.

Freedom of Goods from Transit Dues, &c.

It is specially understood that, in accordance with these provisions, the passage of goods of both Powers will be free from all hindrances and from all transit dues between Lake Nyassa and the Congo State, between Lakes Nyassa and Tanganyika, on Lake Tanganyika, and between that lake and the northern boundary of the two spheres.

Trading and Mineral Concessions.   Real Property Rights.

ART. IX. Trading and mineral concessions, and rights to real property, held by Companies of individuals, subjects of one Power, shall, if their validity is duly established, be recognized in the sphere of the other Power. It is understood that concessions must be worked in accordance with local laws and regulations.

Protection of Missionaries.

ART. X. In all territories in Africa belonging to, or under the influence of either Power, missionaries of both countries shall have full protection.

Religious Toleration and Freedom.

Religious toleration and freedom for all forms of divine worship and religious teaching are guaranteed.

Cession to be made by Sultan of Zanzibar to Germany of Possessions on the Mainland and of Island of Mafia.

ART. XI. Great Britain engages to use all her influence to facilitate a friendly arrangement, by which the Sultan of Zanzibar shall cede absolutely to Germany his Possessions on the mainland comprised in existing Concessions to the German East African Company, and their Dependencies, as well as the Island of Mafia.

It is understood that His Highness will, at the same time, receive an equitable indemnity for the loss of revenue resulting from such cession.

German Recognition of British Protectorate over remaining Dominions of Sultan of Zanzibar, including Islands of Zanzibar and Pemba, and Witu.

Germany engages to recognize a Protectorate of Great Britain over the remaining dominions of the Sultan of Zanzibar, including the Islands of Zanzibar, and Pemba, as well as over the dominions of the Sultan of Witu.

Withdrawal of German Protectorate up to Kismayu.

And the adjacent territory up to Kismayu from which her Protectorate is withdrawn. It is understood that if the cession of the German Coast has not taken place before the assumption by Great Britain of the Protectorate of Zanzibar, Her Majesty's Government will, in assuming

the Protectorate, accept the obligation to use all their influence with
the Sultan to induce him to make that cession at the earliest possible
period in consideration of an equitable indemnity.

ART. XII. *Cession of Heligoland by Great Britain to Germany*. (See
No. 136).

> EDWARD B. MALET.
> H. PERCY ANDERSON.
> v. CAPRIVI.
> K. KRAUEL.

Berlin, 1st July, 1890.

APPENDIX 2 (A)

GENERAL ACT of the Conference of Berlin, relative to the
Development of Trade and Civilization in Africa; the free
Navigation of the Rivers Congo, Niger, &c.; the Supression
of the Slave Trade by Sea and Land; the occupation of
Territory on the African Coasts, &c. Signed at Berlin,
26th February, 1885.

In the Name of Almighty God.
Preamble.

HER Majesty the Queen of the United Kingdom of Great Britain
and Ireland, Empress of India; His Majesty the German Emperor,
King of Prussia; His Majesty the Emperor of Austria, King of Bohemia,
&c., and Apostolic King of Hungary; His Majesty the King of the
Belgians; His Majesty the King of Denmark; His Majesty the King
of Spain; the President of the United States of America; the President
of the French Republic; His Majesty the King of Italy; His Majesty
the King of the Netherlands, Grand Duke of Luxemburg, &c.; His
Majesty the King of Portugal and the Algarves, &c.; His Majesty the
Emperor of all the Russias; His Majesty the King of Sweden and
Norway, &c.; and His Majesty the Emperor of the Ottomans, wishing,
in a spirit of good and mutual accord, to regulate the conditions most
favourable to the development of trade and civilization in certain
regions of Africa, and to assure to all nations the advantages of free
navigation on the two chief rivers of Africa flowing into the Atlantic
Ocean; being desirous, on the other hand, to obviate the misunderstanding and disputes which might in future arise from new acts of
occupation ("prises de possession") on the coast of Africa; and
concerned, at the same time, as to the means of furthering the moral
and material well-being of the native populations, have resolved, on

the invitation addressed to them by the Imperial Government of Germany, in agreement with the Government of the French Republic, to meet for those purposes in Conference at Berlin, and have appointed as their Plenipotentiaries, to wit:—

Her Majesty the Queen of the United Kingdom of Great Britain and Ireland, Empress of India, Sir Edward Baldwin Malet, her Ambassador Extraordinary and Plenipotentiary at the Court of His Majesty the German Emperor, King of Prussia;

His Majesty the German Emperor, King of Prussia, Otho, Prince von Bismarck, his President of the Prussian Council of Ministers, Chancellor of the Empire; Paul, Count von Hatzfeldt, his Minister of State and Secretary of State for Foreign Affairs; Auguste Busch, his Acting Privy Councillor of Legation and Under-Secretary of State for Foreign Affairs; and Henri von Kusserow, Privy Councillor of Legation in the Department for Foreign Affairs;

His Majesty the Emperor of Austria, King of Bohemia, &c., and Apostolic King of Hungary, Emeric, Count Széchényi de Sarvari Felsö-Vidék, Chamberlain and Acting Privy Councillor, his Ambassador Extraordinary and Plenipotentiary at the Court of His Majesty the German Emperor, King of Prussia;

His Majesty the King of the Belgians, Gabriel Auguste Count van der Straten-Ponthoz Envoy Extraordinary and Minister Plenipotentiary at the Court of His Majesty the German Emperor, King of Prussia; and Auguste Baron Lambermont, Minister of State, Envoy Extraordinary and Minister Plenipotentiary;

His Majesty the King of Denmark, Émile de Vind, Chamberlain, his Envoy Extraordinary and Minister Plenipotentiary at the Court of His Majesty the German Emperor, King of Prussia;

His Majesty the King of Spain, Don Francisco Merry y Colom, Count Benomar, his Envoy Extraordinary and Minister Plenipotentiary at the Court of His Majesty the German Emperor, King of Prussia;

The President of the United States of America, John A. Kasson, Envoy Extraordinary and Minister Plenipotentiary of the United States of America at the Court of His Majesty the German Emperor, King of Prussia, and Henry S. Sandford, ex-Minister;

The President of the French Republic, Alphonse, Baron de Courcel, Ambassador Extraordinary and Plenipotentiary of France at the Court of His Majesty the German Emperor King of Prussia;

His Majesty the King of Italy, Edward, Count de Launay, his Ambassador Extraordinary and Plenipotentiary at the Court of His Majesty the German Emperor, King of Prussia;

His Majesty the King of the Netherlands, Grand Duke of Luxemburg, Frederick Philippe, Jonkheer van der Hoeven his Envoy Extraordinary and Minister Plenipotentiary at the Court of His Majesty the German Emperor, King of Prussia;

His Majesty the King of Portugal and the Algarves, &c., Da Serra Gomes, Marquis de Penafiel, Peer of the Realm, his Envoy Extraordinary and Minister Plenipotentiary at the Court of His Majesty the German Emperor, King of Prussia, and Antoine de Serpa Pimentel, Councillor of State and Peer of the Realm;

His Majesty the Emperor of All the Russias, Pierre, Count Kapnist, Privy Councillor, his Envoy Extraordinary and Minister Plenipotentiary at the Court of His Majesty the King of the Netherlands;

His Majesty the King of Sweden and Norway, &c., Gillis, Baron Bilt, Lieutenant-General, his Envoy Extraordinary and Minister Plenipotentiary at the Court of His Majesty the German Emperor, King of Prussia;

His Majesty the Emperor of the Ottomans, Méhémed Saïd Pasha, Vizir and High Dignitary, his Envoy Extraordinary and Plenipotentiary at the Court of His Majesty the German Emperor, King of Prussia;

Who, being provided with full powers, which have been found in good and due form, have successively discussed and adopted:—

Freedom of Trade in Basin of the Congo, &c.

1. A Declaration relative to freedom of trade in the basin of the Congo, its embouchures and circumjacent regions, with other provisions connected therewith.

Slave Trade by Sea or Land.

2. A Declaration relative to the slave trade, and the operations by sea or land which furnish slaves to that trade.

Neutrality of Territories comprised in the Conventional Basin of the Congo.

3. A Declaration relative to the neutrality of the territories comprised in the Conventional basin of the Congo.

Navigation of the Congo, &c.

4. An Act of Navigation for the Congo, which, while having regard to local circumstances, extends to this river, its affluents, and the waters in its system ("eaux qui leur sont assimilées"), the general principles enunciated in Articles CVIII to CXVI of the Final Act of the Congress of Vienna, and intended to regulate, as between the Signatory Powers of that Act, the free navigation of the waterways separating or traversing several States—these said principles having

since then been applied by agreement to certain rivers of Europe and America, but especially to the Danube with the modifications stipulated by the Treaties of Paris (1856) of Berlin (1878) and of London (1871 and 1883).

Navigation of the Niger.

5. An Act of Navigation for the Niger, which, while likewise having regard to local circumstances, extends to this river and its affluents the same principles as set forth in Articles CVIII to CXVI, of the Final Act of the Congress of Vienna.

Future Occupations on the Coast of Africa.

6. A Declaration introducing into international relations certain uniform rules with reference to future occupations on the coast of the African Continent.

And deeming it expedient that all these several documents should be combined in one single instrument, they (the Signatory Powers) have collected them into one General Act, composed of the following Articles:—

CHAPTER I.—DECLARATION RELATIVE TO FREEDOM OF TRADE IN THE BASIN OF THE CONGO, ITS MOUTHS AND CIRCUMJACENT REGIONS, WITH OTHER PROVISIONS CONNECTED THEREWITH.

Freedom of Trade to all Nations.

ART. I. The trade of all nations shall enjoy complete freedom:—

Basin of the Congo Defined.

1. In all the regions forming the basin of the Congo and its outlets. This basin is bounded by the watersheds (or mountain ridges) of the adjacent basins, namely, in particular, those of the Niari, the Ogowé, the Schari, and the Nile on the north; by the eastern watershed line of the affluents of Lake Tanganyika on the east; and by the watersheds of the basins of the Zambesi and the Logé on the south. It therefore comprises all the regions watered by the Congo and its affluents, including Lake Tanganyika, with its eastern tributaries.

Maritime Zone Defined.

2. In the maritime zone extending along the Atlantic Ocean from the parallel situated in 2° 30' of South Latitude to the mouth of the Logé.

Northern Boundary.

The northern boundary will follow the parallel situated in 2° 30' from the coast to the point where it meets the geographical basin of the Congo, avoiding the basin of the Ogowé, to which the provisions of the present Act do not apply.

Southern Boundary.

The southern boundary will follow the course of the Logé to its source, and thence pass eastwards till it joins the geographical basin of the Congo.

Eastern Boundary.

3. In the zone stretching eastwards from the Congo Basin as above defined, to the Indian Ocean from 5 degrees of North Latitude to the mouth of the Zambesi in the south, from which point the line of demarcation will ascend the Zambesi to 5 miles above its confluence with the Shiré, and then follow the watershed between the affluents of Lake Nyassa and those of the Zambesi, till at last it reaches the watershed between the waters of the Zambesi and the Congo.

Free Trade Principles applied to Signatory Powers, and to such Independent States as may approve the same.

It is expressly recognized that in extending the principle of free trade to this eastern zone, the Conference Powers only undertake engagements for themselves, and that in the territories belonging to an independent Sovereign State this principle shall only be applicable in so far as it is approved by such State. But the Powers agree to use their good offices with the Governments established on the African shore of the Indian Ocean for the purpose of obtaining such approval, and in any case of securing the most favourable conditions to the transit (traffic) of all nations.

Free Access of all Flags to Coast-line.

ART. II. All flags, without distinction of nationality, shall have free access to the whole of the coast-line of the territories above enumerated.

Navigation of Rivers; of Congo and its Affluents, and Lakes, Ports, and Canals

To the rivers there running into the sea to all the waters of the Congo and its affluents, including the lakes, and to all the ports situate on the banks of these waters, as well as to all canals which may in future be constructed with intent to unite, the watercourses or lakes within the entire area of the territories described in Article I.

Transport, Coasting Trade, and Boat Traffic.

Those trading under such flags may engage in all sorts of transport, and carry on the coasting trade by sea and river, as well as boat traffic, on the same footing as if they were subjects.

No Taxes to be levied on Wares Imported (with slight exceptions).

ART. III. Wares, of whatever origin, imported into these regions, under whatsoever flag, by sea or river, or overland, shall be subject to no other taxes than such as may be levied as fair compensation for expenditure in the interests of trade, and which for this reason must be equally borne by the subjects themselves and by foreigners of all nationalities.

Differential Duties forbidden.

All differential dues on vessels, as well as on merchandize are forbidden.

No Import or Transit Duties to be levied on Merchandize.

ART. IV. Merchandize imported into these regions shall remain free from import and transit dues.

Question to be reconsidered after 20 years.

The Powers reserve to themselves to determine after the lapse of 20 years whether this freedom of import shall be retained or not.

No Monopolies or Favours to be granted.

ART. V. No Power which exercises or shall exercise sovereign rights in the above-mentioned regions shall be allowed to grant therein a monopoly or favour of any kind in matters of trade.

Protection of Persons and Property, movable and immovable Possessions; Professions.

Foreigners, without distinction, shall enjoy therein with regard to the protection of their persons and effects, the acquisition and transmission of their movable and real property and with regard to the exercise of their professions, the same treatment and the same rights as nationals.

ART. VI. *Provisions relative to Protection of the Natives, of Missionaries and Travellers, as well as relative to Religious Liberty.*

Preservation and Improvement of Native Tribes; Slavery, and the Slave Trade.

All the Powers exercising sovereign rights or influence in the aforesaid territories bind themselves to watch over the preservation of the native tribes, and to care for the improvement of the conditions of their moral and material well-being, and to help in suppressing slavery, and especially the slave trade.

Religious and other Institutions.   Civilization of Natives.

They shall, without distinction of creed or nation, protect and favour all religions, scientific, or charitable institutions, and undertakings created and organized for the above ends, or which aim at instructing the natives and bringing home to them the blessings of civilization.

Protection of Missionaries, Scientists, and Explorers.

Christian missionaries, scientists and explorers, with their followers, property, and collections, shall likewise be the objects of especial protection.

Religious Toleration.

Freedom of conscience and religious toleration are expressly guaranteed to the natives, no less than to subjects and to foreigners.

Public Worship.

The free and public exercise of all forms of Divine worship, and the right to build edifices for religious purposes, and to organize religious missions belonging to all creeds, shall not be limited or fettered in any way whatsoever.

ART. VII. Postal Régime.
Postal Union.

The Convention of the Universal Postal Union, as revised at Paris the 1st June, 1878, shall be applied to the Conventional basin of the Congo.

The Powers who therein do or shall exercise rights of sovereignty or Protectorate engage, as soon as circumstances permit them, to take the measures necessary for the carrying out of the preceding provision.

ART. VIII. Right of Surveillance vested in the International Navigation Commission of the Congo.
Surveillance of International Navigation Commission of the Congo in territories where no Power shall exercise rights of Sovereignty or Protectorate.

In all parts of the territory had in view by the present Declaration, where no Power shall exercise rights of sovereignty or Protectorate, the International Navigation Commission of the Congo, instituted in virtue of Article XVII, shall be charged with supervising the application of the principles proclaimed and perpetuated (" consacrés ") by this Declaration.

In all cases of difference arising relative to the application of the principles established by the present Declaration, the Governments concerned may agree to appeal to the good offices of the International Commission by submitting to it an examination of the facts which shall have occasioned these differences.

CHAP. II.—DECLARATION RELATIVE TO THE SLAVE TRADE.
Suppression of the Slave Trade by Land and Sea; and of Slave Markets.

ART. IX. Seeing that trading in slaves is forbidden in conformity with the principles of international law as recognized by the Signatory Powers, and seeing also that the operations, which, by sea or land, furnish slaves to trade, ought likewise to be regarded as forbidden, the Powers which do or shall exercise sovereign rights or influence in the territories forming the Conventional basin of the Congo declare that these territories may not serve as a market or means of transit for the trade in slaves, of whatever race they may be. Each of the Powers binds itself to employ all the means at its disposal for putting an end to this trade and for punishing those who engage in it.

CHAP. III.—DECLARATION RELATIVE TO THE NEUTRALITY OF THE TERRITORIES COMPRISED IN THE CONVENTIONAL BASIN OF THE CONGO.
Neutrality of Territories and Territorial Waters.

ART. X. In order to give a new guarantee of security to trade and industry, and to encourage, by maintenance of peace, the development of civilization in the countries mentioned in Article I, and placed under the free trade system, the High Signatory Parties to the present Act, and those who shall hereafter adopt it, bind themselves to respect the neutrality of the territories, or portions of territories, belonging to the said countries, comprising therein the territorial waters, so long as the Powers which exercise or shall excercise the rights of sovereignty or Protectorate over those territories, using their option of proclaiming themselves neutral, shall fulfil the duties which neutrality requires.

Hostilities not to extend to Neutralized States.

ART. XI. In case a Power exercising rights of sovereignty or Protectorate in the countries mentioned in Article I, and placed under the free trade system, shall be involved in a war then the High Signatory Parties to the present Act, and those who shall hereafter adopt it, bind themselves to lend their good offices in order that the territories belonging to this Power and comprised in the Conventional tree trade zone shall, by the common consent of this Power and of the other belligerent or belligerents, be placed during the war under the rule of neutrality, and considered as belonging to a non-belligerent State, the belligerents thenceforth abstaining from extending hostilities to the territories thus neutralized, and from using them as a base for warlike operations.

Serious Disagreements between Signatory Powers to be referred to Mediation.

ART. XII. In case a serious disagreement originating on the subject of, or in the limits of, the territories mentioned in Article I, and placed under the free trade system, shall arise between any Signatory Powers of the present Act, or the Powers which may become parties to it, these Powers bind themselves, before appealing to arms, to have recourse to the mediation of one or more of the friendly Powers.

Or to Arbitration

In a similar case the same Powers reserve to themselves the option of having recourse to arbitration.

CHAP. IV.—ACT OF NAVIGATION FOR THE CONGO.

The Congo and its Branches open to the Merchant Vessels of all Nations.

ART. XIII. The navigation of the Congo, without excepting any of its branches or outlets, is, and shall remain, free for the merchant ships of all nations equally, whether carrying cargo or ballast, for the transport of goods or passengers. It shall be regulated by the provisions of this Act of Navigation, and by the Rules to be made in pursuance thereof.

Equality of Treatment to all Nations ; Coasting Trade ; Boat Traffic.

In the exercise of this navigation the subjects and flags of all nations shall in all respects be treated on a footing of perfect equality, not only for the direct navigation from the open sea to the inland ports of the Congo and *vice versâ*, but also for the great and small coasting trade, and for boat traffic on the course of the river.

Privileges; Riverain and non-Riverain States; Companies, Corporations, and Private Persons.

Consequently, on all the course and mouths of the Congo there will be no distinction made between the subjects of Riverain States and those of non-Riverain States, and no exclusive privilege of navigation will be conceded to Companies, Corporations, or private persons whatsoever.

International Law.

These provisions are recognized by the Signatory Powers as becoming henceforth a part of international law.

Congo. No Restrictions or Obligations to be imposed.

ART. XIV. The navigation of the Congo shall not be subject to any restriction or obligation which is not expressly stipulated by the present Act.

No Landing or other Dues.

It shall not be exposed to any landing dues, to any station or depôt tax, or to any charge for breaking bulk, or for compulsory entry into port.

No Transit Dues on Ships or Goods.

In all the extent of the Congo the ships and goods in process of transit on the river shall be submitted to no transit dues, whatever their starting place or destination.

No Maritime or River Tolls to be levied (with certain exceptions).

There shall be levied no maritime or river toll based on the mere fact of navigation, nor any tax on goods aboard of ships. There shall only be levied taxes or duties having the character of an equivalent for services rendered to navigation itself, to wit:—

Harbour Dues on Wharves, &c.

1. Harbour dues on certain local establishments, such as wharves, warehouses, &c., if actually used.

The Tariff of such dues shall be framed according to the cost of constructing and maintaining the said local establishments; and it will be applied without regard to whence vessels come or what they are loaded with.

Pilot Dues.

2. Pilot dues for those stretches of the river where it may be necessary to establish properly-qualified pilots.

The Tariff of these dues shall be fixed and calculated in proportion to the service rendered.

Lighthouse and such like Dues.

3. Charges raised to cover technical and administrative expenses incurred in the general interest of navigation, including lighthouse, beacon, and buoy duties.

The last-mentioned dues shall be based on the tonnage of vessels as shown by the ship's papers, and in accordance with the Rules adopted on the Lower Danube.

No Differential Duties to be levied.
The Tariffs by which the various dues and taxes enumerated in the three preceding paragraphs shall be levied, shall not involve any differential treatment and shall be officially published at each port.

Power reserved of revising Tariffs after 5 years.
The Powers reserve to themselves to consider, after the lapse of 5 years, whether it may be necessary to revise, by common accord, the above-mentioned Tariffs.

Congo. Affluents of the Congo.
ART. XV. The affluents of the Congo shall in all respects be subject to the same rules as the river of which they are tributaries.

Streams, Lakes, and Canals.
And the same rules shall apply to the streams and rivers as well as the lakes and canals in the territories defined in paragraphs 2 and 3 of Article I.

At the same time the powers of the International Commission of the Congo will not extend to the said rivers, streams, lakes, and canals, unless with the assent of the States under whose Sovereignty they are placed. It is well understood, also, that with regard to the territories mentioned in paragraph 3 of Article I, the consent of the Sovereign States owning these territories is reserved.

Roads, Railways, or lateral Canals open to all Nations.
ART. XVI. The roads, railways, or lateral canals which may be constructed with the special object of obviating the innavigability or correcting the imperfection of the river route on certain sections of the course of the Congo, its affluents, and other water-ways placed under a similar system, as laid down in Article XV, shall be considered in their quality of means of communication as dependencies of this river, and as equally open to the traffic of all nations.

Tolls.
And, as on the river itself, so there shall be collected on these roads, railways, and canals only tolls calculated on the cost of construction, maintenance, and management, and on the profits due to the promoters.

As regards the Tariff of these tolls, strangers and the natives of the respective territories shall be treated on a footing of perfect equality.

International Navigation Commission of the Congo.

ART. XVII. There is instituted an International Commission, charged with the execution of the provisions of the present Act of Navigation.

Each Power to be Represented by One Delegate with One Vote only.

The Signatory Powers of this Act, as well as those who may subsequently adhere to it, may always be represented on the said Commission, each by one Delegate. But no Delegate shall have more than one vote at his disposal even in the case of his representing several Governments.

Payment of Delegates, Agents and Employés.

This Delegate will be directly paid by his Government. As for the various agents and employés of the International Commission, their remuneration shall be charged to the amount of the dues collected in conformity with paragraphs 2 and 3 of Article XIV.

The particulars of the said remuneration, as well as the number, grade, and powers of the agents and employés, shall be entered in the Returns to be sent yearly to the Governments represented on the International Commission.

Congo. Inviolability of Members and Agents their Offices and Archives.

ART. XVIII. The members of the International Commission, as well as its appointed agents, are invested with the privilege of inviolability in the exercise of their functions. The same guarantee shall apply to the offices and archives of the Commission.

Congo. Constitution of the Commission.

ART. XIX. The International Commission for the Navigation of the Congo shall be constituted as soon as five of the Signatory Powers of the present General Act shall have appointed their Delegates.

Nomination of Delegates to be notified to German Government.

And pending the Constitution of the Commission the nomination of these Delegates shall be notified to the Imperial Government of Germany, which will see to it that the necessary steps are taken to summon the meeting of the Commission.

Navigation, River Police, Pilot, and Quarantine Rules.

The Commission will at once draw up navigation, river police, pilot, and quarantine Rules.

These Rules as well as the Tariffs to be framed by the Commission, shall, before coming into force, be submitted for approval to the Powers represented on the Commission. The Powers interested will have to communicate their views with as little delay as possible.

Infringement of Rules.

Any infringements of these Rules will be checked by the agents of the International Commission wherever it exercises direct authority, and elsewhere by the Riverain Power.

In the case of an abuse of power, or of an act of injustice, on the part of any agent or employé of the International Commission, the individual who considers himself to be aggrieved in his person or rights may apply to the Consular Agent of his country. The latter will examine his complaint, and if he finds it *primâ facie* reasonable, he will then be entitled to bring it before the Commission. At his instance then, the Commission, represented by at least three of its members, shall, in conjunction with him, inquire into the conduct of its agent or employé. Should the Consular Agent look upon the decision of the Commission as raising questions of law ("objections de droit"), he will report on the subject to his Government, which may then have recourse to the Powers represented on the Commission, and invite them to agree as to the instructions to be given to the Commission.

ART. XX. The International Commission of the Congo, charged in terms of Article XVII with the execution of the present Act of Navigation, shall in particular have power—

Works necessary to assure Navigability of the Congo.

1. To decide what works are necessary to assure the navigability of the Congo in accordance with the needs of international trade.

On those sections of the river where no Power exercises sovereign rights, the International Commission will itself take the necessary measures for assuring the navigability of the river.

On those sections of the river held by a Sovereign Power the International Commission will concert its action ("s'entendra") with the riparian authorities.

Pilot Tariff and Navigation Dues.

2. To fix the pilot tariff and that of the general navigation dues as provided for by paragraphs 2 and 3 of Article XIV.

The Tariffs mentioned in the first paragraph of Article XIV shall be framed by the territorial authorities within the limits prescribed in the said Article.

The levying of the various dues shall be seen to by the international or territorial authorities on whose behalf they are established.

Administration of Revenue.

3. To administer the revenue arising from the application of the preceding paragraph (2).

Quarantine Establishment.

4. To superintend the quarantine establishment created in virtue of Article XXIV.

Appointment of officials and Employés.

5. To appoint officials for the general service of navigation, and also it own proper employés.

Sub-Inspectors.

It will be for the territorial authorities to appoint Sub-Inspectors on sections of the river occupied by a Power, and for the International Commission to do so on the other sections.

The Riverain Power will notify to the International Commission the appointment of Sub-Inspectors, and this Power will undertake the payment of their salaries.

In the exercise of its functions, as above defined and limited the International Commission will be independent of the territorial authorities.

Congo. Employment of War Vessels by Navigation Commission.

ART. XXI. In the accomplishment of its task the International Commission may, if need be, have recourse to the war vessels of the Signatory Powers of this Act, and of those who may in future accede to it, under reserve, however, of the instructions which may be given to the Commanders of these vessels by their respective Governments.

Congo. War Vessels Exempt from Navigation Dues.

ART. XXII. The war vessels of the Signatory Powers of this Act that may enter the Congo are exempt from payment of the navigation dues provided for in paragraph 3 of Article XIV.

Otherwise liable to Payment of Pilot and Harbour Dues.

But unless their intervention has been called for by the International Commission or its agents, in terms of the preceding Article, they shall be liable to the payment of the pilot or harbour dues which may eventually be established.

Congo. Loans for Technical and Administrative Expenses.

ART. XXIII. With the view of providing for the technical and administrative expenses which it may incur, the International Commission created by Article XVII may, in its own name, negotiate loans to be exclusively guaranteed by the revenues raised by the said Commission.

The decisions of the Commission dealing with the conclusion of a loan must be come to by a majority of two-thirds. It is understood that the Governments represented on the Commission shall not in any case be held as assuming any guarantee, or as contracting any egagement or joint liability ("solidarité") with respect to the said loans unless under special Conventions concluded by them to this effect.

The revenue yielded by the dues specified in paragraph 3 of Article XIV shall bear, as a first charge, the payment of the interest and sinking fund of the said loans, according to agreement with the lenders.

Quarantine Establishment at Mouth of the Congo.

ART. XXIV. At the mouth of the Congo there shall be founded, either on the initiative of the Riverain Powers, or by the intervention of the International Commission, a quarantine establishment for the control of vessels passing out of as well as into the river.

Sanitary Control over Vessels.

Later on the Powers will decide whether and on what conditions a sanitary control shall be exercised over vessels engaged in the navigation of the river itself.

Congo.   Freedom of Navigation of the Congo and Territorial Waters during War.

ART. XXV. The provisions of the present Act of Navigation shall remain in force in time of war. Consequently all nations, whether neutral or belligerent, shall be always free, for the purposes of trade, to navigate the Congo, its branches, affluents, and mouths, as well as the territorial waters fronting the embouchure of the river.

Roads, Railways, Lakes, and Canals included.

Traffic will similarly remain free, despite a state of war, on the roads, railways, lakes, and canals mentioned in Articles XV and XVI.

Transport of Contraband of War excepted.

There will be no exception to this principle, except in so far as concerns the transport of articles intended for a belligerent, and in virtue of the law of nations regarded as contraband of war.

Neutrality of Works and Establishments.

All the works and establishments created in pursuance of the present Act, especially the tax-collecting offices and their treasuries, as well as the permanent service staff of these establishments, shall enjoy the benefits of neutrality ("placés sous le régime de la neutralité"), and shall, therefore, be respected and protected by belligerents.

CHAP. V.—ACT OF NAVIGATION FOR THE NIGER.

The Niger and its Branches open to the Merchant Vessels of all Nations.

ART. XXVI. The navigation of the Niger, without excepting any of its branches and outlets, is and shall remain entirely free for the merchant ships of all nations equally, whether with cargo or in ballast, for the transportation of goods and passengers. It shall be regulated by the provision of this Act of Navigation, and by the Rules to be made in pursuance of this Act.

Niger.   Equality of Treatment to all Nations; Coasting Trade; Boat Traffic.

In the exercise of this navigation the subjects and flags of all nations shall be treated, in all circumstances on a footing of perfect equality, not only for the direct navigation from the open sea to the inland ports of the Niger, and *vice versâ*, but for the great and small coasting trade, and for boat trade on the course of the river.

Privileges: Riverain and non-Riverain States; Companies, Corporations, and Private Persons.

Consequently, on all the course and mouths of the Niger there will be no distinction made between the subjects of the Riverain States and those of non-Riverain States; and no exclusive privilege of navigation will be conceded to companies, corporations, or private persons.

International Law.

These provisions are recognised by the Signatory Powers as forming henceforth a part of international law.

No Restrictions or Obligations to be imposed on Navigation.

ART. XXVII. The navigation of the Niger shall not be subject to any restriction or obligation based merely on the fact of navigation.

No Landing or other Dues to be imposed.

It shall not be exposed to any obligation in regard to landing-station or depôt, or for breaking bulk, or for compulsory entry into port.

No Transit Dues on Ships or Goods to be levied.

In all the extent of the Niger the ships and goods in process of transit on the river shall be submitted to no transit dues, whatever their starting place or destination.

No Maritime or River Tolls to be levied (with certain exceptions).

No maritime or river toll shall be levied or based on the sole fact of navigation, nor any tax on goods on board of ships. There shall only be collected taxes or duties which shall be an equivalent for services rendered to navigation itself.

No Differential Duties to be levied.

The Tariff of these taxes or duties shall not warrant any differential treatment.

Affluents of the Niger.

ART. XXVIII. The affluents of the Niger shall be in all respects subject to the same rules as the river of which they are tributaries.

Niger. Roads, Railways, or lateral Canals open to all Nations.

ART. XXIX. The roads, railways, or lateral canals which may be constructed with the special object of obviating the innavigability or correcting the imperfections of the river route on certain sections of the Niger, its affluents, branches, and outlets, shall be considered, in their quality of means of communication, as dependencies of this river, and as equally open to the traffic of all nations.

Tolls.

And, as on the river itself, so there shall be collected on these roads, railways, and canals, only tolls calculated on the cost of construction, maintenance, and management, and on the profits due to the promoters.

As regards the Tariff of these tolls, strangers and the natives of the respective territories shall be treated on a footing of perfect equality.

British Engagements. Waters of the Niger and its Affluents, &c., under British Sovereignty or Protection, to be subject to the principles above described.

ART. XXX. Great Britain undertakes to apply the principles of freedom of navigation enunciated in Articles XXVI, XXVII, XXVIII and XXIX on so much of the waters of the Niger, its affluents, branches, and outlets, as are or may be under her sovereignty or protection.

Rules of Navigation to be established.

The rules which she may establish for the safety and control of navigation shall be drawn up in a way to facilitate, as far as possible, the circulation of merchant ships.

Great Britain not restricted from making any Rules not contrary to above Engagements.

It is understood that nothing in these obligations shall be interpreted as hindering Great Britain from making any Rules of Navigation whatever which shall not be contrary to the spirit of these engagements.

Foreign Merchants and all Trading Nationalities to be protected the same as British Subjects.

Great Britain undertakes to protect foreign merchants and all the trading nationalities on all those portions of the Niger which are or may be under her sovereignty or protection as if they were her own subjects: provided always that such merchants conform to the rules which are or shall be made in virtue of the foregoing.

Niger. French Engagements, with regard to Waters of the River, &c., under her Sovereignty or Protection.

ART. XXXI. France accepts, under the same reservations, and in identical terms, the obligations undertaken in the preceding articles in respect of so much of the waters of the Niger, its affluents, branches, and outlets, as are or may be under her sovereignty or protection.

Engagements of the other Signatory Powers.

ART. XXXII. Each of the other Signatory Powers binds itself in the same way in case it should ever exercise in the future rights of sovereignty or protection over any portion of the waters of the Niger, branches, or outlets.

Freedom of Navigation of the Niger and Territorial Waters during War

ART. XXXIII. The arrangements of the present Act of Navigation will remain in force in time of war. Consequently, the navigation of all neutral or belligerent nations will be in all time free for the usages of commerce on the Niger, its branches, its affluents, its mouths, and outlets, as well as on the territorial waters opposite the mouths and outlets of that river.

Roads, Railways, and Canals included.

The traffic will remain equally free in spite of a state of war on the roads, railways, and canals mentioned in Article XXIX.

Transport of Contraband of War excepted.

There will be an exception to this principle only in that which relates to the transport of articles destined for a belligerent, and considered, in virtue of the law of nations, as articles contraband of war.

CHAP. VI.—DECLARATION RELATIVE TO THE ESSENTIAL CONDITIONS TO BE OBSERVED IN ORDER THAT NEW OCCUPATIONS ON THE COASTS OF THE AFRICAN CONTINENT MAY BE HELD TO BE EFFECTIVE.

Notifications of Acquisitions and Protectorates on Coasts of African Continent.

ART. XXXIV. Any Power which henceforth takes possession of a tract of land on the coasts of the African Continent outside of its present possessions, or which, being hitherto without such possessions, shall acquire them, as well as the Power which assumes a Protectorate there, shall accompany the respective act with a notification thereof, addressed to the other Signatory Powers of the present Act, in order to enable them, if need be, to make good any claims of their own.

Establishment of authority in Territories occupied on Coasts. Protection of existing Rights. Freedom of Trade and Transit.

ART. XXXV. The Signatory Powers of the present Act recognize the obligation to insure the establishment of authority in regions occupied by them on the coasts of the African Continent sufficient to protect existing rights, and, as the case may be, freedom of trade and of transit under the conditions agreed upon.

CHAP. VII.—GENERAL DISPOSITIONS.

Reservation as to Modifications.

ART. XXXVI. The Signatory Powers of the present General Act reserve to themselves to introduce into it subsequently, and by common accord, such modifications and improvements as experience may show to be expedient.

Liberty of other Powers to adhere to Act.

ART. XXXVII. The Powers who have not signed the present General Act shall be free to adhere to its provisions by a separate instrument.

Adhesions to be notified to all the Powers.

The adhesion of each Power shall be notified in diplomatic form to the Government of the German Empire, and by it in turn to all the other Signatory or adhering Powers.

Acceptance of all Obligations and Admission to all Advantages.

Such adhesion shall carry with it full acceptance of all the obligations, as well as admission to all the advantages, stipulated for by the present General Act.

General Act to be Ratified.

ART. XXXVIII. The present General Act shall be ratified with as little delay as possible, the same in no case to exceed a year.

It will come into force for each Power from the date of its ratification by that Power.

Meanwhile, the Signatory Powers of the present General Act bind themselves not to take any steps contrary to its provisions.

Each Power will address its ratification to the Government of the German Empire, by which notice of the fact will be given to all the other Signatory Powers of the present Act.

Where Ratifications are to be deposited.

The ratifications of all the Powers will be deposited in the archives of the Government of the German Empire. When all the ratifications shall have been sent in, there will be drawn up a Deposit Act, in the shape of a Protocol, to be signed by the Representatives of all the Powers which have taken part in the Conference of Berlin, and of which a certified copy will be sent to each of those Powers.

In testimony whereof the several Plenipotentiaries have signed the present General Act and have affixed thereto their seals.

Done at Berlin, the 26th day of February, 1885.

[Here follow the signatures.]

PROTOCOL. *Ratifications of General Act of Berlin Conference of 26th February, 1885. Berlin, 19th April, 1886.*

Ratifications (with the exception of the United States of America) deposited at the Berlin Foreign Office. The United States ratified on 2nd July, 1890.

All the Powers who took part in the Conference of Berlin having, with the exception of the United States of America, ratified the General Act of that Conference, signed at Berlin on the 26th February, 1885, and having delivered their ratifications to the Government of the German Empire, which has deposited them in the Imperial archives, and has so informed the other Signatory Powers, the Undersigned, authorized to this effect by their respective Governments, have met together at the Berlin Foreign Office to draw up the Act of Deposit of these ratifications, in the manner agreed upon by Article XXXVIII of the said General Act.

Count Bismarck explained in a few words the object of the meeting to which he had invited the Representatives of the Powers who had ratified the General Act of the 26th February, 1885. He read Article XXXVIII of the General Act, and observed that the delay provided for by the first paragraph of the said Article had been prolonged, by common consent, at the request of the Government of Austria-Hungary.

Count Bismarck having then formally declared that the General Act had not been ratified by the Government of the United States of America, recalled to mind that this eventuality had been foreseen at the time of the deliberations of the Conference of Berlin, as shown in Annex No. 3 to the Protocol No. 9, and particularly in the extract of the Protocol of the sitting of the Conference of the 31st January, 1885, which forms Annex No. 6 to the said Annex No. 3. He consequently expressed the opinion that the United States of America enter into the category of Powers who may adhere later to the stipulations of the General Act, in the manner and to the effect determined by Article XXXVII of that Act; all the stipulations contained in the General Act would, however, remain in full force and vigour among all the other Signatory Powers of the said Act, and would bind them reciprocally by virtue of their respective ratifications.

The Representatives of Austria-Hungary, Belgium, Denmark, Spain, France, Great Britain, Italy, Holland, Portugal, Russia, Sweden and Norway, and Turkey having declared that they concurred in this view, and that they were authorized to complete, under the conditions explained by Count Bismarck, the formality provided for in Article XXXVIII of the General Act, the ratifications were produced, and after being examined and found in good and due form, Count Bismarck declared that the documents would, in conformity with the conditions of Article XXXVIII, remain deposited in the archives of the Government of the German Empire.

The other members of the meeting took formal note of this deposit.

In witness whereof the present Protocol has been drawn up, a certified copy of which shall be communicated by the Government of the German Empire to each of the other Powers who have ratified the General Act of the 26th February, 1885.

Done at Berlin, read, and approved on the 19th April, 1886.

[Here follow the signatures.]

APPENDIX 2 (B)

CONVENTION between Great Britain and France for the Delimitation of their respective Possessions to the West of the Niger, and of their respective Possessions and Spheres of Influence to the East of that River. Signed at Paris, 14th June, 1898.

Ratifications exchanged at Paris, 13th June, 1899.

THE Government of Her Majesty the Queen of the United Kingdom of Great Britain and Ireland, Empress of India, and the Government of the French Republic, having agreed, in a spirit of mutual good-will, to confirm the Protocol with its four Annexes prepared by their respective Delegates for the delimitation of the British Colonies of the Gold Coast, Lagos, and the other British possessions to the west of the Niger, and of the French possessions of the Ivory Coast, Sudan, and Dahomey, as well as for the delimitation of the British and French possessions and the spheres of influence of the two countries to the east of the Niger, the Undersigned, his Excellency the Right Honourable Sir Edmund Monson, Ambassador Extraordinary and Plenipotentiary of Her Majesty the Queen of the United Kingdom of Great Britain and Ireland, Empress of India, accredited to the President of the French Republic; and his Excellency M. Gabriel Hanotaux, Minister for Foreign Affairs of the French Republic; duly authorized to this effect, confirm the Protocol with its Annexes, drawn up at Paris the 14th day of June, 1898, the text of which is as follows:—

Protocol.

The Undersigned, Martin Gosselin, Minister Plenipotentiary and Secretary of Her Britannic Majesty's Embassy at Paris; William Everett, a Colonel in Her Britannic Majesty's land forces and an Assistant Adjutant-General in the Intelligence Division of the War Office; René Lecomte, Minister Plenipotentiary, Assistant Sub-Director in the Department of Political Affairs in the Ministry of Foreign Affairs; Louis Gustave Binger, Colonial Governor, unattached, Director of African Affairs at the Ministry of the Colonies; delegated respectively by the Government of Her Britannic Majesty and by the Government of the French Republic in order to draw up, in conformity with the Declarations exchanged at London on the 5th August, 1890 and the 15th January, 1896, a draft of definitive delimitation between the British Colonies of the Gold Coast, Lagos, and the other British possessions to the west of the Niger, and the French possessions of the Ivory Coast, the Sudan, and Dahomey, and between the British and

French possessions and the spheres of influence of the two countries to the east of the Niger, have agreed to the following provisions, which they have resolved to submit for the approval of their respective Governments:—

Frontier between Gold Coast Colony and French Ivory Coast and Sudan.

ART. I. The frontier separating the British Colony of the Gold Coast from the French Colonies of the Ivory Coast and Sudan shall start from the northern terminal point of the frontier laid down in the Anglo-French Agreement of the 12th July, 1893, viz., the intersection of the thalweg of the Black Volta with the 9th degree of north latitude, and shall follow the thalweg of this river northward up to its intersection with the 11th degree of north latitude. From this point it shall follow this parallel of latitude eastward as far as the river shown on Map No. 1, annexed to the present Protocol, as passing immediately to the east of the villages of Zwaga (Soauga) and Zebilla (Sebilla), and it shall then follow the thalweg of the western branch of this river up stream to its intersection with the parallel of latitude passing through the village of Sapeliga. From this point the frontier shall follow the northern limits of the lands belonging to Sapeliga as far as the River Nuhau (Nouhau), and shall then follow the thalweg of this river up or down stream, as the case may be, to a point situated 2 miles (3,219 metres) eastward of the road which leads from Gambaga to Tenkrugu (Tingourkou), viâ Bawku (Baukou). Thence it shall rejoin by a straight line the 11th degree of north latitude at the intersection of this parallel with the road which is shown on Map No. 1 as leading from Sansanné-Mango to Pama, viâ Jebigu (Djebiga).

Frontier between Lagos and Dahomey (West of Lower Niger).

ART. II. The frontier between the British Colony of Lagos and the French Colony of Dahomey, which was delimited on the ground by the Anglo-French Boundary Commission of 1895, and which is described in the Report signed by the Commissioners of the two nations on the 12th October, 1896, shall henceforward be recognised as the frontier separating the British and French possessions from the sea to the 9th degree of north latitude.

From the point of intersection of the River Ocpara with the 9th degree of north latitude, as determined by the said Commissioners, the frontier separating the British and French possessions shall proceed in a northerly direction, and follow a line passing west of the lands belonging to the following places, viz., Tabira, Okuta (Okouta), Boria, Tere, Gbani, Ashigere (Yassikéra), and Dekala.

From the most westerly point of the lands belonging to Dekala the frontier shall be drawn in a northerly direction so as to coincide as far as possible with the line indicated on Map No. 1 annexed to the present Protocol, and shall strike the right bank of the Niger at a point situated 10 miles (16.093 metres) up-stream from the centre of the town of Gere (Guiris) (the port of Ilo), measured as the crow flies.

Frontier on the River Niger.

ART. III. From the point specified in Art. II, where the frontier separating the British and French possessions strikes the Niger, viz. a point situated on the right bank of that river, 10 miles (16.093 metres) up-stream from the centre of the town of Gere (Guiris), (the port of Ilo), the frontier shall follow a straight line drawn therefrom at right angles to the right bank as far as its intersection with the median line of the river. It shall then follow the median line of the river, up-stream, as far as its intersection with a line drawn perpendicularly to the left bank from the median line of the mouth of the depression or dry water-course, which, on Map No. 2, annexed to the present Protocol, is called the Dallul Mauri, and is shown thereon as being situated at a distance of about 17 miles (27.359 metres), measured as the crow flies, from a point on the left bank opposite the above-mentioned village of Gere (Guiris).

From this point of intersection the frontier shall follow this perpendicular till it meets the left bank of the river.

Frontier East of the Niger.

ART. IV. To the east of the Niger the frontier separating the British and French possessions shall follow the line indicated on Map No. 2, which is annexed to the present Protocol.

Starting from the point on the left bank of the Niger indicated in the previous Article, viz., the median line of the Dallul Mauri, the frontier shall follow this median line until it meets the circumference of a circle drawn from the centre of the town of Sokoto with a radius of 100 miles (160·932 metres). From this point it shall follow the northern arc of this circle as far as its second intersection with the 14th parallel of north latitude. From this second point of intersection it shall follow this parallel eastward for a distance of 70 miles (112·652 metres); then proceed due south until it reaches the parallel of 13° 20′ north latitude, then eastward along this parallel for a distance of 250 miles (402·230 metres); then due north until it regains the 14th parallel of north latitude; then eastwards along this parallel as far as its intersection with the meridian passing 35′ east of the centre of the town of Kuka, and thence this meridian southward until its intersection with the southern shore of Lake Chad.

The Government of the French Republic recognizes, as falling within the British sphere, the territory to the east of the Niger, comprised within the above-mentioned line, the Anglo-German frontier, and the sea.

The Government of Her Britannic Majesty recognizes, as falling within the French sphere, the northern, eastern, and southern shores of Lake Chad, which are comprised between the point of intersection of the 14th degree of north latitude, with the western shore of the lake and the point of incidence on the shore of the lake of the frontier determined by the Franco-German Convention of the 15th March, 1894.

ART. V. The frontiers set forth in the present Protocol are indicated on the annexed Maps, which are marked 1 and 2 respectively.

The two Governments undertake to appoint within a year as regards the frontiers west of the Niger, and within two years as regards the frontier east of that river, to count in each case from the date of the exchange of ratifications of the Convention which is to be concluded between them for the purpose of confirming the present Protocol, Commissioners who will be charged with delimiting on the spot the lines of demarcation between the British and French possessions, in conformity and in accordance with the spirit of the stipulations of the present Protocol.

With respect to the delimitation of the portion of the Niger in the neighbourhood of Ilo and the Dallul Mauri, referred to in Art. III, the Boundary Commissioners shall, in determining on the spot the river frontier, distribute equitably between the two Contracting Powers such islands as may be found to interfere with the delimitation of the river as defined in Art. III.

It is understood between the two Contracting Powers that no subsequent alteration in the position of the median line of the river shall affect the ownership of the islands assigned to each of the two Powers by the *procès-verbal* of the Commissioners, after being duly approved by the two Governments.

Treatment of Native Chiefs.

ART. VI. The two Contracting Powers engage reciprocally to treat with consideration ("bienveillance") the native Chiefs who, having had Treaties with one of them, shall, in virtue of the present Protocol, come under the sovereignty of the other.

Non-interference in Sphere of other Power.

ART. VII. Each of the two Contracting Powers undertakes not to exercise any political action in the spheres of the other, as defined by Arts. I, II, III, and IV of the present Protocol.

It is understood by this that each Power will not, in the spheres of the other, make territorial acquisitions, conclude Treaties, accept sovereign rights or Protectorates, nor hinder nor dispute the influence of the other.

Lease of Land to French Government.

ART. VIII. Her Britannic Majesty's Government will grant on lease to the Government of the French Republic, for the objects, and on the conditions specified in the form of lease annexed to the present Protocol, two pieces of ground to be selected by the Government of the French Republic in conjunction with Her Britannic Majesty's Government, one of which will be situated in a suitable spot on the right bank of the Niger between Leaba and the junction of the River Moussa (Mochi) with the former river, and the other on one of the mouths of the Niger. Each of these pieces of land shall have a river frontage not exceeding 400 metres in length, and shall form a block, the area of which shall not be less than 10 nor more than 50 hectares in extent. The exact boundaries of these pieces of land shall be shown on a plan annexed to each of the leases.

The conditions upon which the transit of merchandize shall be carried on on the Niger, its affluents, its branches and outlets, as well as between the piece of ground between Leaba and the junction of the River Moussa (Mochi) mentioned above, and the point upon the French frontier to be specified by the Government of the French Republic, will form the subject of Regulations, the details of which shall be discussed by the two Governments immediately after the signature of the present Protocol.

Her Britannic Majesty's Government undertake to give four months' notice to the French Government of any modification in the Regulations in question, in order to afford to the said French Government the opportunity of laying before the British Government any representations which it may wish to make.

Reciprocal Treatment as regards River Navigation, Commerce, Taxes, &c., for Thirty Years from date of Exchange of Ratifications.

ART. IX. Within the limits defined on Map No. 2, which is annexed to the present Protocol, British subjects and British protected persons and French citizens and French protected persons, as far as regards their persons and goods, and the merchandize the produce or the manufacture of Great Britain and France, their respective Colonies, possessions, and Protectorates, shall enjoy for thirty years from the date of the exchange of the ratifications of the Convention mentioned in Art. V the same treatment in all matters of river navigation, of commerce, and of tariff and fiscal treatment and taxes of all kinds.

Subject to this condition, each of the two Contracting Powers shall be free to fix, in its own territory, and as may appear to it most convenient, the tariff and fiscal treatment and taxes of all kinds.

In case neither of the two Contracting Powers shall have notified twelve months before the expiration of the above-mentioned term of thirty years its intention to put an end to the effects of the present Article, it shall remain in force until the expiration of one year from the day on which either of the Contracting Powers shall have denounced it.

In witness whereof, the undersigned Delegates have drawn up and signed the present Protocol.

Done at Paris, in duplicate, the 14th day of June, in the year of our Lord 1898.

> MARTIN GOSSELIN.
> WILLIAM EVERETT.
> RENÉ LECOMTE.
> G. BINGER.

Annexes 1 and 2 (Maps).

Annex 3.

Modification of Conventional Line by Commissioners on the Ground.

Although the delineation of the lines of demarcation on the two maps annexed to the present Protocol are supposed to be generally accurate, it cannot be considered as an absolutely correct representation of those lines until it has been confirmed by new surveys.

It is therefore agreed that the Commissioners or local Delegates of the two countries, hereafter appointed to delimit the whole or part of the frontiers on the ground, shall be guided by the description of the frontier as set forth in the Protocol.

They shall, at the same time, be permitted to modify the said lines of demarcation for the purpose of delineating them with greater accuracy, and also to rectify the position of the watersheds, roads, or rivers, as well as of towns or villages indicated on the maps above referred to.

Any alterations or corrections proposed by common consent by the said Commissioners or Delegates shall be submitted for the approval of their respective Governments.

> MARTIN GOSSELIN.
> WILLIAM EVERETT.
> RENÉ LECOMTE.
> G. BINGER.

Annex 4.

Form of Lease.

1. The Government of Her Britannic Majesty grants in lease to the Government of the French Republic the piece of land situated

of the Niger River, having a river frontage   in length, and forming a block of hectares in extent, the exact boundaries of which are shown on the plan annexed to this lease.

2. The lease shall run for thirty years uninterruptedly, commencing from the   , but in case neither of the two Contracting Powers shall have notified twelve months before the expiration of the above-mentioned term of thirty years its intention to put an end to the present lease, it shall remain in force until the expiration of one year from the day on which either of the Contracting Powers shall have denounced it.

3. The said land shall be subject to the laws for the time being in force in the British Protectorate of the Niger districts.

4. A portion of the land so leased, which shall not exceed 10 hectares in extent, shall be used exclusively for the purposes of the landing, storage, and transhipment of goods, and for such purposes as may be considered subsidiary thereto, and the only permanent residents shall be the persons employed in the charge and for the security of such goods, their families, and servants.

5. The Government of the French Republic binds itself—

(*a*) To fence in that portion of the said land referred to in Art. 4 of this lease (with the exception of the side which faces the River Niger) by a wall, or by a stockade, or by any other sort of continuous fence, which shall not be less in height than 3 metres. There shall be one door only on each of the three sides of the fence.

(*b*) Not to permit on the said portion of land the receipt or exit of any goods in contravention of the British Customs Regulations. Any act in violation of this stipulation shall be considered as evasion of custom duties, and shall be punished accordingly.

(*c*) Not to sell nor allow the sale of any goods in retail in the said portion of land. The sale of quantities less in weight or measure than 1,000 kilog., 1,000 litres, or 1,000 metres is held to be sale in retail. It is understood that this stipulation shall not apply to goods in transit.

(*d*) The Government of the French Republic, or its sub-lessees or agents, shall have the right to build on the said portion of land, warehouses, houses for offices, and other buildings necessary for operations of landing, storing, and transhipping goods, and also to construct on that part of the foreshore of the River Niger comprised in the lease, quays, bridges, and docks, and any other works required in connection with the said operations, provided that the designs of all works so to be constructed on the foreshore of the river are furnished to the British authorities for examination, in order to ascertain that these works would not in any way inconvenience the navigation of the river, or be in conflict with the rights of others or with the Customs system.

(e) It is understood that the shipping, landing, and storing of goods on the said portion of land shall be conducted in all respects in accordance with the laws for the time being in force in the British Protectorate of the Niger districts.

6. The Government of the French Republic binds itself to pay annually to Her Majesty's Government, on the 1st January of each year, a rent of 1 fr.

7. The Government of the French Republic shall have the right to sublet the whole or any portion of the land passing under this lease, provided that the sub-lessess shall not use the land for any other purposes than those stipulated in this lease, and that the said Government shall remain responsible to the Government of Her Britannic Majesty for the observance of the stipulations of this lease.

8. The Government of Her Britannic Majesty binds itself to fulfil towards the lessee all duties incumbent upon it as owner of the said land.

9. At the expiration of the term of thirty years specified in Art. 2 of this lease, the French Government, or its sub-lessees, may remain in possession and in the enjoyment for a period of time which, together with the said terms of thirty years, shall not exceed ninety-nine years of the constructions and installations which shall have been made on the leased land. Nevertheless, the Government of Her Britannic Majesty reserves to itself, on the expiration or determination of the lease, in accordance with the conditions specified in Art. 2, the right of purchasing such constructions and installations at a valuation to be determined by experts who will be appointed by the two Governments, on the understanding that notification of their intention be furnished to the French Government ten months, at latest, before the expiration or determination of the lease. In case of disagreement between them, the experts shall choose a referee, whose decision shall be final.

In calculating the value of the above-mentioned constructions and installations, the experts shall be guided by the following considerations:—

(a) In the event of the lease expiring at the end of the first thirty years, the purchase value of the property to be sold shall be the full market value.

(b) In the event of the lease being determined at any time after thirty years, the value of the property to be sold shall be the full market value less a fraction, whose numerator shall be the number of years the lease has run, minus thirty, and whose denominator shall be sixty-nine.

10. The land comprised in the lease shall be measured and marked out without delay.

11. If a difference of opinion should arise between the two Governments as to the interpretation of the lease, or as to any matter arising in connection therewith, it shall be settled by the arbitration of a jurisconsult of third nationality, to be agreed upon by the two Governments.

MARTIN GOSSELIN.
WILLIAM EVERETT.
RENÉ LACOMTE.
G. BINGER.

The present Convention shall be ratified, and the ratifications exchanged at Paris within the period of six months, or sooner if possible.

In witness whereof the Undersigned have signed the present Convention and have affixed thereto their seals.

Done in duplicate, at Paris, the 14th June, 1898.

(L.S.) EDMUND MONSON.
(L.S.) G. HANOTAUX.

APPENDIX 2 (C)

DECLARATION completing the Convention between Great Britain and France of 14th June, 1898 (Spheres of Influence in Central Africa and the Soudan). Signed at London, 21st March, 1899.

[Ratifications exchanged at Paris, 13th June, 1899.]

THE Undersigned, duly authorized by their Governments, have signed the following Declaration:—

The IVth Article of the Convention of the 14th June, 1898 shall be completed by the following provisions, which shall be considered as forming an integral part of it—

1. Her Britannic Majesty's Government engages not to acquire either territory or political influence to the west of the line of frontier defined in the following paragraph, and the Government of the French Republic engages not to acquire either territory or political influence to the east of the same line.

2. The line of frontier shall start from the point where the boundary between the Congo Free State and French territory meets the water-parting between the watershed of the Nile and that of the Congo and its affluents. It shall follow in principle that water-parting up to its intersection with the 11th parallel of north latitude. From this point

it shall be drawn as far as the 15th parallel in such manner as to separate, in principle, the Kingdom of Wadai from what constituted in 1882 the Province of Darfur; but it shall in no case be so drawn as to pass to the west beyond the 21st degree of longitude east of Greenwich (18° 40' east of Paris), or to the east beyond the 23rd degree of longitude east of Greenwich (20° 40' east of Paris).

3. It is understood, in principle, that to the north of the 15th parallel the French zone shall be limited to the north-east and east by a line which shall start from the point of intersection of the Tropic of Cancer with the 16th degree of longitude east of Greenwich (13° 40' east of Paris), shall run thence to the south-east until it meets the 24th degree of longitude east of Greenwich (21° 40' east of Paris), and shall then follow the 24th degree until it meets, to the north of the 15th parallel of latitude, the frontier of Darfur as it shall eventually be fixed.

4. The two Governments engage to appoint Commissioners who shall be charged to delimit on the spot a frontier-line in accordance with the indications given in paragraph 2 of this Declaration. The result of their work shall be submitted for the approbation of their respective Governments.

It is agreed that the provisions of Art. IX of the Convention of the 14th June, 1898, shall apply equally to the territories situated to the south of the 14° 20' parallel of north latitude, and to the north of the 5th parallel of north latitude, between the 14° 20' meridian of longitude east of Greenwich (12th degree east of Paris) and the course of the Upper Nile.

Done at London, the 21st March, 1899.

SALISBURY.
PAUL CAMBON.

APPENDIX 3

TEXT of Convention between Great Britain, Germany, Austria-Hungary, Spain, France, Italy, The Netherlands, Russia, and Turkey, respecting the Free Navigation of the Suez Maritime Canal. 29th October, 1888.

(Preamble omitted as inessential)

ART. I. The Suez Maritime Canal shall always be free and open, in time of war as in time of peace, to every vessel of commerce or of war, without distinction of flag.

Consequently, the High Contracting Parties agree not in any way to interfere with the free use of the Canal, in time of war as in time of peace.

The Canal shall never be subjected to the exercise of the right of blockade.

ART. II. The High Contracting Parties, recognizing that the Fresh Water Canal is indispensable to the Maritime Canal, take note of the engagements of His Highness the Khedive towards the Universal Suez Canal Company as regards the Fresh Water Canal; which engagements are stipulated in a Convention bearing the date of 18th March 1863, containing an *exposé* and four Articles.

They undertake not to interfere in any way with the security of that Canal and its branches, the working of which shall not be exposed to any attempt at obstruction.

ART. III. The High Contracting Parties likewise undertake to respect the plant, establishments, buildings, and works of the Maritime Canal and of the Fresh Water Canal.

ART. IV. The Maritime Canal remaining open in time of war as a free passage, even to ships of war of belligerents, according to the terms of Article I of the present Treaty, the High Contracting Parties agree that no right of war, no act of hostility, nor any act having for its object to obstruct the free navigation of the Canal, shall be committed in the Canal and its ports of access, as well as within a radius of three marine miles from those parts, even though the Ottoman Empire should be one of the belligerent Powers.

Vessels of war of belligerents shall not revictual or take in stores in the Canal and its ports of access, except in so far as may be strictly necessary. The transit of the aforesaid vessels through the Canal shall be effected with the least possible delay, in accordance with the Regulations in force, and without any other intermission than that resulting from the necessities of the service.

Their stay at Port Said and in the roadstead of Suez shall not exceed twenty-four hours, except in case of distress. In such case they shall be bound to leave as soon as possible. An interval of twenty-four hours shall always elapse between the sailing of a belligerent ship from one of the ports of access and the departure of a ship belonging to the hostile Power.

ART. V. In time of war belligerent Powers shall not disembark nor embark within the Canal and its ports of access either troops, munitions, or materials of war. But in case of an accidental hindrance in the Canal, men may be embarked or disembarked at the ports of access by detachments not exceeding 1,000 men, with a corresponding amount of war material.

ART. VI. Prizes shall be subjected, in all respects, to the same rules as the vessels of war of belligerents.

ART. VII. The Powers shall not keep any vessel of war in the waters of the Canal (including Lake Timsah and the Bitter Lakes).

Nevertheless, they may station vessels of war in the ports of access of Port Said and Suez, the number of which shall not exceed two for each Power.

This right shall not be exercised by belligerents.

ART. VIII. The Agents in Egypt of the Signatory Powers of the present Treaty shall be charged to watch over its execution. In case of any event threatening the security or the free passage of the Canal, they shall meet on the summons of three of their number under the presidency of their Doyen, in order to proceed to the necessary verifications. They shall inform the Khedival Government of the danger which they may have perceived, in order that that Government may take proper steps to insure the protection and the free use of the Canal. Under any circumstances, they shall meet once a year to take note of the due execution of the Treaty.

The last-mentioned meetings shall take place under the presidency of a Special Commissioner nominated for that purpose by the Imperial Ottoman Government. A Commissioner of the Khedive may also take part in the meeting, and may preside over it in case of the absence of the Ottoman Commissioner.

They shall especially demand the suppression of any work or the dispersion of any assemblage on either bank of the Canal, the object or effect of which might be to interfere with the liberty and the entire security of the navigation.

ART. IX. The Egyptian Government shall, within the limits of its powers resulting from the Firmans, and under the conditions provided for in the present Treaty, take the necessary measures for insuring the execution of the said Treaty.

In case the Egyptian Government shall not have sufficient means at its disposal, it shall call upon the Imperial Ottoman Government, which shall take the necessary measures to respond to such appeal; shall give notice thereof to the Signatory Powers of the Declaration of London of the 17th March, 1885; and shall, if necessary, concert with them on the subject.

The provisions of Articles IV, V, VII, and VIII shall not interfere with the measures which shall be taken in virtue of the present Article.

ART. X. Similarly, the provisions of Articles IV, V, VII, and VIII, shall not interfere with the measures which His Majesty the Sultan and His Highness the Khedive, in the name of His Imperial Majesty, and within the limits of the Firmans granted, might find it necessary to take for securing by their own forces the defence of Egypt and the maintenance of public order.

In case His Imperial Majesty the Sultan, or His Highness the

Khedive, should find it necessary to avail themselves of the exceptions for which this Article provides, the Signatory Powers of the Declaration of London shall be notified thereof by the Imperial Ottoman Government.

It is likewise understood that the provisions of the four Articles aforesaid shall in no case occasion any obstacle to the measures which the Imperial Ottoman Government may think it necessary to take in order to insure by its own forces the defence of its other possessions situated on the eastern coast of the Red Sea.

ART. XI. The measures which shall be taken in the cases provided for by Articles IX and X of the present Treaty shall not interfere with the free use of the Canal. In the same cases, the erection of permanent fortifications contrary to the provisions of Article VIII is prohibited.

ART. XII. The High Contracting Parties, by application of the principle of equality as regards the free use of the Canal, a principle which forms one of the bases of the present Treaty, agree that none of them shall endeavour to obtain with respect to the Canal territorial or commercial advantages or privileges in any international arrangements which may be concluded. Moreover, the rights of Turkey as the territorial Power are reserved.

ART. XIII. With the exception of the obligations expressly provided by the clauses of the present Treaty, the sovereign rights of His Imperial Majesty the Sultan and the rights and immunities of his Highness the Khedive, resulting from the Firmans, are in no way affected.

ART. XIV. The High Contracting Parties agree that the engagements resulting from the present Treaty shall not be limited by the duration of the Acts of Concession of the Universal Suez Canal Company.

ART. XV. The stipulations of the present Treaty shall not interfere with the sanitary measures in force in Egypt.

ART. XVI. The High Contracting Parties undertake to bring the present Treaty to the knowledge of the States which have not signed it, inviting them to accede to it.

ART. XVII. The present Treaty shall be ratified, and the ratifications shall be exchanged at Constantinople, within the space of one month, or sooner, if possible.

In faith of which the respective Plenipotentiaries have signed the present Treaty, and have affixed to it the seal of their arms.

> Done at Constantinople,
> the 29th day of the month of
> October in the year 1888.

ACKNOWLEDGEMENTS

The compiler of these volumes has not intended to provide an exhaustive presentation of every document with all the linguistic variants chronicled and discussed. The aim has been to take the texts accepted by the English-speaking world and make them available for those eager to have a treaty 'vade-mecum' for the period 1814 to 1914 on the key aspects of then current problems. Anyone wishing to savour further nuances should go to the volumes of texts from which this collection has been drawn. My debt to them hardly needs stressing. They are: Hertslet, E.: The Map of Africa by Treaty (2 vols, 1894); Hertslet, E.: The Map of Europe by Treaty (4 vols, 1875-91); Mayers, W. F.: Treaties between the Empire of Africa and Foreign Powers, (1897); Miller, H.: Treaties and Other International Acts of the United States of America (1931); Washington, Dept of State: Treaties and Other International Agreements of the United States of America (1968).

Thanks are also due to Professor Ernst Helmreich for his advice and help during the preparation of the work.

CHRONOLOGICAL Index of references to treaties &c.

Numbers in brackets refer to the numbers given to the treaties printed in these volumes.

GENERAL INDEX

Numbers in brackets refer to the treaty numbers in these volumes.

Pages 1-459 are in Vol 1; Pages 460 to end in Vol 2.

internal relations, (5) 71,
(20) 151, 155-6, 158, 166
Jews, civil rights, (4) 38
and Lauenburg, (50) 295
laws, (4) 35, (5) 70, (20)
149-67
Mediatised districts, Circle
of Westphalia, relations with
Prussian monarchy, (5) 64
Mediatised Princes, rights of,
(4) 36-7, (20) 165-6
member states
equality, (4) 35, (5) 67
internal administration,
(20) 158, 163-5
internal order, (20) 157-8
rights and obligations,
(20) 151, 152, 154-5
sovereign powers, (20) 164
navigation, regulation between
states, (4) 40
neutrality in wars between
foreign powers, (20) 162
Nobility of the Empire,
rights of, (4) 37
object of, (4) 35, (5) 67,
(20) 151
Oldenburg, withdrawal of,
435
Peace, maintenance of, (4) 35,
(5) 71, (20) 155-7, 158-60
peace negotiations, (20) 162
powers, (20) 151-2
and Schleswig, (47) 286, (48)
290
territorial arrangements,
(7) 99-104
territory
boundary between Danish States
within and without, (47) 287
boundary with France, (1)
2-3, 5, (12) 130
tribunals, (4) 35-6, (5) 71,
(20) 156, 158
Germany
alliance with
Austria-Hungary, 1879, (117)
587-91
in relation to League of
the Three Emperors, (118)
591-2
renewal, 1883, (127) 629-30

renewal. 1902, (159) 732
Austria-Hungary and Italy
(Triple), 1882, (124) 611-13
Second Treaty, 1887, (131)
639-43
supplementary agreement of
Austria-Hungary and Italy,
1909, (174) 812-13
Third Treaty, 1891, (138)
658-62
Franco-Russian
understanding concerning,
1892, (139) 662-5
Fourth Treaty, 1902, (161)
738-43
Fifth Treaty, 1912, (184)
833-8
Naval Agreement, 1913, (191)
854-63
Austria-Hungary and
Roumania, 1883 (by
accession), (128) 631-2
Austria-Hungary and
Roumania, 1892 (by
accession), (140) 666-7
prolongation, 1896, (145)
681-2
renewal, 1902, (158) 729-30
renewal, 1913, (185) 840-1
Austria-Hungary and Russia,
1873 (by accession), (102) 509
Austria-Hungary and Russia
(League of the Three
Emperors), 1881, (121) 603-7
renewal, 1884, (129) 634-5
Russia ('Reinsurance
Treaty'), 1887, (133) 645-7
canals, reciprocal rights with
France, (100) 498
civil rights, (96) 465, (100) 502
commerce
in Africa, 878-9
in China
Anglo-German agreement,
(153) 713-14
'Open Door' policy, (152)
699-702
with France, (100) 501-2
in Turkey, Anglo-German
agreement re petroleum,
(193) 867-9
finance